MAN ON THE SPOT

By the same author

I Belong to Glasgow (Nexus Press, 1975)
Albania Who Cares? (Autumn House 1992, 2nd Edition 1993)

MAN ON THE SPOT

A Broadcaster's Story

Bill Hamilton

Book Guild Publishing
Sussex, England

First published in Great Britain in 2010 by
The Book Guild Ltd
Pavilion View
19 New Road
Brighton, BN1 1UF

Typesetting in Garamond by
Keyboard Services, Luton, Bedfordshire

Printed and bound in Great Britain by
CPI Antony Rowe

A catalogue record for this book is available from
The British Library

ISBN 978 1 84624 517 6

This book is dedicated to all who have helped and guided me throughout my life and in particular to the memory of my loving and sacrificial parents, Jim and Emily.

Contents

Acknowledgements

My sincere thanks go to John Arthur, Adrian Gilbert, Sue Barrand and Mary Simmonite for their support and encouragement; to Mira Shuteriqi, Vjollca Dedej and Mira Warren for their ready assistance with research and translation and for the enormous work undertaken on my visits to Albania; to Andy Anderson, Judy Caulfield, Gareth M. Davies, Brian Harrison, David Helme and my brother Douglas for their help in prompting my, at times, imperfect memory; to Bhasker Solanki, Brian Staveley, Bob Prabhu and George MacAulay for the use of photographs; to my family for their patience and forbearance, including grandson Stevie who rescued me from at least one computer disaster; to Maureen Kennedy for reading my manuscript thoroughly and suggesting some valuable improvements to the text; and to all at Book Guild for their kindly and professional approach to this publication, particularly designer Kieran Hood, Joanna Bentley, Janet Wrench, Laura Lockington and Jessica Haggerty.

Introduction

Journalism can never be silent: that is its greatest virtue and its greatest fault. It must speak, and speak immediately, while the echoes of wonder, the claims of triumph and the signs of horror are still in the air.

Henry Anatole Grunwald (former managing editor of *Time* magazine)

Journalists don't rate highly in the popularity stakes. Opinion polls frequently place them alongside politicians, estate agents and double glazing salesmen. Football referees fare even worse, lampooned as incompetent buffoons, ridiculed by fans and abused and disrespected by the players under their control. At least that's what the world would have you believe.

I have done both jobs for the past 50 years and have survived intact. What's more, my own experiences in the field are somewhat at odds with such ubiquitous conceptions. For every pedlar of poor, ill-informed and second-rate journalism, there is another passionately committed to an honourable profession – a teller of the truth, an informer of the facts, an eye on the elite and a voice for the voiceless. For every referee who runs away from a sport he can no longer handle, there is another made of sterner stuff with the moral fibre, courage, fitness and tenacity required to reach the top.

My passage to the apex of my trade was an old-fashioned one. For me there were no academies of excellence, BBC news trainee schemes or fast-track entry from Oxford or Cambridge. I started on the bottom rung of the ladder and progressed via weekly and evening papers into regional and national radio and television as a reporter, news editor and correspondent. I owe whatever success I achieved to the dedication and professionalism of a series of editors who rewarded my unbridled enthusiasm for the job by showing their faith in my ability and allowing me to be set loose on a myriad of diverse assignments.

1

In an odd kind of way, proficient journalism and refereeing have a common denominator, an emphasis on scrupulous impartiality. Nowhere is that more apposite than at the BBC which, despite frequent attacks from politicians, remains a world-renowned trademark for quality, professionalism and innovation. It forms the very basis of the public's trust without which the Corporation simply could not function. I was fortunate to spend more than twenty years of my career in 'Auntie's' fold entrusted with telling and occasionally unearthing some of the most remarkable happenings at home and abroad, occupying a front row seat to history in the making and always with an undying curiosity about the world around me.

Life as a television reporter can be a very shallow existence, dipping in and out of people's lives, rigging and de-rigging equipment at such a rate of knots that sometimes it's a miracle that you have been able to keep abreast of events. It is too easy to become little more than a fireman engaged in a race against time to get the images and the story to the satellite point in time for the next news of the day. Much has changed in the past two decades thanks to the brave new world of technological revolution. Ten digital channels now take the place previously held by just one analogue channel. The 'digi box', Freeview, the Net, Twitter, blogging and the BlackBerry have transformed the way we receive our news.

Where does the humble journalist of an earlier generation stand in all this turmoil? 150 words a minute shorthand, the constant clatter of the old Olivetti typewriter and the ability to ask simple, straightforward questions have been superseded by such concepts as the mission to explain, producer choice, multi-skilling and bi-mediality. In the broadcasting industry, restrictive practices have long since been banished to the annals of history. Today you have to learn how to shoot and edit pictures as well as how to voice over them and be as competent painting the scene in a radio studio as complementing the images on television.

With an emphasis on 'live' television, correspondents and reporters are now in increasing danger of becoming part of the story as they pop up at the scene or are marched into a studio and asked not just to dispense the latest information but actively encouraged to express their impressions about what they have witnessed. Often their delivery begins in a deferential way as they turn towards the newsreader – better known today as the programme 'anchor' – and address him (or her) by their first name. It seems to me an unhealthy exercise in indulgence, reminiscent of an errant schoolboy being summoned to the headmaster's office, and an irritating prelude to the most important job – delivering the salient facts directly to the viewer.

News is what happens outwith broadcasters but inevitably we can get drawn in and, of course, we are affected by what we see, sometimes profoundly, physically and emotionally. Whatever others may think, few journalists are devoid of normal human emotions when swiftly and suddenly airlifted into a famine, an earthquake or a full-scale war.

Certain images stick in your mind for a lifetime. They can haunt you in your dreams. The experience may have been fleeting but the impact of that short-term involvement can be very powerful. The reporter has to be able to combine sympathy and empathy with a single-minded determination that will carry him through a traumatic event.

Over the past 50 years I have encountered many dreadful sights. In Albania, children left in dank, dark rooms of degrading institutions until starvation or cold kills; in Sudan, witnessing entire villages put to the torch with the few survivors wandering aimlessly among streets and homes reduced to blackened shells; in Beirut, buildings being pounded relentlessly with shell and mortar; in drought-ravaged Africa, standing on the cracked bed of Zimbabwe's Lake Kyle where in normal times I would have been submerged by 100ft of water. Even at home, there was a chilling numbness in the aftermath of the Dunblane massacre, a senseless carnage of so many innocent young children carried out by a deranged gunman bearing my own surname.

I have also seen the power of television news to galvanize people into responding to some of life's greatest tragedies ... schoolchildren handing over their pocket money to buy life-saving medical equipment; doctors, therapists and teachers offering professional help; royalty and stars of stage and screen making personal visits to soothe the pain of vulnerable children; and ordinary men and women moved sufficiently to give up job and home to answer the cry for long-term practical assistance in several of the poorest and most dangerous areas of the world. Such sacrifices are a powerful antidote to the concern of the older generation in particular that the daily diet of news is much too depressing.

A good friend of mine, Robin Bell-Taylor, farms for the Crown Estates in Hertfordshire. He often describes his work as 'feeding the nation'. There is a correlation with the journalist's job there too as he sets about feeding the public's insatiable appetite for news and information. In my earnest quest to uncover a good story, I have confronted the principled, the bad and the bizarre in relatively equal measure and that also applies to my experiences on the football field.

The years may be passing with indecent haste but as yet, I have no intention of blowing the final whistle on either career. What follows is a story of a journalist who is not growing OLD, just growing UP.

1

City of Discovery

Childhood is measured out by sounds and smells and sights before the dark hour of reason grows.

Sir John Betjeman

In 1985 Dundee began to be marketed as 'The City of Discovery'. It was the year that the Antarctic explorer Captain Robert Falcon Scott's ship of the same name was transported from the Thames to be given pride of place in a custom-built dock on the banks of the River Tay. Thousands turned out to welcome her home. RSS *Discovery* had been launched at the Panmure Shipyard in 1901 by men renowned for their expertise in building sturdy wooden ships for the whaling industry and was strengthened with essential design features that allowed her to survive the extreme polar conditions.

Till this exercise in rebranding instigated by *Discovery's* return, Dundee had been universally known as the city of the 3 Js, in recognition of its three main industries during the greater part of the twentieth century – namely, jute, jam and journalism.

As a boy I used to watch the big cargo ships unloading the bales of raw jute which had arrived from India ready to be transported to any one of thirty mills where it would be carded, spun and woven for use in sails, ropes, sacks, tents and carpets. On the jam front, I spent many a day slaving in the berry fields during the summer holidays, picking the rasps and strawberries that would make up enough pots to fill our family's larder and most of our neighbours' for months ahead while the pungent orangey smell of Keiller's marmalade factory wafted across our street for hours at a time. Horror of horrors, the distinctive white glass jars of Dundee Marmalade can still be seen on the supermarket shelves but the zesty breakfast treat is now manufactured in Manchester!

With the demise of jute, only the third J remains. Journalism still

5

thrives in Dundee, home of D C Thomson with 2,000 employees producing more than 200 million newspapers, magazines and comics each year. As a boy, the idea of entering the profession never crossed my mind. I was still on my own voyage of discovery.

I was a wartime baby, born in September 1943 at a nursing home called Fernbrae in Dundee's west end. Thankfully, in a city that has handed over much of its historical past to the bulldozer, the partly listed building stands in a conservation area overlooking the Tay and is now a private hospital.

My father, James Hamilton, often known as Hamish, had served as an auxiliary policeman at the start of the war and was a keen radio amateur registered with the Radio Society of Great Britain and proud of his own call sign. He was just the sort of material the Admiralty was looking for when it put out a call for radio technicians to trace faults and swiftly repair boffin-constructed radar sets. Based at Royal Naval establishments in Hampshire and frequently at sea, my father, commissioned as a Lieutenant, barely set eyes on me till the end of the war. By then, he had undergone a serious operation. Working on a radar mast, his ship came under attack from a German U-boat forcing the captain to order an emergency turn. Dad was hurled on to the bridge, his back shattered in the fall but a naval surgeon taking a bone graft from his leg put him back together again and shouted 'you'll get 25 years out of this.' If that seemed an optimistic prediction then my father outlived most of his peers, reaching the grand old age of 90.

In the last years of the war, he had proved an effective teacher of radar. Among his pupils was a young First Lieutenant known simply as Philip of Greece. Though Philip was courting the future Queen Elizabeth at the time, father refused requests to allow him to skip off early from classes, much to the chagrin of Philip's princess and the naval authorities.

After the war, dad became an officer in the Royal Naval Reserve rising to the rank of Commander (Electrical) of the Tay Division and twice carrying off a prestigious national trophy from HMS Collingwood. Training nights were held on board the *Unicorn*, which at anchor in the Earl Grey Dock, was Britain's oldest commissioned vessel afloat. Frequently, at weekends the officers, ratings and wrens would sail out of the Tay estuary into the North Sea on the minesweeper HMS *Montrose*. There were occasional family days when we would be invited to take a closer look at dad's shipborne radar equipment, enjoy the roast pork cooked in the galley and then, as the waves began to pound the side of the vessel, take a death-like grip of the handrail before proceeding to lose our lunch over the leeward side.

Dad had met my mother, Emily, at a bus stop when both were on their way to Esperanto classes. Like many others at that time they thought the ability to use an international language would be of use in the new world order but somehow it never really took off.

While my father was absent from the family home, mum did all she could to present a sense of security for my elder brother Douglas and myself. Everything was on ration and coupons soon ran out. Material was hard to come by and versatility was the name of the game. Like most other women in our street, she was a good seamstress and dressmaker. Her dexterous hands made my baby clothes out of curtains and dusters or by cutting up larger garments. Tailored coats were produced, trimmed with velvet collars. Buttons were made out of casein found in milk but which often broke in the wash.

As a child, mum had been brought up with a sense of inner discipline which was further accentuated by watching one of the more notable neighbours at work. Those were the days when the women of the house scrubbed their doorsteps daily and then trimmed them with white clay lines. One turned the chore into a personal crusade, the clay spelling out a potent message:

Annie Clunie, Buttars Loan;
Temperance makes a happy home!

Goodness knows what her reaction would be today as a pub and a bookmakers now stand on the site!

We had a bomb shelter in the back garden of our council house in Glenprosen Terrace, the only one in our street that had an internal light. It was shared by a policeman's widow who lived downstairs and who gave mum's boys a hard time. Once when I was simply retrieving a tennis ball from her lawn, she flew into a tantrum and reported the family to the city housing department. Mother was furious. Red-faced with her young son in tow, she was ushered into a bare-walled office and forced to make a public apology.

Considering it had shipyards, munitions factories and jute mills that were making millions of sandbags plus the Tay Rail Bridge – at that time the longest in Europe – Dundee escaped relatively lightly in bombing raids by the Luftwaffe. The city was also home to the Royal Navy's 9th Submarine Flotilla, a large international force composed of British units supplemented by Free French, Dutch, Norwegian and Polish crews whose countries had been overrun by the Nazis. They had a vital role harrying the German supply convoys off Norway and were involved in some of the most daring naval operations of the war. I was not yet a year old when the sirens sounded for the last time. By then, the allied advance through Europe was well under way and Herr Hitler, staring defeat in the face, did not place sorting out the resilient folk of Dundee among his top priorities.

Home at last, dad trained to become a quantity surveyor and was given a partnership in my grandfather's business. I loved travelling by tramcar to grandpa's tenement flat, the last in his part of town to be converted to electricity. Under the gas lamps, I had fun winding up the old gramophone, changing the steel phonograph needles and listening to Willie McCulloch's classic Scots monologues such as 'Mrs Montgomerie's Wee Shop' or 'Deputation to the Minister'. If we stayed up late and the National Anthem came on the radio, we all had to get up off the sofa and stand to attention.

With money extremely tight, savings were made wherever possible. Monday was washday and we could expect a plate of stovies – tatties and stew made up of left-over meat from our Sunday treat all thrown into one pot. With hot water at a premium, baths were conducted in the kitchen sink or in a baby bath placed in front of the coal fire until I outgrew both. By then, the main entertainment of the day was provided by tuning the wireless to *Listen with Mother* with its soothing signature tune from Fauré's *Dolly Suite* and the famous opening line 'Are you sitting comfortably? Then I'll begin.'

My parents made huge sacrifices to ensure Douglas and I could gain access to the best possible education. Their hard-earned savings allowed us to attend a fee-paying school, Dundee High. I entered Primary One while still just four years old and said goodbye in the Fifth Form thirteen years later. I enjoyed school life and built many lasting friendships with my classmates. We were given every encouragement by teachers who took a great interest in their charges; men and women whose warm and occasionally eccentric personalities left an indelible mark while their leather belts often created another kind of warmth just to remind us that discipline goes hand-in-hand with education.

Extra-curricular activities included the Combined Cadet Force where I first learnt how to fire a rifle. Returning to the school 40 years later, I was amazed to find a tiny hole in the roof of the gym at the very spot where I had despatched a bullet after my grip had slipped in sheer desperation to hit the target.

Sharing a bedroom with my brother meant that when he contracted scarlet fever, the infection spread quickly. Just five at the time, I was terrified as the ambulancemen climbed the stairs to carry me off to a hospital where the matron reigned supreme and my parents had to stand outside in the bitter winter cold to talk to their disconsolate son through a heavy pane of glass. After a course of penicillin injections, I began to feel a little better but was so distraught at my isolation that I started crying for my mother.

'Oh, we have a surprise for you,' one of the nurses shouted, 'your mum's just arrived next door in the women's ward. She's caught the fever too!'

Holidays always involved a two-day trip to Southsea with dad combining a fortnight's break with his annual naval training exercise at HMS Collingwood. En route, we would generally stay overnight in the Lake District. There, my father would recall the day when riding a tandem, he and his companion had been struck by lightning whilst descending the Kirkstone Pass towards Lake Windermere. Rescued – relatively uninjured but in a state of severe shock – by a passing motorist, they were given a hot meal by the local constabulary before spending the night as VIP guests in an Ambleside police cell.

Going to the pictures was a real treat in Dundee. By the time I was twelve, there were 27 cinemas to choose from and many had exotic names like La Scala, Rialto, Kinnaird, Tivoli, Princess, Victoria and Broadway. Occasionally, my parents would allow me to go on my own. Standing in the queue outside waiting for the film to start, I would sneak up to a responsible-looking adult and ask if I could tag on behind so that I could get in for half price. In the Fifties, it never dawned on me or my parents that I might have been putting my welfare at considerable risk.

By then I had become a member of the Boys' Brigade. The 4th Dundee Company was based at St Mark's Church on the other side of town but I was able to ride on the tram from its northern terminus at Maryfield. Climbing aboard, I took great delight ascending the stairs to the upper deck and then switching all the reversible wooden seats to face the direction of travel. I'm not sure though that the hierarchy of the Transport Department would have been enamoured by another little prank in which I freely indulged. This entailed placing a copper halfpenny on one of the rails and watching several tons of tram pass over it, enabling the coin to be converted into the size of an unconvincing penny. Not a sensible trick really, for a ha'penny worth of sweets was much preferable to a squashed penny. The last Dundee tram ran to

Lochee in October 1956 and my brother managed to get hold of two precious souvenirs, a brake handle and a destination board which became the pride and joy of the home-made street go-kart for years to come.

Boys' Brigade activity filled most of the weekend. Drill parade on Friday night, football Saturday afternoon, activity and games club Saturday evening and Bible Class Sunday morning. There were outdoor camps in the summer and hikes and Battalion events throughout the rest of the year. The company captain, Walter Brown, was an inspirational figure, full of ideas for young lads seeking excitement and adventure but also aware of the need for each of them to accept responsibility for his actions. He worked for a big timber company and each Christmas huge tree trunks of every description would arrive at the Church Hall and Walter's boys would be equipped with axes to provide dozens of pensioners with box loads of firewood for Christmas. Goodness knows what the Health and Safety Executive would have to say about the whole episode today! Clutching the boxes in both hands as we left the hall, the beneficent Mr Brown would then pop a quarter pound of tea on top and hand over a long list of addresses. As luck would have it, most of the kindly old pensioners were to be found way up on the fourth floor of the Victorian stone-built tenements.

Behind each group of tenements there was a courtyard sometimes visited by a 'crooner', who having entertained the tenants with a song or two from his extensive repertoire, would remove his cap and try to catch a shower of coppers sent raining down in great glee by the children of the block.

On Saturday nights Mr Brown would invite visitors to join in the club activities. One day, he introduced me to a blind boy and placed half a crown in my hand. 'Buy him an ice cream from the parlour at the top of the road and make sure he enjoys himself for the rest of the evening.' Over the years, the boys built a magnificent model railway that became the pride of the city, so much so that at least two department stores engaged in an ongoing battle to lure the BB company into setting it up as a huge working display to attract customers during the Christmas rush. The boys devoted hours of their holidays working the controls and embellishing the layout.

Trains have been a lifelong passion. I used to spend the summer buying weekly runabout tickets, enjoying the last years of the steam age with the latest timetable and a couple of jam sandwiches in a box tucked under my arm and exploring all that the railways had to offer before Dr Beeching wielded his infamous axe. When a diesel railbus was introduced on the Gleneagles to Comrie branch, drivers became infuriated by my constant presence at unmanned request halts where a frantic wave of the hand forced them to apply the brakes. As the steps were lowered, there were frequent cries of 'oh no, not you again!'

My popularity quickly waned too, with the conductors of Dundee Corporation who repeatedly threw me off the tram or bus for my inability to stump up the 1d fare. Temptation at the tuck shop meant it had already disappeared from my pocket. The trick was to sit in the front seat upstairs. By the time the conductor had walked the entire distance of the upper deck, the bus was that little bit nearer home which resulted in a shorter walk after the humiliation of my dismissal. If my parents found out what I had been up to, then I knew what was coming – a good clip around the ear.

They were rightly sticklers for discipline and it did neither Douglas nor me the slightest harm. Shoes and boots would have to be polished before we left home, BB and cadet uniforms made to sparkle and our hair combed in the coal cellar to avoid any dandruff falling on the floor. Then along with a drop of water, we rubbed in a yellow cream called Pragmatar into the scalp.

My great aunt Jessie came to stay with us when we moved to a new semi in Mains Loan. A spinster, she had been employed as a nanny by some very influential families in the USA and Canada. Once a week, an octogenarian friend came to visit and I would be invited into auntie's room to prepare toast by hanging the bread at the end of a long fork and holding it in front of the gas fire.

In my teenage years, we welcomed a new arrival, a miniature grey poodle named Peter. Like me, he had a great affection for football and loved to join in kick-abouts on all the local parks. In later years, when I was working for the evening paper in Hartlepool, he arrived with my parents one weekend and was being looked after by an elderly babysitter employed by some friends while we all went into town for a meal.

On our return, he had gone – utterly lost, we thought, wandering aimlessly in a large town he did not know. Three days later, Peter turned up on the front doorstep black as the ace of spades, having apparently bedded down in a cemetery two miles away and then batteries recharged, intuitively finding his way back.

My brother by now, was the proud owner of a grown-up's dinky – a BSA Bantam 125cc motor cycle – which could reach speeds of up to 40 miles an hour if you were lucky and performed over 100 miles to the gallon. Sadly, there was just one seat so little brother couldn't ride pillion. Leaving college, Douglas became a radar technician with the RAF before GEC/Marconi put him in charge of the fire control and missile systems for the lifetime of Britain's Polaris submarine fleet. In 1997 I was immensely proud to join him at Buckingham Palace after he had been awarded the MBE on the recommendation of the Royal Navy for whom he served as consultant on the entire Polaris programme.

My early leanings were towards the ministry. Cousin Judy had even sent me a dog collar to wear when conducting services for my housebound aunt in her front bedroom. There were hymns, prayers, bible readings, even a short sermon, but the results of my Highers – the Scottish equivalent of A Levels – were not good enough for entry to a university theology degree course. My mind and ambition were now moving in an entirely different direction, one that would bring together two of the great passions in my life – football and a newly acquired fascination for journalism.

My father had fired my enthusiasm for the game. I was just seven years old when he first took me to Dens Park to see the legendary Billy Steel. Dundee had paid a record Scottish transfer fee of £23,000 to bring him north from Derby County. An exceptionally talented inside-forward, Steel exuded a style and authority that would have the clubs of today wrangling over his signature. I was amazed at his ability and he knew exactly how to set the terraces alight, combining a brilliant footballing brain with a tireless work ethic and an explosive shot. He helped Dundee win back-to-back League Cups and also played in the Scottish Cup Final. With the two closest professional clubs geographically in Britain – the Tannadice Terrors of Dundee United were just across the street – football was an essential part of city life.

There were also twelve junior clubs in the city. In a first stab at journalism I wrote a programme for one of them, Osborne FC, and also manned the turnstiles, a helpful exercise in brushing up my arithmetic.

I had an exciting and invigorating childhood guided by self-sacrificing parents, who did everything they could to prepare me for the rigours of life ahead. The only question that remained to be answered was had I made the right choices? The answer would not be delayed for long.

2

Don't Shoot the Ref!

I never comment on referees and I'm not going to break the habit of a lifetime for that prat.

Ron Atkinson

It all began at six o'clock on Christmas morning 1957. That's when I awoke to find Santa Claus had somehow managed to prise open my stocking wide enough to hold *The FA Book for Boys*, one of the most sought-after annuals for any soccer-mad youngster – provided you lived south of Hadrian's Wall!

Sliding down a chimney in Dundee with such an offering was considered akin to an act of treachery on the part of Father Christmas. In the days when Scotland v England matches were still the highlight of the soccer calendar, no young Scot could possibly expect anything but disdainful looks from his peers whilst flicking through a book emanating from the powerhouse of English football.

My eyes were drawn to an article entitled 'Perhaps YOU could become a referee?' Most readers would probably have run a mile rather than even contemplate such a horrendous suggestion but I had very good reason to read on.

As a pupil in the Third Form at Dundee High School, I was told I had three choices of the winter sport in which I might wish to indulge – rugby or rugby or rugby. Perhaps I was a coward but I did not take kindly to offering up my delicate frame to the wildest opponent in a scrum, ruck or maul. Not that things improved when deciding a burst of speed might make the wing my best position. Now I found myself a target for ferocious defenders whose strength and stamina seemed to me to be powerful pointers to the wholesomeness of school dinners fifty years and more before an eminent TV chef used the power of his celebrity to bring about a revolution in the dining hall.

Fortunately, I had an ace up my sleeve. As an enthusiastic member of The Boys' Brigade, I was given the opportunity to play *association* football on Saturday afternoons. Here, the spirit was most definitely willing but the skill factor was as close as you will ever get to non-existent.

As a twelve-year-old I had watched the city's two professional sides, Dundee and Dundee United, playing at home on alternate Saturdays and produced my own handwritten sports paper which I endeavoured to get into my father's hands before the Dundee *Sporting Post* came tumbling through the letterbox.

I would fold two sheets of A4 paper to provide eight pages of sports material, reports from an imaginary league which I administered from our dining-room table, and a front and back page account of the match I had watched that afternoon complete with picture cigarette cards of players who had taken part.

When I started playing for the BB side, my own game became the highlight. In the early weeks of 1957, I was handed the captaincy of the team and in one game, to my absolute astonishment, I managed to burst into the penalty area to meet a cross from the left. The ball spun off my right foot and looked to be soaring up and over when it was suddenly caught by the wind, deceived the goalkeeper and dropped just under the crossbar.

I was in seventh heaven and rushing home after the game, produced a banner headline 'HAMILTON WONDER GOAL', followed by a more telling subhead, 'But 4th BB go down 13–2.'

Little wonder then that the refereeing article the following Christmas had caught my eye.

The author John Degg's opening words commanded instant appeal. 'Not everyone can become a good player – however hard they try. Some, even while still in their teens, can make their most valuable contribution to the game as referees.' This was followed by an interesting rider. 'This is something for which you should certainly take advice from your Sports Master.'

Little did I know that Dallas Allardice, shortly to become Head of PE at Dundee High, a war hero and a former rugby international, had once played football for Huntly in the semi-professional Highland League. His were always words of encouragement.

As for Father Christmas, I had not expected that the chubby old man of jolly countenance would also list diplomacy and political correctness among his many attributes ... for tugging at the lower woollen strands of my stocking, I released a second annual that would be the envy of

14

all the boys in our street, Hugh Taylor's lavishly illustrated *Scottish Football Book.*

Would there be a similar article on refereeing north of the border, I wondered? Skipping eagerly forward to Page 140 provided the answer with a striking headline 'DON'T SHOOT THE REF!'

At first glance, it didn't look very encouraging. Reading on, the tone only served to endorse the view of so many of my friends that referees were picked with a pin from a queue of psychiatrists' discards. There were suggestions that the fellow who wanted to become a referee would face difficulties which would make the voyage of *Ulysses* as pleasant as a cruise round Rothesay Bay. Just to tempt me a little more I read that if I ventured forth on this noble path I would earn more jeers than cheers, be ill-paid, insulted, sometimes assaulted, accused of corruption, blindness, imbecility and spied on more often than James Bond.

Could things get any worse, I wondered? Yes, they certainly could! The writer of the article decided to cite a description of a referee penned by Dr Percy Young, a famous musician and billed as soccer's most charming essayist:

> *Of all the blear-eyed nincompoops that ever appeared in spindle-shanks on the turf in the guise of a referee, the cachinnatory cough-drop who attempted the job on Saturday was the worst we have ever seen.*
>
> *His asinine imbecility was only equalled by his mountebank costume and his general appearance and get-up reminded one more of a baked frog than a man. No worse tub-thumping, pot-bellied, jerry-built jackass ever tried to perform as a referee.*
>
> *His lugubrious tenebrousness and his monotonous squeaking on the whistle were a trial to the soul.*
>
> *Encased in a dull psychological envelopment of weird chaotic misunderstandings of the rules, he gyrated in a ludicrously painful manner up and down the field, and his addle-headed, flat-chested, splay-footed, cross-eyed, unkempt, unshaven, bow-legged, hump-backed, lop-eared, scraggy, imbecile and idiotic decision when he ruled Jones' second goal offside, filled the audience – players and spectators alike – with disgust.*

Phew! It seemed to me the hymn of hate so often directed at referees had mounted to nothing less than a savage battle-cry. Yet, if it really was that bad then maybe they needed a few more recruits in the front line ... and fast!

15

The *FA Book for Boys* had been far more upbeat and so – act of treason or not – I wrote to the Secretary of The Football Association at Lancaster Gate, London, asking for more details. Within a few days I received a beautiful handwritten note from Sir Stanley Rous with instructions of whom to approach in Dundee and aged just 14, I became Scotland's youngest football referee.

This was confirmed by a knock at the front door of my home in Mains Loan. Standing there, were reporters and photographers from two daily newspapers. Could I don my kit, stick a whistle in my mouth and get out into the back garden for a photo? This little exercise took no more than ten minutes, but as the journalists sat in our lounge drinking my mother's coffee for the best part of three hours, a thought flashed through my mind: 'I must try journalism as a career!'

I had attended the referees' courses, sat an oral and written examination and undertaken some serious physical training but was told I would have to wait until 16 before I could qualify for my referee's badge as I was still considered too young to take control of matches under the auspices of the Scottish Football Association. But with a desperate shortage of match officials, The Angus Amateur League was more than willing to let me take charge of Under-18 games, and each Tuesday, in a frenzy of excitement, I would furtively ease my way out of the school gates at playtime to get my hands on a copy of *The Evening Telegraph* listing all refereeing appointments for the upcoming weekend.

Without a place in any of the school rugby XVs through a combination of choice and limited ability, I also had Saturday mornings free to referee school games. This turned out to be a great learning curve and the schools liked the arrangement too, as it meant that teachers, who invariably found they had to take charge of these games, could revert to a coaching role from the touchline. Cup Final appointments began to roll in, though unlike more recent times, the players and referee never received a medal – but this was Scotland! The winning side had to be content with the one piece of silverware which by Monday morning had been securely locked away in the headmaster's glass cabinet.

One evening returning home from school, I received an unexpected phone call complimenting me on my handling of these games and asking whether I would be willing to referee the Scottish Schoolboys Cup semi-final between Dundee and Edinburgh at Glenesk Park.

Though thrilled at the prospect, I also felt uncomfortable. Living in Dundee, I thought, might lead to questions about my neutrality, especially if some controversial incident was to arise during the match. I expressed my inner fears to more experienced colleagues whose advice was 'to concentrate one hundred per cent on the game and forget everything else. In any case, Edinburgh is a much larger city with far more talented players to choose from, so the result is really a foregone conclusion.'

As events began to unfold on that memorable night, nothing could have been further from the truth. It was an electrifying match in which Dundee overwhelmed their opponents with their tactical superiority and swift passing game crowned by five goals from the boot of a fourteen-year-old called Peter Lorimer. How well or otherwise I had performed was no longer of the slightest importance. Every professional scout in the land was now on the heels of this prolific striker who had scored 176 goals during the season for Stobswell School.

Manchester United were desperate to sign him but in the end, Leeds United's Don Revie beat almost 30 other top-class clubs to Lorimer's signature, driving all through the night to Dundee and receiving a speeding ticket for his trouble. Peter's parents were persuaded that their son was taking the right step but neither he, nor they, could have contemplated that he would go on to play 690 times for Leeds and score a club record 238 goals. What I had witnessed on that grey Dundee evening was the launch pad to a superlative career by the player regarded as having the hardest shot in football history.

Now mine host at The Commercial Inn in the Holbeck area of Leeds and a member of the United Board of Directors, Peter is often asked about his innate ability to score such spectacular goals.

'When I kicked a ball, I didn't have to think about rhythm or power,' he insists. 'It was an automatic reaction and a gift for which I will always be grateful.'

During holiday periods, I would cycle around all the senior grounds in the city, looking for opportunities to leap on to the field and take charge of proceedings. At one point, by sheer chance, I came across Dundee United about to play a pre-season match behind closed doors at a secret location.

Cheekily, I approached their new manager, Jerry Kerr, who was to become a United legend, and asked whether I might referee the game. 'Oh, go on then sonny, let's see what you can do and remember don't stand for any nonsense from these fellas!'

The match that Monday afternoon went well and fortunately I experienced few problems and received many compliments from a bunch of well-disciplined, full-time professionals who were also more than willing to add their names to my greatly treasured autograph book.

What I didn't expect was a personal visit by the Dundee United manager to my home the following Thursday just minutes after I had finished my evening paper round.

He told my parents that he had been very impressed by my ability and, turning to me, asked warmly, 'Would you like to referee the club's pre-season friendly at Tannadice Park on Saturday?'

I could hardly take it in. I had now turned 16 but the prospect of controlling 22 professional footballers in front of a 6,000 crowd was mind-boggling. My school friends and teachers simply didn't believe me when, in my excitement, I told them of what Saturday had in store. They all thought I was living in a fantasy world.

When the big day arrived, I was up at the crack of dawn, polishing my boots for the umpteenth time, checking and rechecking that every possible piece of kit required was neatly packed into my sports bag. Back and forward I went to the toilet, up and down the stairs until at 10 am, I could wait no longer and asked my father if, on this one occasion, he might proffer me a lift to the ground.

'But we'll be there in just five minutes,' he exclaimed, 'and the match doesn't kick off till three o'clock!'

Fortunately, it was a fine day with the sun shining through a virtually cloudless sky. Just as well, as I waited nearly two hours for the groundsman to appear and let me in. When I told him what part I would be playing in the day's proceedings, I was again met with a look of disbelief, but he was kind enough to furnish me with a glass of lemonade to help calm my nerves.

By 1.30 pm I had made myself at home in the officials' dressing room when suddenly the door burst open and striding into the room came one of Scotland's best-known referees, John Gordon of Newport-on-Tay, who would later officiate at the 1978 World Cup in Argentina, and his two SFA linesmen.

'What are you doing in here, young Bill?' John enquired. I was lost for words. Here was the biggest moment of my life disintegrating before my very eyes. I knew John very well. He had been my referees' tutor and had helped supervise the written examination.

'Oh, I've been asked to referee this afternoon's match,' I replied meekly.

'You've what?' John replied, the underlying tone of his voice indicating his utter disbelief. I was totally crestfallen. What would I tell my friends now? Were they right? Was this whole episode just a figment of my imagination?

Just then there was a knock at the door. The Dundee United manager asked if he could come in. Recognising at once my obvious distress, he put a comforting arm around my shoulder. 'I'm so sorry Bill. I did not realize that the club secretary had fixed up all three officials for this afternoon. Perhaps you would like to be my guest and take a seat in the directors' box.'

At that point, he turned to John Gordon, and stated that unusually, even for a pre-season friendly, he wanted the match to be played in three half-hour segments rather than the normal two halves of forty-five minutes. Quick as lightning, John turned to me and said:

'I'll tell you what Bill, how about you refereeing the middle half hour. You'll have two experienced linesmen, so no need to fear. I'm sure you'll carry it all off splendidly.'

'Sure thing,' I said, butterflies quickly returning to my stomach. The actual half-hour passed by in a flash. It was by far the most exciting part of the game. Four goals, flowing, attacking football with no unsavoury incidents of note. Walking out there as a schoolboy, in front of several thousand spectators, was a thrill I shall never forget and, of course, reading about it afterwards in the *Dundee Sporting Post*.

It would be a long time before I would ever tread the turf of a professional club again. For the first two seasons, my sphere of operations were the park pitches of Dundee immaculately prepared under the direction of one of the country's finest Parks Superintendents, Alex Dow. Sawdust bought in large quantities from local sawmills was used to mark out the pitch. Even on a grey, dreich day, the distinctive orange/yellow lines stood out sharply, a contrast to some of the lime products used extensively today which have been known to kill the grass and leave brown marks when the white has worn off.

Alas, only one appurtenance was missing ... goal nets, whose absence would soon plunge me headlong into controversy and within a whisker of quitting the hobby I had barely begun.

To make matters worse, the occasion was my very first Amateur League Cup final. Seventy minutes into the game at windswept Caird Park, and the score at 1–1, as the linesman on the right-hand diagonal, I indicated as instructed to the match referee Allan Gall, one of my closest friends, that in my opinion the whole of the ball had crossed the goal line between the posts and underneath the crossbar.

Uproar ensued as, by all accounts, the ball had been sent several yards wide of the goal. Despite my earnest prayers that the side ahead would score again, the match ended 2–1 ... the cue for my quick-thinking father to race his Austin Westminster across the park, back door flung open, to set up the great escape in the nick of time!

Come to think of it, I'm still waiting for my half-crown fee for that game. I often reflect on just how many Mars Bars that would have bought in the late 1950s.

This unsavoury incident could – perhaps it ought – to have brought my refereeing career to an abrupt halt. But I had older friends and colleagues who reminded me of the size of investment in each new referee.

Over fifty seasons later, I'm still there, just as enthusiastic as on Day One, if a mite more mature.

Searching through an old trunk in the attic of my St Albans home, I came across all my old match cards which propelled me into doing some sums on my pocket calculator. I discovered I had officiated at well over 2,000 matches which at 90 minutes per game, excluding extra time, amounts to the equivalent of four solid months of refereeing. As for the total mileage run during games – approximately five miles per game – that would have taken me as far as Australia. Ah, but there's the rub, at 66 how do I get back again?

There have been some memorable moments along the way including the day I watched a substitute defender down several cans of beer in the dug-out before foolishly allowing him to come on for the last quarter of the match. I need not have worried. Within two minutes, he was back from whence he started, first having been shown a yellow card for disputing an offside decision from the other end of the pitch – a good 110 yards away – and then sent off for removing a corner flag and using it as a support to keep himself upright.

One of the most frightening and bizarre incidents occurred in the Kincardine fishing village of Gourdon which unusually found itself thrust on to the soccer map after its football team's long and distinguished run in the Scottish Amateur Cup. Now residing in Aberdeenshire, I was appointed to take charge of their match against Dundee Camperdown, a team principally comprised of players from an inner city housing estate.

They arrived in good time for the appointed 2 pm kick-off but so too, did a host of regulars from Gourdon's Harbour Bar keen to see what the cream of local football talent could achieve against one of the competition's favourites. To help fortify themselves for the long exhausting uphill climb from the picturesque harbour to the ground, perched on a cliff towering over the village, some had downed one whisky too many. Clearly, they had no intention of playing only a passive role in the biggest day in the history of Gourdon Selbie FC.

As I called the two captains to the centre circle to toss the coin and get proceedings under way, I spotted a number of revellers in high spirits behind the goal Gourdon would be defending. My first thought was that such raucous, impassioned and unpredictable behaviour would add some colour and extra spice to what I was certain would be a frenetic and highly charged cup tie.

The match was just 15 minutes old when pandemonium broke loose. With the score still 0–0 and with the visiting side's centre-forward having rounded the keeper and bearing down on an open goal, one of the ribald corps of supporters leapt the boundary rope and quick as a flash upended the striker with one of the most timely and effective sliding tackles I have ever seen.

Within seconds I was surrounded by a furious mob of Dundee players urging me to abandon the game. Was this to be an inglorious end to Gourdon's unexpected bid to lift one of amateur football's most coveted trophies? Would this fishing community be plunged into a corporate sense of shame? And more importantly from my point of view, would I ever get out of the place alive should I blow time on the proceedings?

Like most of those around me, I was still in a state of shock. I had never witnessed such a bizarre and absurd incident before and knew it was never likely to be repeated during the rest of my refereeing career. Yet, I had to make a decision – and quickly – before things got completely out of hand.

Barely a minute had passed when the answer appeared in the shape of a 6ft 2in Police Constable who had unexpectedly arrived from the nearby town of Inverbervie. The culprit and his friends identified, they were immediately escorted from the scene, the security tightened and the match restarted with a dropped ball, under the Laws of the Game the only possible resumption where a goal has been prevented by an 'outside agent'.

I was particularly anxious to get play under way as swiftly as possible so that the minds and concentration of the players were again fully focused on the match. In the event, Dundee Camperdown emerged as the victors in a thrilling end-to-end cup tie. Needless to say, on this occasion, I politely turned down the post match hospitality – a drink at the Harbour Bar. The very mention of the place was enough to send an almighty shiver down my spine. My only intent was to get out of the ground and on my way home at the rate of knots!

South of the border, I made rapid progress up the refereeing ladder. I had already been promoted to a Class 1 official by my mid-20s and was officiating in regional leagues in the North East and in the FA

Amateur Cup. Among those who viewed my progress with interest was Lawrie McMenemy, then coach of Bishop Auckland and later to lead Southampton to one of the biggest FA Cup Final shocks of all time, a 1–0 win over Manchester United.

The game which clinched my promotion was another cup tie played in a mining community near Ashington in Northumberland.

An assessor had been despatched from Newcastle to monitor my performance and though marks awarded to the referee by competing clubs have a distinct bearing on promotion prospects, the assessor's verdict is the most important one.

Today young referees are monitored over a number of matches. In the 1960s such well-structured procedures were still not in place. Sometimes you were lucky to get even two assessments during the course of a season and some of those doing the assessing would hide behind a tree or a burger van rather than have their presence revealed.

In this particular game, the assessor did approach me at the end of the match. He said I had done well and that he was impressed with my performance. He also mentioned that he would be recommending that I should be promoted to Class 1.

This was followed by an unusual request. Could he possibly have a lift home to Newcastle? Having heard such encouraging news, I was more than happy to oblige. Getting to the ground had apparently posed serious problems for him. He'd been required to change buses three times en route and, with no coordination of the timetables, was left waiting for well over an hour at one of the stops as a heavy downpour ensured he was soaked through.

A second heavy shower during the game did nothing to lift his spirits but at least now, he did not have to endure a second nightmare journey back to his front door – or so we thought! On reaching my Ford Anglia parked outside the clubhouse, we found one of the rear tyres had been slashed. Obviously, someone at the game had not shared the assessor's opinion of my performance. Thankfully, I had a spare in the boot and the assessor insisted that as he was already soaked to the skin, he was not too troubled about getting his hands dirty.

Fortunately, in over half a century of refereeing, I have not experienced a single physical assault. Not all are so lucky. In some parts of the country, abuse directed at officials – some of them still taking their first tentative steps in the game – has reached such a level that the Football Association has received calls asking for counselling to be made available for the victims. I know of colleagues who have suffered broken cheek bones, fractured jaws, been spat at, punched to the ground, kicked in the face and even had their clothes set on fire.

As a referee, you always have to be prepared for the unexpected. In a Spartan South Midlands League game at Pitstone & Ivinghoe, I was on the point of dismissing a Sun Postal Sports player from the Field of Play for head-butting an opponent when a spectator started shouting abuse in his direction. Suddenly, the captain of the visiting side made a beeline for the technical area and grabbed hold of an oak fold-up chair which he then proceeded to hurl at the startled fan, missing him by a matter of inches.

Two red cards shown in a matter of seconds and a delayed restart to the match until the two offenders were safely tucked away in the dressing room.

In another match at Leighton Town, a player was anxious to know from which point of the touchline should he take a throw-in. 'Right there,' I shouted, 'just in front of that gorgeous girl in the front row of the stand.'

Moments later, I was stopped in my tracks as her husband bounded on to the side of the pitch, his face turning crimson with rage, as he screamed: 'What was that you were saying about my wife?'

Arriving at one ground in North East Fife, I was horrified to find the referee's changing room was situated in a crumbling cowshed. The animals had been evacuated but the dark, dingy room had been filled to the rafters with a huge pile of manure. In one corner lay a bench and above it an iron hook, presumably to attach my clothes to a flyblown wooden pillar. Running on to the pitch, I may have appeared to the players as the epitome of unruffled authority but reeking of horse dung soon altered that assessment – a real confidence booster if ever I encountered one!

A trip to the local park at the weekend to watch a youth game can be a chastening experience. I have seen parents screaming abuse at teenage referees taking charge of Under-12 games. Is it any wonder that some of them revert back to doing a paper round on a Saturday morning rather than subject themselves to such vitriol?

Grass roots football cannot afford to allow violence and intimidation to take such a heavy toll. Since the turn of the millennium, 7,000 referees a season have quit the game and the Football Association has been forced to find new initiatives to stem such a dreadful haemorrhaging of young talent.

One of the saving graces has been the formation of referee academies which have resulted from a partnership between the Football Association, the county football associations and the country's professional clubs. In my county of Hertfordshire for instance, Arsenal and Watford play competitive games every week at Under-18 down to Under-12 level against teams from other League clubs. These are not 'win at all costs' games, rather an opportunity for the professional sides to develop the skills of some of the most prodigious young footballers within 90 minutes' travelling distance from the club.

When the lads are approaching 16, the club will sit down with the player and his parents to decide the best way forward. Many are rejected. The lucky ones are offered a scholarship and will be expected to continue their education studying for A Levels or BTech Diplomas at a local college.

The academy games provide the ideal situation for the young inexperienced referee who can progress in a safe and protected environment. Parents who misbehave are asked to leave and told if such conduct is repeated, their son will be sent on his way too.

Mentors, mainly experienced referees, offer on the spot help and guidance but if they find youngsters under their tutelage turning up at the ground with dirty boots, they're sent home. If they arrive late for the pre-match briefing, the same fate may well await them.

Discipline, self-respect and a willingness to work together as a team with their assistant referees are other attributes necessary to identify a pathway from starting in grass roots football all the way to the Premiership. Only a small number will ever make the grade but the academy scheme certainly provides a good starting point.

The young referee must also commit to regular training sessions. These cover areas such as diet, fitness, decision making and how to manage unexpected situations that may arise.

They are important steps in the drive to keep more young referees on board. The sadness is that those who are most critical of the referee's role would never contemplate doing the job themselves. That is particularly true of professional footballers coming to the end of their careers. Because they've played the game at a level of such intensity, it is often suggested their experience would be invaluable as referees and that they should be fast-tracked to the top of the game. I certainly have my reservations on that score but in any case, you can literally count on the fingers of one hand the number of former professionals who have given more than a moment's consideration to taking up the whistle.

Normally, as a linesman or assistant referee as he's called today, it's a bit easier to dodge the humour or more likely, the derision of the Press. Recently though, one satirist by the name of Bill Scholes, had a real go at my expense and had me laughing well into the night.

It is not uncommon at Welwyn Garden City for low flying aircraft to add interest to a game of football. At today's Spartan South Midlands Premier Division game, one of the linos (sorry, assistant referees) was heard to remark how nice it was to have arranged a flying display for the League Committee members. It was pointed out to the Mad Scot on the line, nicely, that the aircraft had probably mistaken his rigorous flag waving for instructions to land. He was so successful that at one stage there were 2 Cessnas, a Piper Apache and an Aeronca circling the ground waiting instructions, whilst slightly higher two Boeing 737s and an Airbus could be seen patiently stacking as they waited their turn!

For more than a decade now, I have travelled each year to Denmark having been invited to referee at one of the largest and most colourful youth tournaments in the world. Few other experiences in life compare with the Dana Cup when it comes to rolling pain and pleasure into one.

This competition regularly attracts more than 800 teams from over 40 countries. Collectively, they play over 2,000 games in five days. The tournament is held at the town of Hjorring in Northern Jutland. Just 25,000 people live there, but during Dana Cup week the population more than doubles. It never ceases to amaze me that such a small town can find the necessary infrastructure to hold an event on this scale.

This is organisation of the highest order. For one week of the year, a smart, upmarket Danish municipality manifests itself as the crossroads of the world, a sporting challenge and cultural experience where young players – girls as well as boys – regardless of borders, skin colour, politics or religion, can meet in a safe environment. This is a competition where teams from all five continents can match themselves against others of the same age and where the battle for trophies gives the competition its pulse and energy. From the Ural Mountains to New Zealand, from Iceland to Argentina, all the participants have been touched in some way by the Dana Cup experience.

Here you see Moldovan boys in holed shorts and ill-fitting boots mixing with their more fortunate counterparts from the USA resplendent in the very latest gear, while on the pitch, the Brazilians are putting their ball wizardry to the test against the familiar route one approach of the Norwegians. What a privilege to be given the job of refereeing the Uruguayans and Taiwanese as they meet for the first and perhaps the last time in life.

The organisers even subsidise a handful of clubs to travel from some of the poorest and most remote parts of Africa, boys who had rarely travelled out of their own villages in countries like Somalia, Malawi or Sierra Leone, still in a state of disbelief after being flown thousands of miles across the world to face opposition from England, Germany or Australia.

Schools, village halls and sports clubs from miles around are commandeered to house the 20,000 participants including coaches, physiotherapists and referees. Parents rent tents, caravans or wooden chalets. Then there are the Danes who lavish hospitality on their guests and can find no suitable substitute for their two addictions which are rather contradictory bedfellows – football and beer.

The referees too, are football addicts – how else can you account for the sheer madness involved in accepting the unrelenting daily demands of the job. Matches may be curtailed to just an hour's play but you can find yourself allotted four fixtures in a single day and then have to roll out your sleeping bag each night to fight for every inch of space on a hall floor accommodating up to 120 fellow-referees. Worse still is the need to don a pair of ear plugs to avoid the nightly cacophony provided by a worldwide array of heavy snorers.

Great friendships have sprung up over the years with refereeing colleagues from Cologne and Milan, from Helsinki and Budapest and from Miami and Accra. This is a truly international group of friends coming together to celebrate the game they love and to soak up all that accompanies such a frenetic week of competition.

Travelling the world as a BBC Correspondent, I always ensured I kept a whistle in my pocket. It worked a treat, such is the universal appeal of the sport. In one Albanian village, I found 40 excited youngsters using a sheep's head as a football. When I replaced it with a Mitre ball which I'd brought from England, the excitement of the moment brought screams of joy and another hundred lads scurrying from their crumbling apartment blocks to join in. Even years of experience cannot prepare you for refereeing a match with 70 players a side!

It was a situation I found repeated time and time again as, whistle in hand, I got play under way in a Palestinian refugee camp, among Zulu children in South Africa and in the rat-infested slum dwellings of Rio de Janeiro. Grass may be the ideal surface but football can be played anywhere … a small clearing in the bush, a back yard, against a brick wall or wooden fence. A broken bucket or an old plastic bag can take the place of a ball and a few rolled-up socks, a jumper or a couple of empty cans used to form the goal. For tens of thousands of the world's poor, football is not just another game. It is a passionate and emotional experience that unites and holds together not just for 90 minutes but long after the game is over.

What a contrast to the fortunes of the players in England's Premier Division, some of whom earn more in a single week than many of the world's youngsters can hope to earn in their entire lifetime! With so much money floating around in the professional game, I often pondered why referees were the last people in sport to attract sponsorship. I could not understand why businesses seemed to be so reluctant to have their logo emblazoned across our chests.

I thought we might have attracted an optician or two since we are all blind, an orphanage or two since our parentage is called into question every Saturday or even an undertaker or two – after all, we do wear black and our detractors could be granted their final wish.

It was a pleasant surprise then to see Specsavers finally coming forward to sponsor referees in Scotland, Holland and Denmark. Yet given the pathological hatred some fans seem to have for the man in the middle, the idea of being whisked to safety thousands of miles away by Air Asia, recent sponsor of England's Premier League referees, could be viewed as the preferable option!

The low-cost airline invested a considerable sum into improving the training methods of the elite group of match officials as well as investigations into new technology and the development of up-and-coming referees.

They also very graciously made a contribution towards the cost of a gala dinner hosted by my good friend John Motson, BBC's 'Voice of Football', to mark my 50th season as an active referee. The event gave fellow broadcaster Alan Parry, the only TV football commentator to have worked for BBC, ITV and Sky Sports, a rare opportunity to launch a humorous onslaught against the referee fraternity, only to find himself the butt of a most eloquent response by Harrow School Housemaster David Elleray, President of the Referees Association and for many years England's highest-profile and most highly regarded FIFA referee.

David presented me with the Football Association's Gold Medal for 50 years' service to the game, while Mark Halsey who had made a special day-return trip from Bolton, handed over a referee shirt signed by every one of the Premier League match officials. There were also surprise presentations from two of the finest referee administrators, my good friends Mike Taylor and Eric Harrison.

A few weeks later I received an invitation from Keith Hackett, the man who refereed the Centenary FA Challenge Cup Final at Wembley and had become General Manager of the Professional Game Match Officials Board, to join the Premiership's Select Group referees at Barnsdale on Rutland Water.

An opportunity to meet the best in the business, I thought, and a splendid location to spend two restful days. Not a bit of it. I was despatched with track suit and trainers to an RAF camp where the fitness instructor took great pleasure in watching me pant and grimace as I was subjected to the speed endurance training specially devised for our professional referees.

On the pitch and in the gym, their performance was appraised continuously under the watchful gaze of sports scientist Matt Weston. Whatever else you may say about our top referees, you certainly can't accuse them of a lack of fitness.

Computer monitoring has shown they cover up to 13 kilometres per game and it's vital that a referee is as close to the action as possible when it comes to 'selling a decision' to a player. If you're ten metres away, they'll accept it much more easily than if you're 30 to 40 metres from the incident.

Weston's own observation is that the dedication of our leading referees matches that of any professional athlete with whom he has ever worked. Each referee also wears a lightweight telemetric heart monitor equipped with electrodes. The information it transmits not only shows how much effort has been put in but ensures the aims of the training sessions are met in full.

New technology has led to so many advances but has also added to the pressure on referees. I often think of some of my eminent predecessors. Men like Jack Mowat, Tiny Wharton and Ken Aston. Some suggest they were of a higher order and made fewer mistakes. What nonsense! They were fortunate to be around at a time before television coverage of the game had got fully into its stride. Television's role in the denigration of referees is pivotal and I say that as one who spent over 40 years in the broadcasting business.

Action replays showing camera shots from any of six different angles have put referees under pressure as never before. The majority of the decisions they have been shown to have got right are rarely a discussion point for the panel of studio experts but make one mistake, and it becomes open house for the critics. Occasionally, a referee will be dropped from the next weekend's fixture for getting a decision wrong. The intention is this should be seen as a 'kick up the backside' and a warning to other officials, but it serves to give managers and players licence to have a go at referees if they disagree with their decisions.

Imagine if the same fate was to await Wayne Rooney or Didier Drogba every time they missed an open goal. Referees are not robots. They are human beings who are just as fallible as any of their contemporaries.

That said, I cannot think of any more agreeable way of spending a Saturday afternoon. Mentally and physically, there is no better exercise to keep you on your toes for 90 minutes. Experience teaches you a great deal about man management and you need to use your own personality to advantage. A sense of humour too, never goes amiss nor does exercising your faith. I always try to say a prayer in the dressing room before I go out. It's a helpful experience, for whatever happens, it puts the game into perspective. There are far more important things in life than football. The abuse I might be subjected to on any given weekend is nothing compared with what Our Lord went through.

I have been fortunate to have refereed representative games at the two Wembley Stadiums – old and new – including a full-blooded affair between the staff and pupils of *Grange Hill* and the stars of *Coronation Street* and *EastEnders* (I'd rather wished they'd reserved some of the night's antics for the small screen!) and to have trodden the turf of the hugely impressive Millennium Stadium in Cardiff, but so far I have not had the honour of officiating at Hampden Park in Glasgow. Alas, after 52 years in the middle, the home of Scottish football may have eluded my grasp.

3

Weekly Adventures

Newspapers always excite curiosity. No-one ever puts one down without the feeling of disappointment.

Charles Lamb

Long before daylight I had taken up residence at the foot of the stairs, my heart throbbing with excitement as I awaited the arrival of the morning post. At last I could hear the familiar footsteps of the postman approaching the front door. On to the doormat, it dropped – an envelope clearly marked 'D C Thomson'. After a rigorous interview and an even tougher initiative test at the home of one of Scotland's publishing giants, I was only seconds away from discovering my fate.

The letter contained but one sentence. 'I regret to tell you that you have been unsuccessful in obtaining the position for which you were an applicant.'

I can only imagine from such a terse response they must have considered I fell far short of the standard required. Such feelings of failure and rejection were aggravated by the dread of what to tell my parents who had invested so much of their limited resources into ensuring my brother and I had enjoyed the benefits of a fee-paying education.

When a rejection occurs it is far too easy to get trapped in a negative mindset and to accept it as a dismal forecast of your future. I have seen it in so many walks of life and sadly, many seem incapable of turning their energies towards creating success rather than running away from failure.

My father was adamant. 'You've made up your mind that you want to be a journalist so jolly well get on with it!' Easier said than done.

By continuing to don my school uniform, I could still take advantage of the penny fare on the fleet of Routemaster buses which by now had

31

replaced the vintage trams as a means of getting into the city from the genteel suburb of Maryfield. The reference library in Dundee's Albert Institute, founded in memory of the Prince Consort, was one of the finest of its kind in the country. Many times, with important school examinations pending, I would ascend the granite steps and push through the revolving doors in my haste to remove bulky volumes from their shelves. Forty minutes would be enough to quickly scan the pages and commit to memory concise summaries of a Shakespeare play or famous Scottish novels such as Sir Walter Scott's *Ivanhoe* or Stevenson's *Kidnapped*.

The task this time was to locate the most recent edition of *Willings Press Guide*, still the first port of call for anyone wanting instant access to important newspaper contacts.

I noted the names of all the Scottish editors and their office addresses. Within a week, I had 120 letters winging their way to every one of them.

More than a hundred took the trouble to reply. Some were sympathetic, several wished me luck but all but four stated categorically 'no vacancies for trainees'.

It's very easy to become discouraged when faced with a barrage of refusals, but with a handful at least willing to put my name on file, there was still room for a modicum of optimism. Whoever said discretion is the better part of valour, I decided, was just plain wrong. Each of the editors must receive an enthusiastic phone call and a personal plea to 'come and spend a day with you'.

The ploy paid off handsomely. One of the four said 'yes'. I arrived on his doorstep the following week, three newly sharpened HB pencils in my top pocket and a notebook in my hand, ready for action. The day itself remains a blur. Determined to pack as much information as I could into eight hours meant I was running in several directions at once, but I did get a general feel of what went on in an editorial department and in the organised chaos of the caseroom where the screeds of copy jotted down by the reporters was laboriously hand-set, character by character, by skilled compositors.

I was just 17 but my enthusiasm seemed to have left its mark. 'There's no job for a junior at the moment but if anything should come up, be sure we'll get in touch – maybe even give you an interview.'

Hurrying home from Cupar with a copy of the latest edition of *The Fife Herald* under my arm, the thought suddenly struck me that all my school education had one glaring omission. Boys were not taught shorthand or typing – those subjects were exclusively the province of the girls at Dundee High.

Realising that this could be a major handicap to ever obtaining a job in journalism, I immediately enrolled on a Pitmans course at Bruce's Business College. I arrived on the first day to find myself the only boy alongside 26 girls. How I would have relished that scenario today but more than a little bashful in my tender years – no doubt enhanced by my Presbyterian upbringing – I made a habit of arriving late and leaving early.

It soon became crystal clear that most of the girls had a much greater aptitude for mastering the art of grammalogues to facilitate speed, so convenient to use when taking dictation. Mastering the typewriter keyboard I found a much easier exercise.

My failure to follow suit with shorthand was a sure recipe for problems ahead.

I had attended the college barely four months when the call came. Duncan Campbell, the approachable, self-effacing and hugely encouraging editor of the *Fife Herald* wanted to see me. One of his three reporters had left for a senior job elsewhere, another had been promoted, so now he needed a trainee. My name was included on his shortlist.

The interview went well. I was now 18 and a mite more mature. My enthusiasm was still unrestrained. I had read every available book on journalism and I had endeavoured to learn the art of shorthand and typing. I was given a page of gobbledegook purported to be the annual report of a local institution and told to reassemble it into something vaguely readable. The editor seemed impressed and to my surprise eliminated the need for another night at the foot of the stairs awaiting the postman's arrival, by offering me the job that very afternoon. Still shaking with excitement, I had difficulty pressing the A & B buttons in the telephone kiosk on the way back to the station, so decided that on this occasion my parents would not object to a transfer charge call to hear the news.

On Monday 5 February 1962, I arrived at the Burnside works of the *Fife Herald*. The building was over a hundred years old and showing many signs of decay. Yet there was something subtly exotic about the old wooden office that housed the three reporters, the editorial files, the oak desks, layers of carbon paper, the Olivetti typewriters and the Bakelite phones. The smell was most agreeable ... an intoxicating odour provided by a mixture of the solid wood, layers of dust and the mellow, dry corn fragrance of old books.

Next door was Duncan Campbell's office, the room to which we had to personally convey our stories for his perusal and to receive in return encouragement, advice or constructive criticism. Once he had edited and headlined the items, they were taken in turn to the caseroom which today would have been a front line target for any noise abatement society. Here, the aroma was of an entirely different nature, the room exuding the smell of hot metal and oil … and dominating everything – those dinosaurs, the linotype machines. The printing process was cumbersome and these large and complicated devices set the type one line at a time. The operators used a keyboard to key in the letters, then each line set up had molten lead at over 200 °C run into it to form a 'slug' which then went into a 'galley' for printing. I had heard it said that many a printer's devil believed that purgatory could never be so grim as a composing room. I guess for most compositors the age of computers and new technology simply could not come quickly enough.

From Day 1, my two reporting colleagues kept reminding me that I was the highest paid junior the newspaper had ever employed – five pounds, ten shillings for what often turned out to be a six-day week. Leaving a NCP car park in Central London the other day with a £24 bill, it suddenly struck me that represented the equivalent of four weeks' work in 1962!

On top, the journalists were allowed a very small percentage of a linage fee paid by the national newspapers for stories we telephoned to their newsrooms each day. In my case, I was entitled to no payment at all for the first six months before finally qualifying to collect just 5 per cent of the money paid to the paper which, with its sister publications the *Fife News* and *St Andrews Citizen*, was owned by the Innes family.

I remember once having my expenses queried because I had spent 3/6d on a plate of bacon, egg and chips. I had worked from eight in the morning covering cases at the local Sheriff Court, attending a farmers' meeting and covering an East of Scotland League cricket match for both our own paper and the sports edition of the *Edinburgh Evening Dispatch*.

As a member of Cupar Cricket Club, Mr Innes was at pains to point out that the teas there cost just 1/9p. Maybe he thought a mere stripling like me could survive on half a meat paste sandwich and a cup cake for an entire 12-hour shift!

For the most part though, I was counting my good fortune. I had reached the first step of the journalistic ladder and was relishing all the opportunities and excitement it afforded.

On a weekly paper, you get the chance to try your hand at everything – courts, councils, agriculture, crime, features, sport … the list is endless. The job of the reporter is to develop a keen news sense, find things out, establish what is the truth and have a passion for precision. An enquiring mind, an outgoing nature and an ability to get to the core of an issue are essential attributes, so too, a very real sense of urgency. Even weeklies have deadlines to meet and woe betide the reporter who fails to file his copy on time.

Duncan Campbell and his chief reporter, Sadie Cullum, rewarded my enthusiasm by pushing me further down the road of discovery. More responsibility, a sense of worth and bigger stories soon become a necessity when you've spent the first few weeks listing in meticulous detail all the winners in the jam-making competition or ensuring you have properly deciphered the minister's scrawl intimating the names of the babies baptised at the local parish kirk. Missing out the twelfth name to be prised out of the black bag at the Scottish Women's Rural Institute weekly prize draw would bring an irate phone call to the Editor and a request that the offending junior be suitably chastised or even worse – sacked for gross incompetency.

Through it all, Duncan Campbell remained calm and stoical. To me, he was an inspirational figure who had a genuine and compassionate interest in those who worked for him and with him. There was a streak of boldness too. I can well remember an occasion when the managing director of a firm which spent considerable sums of money on placing adverts in the paper made a personal visit to the Burnside works in a desperate attempt to have all coverage of his latest motoring conviction omitted from next week's edition. To his fury, the report was published in full. It's amazing the lengths to which some people are prepared to go to try to prevent their neighbours and business clients discovering just how they fall foul of the law.

My first 'scoop' resulted directly from a visit I paid each week to Fisher and Donaldson, a fourth-generation family bakery business in Cupar's Crossgate. One of the employees there used to provide me with snippets of information about the town's boxing club. One particular week he said he had lined up something special and asked that I visit the club with a photographer the following Thursday.

This request was not without its difficulties. Getting pictures into the *Fife Herald* was always the subject of considerable debate. The problem was that the photographs had to be sent 30 miles by bus to the *Perthshire Advertiser* where photo lithographic block-making in zinc was performed and the block then returned to Cupar for insertion in the appropriate page. This little exercise, of course, was a costly procedure and the proprietor was keen for others to pay the bill. One of his tricks was to ask all newly married couples to send a cheque for 15s to cover the cost of having their wedding picture published!

In the event, I persuaded the editor that this was an assignment that we simply could not afford to miss. My source had never failed me and so confident was I that we would get a prodigious exclusive that I told Duncan Campbell: 'If I let you down on this one, you can deduct the fifteen bob from my weekly pay packet.'

On entering the club, I was introduced to a young man called George Smith and his two teenage brothers, Bill and Christopher, who lived in the Fife village of Springfield. All three suffered from a rare congenital condition called *aniridia* which had led to the onset of glaucoma and other eye complications rendering them almost totally blind.

George, now 22, had become an easy target for bullies who roamed local bus stations on Saturday nights. Twice he found himself the victim of vicious assaults in Cupar and he was also badly beaten during a visit to the new town of Glenrothes.

The police were unable to track down those responsible, a sorry situation that was compounded by the fact that George's blindness made it impossible to identify any possible suspects. But not all was lost. The police constable sent to the family home to take statements was able to offer some sound advice. 'What you need young George,' he said, 'is to learn some basic self-defence techniques.' Angus McKinnon knew what he was talking about. He was a former RAF middleweight boxing champion.

'Let's be having you down to the Cupar club next Thursday,' was his parting shot.

'Sure thing,' George replied, 'and would you mind if I bring my younger brothers too?'

Little did the PC – or I for that matter – realise just how events would turn out that memorable evening.

George was kitted out with long satin boxing shorts and a pair of all-leather sparring gloves. A few tips from the ex-champion and we waited to see just what George could do. By now, the photographer had manoeuvred himself into the perfect ringside position and I offered up a silent prayer that he would capture a good shot of the action.

What happened next defied belief. Our blind friend first rocked the former champion with a fierce right hook which left a nasty cut under his left eye and then followed up with another that had him staggering backwards on to the ropes and then to the canvas.

Fortunately, PC McKinnon quickly recovered but I don't know who was more elated – George who would have a ready answer for any future bully or me who had secured a memorable scoop.

The problem was that there were six days to go before publication and the bakery employee who had been the source of my story was the next-door neighbour and best friend of Dave Simpson, the senior and highly respected reporter at the Cupar office of the daily *Dundee Courier*. Would he keep his promise not to tell?

My predicament was certainly not helped when having missed the last bus to Cupar from the photographer's home in Ceres, I started trudging the long four miles home carrying an envelope containing the picture of the blind boxer's stunning blow.

I had walked barely a mile when a familiar grey Morris Minor approached from behind, the driver sounding his horn. Dave Simpson pulled his car to a halt and flung open the passenger door. 'What are you doing out at this time of night?' he enquired. 'Get in and I'll take you back to town.'

Glancing down at the big brown envelope marked 'PHOTOGRAPHS, HANDLE WITH CARE', he enquired what was inside. 'Oh nothing,' I said. 'Just a couple of family portraits I was showing to a friend.'

For someone with such an enquiring nature – the consummate professional – I was amazed he didn't ask to see the pictures. Within minutes, we had arrived back in Cupar. I jumped out of the car in such a hurry, I nearly dropped the envelope in the roadside gutter.

When the next edition of *The Fife Herald* hit the streets, Dave Simpson's neighbour had a lot of explaining to do and confirmation of the value of my scoop was seeing the story appearing the next day almost word for word in *The Dundee Courier*.

Those were the days when people took great pride in their own communities. Before local government streamlining and re-organisation stripped such upstanding burghs as Auchtermuchty, Falkland, Ladybank and Newburgh of their councils, provosts, ermine, scarlet robes and chains of office.

I often wondered if in his later years, Edward Heath ever regretted his Government's decision to abolish such great powerhouses of decision-making where water from the local reservoir was sold to a neighbouring burgh less well endowed and where the merits of deploying a clear or pearl light bulb in the public loo could so easily become the subject of a heated half-hour debate!

The Councillors may all have been elected as Independents but they were very effective in fighting the corner of those to whom they were accountable – sometimes too passionate in their arguments which gave rise to suspicions that their political allegiance might have lain elsewhere.

Unlike the situation in England, where the office of Mayor welcomed a new incumbent each year, Scottish Burghs allowed their Provost to enjoy a three-year term of office ... some were even re-appointed for two further terms or more. This meant they emerged as virtual institutions in their own right and became far more difficult to replace. Suggesting the time had come for a change of face would require more than a degree of courage on the part of a fellow councillor ... I even heard the word 'treachery' used to describe the rebellious attempt to have one Scottish provost stand down on the grounds that his growing popularity around town was an unhealthy phenomenon.

The Provosts often represented their burghs on the County Council too ... how they managed to hold down responsible full-time jobs seemed to me to be something of a mystery. Take Angus Goodall, the civic leader of the small North Fife burgh of Newburgh. In the 1960s, he managed the workforce at the town's linoleum works, presided over the Town Council and was making frequent trips to Cupar to sit on a range of county committees.

To cover meetings at Newburgh Town Hall, I had to travel by an Alexanders Bluebird bus, but such were the vagaries of the timetable, I always arrived a few minutes after the meeting had got under way. The bench on which I had to sit was immediately behind the Provost's chair at the very far end of the room which meant I had to tiptoe past the Bailies and other councillors lest I inadvertently interrupted proceedings.

One councillor, recently elected, was a little more brazen than the others. As I sidled through the narrow gap between his seat and the wall, a hand would suddenly be outstretched in my direction. Not for a second did anyone in the room suspect there might be an ulterior motive behind this seemingly friendly welcome.

Yet, thrust into the palm of my hand, a tiny crumpled piece of paper which unfolded to ten times its size, contained verbatim speeches that the ebullient and oft rebellious councillor Angus Murray intended to deliver, right down to the last comma. He had obviously heard of my constant struggle with the intricacies of shorthand and was determined to avoid any possibility of being misquoted in next week's edition.

Provost Goodall found the councillor less beneficent, with his brusque manner an unhealthy threat to a troublesome heart condition. Occasionally, debates would be temporarily suspended while the provost was dispensed two heart pills from a silver salver which, together with a glass of the purest Fife water, was carried ceremoniously into the council chamber by the Town Clerk.

One particular evening a heated row over council housing threatened to run out of control. With Angus Murray on the attack, the provost suddenly slumped forward in his seat, his head crashing against the wooden table. My first thought was that he had finally succumbed to heart failure. Just seconds later, the chimes of an ice cream van wafted through the open window. 'Ah, there's Mr Whippy awa' past!' the Provost exclaimed, bursting back into life, 'maybe you could do with a cone, Mr Murray, to cool your flaming tongue!'

Later, the two independent spirits were to forge a great friendship. Sadly, the demise of Scotland's small burghs in 1975 led to a huge loss of identity and self-esteem. Many of Scotland's traditions have been sacrificed on the altar of distant bureaucratic local government. More's the pity.

My shorthand handicap was to lead to a much more serious incident towards the end of my first year at *The Fife Herald*. By now, I was being given more onerous tasks including reporting many of the big debates at County Hall. One of my reports carried on the front page brought an irate phone call from the Convener of Fife County Council, Mr John McWilliam. He took exception to certain details, complained to the editor that he had been misquoted, and called for an immediate retraction. He also demanded that I meet him in his office that very afternoon to explain myself. I knew at once that my job was on the line.

My saving grace was that Duncan Campbell was far from pleased with the manner in which the convener had delivered his complaint. I was asked to bring my notebook into the editor's office.

'Okay Bill, let's see your note of the meeting.' My hands were trembling, my heart missed a beat as I placed the evidence on his desk. 'What do you call this?' he asked, his red cheeks displaying all the signs of exasperation. The page was full of blank spaces with the odd indecipherable scrawl sandwiched between half a dozen shorthand symbols.

'Bring me a copy of the newspaper with your report!' Turning over a new page in the notebook, the Editor carefully transcribed each quote into an accurate shorthand record.

'Now take that to the Convener and tell him you got it absolutely right. But first, phone up the college and see how quickly they can get you on to the next shorthand course!'

Not only had I survived but to my utter amazement that very day I was to receive an unreserved apology from the most powerful politician in the county of Fife.

Though I had stayed in 'digs' for the first few months of my journalistic career, I was eventually allowed to travel back and forth to my home in Dundee. The train journey lasted little over twenty minutes and crossed the Tay Bridge – nearly two and a quarter miles in length – which replaced Sir Thomas Bouch's original construction. This had taken six years to build and collapsed during a violent storm in December 1879 dragging in its wake a train and 75 passengers. The train plunged into the murky waters of Scotland's longest river, leaving no survivors.

Today, entering the bridge's central span, The High Girders, and glancing downstream at the stumps of the original bridge piers still visible on the surface of the river even at high tide, serves as a stark reminder of our mortality.

It also brings to mind the most infamous writings of the Dundee poet William Topaz McGonagall, whom the satirical magazine *Punch* described as 'the greatest bad verse writer of his age', and his most ardent followers add, 'or of any other age.'

His greatest disappointment in life was being turned away from Balmoral Castle after a four-day hike from Dundee, seeking an audience with his beloved Queen Victoria. Yet one can readily see why Her Majesty would not have been amused by such a visit when just a year later he penned yet another comical set of rhyming couplets to convey the shock experienced by the people of his home town when they awoke to news of the bridge's collapse.

> *Beautiful Railway Bridge of the Silv'ry Tay!*
> *Alas! I am very sorry to say*
> *That ninety lives have been taken away*
> *On the last Sabbath day of 1879,*
> *Which will be remembered for a very long time.*

If that wasn't bad enough, then how about the pronouncement that:

> *As soon as the catastrophe came to be known*
> *The alarm from mouth to mouth was blown,*
> *And the cry rang out all o'er the town,*
> *Good Heavens! The Tay Bridge is blown down.*

One of the quirks of British nature is our great sympathy for the underdog. In McGonagall's case, it has been defined as a celebration of human inadequacy. Stephen Pile in his *Book of Heroic Failures* claims that the people of Dundee recognised that the poet was 'so giftedly bad he backed unwittingly into genius'.

It was a thought that certainly crossed my mind when I was invited to the first dinner of the No.0 Club of the Fraternity of Weavers held in appreciation of that very genius at the Station Hotel in Ladybank. The chief criticisms of his poetry, that he was deaf to poetic metaphor and unable to scan correctly became all too evident, as each diner in turn, fortified by a tipple of his favourite malt, began to recite the tortuous verse that made McGonagall the perfect target for the practical jokers of his day.

Today, McGonagall's home city maintains several reminders of his life. The William McGonagall Appreciation Society has an active membership of well over 150. At one of their suppers, the courses were served in reverse order, starting with coffee and ending with the starters.

Like McGonagall I had always been a train enthusiast, but was now old enough to drive a car. However, given my meagre earnings, I knew I could not entertain the notion of buying an 'old banger'. Fortunately, my father was quite willing to allow me to learn the rudiments of driving from behind the wheel of his Austin Westminster. By mid-evening, most of the vast workforce serving the factories on the sprawling Dundee trading estates had finished work for the day, leaving behind empty roads and deserted cul-de-sacs ideal for rehearsing the complete gamut of driving manoeuvres.

Sometimes dad's tolerance level was stretched to its absolute limit as I cranked my way through the various gears or occasionally mistook the accelerator for the brake pedal which would later earn a clip around the ear. When he felt I had progressed sufficiently, I was allowed to enrol for a series of lessons with the local driving school in Cupar.

Before long, the time of reckoning had arrived. Many questioned whether Cupar was really a true test of one's driving abilities. As I remember it, unlike today, there wasn't a single traffic light in the town. To make up for the lack of obstacles on the test route, I succeeded in mounting a grass verge whilst reversing, stalling at a road junction and hitting the kerb on both sides of the road attempting a three-point turn. The examiner was not impressed and urged me to exercise extreme caution in my efforts to return him to the starting point in one piece!

'You need a lot more practice especially in traffic. I would not expect to see you again for quite some time.'

Back in the car park the instructor scratched his head in seeming disbelief that one of his pupils could fail so miserably but, defying the examiner's advice, he asked me to apply for another test at once, not that he – or I for that matter – expected that a second chance would arise within three weeks.

The omens were not good. To add to my nervous state, ten minutes before the scheduled time, the heavens opened. Torrential rain, high winds and overhead, fork lightning accompanied by sharp, loud cracks of thunder, heralded my arrival in the car park.

I fully expected the test would be cancelled. Not a bit of it. At precisely 12 noon, the door of the examiner's hut opened, an umbrella was hastily raised and I could just make out a familiar figure heading in my direction. My heart sank. He would surely recognise me and wonder how I had the gall to subject him to another 40 minutes of living hell.

To the contrary, the examiner was calmness personified. 'I'm sure I don't need to tell you that the conditions today demand extreme caution. Now please drive off in your normal fashion.'

I had not gone more than 20 yards when his hand slammed down on the dashboard. Clearly, he wanted to ensure the emergency stop was out of the way before I hit the open road.

Remembering the route we had taken last time, I guessed he might soon ask me to turn right into Lady Wynd. This was a one-way street and I knew that on reaching the T-junction at the bottom I would have to choose the correct lane for whichever direction the test route was to follow next.

I need not have worried. For no sooner had we turned into the wynd than the test came to a complete standstill little over 500 yards from the start. A funeral cortege consisting of half a dozen cars was blocking one side of the road, whilst on the opposite side vehicles of every description were parked nose to tail almost as far as the eye could see.

Realizing there was no way through, the examiner asked if I had considered putting the car into reverse. 'I can't do that,' I insisted, 'as this is a one-way street.'

'Quite right, Mr Hamilton. So let's find out how much you know about the Highway Code.' By the time the cortege was on the move, nearly 30 minutes had elapsed. I had answered somewhere in the region of 50 questions and the examiner was becoming increasingly anxious that the test timetable for the rest of the day might run way out of kilter.

Another 500 yards was sufficient to accommodate the hill start, reverse and three-point turn. 'We're not looking for perfect drivers, just careful ones.' The examination of my driving skills was over and a pass certificate placed in my hand. It must have been the shortest test route on record.

Hurrying back to Dundee that evening, I found my father surprisingly agreeable to my request that I take his Austin downtown to see how I could cope driving alone in a bustling city centre. It proved a rude awakening.

Unlike Cupar, there were traffic lights at every major junction and for the next hour I seemed to have forgotten everything I'd ever learned. Stage fright set in as impatient bus and lorry drivers – horns blaring – wondered if I would ever get on the move.

Worse was to follow, a mile from home an errant schoolboy suddenly dashed out in front of the car. On leaving the vehicle, I found his school satchel dangling from the end of the front bumper. The relief on seeing him grinning from the pavement opposite was indescribable. It may not have been my fault but I knew it would be some considerable time before I would have the confidence to drive alone again.

By now, I had served an apprenticeship on a weekly paper of just over eighteen months. Though I still had much to learn about journalism, I was already getting itchy feet, a sign that maybe it was time for a fresh and more demanding challenge.

Once again, I found myself bounding up the steps of Dundee's Reference Library, not this time to engross in English literature studies but to grasp a copy of *The UK Press Gazette* which listed all the journalistic vacancies in the country.

My eye was immediately drawn to an advert for a Sports Reporter/Sub Editor for the attractively named *Northern Daily Mail* based at West Hartlepool, then part of County Durham. I had never been there but the name of the town's football team, Hartlepools United, was familiar enough. Whenever they played at home, my father always listed their match on the 'Four Aways' section of the pools coupon. Such was their miserable record on their own ground, it was one result you could always be assured would come up trumps!

I thought hard and long about applying. It would mean leaving home for the first time to an area I knew absolutely nothing about. Not only that, in 1963 the town had one of the highest unemployment rates in the United Kingdom. I wrote my application letter that night and decided to sleep on my decision. But waking the following morning at 3 am, I threw a coat over my pyjamas and made a beeline for the nearest postbox. It was the point of no return.

4

Life at the Bottom

People said you could drop off the end of the world if you went to Hartlepool. Sometimes I wished I had!

Brian Clough

One of the real pleasures of travelling by rail in the early sixties was the opportunity to take a stroll down the corridor of a long distance train and peer into the carriage compartments, each of which accommodated six people comfortably or eight at a squeeze. It was a wonderful way of weighing up who might be an ideal travelling companion from a choice of over two hundred possibilities.

A mere glance through the glass-plated compartment door would provide some valuable clues as to the likely topic of conversation. Sandwiched between the cases on the luggage rack, the eye might spot a violin case, a set of golf clubs or a bottle of Scotch. Not everyone, of course, welcomed such an intrusion and if your opening line brought only a peremptory nod followed by a desperate scramble to find that discarded newspaper then it was time to up sticks and move elsewhere.

As I boarded the early morning London train at Dundee Tay Bridge Station in August 1963, my corridor promenading was a little shorter than usual. Hardly surprising considering two extremely attractive young ladies were heading for the door of the second-class carriage that had juddered to a halt at the very spot where I was standing on the platform.

In true chivalrous fashion, I took hold of their suitcases and slid open the door of the first empty compartment. Their luggage safely stored, I read the girls' jaunty demeanour and ready smile as a signal that they wouldn't find my company too disagreeable. 'Where are you from?' I asked politely.

'Oh, I don't suppose you would know the place – British West Hartlepool.'

It's amazing the coincidences you come across in everyday life. But this was a very timely one. Though I was carrying a notebook crammed with every scrap of information I could find on the town, its industries and its people, what an opportunity now to learn so much more – revelations that might just improve my chances of landing a job on the *Northern Daily Mail.*

I was intrigued with the prefix the girls had given the place. Why *British* West Hartlepool? They didn't have an answer and, to be honest, to this day I've haven't met anyone who has come up with a convincing response to the question.

Among those thought to be responsible was comedian Jimmy Edwards with his 1950s radio sketch called *Night Train to West Hartlepool.* Others supposed the culprit to be the band leader Victor Silvester who came up with a number *British Honduras, British East Africa and British West Hartlepool.* Benny Hill and Tony Hancock were also known to have satirised the town in comedy skits. But local historians say it's a term more likely to have been used by Lascar sailors arriving from the Indian subcontinent at the beginning of the twentieth century.

Alighting from the train – I wondered whether the place had moved on since then. I had been told by my travelling companions that the newspaper office was but a short stroll from the station and town centre, so immediately enquired from the first passer-by directions to the main street.

'You're standing in it,' was his curt reply.

I thought he must be joking. 'But this is a town of close on 100,000 people. Where are the shops?'

He pointed to a Chinese restaurant that had recently opened its doors in Church Street. 'They do a darned good three-course lunch for three bob in there.'

When I explained that food was not my first consideration as I had an interview in half an hour's time at the local evening paper, his face suddenly lit up.

'Ah, then you're a lucky man. Top of the street ... a big whitewashed building ... you can't miss it ... best looking office in town, right opposite the bus station. Hope it goes well.'

It did. Within minutes of arriving, I was ushered into a smartly furnished office for a face to face interview with none other than the Editor in Chief of Portsmouth and Sunderland newspapers, Charles Cowley. He put me at my ease straight away, asked about my sporting interests and what I knew about the area. He then glanced at some of the cuttings I had brought along to give him an idea of the range of stories to which I had been assigned during my short apprenticeship at the *Fife Herald.*

I had not realised just how influential a journalist Mr Cowley had become. He had edited the *Mail's* two sister papers, *The Evening News, Portsmouth* and the *Sunderland Echo.* I was soon to discover that he had a gifted pen which he turned with equal ease to matters of grave public concern or to light-hearted comment. During our tête-à-tête, he revealed a whole range of sports in which he took a special interest. They included amateur boxing and swimming, in both of which he had excelled as a younger man.

I can't say why but we just seemed to 'click', so much so that he offered me the Sports Reporter/Sub Editor job there and then. I was so surprised that I asked for a day to think things over, talk to my parents and be absolutely sure in my own mind that this was the right move. I asked if I might be given a tour of the building.

'Why, of course,' Mr Cowley said, 'you have a good look round and ask any questions you like.'

The building was buzzing with activity. If my first impression of Hartlepool was of a town literally dying on its feet then this place was the antithesis – teleprinters spewing out news from around the country and the world, courtesy of the Press Association, subs busily writing telling headlines to keep the conveyor belt of news production running smoothly, everyone working at a frenetic pace with four editions of the paper to roll off the presses in a single afternoon. To watch all this with the minutes ticking away towards the next deadline promoted a feeling of excitement and intensity. Two of the editions headed for towns and villages along the North East coast and into the Durham coalfields with deliveries to such austere-sounding places as Blackhall, Deaf Hill and Trimdon, the latter two later to emerge into prominence as pit village satellites of Tony Blair's Sedgefield constituency.

Yet stepping outside again on to the streets of West Hartlepool, it took just a few minutes to unwind and to realise that the people here were living in a different world where poverty and unemployment were taking their toll.

Just months before, Gray's Shipyard had shut down in its centenary year bringing the shipbuilding industry to a close. With the demise of one of the town's largest employers, hundreds more had now joined the dole queues.

At its peak, Gray's workforce totalled over 3,500 men in the yards and another 1,500 in the engine works. Winner of the Blue Riband for output on six occasions, the yard was one of the most productive in the country during the Second World War with the launch of 90 ships – an impressive record.

The dockyard cranes though were still at work. Ships were offloading timber from the Baltic states and exporting cargoes of coke and coal.

There was time for a fleeting visit to the Victoria Ground, home of Hartlepools United. It was much worse than I had imagined. No floodlights, home dressing room nothing more than a glorified portacabin, and a crumbling old wooden stand. This had been intended only as a temporary replacement for the one destroyed by a bomb dropped by a German Zeppelin airship during the Great War. A claim of £2,500 was made but not a penny was received from the German Government! It would be the late 1980s before the replacement was finally demolished after the tightening of fire regulations following the disastrous Bradford fire. Little wonder, I thought, that the club was struggling for its life in the Football League.

To the east of the ground lay old Hartlepool, known locally as the Headland, which until the merger of the two towns into a single new authority in 1967 was still a borough in its own right. It had been the site of an Anglo-Saxon monastery founded by St Bega in AD 640 but later destroyed in a Danish invasion. In the twelfth century the Church of St Hilda was built and is now the crowning glory of the Headland.

The old town too had taken a battering during the First World War as three heavy German cruisers, *Blücher, Seyditz and Moltke,* aiming for the vast docks complex, rained down more than a thousand shells during their first attack on British soil. 119 people were killed.

Taking a stroll along the seafront provided the opportunity for reflection until the biting chill of the easterly wind blowing in from the North Sea prompted a swift return to the railway station and the start of a long, thoughtful journey home.

One subject I had been careful not to raise during my interview was the tale most associated with Hartlepool, the hanging of a monkey as a French spy.

Every reference I found of the town seemed to mention it. According to legend, during the Napoleonic Wars, fishermen from Hartlepool watched as a French warship was wrecked off the coast. The sole survivor was a monkey, wearing a French uniform, no doubt to amuse the ship's company. On finding the monkey, it was decided to hold an impromptu trial on the beach. Unfamiliar with what a Frenchman looked like and unable to understand the creature's jabbering, they came to the conclusion that the monkey was a French spy and sentenced him to death. The mast of one of the fishing cobles is said to have provided a convenient gallows.

In more recent times, the town's football fans have been daubed with the nickname 'Monkey Hangers' while their mascot became *H'Angus the monkey*. The man in the costume, Stuart Drummond, stood as a candidate for the first directly elected Mayor of Hartlepool in 2002 with his campaign slogan 'free bananas for schoolchildren'. To widespread surprise, he won and was then re-elected by a landslide three years later.

The monkey hanging legend has a special place in North East folklore and has been an inspiration to a number of song writers. Surprisingly, many of them, including the writer of this verse, have chosen to remain anonymous.

In former times, mid war an' strife,
The French invasion threatened life,
An' all was armed to the knife,
The fishermen hung the monkey O!
The fishermen with courage high,
Seized on the monkey for a spy;
'Hang him!' says yen, says another, 'He'll die!'
They did and they hung the monkey O!
They tried every means to make him speak
And tortured the monkey till loud he did speak;
Says yen 'that's French' says another 'it's Greek'
For the fishermen had got drunky O!
'He's all ower hair!' some chap did cry,
E'en up te summat cute an' sly,
Wiv a cod's head then they closed an eye
Afore they hung the Monkey O!

In the summer of 2005 a leg bone found washed ashore at Seaton Carew on the outskirts of the town brought great excitement. At first it was thought it had belonged to a monkey, giving credence to the legend. However, scientific tests revealed the bone to be from a prehistoric red deer.

My parents and closest friends urged me to take up the job I'd been offered. They saw it as a wonderful opportunity to expand my journalistic career and, as I had all but forgotten the rudiments of French I had learned at school, there seemed little chance in my case of being mistaken for anything remotely resembling a Gallic spy!

The sports desk of *The Northern Daily Mail* comprised a team of just two. The Sports Editor was an extremely affable New Zealander from Christchurch with a very distinguished sounding name, Hedley Mortlock. He was an expert on rugby and later whilst working on the *Sun* covered the infamous All Blacks tour to Britain in 1972–3 when Keith Murdoch was sent home for punching a Cardiff security guard just hours after scoring New Zealand's only try in a 19–16 win over Wales.

Alas, Hedley's knowledge of association football was as limited as the ability of Hartlepools United to extricate themselves from a yearly round of re-election applications to the Football League, a fate that awaited those clubs who finished in the bottom four of the old Fourth Division. By the summer of 1964 these had amounted to five in a row and it was just as well that the club had friends in the higher echelons of the game. Without their votes, the side would have faced a sorry exit from League football and all that meant for the town. Hartlepools' good fortune contrasted starkly with that of another North East club, Gateshead, who had only applied for re-election twice in a relatively successful 30-year period, but in 1960 were nevertheless unceremoniously removed in favour of the more geographically acceptable Peterborough United.

At the start of the 1963–4 season, Hedley took up his position in the Press Box at the Victoria Ground to relay by telephone to a copy typist at the *Mail* office his running commentary on a pre-season friendly. The tried and tested system was for the type-written words to be rushed to a sub-editor's desk before being despatched to the composing room by a pneumatic air tube system, ready to be set in type for the *Football Mail*. This was one of the many green or pink sports papers that used to reach the streets of nearly every town in Britain that boasted an evening paper, in little more than half an hour after the final whistle.

Unfortunately for 'Mort', the ball was of the wrong shape and panic set in. Minutes went by without any 'copy' being received, causing a state of alarm at the subs desk. How were they going to fill all those glaring gaps in the front and back pages? It proved a field day for the photo department. Pictures from the match had to be supplemented with huge double column images of players 'snapped' at a recent training session which were hurriedly summoned from the files. A disaster had been averted, though the front page of the paper looked more like a tame edition of *Picture Post*!

On Monday morning, 'Mort' offered to resign but he gained the sympathy of the editor and went home that evening clutching every book he could muster on association football. By the time the first League game of the season was under way, my Kiwi colleague had established a degree of confidence to equal his natural charm, while his new found knowledge, understanding and insight of the game made him far better equipped to do his job than the anaemic players whose embarrassing performances once again produced a season of abysmal failure.

In my early months with the paper, I was given the job of covering Hartlepools Reserves home and away. This was a little less stressful and, supplemented by a number of part-time and amateur players, the side's results were a good deal more promising than those of the first team.

Hedley Mortlock and I were responsible for providing four pages of sport each evening plus a heavy schedule writing, subbing and headlining the inside pages of the *Football Mail.* We were aided in this by receiving copy from reporters covering the fortunes of Sunderland, Middlesbrough and the area's two big Rugby Union clubs, plus a host of freelances who brought us the latest news and developments from non-League sides stretching from the Wear to the Tees. This left only the front, back and middle pages to carry up to the minute reports of the Saturday afternoon games and, of course, a full results service and the updated League tables.

Each day, the local news and sport was supplemented by breaking news stories from across the UK which arrived from a network of dedicated journalists via the Press Association wire telegraph service. The teleprinters situated in the roof of the building were chattering away day and night, providing a news service from correspondents worldwide and you could always rely on a wired photograph of a major event arriving in good time to meet the various editions.

In order to speed the process of delivery, different numbered folios of the same story might emerge on separate printers, which meant they would descend the chute into the sub-editors' room out of sequence. This irritated the Chief Sub, George Anderson, to such an extent that he used to bend his body into an unfeasibly contorted position as he yelled up the chute to the operator above: 'Ossie, John anybody ... help me. I've got Beatles 1, 2 and 4. Page 3 is missing, what's happened?' So used had they become to these quite unnecessary interruptions from below, that the operators could be heard shouting such responses as, 'It's tea break time in London. We've run out of paper, or The Beatles have asked for page 3 to be retracted!'

George's one great asset was his ability to delegate responsibility to others. He could work himself into a frenzy, complaining he was overloaded with work and cajoling others to relieve him of his burden. In fact, for much of the day he sat with arms folded, banging loose change from his pocket up and down on his desk. Being the newest recruit in the room, I knew I would be the target for his next call.

'Here's my tuppence halfpenny, Willie ... off you go to the canteen – tea, no sugar please.' Protestations that I was up against the clock in my efforts to get the back page lead completed were politely dismissed.

As George's deputy, Rowley Middleton was also at the receiving end of his mild rebukes. If he was missing from the room even for a few minutes, perhaps to collect some copy from the reporters' office, Rowley, who liked a punt at the best of times, would be accused of having deserted his post to place a few bob on a horse in the 3.15 race at Sandown.

Nevertheless, together with other engaging characters such as Dick Jacques with his encyclopaedic knowledge of sport, these experienced journalists created a warm and friendly atmosphere and no little encouragement.

As the 1964-5 season began, Hedley Mortlock had been offered a job on the *Sun* and suddenly, I found myself promoted to Sports Editor and a place in the front of the Hartlepools United coach as the ill-fated club was given yet another chance to throw off its Cinderella image and finally escape re-election at the sixth time of asking.

I was asked to write under the pseudonym 'Sentinel' to maintain a long-running tradition. In the literal sense then, I was a look-out man, a sentry employed to observe the approach of danger and to watch for something to happen. It was a pen name that certainly fitted the bill.

By now, Hartlepools' Manager, Bob Gurney, had been sacked – the fourth in three years – and replaced by Alvan 'Tiger' Williams, at 31 the youngest boss in League football. The son of a vicar from Anglesey, he had arrived as trainer-coach the previous season and then offered the manager's job on a month's trial by Chairman Ernie Ord. The two men were a complete contrast – the chairman short, wily and entrepreneurial; the manager, tall, fiery, intimidating and with hands as big as spades.

Alvan had once been on Bolton Wanderers' books and while at Burnden Park worked on the ground staff, training with such fine internationals as Nat Lofthouse, Willy Moir and Bobby Langton before National Service intervened. Later he was to make his name as a rugged, no nonsense centre-half for Wrexham, Bradford Park Avenue, Exeter City and Bangor.

Mr Ord, as he insisted in being addressed, owned the only Rolls-

Royce in town. In the early sixties, he also ran West Hartlepool on 'tick' as the director of a check trading company. In lower-income regions like the North East, such businesses were highly profitable. In the struggle to feed and clothe themselves, clients would be issued with a £10 ticket which they could exchange at local stores. The check trading companies then sent out agents to customers' homes to collect weekly fees on the vouchers, sometimes as low as half a crown a week. While interest rates could range up to 70 per cent on an annualised basis, such companies provided credit access to consumers who were otherwise unable to procure loans from traditional banking sources.

Ernie Ord would visit the Victoria Ground every morning in his Rolls Silver Cloud, but on the day Alvan was appointed the price of petrol went up. Not to be outdone, the chairman arrived at the ground in a brand new Hillman Imp. His greeting to his new manager was: 'The Government won't beat me, my Rolls is staying in the garage.'

In April 1964 allegations were made that Hartlepools' players had been involved in a bribery scandal and had deliberately thrown a League match. This led to the club dismissing the players cited, leaving Alvan with only seven professionals. Finally, after the Chairman resigned and then demanded his reinstatement for the third time, some cash was released for players and the full-time playing staff increased to 16.

One of these was Ambrose (Amby) Fogarty who was in a class of his own and one of the finest players ever to appear in the club's blue and white stripes. He was Hartlepools' record signing when moving from Sunderland for £10,000 and went on to make over a hundred appearances. In 1964 he became the first Pools international when he won the last of his eleven caps for Ireland against Spain.

I enjoyed sitting next to him on the team bus. He was always an upbeat character, intelligent, colourful and full of Irish wit and humour. He was also an exceedingly good source of information about what was going on inside the club. The manager was quick to identify the source of some of my exclusives and thereafter despatched me to sit on the single seat at the front of the coach adjacent to Ted the driver.

For the first few months of the season, Hartlepools' results followed a familiar pattern and by November the club found itself once again consigned to the basement of the Fourth Division. Sentinel's life was becoming one of despair. Return trips from Oxford, Rochdale, Notts County and Bradford resembled a funeral cortege. My running reports for the *Football Mail* were attracting depressing headlines. The newsboys who used to grab handfuls of the green 'un and race off to the pubs in the hope of selling the lot in half an hour found their cries of 'Footy Mail' through the front door of such celebrated drinking dens as The Devon being met with angry responses of 'bugger off!'.

Those who didn't already know the final result just had to take one glance at the front page where 'The Docker' gave the game away. He was a cartoon character in a flat cap, swinging on a pit prop hanging off a crane. To herald a Pools United win, he would be seen with thumb up and grinning ear to ear. Pointing sideways signified a draw and alas, the caricature that appeared all too frequently, glum face and thumb down, indicating yet another loss. At least the two of us were on the same wavelength!

One autumn weekend brought games at Newport County on the Saturday and then Torquay on the Monday evening. Pressure was building, the manager knew his job was under threat and the players were beginning to realize that the curtain might be closing on their life as full-time professionals by the end of a disastrous season. The warnings went unheeded. Pools lost 2–0 to ten-men Newport and 2–1 at Torquay. The performance at the Devon resort was a distinct improvement on recent form but the atmosphere was still one of foreboding. The pirate radio station *Caroline,* then 'all the rage' transmitting the best of pop music from a ship anchored in international waters off the Suffolk coast, also became the favourite of the Pools team. When the coach driver Ted stopped en route to Bristol to refuel, Alvan popped into the service station to replenish his supply of cigars. On his return, he found the sounds of *Radio Caroline* blasting through the speakers and immediately demanded that the driver turn the radio off. A blazing row ensued with Ted refusing to drive the bus any further, removing the keys from the ignition and walking off down the road. It took a considerable amount of time and some sweet talking to persuade him to resume his seat behind the wheel, this time without the musical accompaniment.

The more miserable the results, the harder the job became. Having given the players a piece of his mind in the dressing room, the manager now turned his wrath upon me. However much Alvan may have wished that I could have found some positives to report in a 5–0 pummelling at Brighton, there was not a single flash of inspiration to be seen from anyone in a Pools shirt. Mr Ord, who rarely travelled to away games, was obviously far from enamoured with my critical summary on the performance which appeared at the end of my *Football Mail* report. He immediately phoned the hotel where the team had arrived for dinner for a heated exchange of words with his manager.

Making my own way back from the Goldstone Ground to join them, I was immediately pinned against the wall by Alvan, his face crimson with rage. Luckily, I managed to get out of the way just in the nick of time with the steel tip of his umbrella heading straight for my belly button! The 300-mile journey back to Hartlepool that night was one of the most wretched I have ever encountered. Still fuming over his side's performance, the manager refused all requests to stop the bus even for those desperate for a pee – Alvan certainly had his own unique way of keeping his players happy!

Worse was to follow. Arriving early one Saturday morning to catch the coach for the away fixture at Barrow, I found the manager in a foul mood, roaring his disapproval of an article I had written the previous evening about a player whom a previously reliable source had indicated was now a transfer target for the club.

At first, it seemed I was to be barred from boarding the bus, this despite the fact that the *Mail* paid the club in full for all my travel costs. Eventually Alvan relented, but when we pulled into the Lakeside Hotel at Windermere for lunch, I was despatched to a table in the far corner of the restaurant and served a good 30 minutes after the main party. I had hardly cut into my sirloin steak when I was being summoned back to the car park. Having a sweet tooth, I was totally distraught that the peach melba would have to wait for a more agreeable day!

Being young and still wet behind the ears, I decided it best not to raise the issue with the Editor, Fred Dines. He was a kindly man whose main interest in my progress was a daily enquiry as to how much headway I had been making with my shorthand whilst attending a day release course organised by the National Council for the Training of Journalists at Monkwearmouth College in Sunderland. The continuing inability to increase my speed was still the bane of my journalistic life.

One morning, however, Alvan went too far, issuing a series of threats during a phone conversation about what was in store for me if I didn't change my ways. My predecessor, 'Mort', had once been banned from the ground and had to report the match from the terraces when the Chairman took a dislike to the *Mail's* reporting of events, while another who had also once written under the pen name 'Sentinel' had been thrown fully clothed into the showers by an irate forward who didn't take too kindly to criticism of his abilities as a striker. Given that level of intimidation and retribution, I feared what fate might be in store for me and so this time, headed straight for the Editor's office.

Mr Dines was extremely supportive and put a call through to the

Hartlepools' Chairman. Within the hour, Mr Ord had joined us. Coffee cup in hand, lace handkerchief tucked up under his gold watch, he raised a sympathetic smile.

'You will be getting a call from my manager firstly to apologise and then to invite you to dinner.'

Three days later, the three of us sat down to a four-course meal at The Grand Hotel, one of the town's most imposing Victorian buildings offering the finest in food and service.

Alvan offered to pick me up in his Jaguar and in the presence of his Chairman was the most genial of hosts, handing me the extensive menu and list of fine wines and declaring: 'Never mind the cost, choose whatever takes your fancy.'

When the head waiter rushed to the table to inform Mr Ord that a call was waiting for him in reception, Alvan's face suddenly changed. Though he didn't say anything, his demeanour left me in no doubt that he viewed the whole experience as one of humiliation. It was a defining moment in a season that for both of us was suddenly and unexpectedly to take a decided turn for the better.

One of the most dreaded trips for any sixties side was to take on the Lions of Millwall at The Den with its intimidating, fortress-like reputation. The South London club were six months into an incredible three-year unbeaten home run stretching to 59 games. To everyone's surprise, Pools had the audacity to hold them to a goalless draw, almost as great a shock as their 1–0 win over the same opposition in front of their largest home crowd of over 10,000 the previous October, a result that at the time had mistakenly led their fans to believe promotion might be a realistic target.

We had now advanced to February 1965 and the players' belief in their own ability had suddenly come flooding back. Unexpected triumphs at Crewe and then in the local derby at Darlington saw Pools reaching the dizzy heights of 12th place in the League. Alvan was a changed personality. That tough, uncompromising stance and outward abrasiveness had been replaced with a willingness to communicate ... yes, even with *Sentinel,* who in turn had now to rediscover more positive phrases to describe the team's turn of fortune.

Pulling out yet another mild and elegant Panatella from his box of cigars, Alvan was clearly becoming a trifle more ambitious.

'You'll want to know me, Willie, when I'm manager of Wolves.'

The season ended with Hartlepools United in a creditable fifteenth position, thirteen points clear of the bottom four. It may have taken six years but at long last that unenviable and unsurpassed record of five successive re-election applications was at an end. It called for a celebration, though no-one had expected that the town would go to the lengths of throwing a Civic Reception in their honour. Normally these are reserved for FA Cup winners and Olympic Gold Medallists.

The Mayor, Barbara Mann, though was ecstatic about the club securing its place in the Fourth Division for the following season. As glasses were raised, Mrs Mann was fulsome in her praise of the team's efforts.

'Football is an essential part of our life in the North East,' she declared, 'and there's no doubt that a side which is on the upgrade has a remarkable psychological effect. By having a more successful team after five years in the doldrums, we have improved output in every field of local industry.'

Within days, the champagne corks were popping in the Williams household too. Having achieved such a sudden turnaround in Hartlepools' fortunes, Alvan was now the target for other clubs looking for a new manager. And so it was off to Third Division Southend United and later back to his Welsh roots as manager of Wrexham where he carried out a root and branch restructuring of the club. The team ended his first season in charge just six points adrift of a promotion spot but the following season he was gone, having resigned following a contractual dispute with the directors.

After leaving Wrexham, Alvan sought no further involvement in the game, returning to Anglesey where he converted an old vicarage into a hotel near Llangefni. He later remarried and with his wife Liz worked in Blackpool before managing a number of pubs in London. Outside one of these, the Robert Lee in Tottenham, a 19-year-old student died shortly after being ejected for drunkenness. Alvan and two others were charged with his murder. Though he was acquitted on that charge, Alvan was found guilty of affray and handed a suspended sentence.

He was defended in court by Oliver Popplewell QC who, as a High Court Judge, was later to chair the inquiry into the tragic fire at Bradford City's football ground.

Returning to Wales, Alvan became 'Mine Host' at the Ship Inn in Bala. On his retirement, celebrated Welsh football historian, Gareth M. Davies recommended that 'Tiger' should be given a special award for his services to the game. The Welsh FA agreed and though in failing health, Alvan set off for Cardiff to receive an accolade for a lifetime's service to football.

It was one of his last acts. A few weeks later, he suffered a massive heart attack and fell to his death down the stairs of the retirement home he and his wife had just purchased in the village of Llandderfel.

Intimidating he may have been, hard as granite on the field and in the dressing room, but when he let go of his tough exterior Alvan Williams could be charm personified. I owe him a debt of gratitude, for by putting me in touch with my own vulnerability at such an early stage in my career, I was propelled into finding a tougher and more competitive edge to my character.

Alvan was replaced at the Victoria Ground by former Liverpool player Geoff Twentyman but the club dispensed with his services after a mere four months. Ironically, Twentyman returned to Liverpool as the club's Chief Scout and is credited with bringing such outstanding talents as Ian Rush, Phil Neal and Alan Hansen to Anfield.

In yet another audacious move, Ernie Ord then tried to woo Alvan Williams back for a second stint as manager but had to settle instead for the second-choice candidate, a brash young man by the name of Brian Clough whose Sunderland career had been so cruelly cut short by a bad knee injury after a collision with the Bury goalkeeper. Clough even had the nerve to demand that the chairman allow him to bring in an assistant from Burton Albion, one Peter Taylor.

Taylor confided that the job saved Clough's life.

'He was a no-hoper, jobless, boozing heavily and on his way out.'

In his memoirs, Clough recalled his time at Hartlepools: 'People said you could drop off the end of the world if you went there. Sometimes I wished I had!' Luckily, he never contemplated such a fate when taking lessons in driving the team bus as an economy measure. In his typical showman way, he invited the media to come and watch him trundle the bus about town. It certainly gained him lots of publicity though he was never actually asked to drive the coach to away games.

Clough was just 29 when he took the job and, along with Taylor, instilled a sense of pride while building a side that went on to gain the first promotion in the club's history under his successor, Gus McLean. By now I was at Tyne Tees Television and had the pleasure of joining the players on the team coach as they returned from the decisive game at Swansea. Clough and Taylor had moved on, too, to Derby County then in the Second Division. Just three years later, they had won the First Division title and a legend was born. Clough repeated the feat at Nottingham Forest and of course, 'Ole Big Head' was to lift the European Cup in successive seasons.

The 'best manager England never had' is one of the favourite descriptions of the man who cut his managerial teeth at Hartlepools. Clough, of course, had his own ready answer to that one.

'I'm sure the England selectors thought if they took me on and gave me the job, I'd want to run the show. They were shrewd because that's exactly what I would have done.'

Early in April 1966 I managed to obtain a ticket for the Press Box at Hampden Park as Scotland faced the auld enemy, as ever the climax of the Home International Championship. With England hosting the World Cup that summer, the game was expected to give everyone an opportunity to form a view of their chances of winning the coveted Jules Rimet trophy.

A crowd of 134,000 people made their way to the ground in Glasgow's south side, many of them by car. Nearby parks had vehicles lined up hundreds deep and stretching back the best part of half a mile. I had left my first car, a Standard 8 that had seen better times, behind in Hartlepool. On my last venture north to Scotland, I was responsible for leaving a 200-mile trail of the black stuff due to cracked seals and gaskets and found myself having to pour in two pints of oil for every gallon of petrol.

So this time, I hired a Ford Anglia for the trip across the border. I arrived in plenty of time to find a space in the sprawling car park and headed for the stadium. Climbing the stairs to the Press Box, I ran straight into a familiar face, Ray Robertson then a very distinguished sports writer for the *Northern Echo*.

He was on the third day of his honeymoon and his idea of married bliss was to sportingly offer to take his bride Joan to Glasgow to allow her to indulge in a spot of shopping while he ran off to the game! Having arranged to meet up again in Argyle Street at 6 pm sharp, Ray was becoming very agitated as the second half got under way. He had realised that given the size of the crowd, he would need to slip away early to catch the train from Mount Florida station back into the city centre.

As the goals rained in during an incredible second period – England finally silencing the Tartan Army with a 4–3 triumph – I told Ray to sit back and enjoy the unfolding drama with the promise that I would drive him back to the rendezvous point with plenty of time to spare. We waited as vehicles of every shape and size began to snake out of the nearby park but when our column finally began to move, the Anglia refused to budge. Try as we might, our efforts to get the engine started ended in abject failure and it was well after 7 pm before the AA arrived to put us out of our misery.

Not only had I ruined someone's honeymoon, I had visions of ending a marriage before it had even started! Reaching the hotel opposite Glasgow Central Station, Ray almost tripped himself up on the steps as flustered and embarrassed, he dashed through the front door.

I don't know which of us was the more pleased to have survived the disaster. Happily, Ray and Joan have now been married for over 40 years with two children and five grandchildren but for Ray, the merest mention of the words Hampden Park and Bill Hamilton is enough to induce a cold sweat and knotted stomach.

After the amalgamation of the two Boroughs of Hartlepool and West Hartlepool in the late 1960s, the club dropped the 's' from the end of its name. It is now known simply as Hartlepool United with a completely refurbished stadium and a more ambitious team which has won two promotions and engaged in giant-killing acts in the FA Cup. It's a revival in fortunes that has matched that of the town which has replaced its decaying buildings and redundant works with new service industries and a £60-million marina attracting thousands of visitors.

However, the wind of change has sadly blown one tradition out the window. Like scores of other Saturday papers, the *Football Mail* – or green 'un – is no more, a sad victim of the electronic revolution. What a shame! It just doesn't seem right that 'The Docker' swinging from his old pip prop, has been denied the opportunity of indulging in one final 'thumbs up' to signify better days for his beloved Hartlepool.

5

Ha' Ye Seen Owt Wullie?

Ha'way-tha-lads. I'm very grateful to be a Geordie now.

President Jimmy Carter on being made a Freeman of Newcastle

They don't come any more popular than Our 'Enery, British boxing's first and only Knight of the Realm. Nearly forty years since hanging up his gloves, Henry Cooper's enduring modesty, dignity and innate ability to get along with people contrasts starkly with the arrogance and indifference of so many in professional sport today.

Few of my generation will forget a June night in 1963 when for a few brief moments the Cockney heavyweight looked to have changed the course of boxing history. In front of 35,000 fans at Wembley Stadium, his famous left hook sent the then Louisville Lip, Cassius Clay, crashing to the floor only for the brash young American to be saved by the bell at the end of the fourth round. A cut above Cooper's left eye brought the contest to a close in the fifth but that night turned Cooper into a national icon.

Three years later he was to be given a second chance at Clay – by now the legendary Muhammad Ali – this time for boxing's most prestigious prize, the world heavyweight title. The champion though had learned his lesson. A growing respect for Cooper ensured he would not feel the sting of Henry's Hammer again and another deep gash over the Londoner's left eye meant the fight ended the same way as before.

When British boxing fans talk of Cooper, it isn't the second encounter they recall. But for me, the night of 21 May 1966 was one that would change the whole course of my journalistic career. I had been invited to watch a live transmission of the fight from Arsenal's Highbury stadium on the largest cinema screen in Newcastle. Backstage, the wine was flowing freely as the North East's leading sports writers tucked into the smoked salmon sandwiches washed down with a glass of Dom Perignon.

Not wanting to invade what was fast appearing as an intimate little gathering of buddies, I struck up a conversation with an immaculately dressed young man whose primary concern was to keep the dollop of fresh cream decorating the top of his strawberry tart from staining his skinny-striped jacquard necktie.

He introduced himself as Allan Powell and said he had recently moved to the newsroom of Tyne Tees Television from the *Shields Gazette* where he had been Deputy Chief Sub-Editor. Even though I was still only 22, I had a burning ambition to find a route into television and listened enviously as Allan recounted tales of life on the second floor of the City Road studios in Newcastle, reconstructed from the shell of two disused furniture warehouses.

'What's more, I've heard they're holding auditions for a news journalist/reporter on Tuesday. Why don't you try to get your name on the list?'

First thing Monday morning, I was on the phone to the News Editor, Brian Harrison. I could feel a pang of sympathy at the other end of the line.

'You've left it a bit late,' he said. 'I really don't know what I can do other than pass your name on.'

'But when do the auditions begin?' I asked cheekily.

'Well, I expect you'd better get here by eleven,' was the hesitant response from someone who clearly felt I was pushing my luck a little too far.

I thought it wise to keep my unreliable Ford Anglia at home for the day. It had developed a rather disconcerting habit of shuddering wildly as the speedometer needle reached 40 miles an hour despite repeated attempts by a back-street garage mechanic to erase the problem. This was a day to let the train take the strain.

Consternation on arrival at the Tyne Tees reception desk, as no-one recognised my name and a succession of frantic phone calls around various departments could shed no light on the matter. What's more, seven other candidates had arrived as early as 9 am and were now huddled together in a tiny office, being marshalled in military precision by an ex-Army officer Neville Jackson who had recently taken over as the station's Head of News.

Before I could join them, I had to persuade anyone who would listen that I was a genuine candidate. Finding me a little tiresome, a commissionaire suggested I make my way upstairs to the make-up department where I would be 'seen to!'. Quite what that meant I was not sure, but in trepidation I crept through an open door and was immediately despatched to a high chair not dissimilar to one I regularly encountered during monthly visits to the barbers.

On discovering the purpose of my visit, the make-up artist was kindness personified. As she powdered and pampered my facial features in a bold attempt to enhance my appearance, she also allowed me to benefit from her own brand of positive psychology suggesting that whatever else happened, I must remain calm, focused and confident.

No-one arrived to usher me to the room where Mr Jackson was busily barking out instructions to be followed by the other candidates. 'And who are you then?' he asked, clearly annoyed that his train of thought had been interrupted by this mere slip of a lad bursting into the office, desperately looking for a vacant chair.

When I explained the circumstances that had propelled me from a cinema hospitality suite to a place alongside seven other television hopefuls, he began to mellow. On reflection, I think he was quietly impressed by my map-reading skills as I negotiated all the rabbit warrens to reach his 'command room' in a matter of minutes. After all, personal initiative is one of the hallmarks of a good British soldier.

Fortunately, Neville Jackson had a spare 'battle plan' which he hurled in my direction. It comprised a bulletin put together from some old news scripts specially chosen because they were nothing short of a minefield for anyone unable to discover the proper pronunciation of place names such as Grosmont, Cambois, Bellingham and Houghton le Spring. They even threw in Kirkcudbright for good measure though I was quite unable to fathom what connection this ancient Scottish burgh had with the North East. Surnames too, were readily introduced into the mix, real shockers like Featherstonehaugh (Fan-shaw) and Beauchamp (Beech-um).

I was a bundle of nerves as I scanned the pages that would shortly have to be read to camera. Then, glancing round the room, I recognised several of my competitors. All were thoroughly seasoned journalists with an impressive track record. Suddenly, I felt at ease. Against such a formidable line-up what realistic chance had I of winning the prize?

Besides, I had never physically seen the inside of a television studio and could not even begin to imagine the terrors it held for someone so young and still relatively immature. I consoled myself with the thought that I was enjoying a day out and a once in a lifetime experience.

Having started the day as a 'non person', I was told I would now be the last to be called, as my name was hurriedly scribbled right at the bottom of Mr Jackson's running order. One by one, the candidates left the room to return some ten minutes later. For some, the whole experience had proved too much, a couple had felt intimidated, others thought they had given it their best shot. Alarmingly, two of them said that after they had finished reading the bulletin, they had been asked to look directly into the camera and talk about themselves for a period of two minutes.

What on earth could I say that would be of the remotest interest to Mr Jackson and his cohorts who would be sitting in judgement in the control room that I guessed must be sited alongside the studio? As I glanced through the news script one last time and tried to get my tongue around those unpronounceable names, I made a tactical decision that I thought might make its mark with our 'newsroom general'. The office door opened one last time and I was invited to begin the short walk to Studio 2.

Waiting to greet me was a tall, straight-backed Scotsman with a goatee beard who introduced himself as the floor manager. Bob Hughes was clearly proud of his origins and smiling broadly on discovering that a fellow Scot was about to be put to the test. 'There's absolutely nothing to worry about. Just sit down there lad, start reading what you've got in your hand and don't forget to look into that camera. Got it?'

I could scarcely believe my luck. Every time I had rehearsed the script in the next door office, I had stumbled over words, found myself fighting for breath and even jumbled the pages in the wrong order. This time, everything seemed to go right – correct pronunciations, proper emphasis on the key words and I had reached the last sentence as the indication came that I had but five seconds left.

'That's the spirit son,' Bob shouted as he approached the desk to remove the typewritten bulletin from my grasp. 'Now then, the director has asked me if you would be so good as to talk about yourself for a couple of minutes. Make it interesting lad, let's hear what makes you tick. I'll be giving you a series of signals to indicate how long you have to go. This one for 30 seconds, this for 15 and then using the fingers of both hands I will count you down to zero. Have you got it?'

Almost before I had a chance to draw breath, the red light on top of the camera was on and I was given the signal to start.

'Being a Scot bound by the strictures of a fundamentalist upbringing, it would seem my parents were hoping I would become involved in the ministerial life of the church...' Out of the corner of my eye, I was able to catch a glimpse of Jackson and other members of the newsroom hierarchy behind the control room window shaking their heads in disbelief.

It was exactly the response I had hoped for and the cue for an immediate change of tack.

'Of course, that's not the way I saw it...' I exclaimed with all the vitality and enthusiasm I could muster in a ploy designed to grab the attention of those who must surely have been well on the road to writing me off as a lost cause. The job now was to use the remaining minute and three quarters to create an invigorating and exciting picture of how I saw my life developing in the relatively new and challenging world of television journalism.

Bob Hughes sent me on my way with a warm handshake. Neville Jackson was more poker-faced and non-committal.

'We'll be in touch with everyone as soon as we make a decision and don't forget to fill out an expenses form.'

I left the building feeling I had performed better than expected and had nothing about which to be ashamed. It had been an enjoyable 'away day' with my train fare paid and a chance to see the workings of a television studio for the first, and perhaps the last, time in my life.

Three weeks passed and I had heard nothing. I was even beginning to wonder whether this escapade to Newcastle had been nothing more than a figment of my imagination.

Settling back to life as Sports Editor of the *Hartlepool Mail*, I had become increasingly annoyed by the refusal of several secretaries of local football sides to abide by the deadline imposed for having their team news included in the Friday night edition of the paper. I had threatened to take decisive action despite the Editor's plea to tread softly.

One secretary in particular had failed to heed several warnings.

'Mr Jackson,' I screamed at him down the phone, 'how many times have I told you that your team must be sent to me in writing. I haven't the time to take down the details over the phone. Imagine if every one of 60 other secretaries tried to do it this way. I'm afraid as you don't listen to anything I say, I've no option but to put a stop to this call.'

'I've no idea what you're talking about,' came the exasperated voice on the other end of the phone. 'This is NEVILLE Jackson of Tyne Tees Television. I thought you would like to know you have been chosen as our new reporter. Do you want the job or not?'

It was an embarrassment I would not be allowed to forget. An August starting date was set as my three-year indenture agreement with the paper had still two months to run. This included the three-week period of the 1966 World Cup for which I had obtained accreditation. Though sent to cover West Hartlepool's progress in a North Yorkshire and South

Durham cricket fixture on the momentous day when England beat West Germany in the Wembley final, I did have the privilege of watching one of the biggest football shocks of all time.

A crowd of 18,000 crammed into Middlesbrough's Ayresome Park to watch Italy make short work of North Korea. At least that's what everyone thought until Park Doo-Ik wrote himself into the record books with an incredible winning goal against an Italian side studded with such celebrities as Rivera, Mazzola and Facchetti. The Koreans were so small that one Boro fan sitting nearby said it was like watching a team of jockeys.

Italy returned home under cover of darkness but could not escape a reception of rotten fruit hurled at their players at Genoa Airport while North Korea went on to a quarter final at Goodison Park in Liverpool. There they raced into an amazing 3–0 lead against Portugal before 'The Black Panther' Eusebio took a hand in proceedings and struck four times to turn the game around and give Portugal a 5-3 victory.

At Tyne Tees Television I would be given the chance to cover both news and sport. The ITV station was still a relatively young one and I reckoned two of the major reasons I had been given the job was that, at 22, I was not yet set in my ways and could more readily adapt to the requirements of the post than older colleagues. And, of course, the more obvious one – they would not have to pay me so much!

Programme budgets were tight and in the early days there were no taped programmes. Every programme went out live and if there were any mistakes, they were there for everyone to see. Two brothers from Sunderland, George and Alfred Black, sons of the famous impresario George Black, became joint programme directors ensuring that from the station's opening in 1959 to the mid-sixties, light entertainment was 'king'. The City Road studios reverberated with the sound of music, singing, dancing and comedy. Programmes included *The One O'Clock Show* which went out live for 40 minutes, five days a week, a hectic schedule but a successful one as thousands of children in the North East used to go home for their lunch which was cooked in their mothers' relaxation time. The Head of Sales was convinced he could sell air time at one o'clock in the afternoon. He was right.

The company had also found a lucrative way of increasing advertising revenue. They introduced advertising magazines purported to be programmes but simply based on out-and-out selling. They were given names such as *Hi There, Mary Goes to Market* and *Ned's Shed* and scripted in such a way that a loose story line ran through them, always linking one product to the next.

Ned would be digging a trench with a new spade on his supposed Northumberland allotment when his neighbour Knocker Brown suddenly appeared on the scene to ask him where he got the spade from and how much it cost. The script was totally superficial and they had to keep inventing ways of introducing new products. Ned would accidentally trip over a wheelbarrow which prompted him to say, 'Oh this is my new barrow. Do you like it? You can buy one just like this at Shepherds of Gateshead.' And there would be a whole host of items in and around the shed, all of them given a mention, priced and the viewer told precisely from where they could be purchased. It was a purely money-making venture which endorsed as many as a dozen products in a 15-minute programme. Eventually, ITV's first regulatory body, the Independent Television Authority, stepped in to kick the whole ridiculous scenario firmly into touch. In the last episode, Ned's Shed was set on fire much to the delight of the production staff!

With its franchise coming up for renewal, Tyne Tees was forced to make changes. The station had become a small island of journalism in a very large sea of show business. Now the newsroom became the focus of attention. It would grow substantially in size and importance.

For the first month, I kept my head down, learning as much as I could about how television news actually works. I soon discovered it demanded a team effort where everyone had to pull together – cameraman, sound recordist, lighting engineer, film editor, link writer. Unlike newspapers, reporters did not operate on their own. Most importantly, television was all about pictures. Everything that you scripted had to complement those images faithfully recorded on the celluloid. And one real bonus, shorthand – so long my arch-nemesis – would no longer be a major requirement now that I would have a trusty microphone in my hand.

I was eager to get out 'on the road' but Neville Jackson had not yet written my name in his list of 'front line battle troops'. Then ten days after my arrival, my big break came. With roast lamb just one of three specials on the canteen menu, everyone had deserted the newsroom to jostle for position in the queue. I was left behind to man the news desk with strict instructions to call the canteen if anything even barely resembling a major story should rear its head.

Barely a couple of minutes had passed when the phone rang. An agitated member of the public was desperate to let us know that there was a considerable amount of police activity outside a fish and chip shop in Sunderland. 'I think there's been a robbery of some sort and it looks as though people have been hurt.' I took the man's name and address and promised that if he was right, a tip-off fee would be in the post.

The nature of the call meant there wasn't a minute to lose. I dashed to the canteen, told them I was on my way and would someone please arrange for a camera crew to liaise with me outside the 'chippy'. Arriving at the shop in Southwick Road, I found Eleanor Spence, the owner's wife still in a state of shock. She had been in the back room when a masked raider ran into the shop holding up her assistant Jean Mason at gunpoint. He screamed that the weapon was loaded and immediately made for the till. Showing remarkable presence of mind, Mrs Spence managed to push the gun away and threatened to throw boiling fat from the fryer over the intruder. Her cool head and brave intervention paid off as the man fled empty-handed.

If this was to be my debut as a television news reporter then I knew I had all the makings of a first-class story. It took on even more significance with reports that a nationwide hunt for Britain's most wanted man, Harry Roberts, later convicted for the shooting of three London policemen, was being centred on County Durham after reports that someone answering his description had been seen heading north up the A1 in a car displaying GB plates. The police were taking no chances with every lead being followed up with renewed vigour. Could the masked gunman possibly have been Roberts desperate to get his hands on some ready cash after weeks on the run?

As I started to plan the shape of my story in my head, the camera crew arrived. I introduced myself as Bill Hamilton, the new boy on the block.

'That's funny,' they said. 'We were told Harold Williamson was the reporter on this one. Never mind, let's get rolling.'

And so my first interview began but, just as Mrs Spence was in full flow describing how she had successfully foiled the gunman, into the shop walked the said Harold Williamson. Alas, in my ignorance, I had not realised he was employed by the opposition. To everyone's astonishment, my interview was being recorded by the BBC!

When the laughter finally died down, Harold handed me the film – as it transpired a very fortunate gesture – for by the time the Tyne Tees crew arrived, Mrs Spence's husband had decided he'd had quite enough of the media for one day and wanted us off the premises.

Though we were in the communications business, getting hold of reporters and camera crews was often fraught with problems. With telephone booths out of commission – wires cut, coin boxes smashed by would-be thieves or waiting to be emptied by the GPO – getting hold of a public phone often became a near impossible task – unless of course, you managed to synchronise your call with pub opening hours. Often, it was a case of knocking on someone's door and hoping that the lady of the house took pity on you.

What a relief then when the first pagers were introduced, allowing you to send and receive messages, though not in written form. The whole process became quite sophisticated. You could buzz someone and send a series of numbers. There were three vital ones:

1 – drop everything and get in touch with the office as fast as you can.
2 – finish what you're doing and then there's another job for you.
3 – complete assignment and come back.

A second digit indicated the area of your next job. Every sizeable town in Northumberland, Durham, Teesside and North Yorkshire was given its own unique code, so if the second number indicated Berwick upon Tweed, you would head in that direction before getting to a phone to find out the precise location.

Lighting outside locations on dark winter nights had also brought its problems. Apart from a small hand-held light known as a 'hand basher', there was simply no way of illuminating the scene. That's until someone came up with the idea of using flares. These operated like giant fireworks and each was of similar size and shape to a policeman's truncheon. Pushed into soft ground, they'd burn for about five minutes.

Their use often caused alarm and general mayhem. One set off near the North Sea coast was spotted by the Coastguard and sparked a major alert. The lifeboat was launched and a helicopter put on standby.

On another occasion, cameraman Bob Herrick was enjoying a drink in a well-known hostelry by Paddy's Market on Newcastle's Quayside when he spotted a huge building ablaze on the south bank of the river at Gateshead. He rushed across the Tyne Bridge and set a flare alight only to encounter the Fire Chief seething with indignation. 'It took us two hours to extinguish the fire. Now it has all started up again!' Unperturbed, Bob tried the same ploy at the Monte Carlo rally a few days later. This time he approached a gendarme in pristine uniform and asked whether he would consider holding a flare for him. *'Je serais enchanté pour vous aider'* ('I would be delighted to help you') came the reply. Five minutes later the intrepid volunteer was completely covered in one huge layer of ash!

The practice was discontinued shortly after another embarrassing incident during the filming of an event in the grounds of Durham Cathedral. No sooner had the camera started to roll than a party of American visitors arrived on the scene. One of them came across to express his thanks to the cameraman for illuminating the building believing it was being done for their benefit. From the road some distance away, smoke could be seen rising and half a dozen fire engines arrived within minutes. They thought the Cathedral was on fire!

News Editor Brian Harrison was a constant source of encouragement. He had an impressive track record both in news and sport moving from the *Evening Chronicle* to edit Tyne Tees first Sports programme. Middlesbrough FC decided that their prolific goalscorer, the legendary Brian Clough, should be allowed to appear live in the studio on the opening day. The budget for the entire programme was just £20. On meeting him at Newcastle Station, Harrison said: 'Brian, we have three choices here. We can get a taxi, we can climb aboard a bus or we can walk.'

'How far to the studios?' Clough asked. When told it was about a mile, the show's first VIP guest said: 'Then let's walk.' Harrison was mightily relieved. As they strode through the city, his immediate thought was that he had saved 10 per cent of the programme budget.

'Clough's appearance fee was a fiver. The man who was the goal machine of his day even paid his own train fare. We couldn't afford that. And he agreed to walk back to the station. Could you imagine that happening with any of the football stars of today? You'd be laughed out of court!'

On moving to Tyneside, I first stayed with a delightful couple in the village of Earsdon near Whitley Bay but after a few months they politely asked whether I might find alternative accommodation for three weeks as they were expecting a visit from a relation living in Canada.

While making my way to the railway station at Backworth, I heard the strains of a Salvation Army Band playing one of my favourite hymns. I felt drawn into the tiny hall of Shiremoor Corps and was moved by both the service and the extent of the welcome afforded.

As I prepared to leave, the Bandmaster came running after me.

'Where are you going lad?' he asked.

I explained that I was setting off for Newcastle in search of a temporary flat.

'Don't be silly lad. It's time for Sunday lunch and we'd love you to join us. Oh, and by the way, looking for a flat is quite an unnecessary business. We have a spare room. Stay for as long as you like.' I had heard of Geordie hospitality but this was quite unexpected and overwhelming. Instead of three weeks, I stayed with Bram and Nancy Scott at their seafront home for four years!

At first, I could not understand why I never saw Bram at the breakfast table. Perhaps he liked a long lie-in. That was till his wife explained that he had already completed half a day's work before I was even out of bed. Bram was a fruit and vegetable retailer and was off to the market at four o'clock every morning. Clearly I had to be taught a lesson, so for the next fortnight, he would bound into the bedroom, draw back the curtains and open the window. 'God's given you another day lad, so let's have you up and making use of it!'

His influence and example led to my joining the Salvation Army and I was given the job of running the Sunday School. Here, the Ford Anglia was pressed into service again as on Sunday afternoons I drove it into a nearby council estate, sounding the horn just like a passing ice cream van. Children of all ages would come rushing out of the gates, their parents more than pleased that they would be off their hands and spending the next hour learning the good news about God and the way he wants us to live. Sadly, but necessarily, it's not an exercise that could be sanctioned in today's world where public concern over the safety of our children has now led to a whole raft of heightened security procedures.

Bram's son John ran a hairdressing salon. Occasionally calling in on a Saturday morning, I found it proved a wonderful source of news and revelation as an array of ladies nestled under the driers awaiting perms, highlights, precision cutting or just a simple shampoo and set. Visiting the area during the 50th Anniversary of Tyne Tees Television in 2009, I found John and his assistant Kathy still at work pampering the same ladies with their latest range of innovative creations. The styles may have changed and the hair become a little greyer, but to my surprise these loyal customers immediately recognised this knavish malapert with a twinkle in his eye who had once invaded their privacy in search of a scoop and disclosed once again that they had lost nothing of that innate ability to unearth a good story.

The North East has always been a fund of good stories. As an incomer I thought I would be at a distinct disadvantage on the reporter's beat. Not a bit of it. Wherever I went, doors opened, opinions were freely expressed and you could always count on a kettle being put on the hob for a farewell cuppa to send you on your way. Whatever the rivalries between the Geordies of Newcastle, the Mackems of Sunderland or the newly daubed Smoggies of Middlesbrough, there is a genuine sense of pride in the region and the achievements of its people. In the 1960s thousands of them were still engaged in building some of the world's finest ships or digging deep into the bowels of the earth for coal.

I was young, optimistic and smitten by the television bug. It was a fantastic learning curve and I eagerly grabbed every opportunity that came my way. Before long, it was decided I should be allowed to present the Friday sports spot which would fill the last ten minutes of the evening news programme anchored by Bob Langley, one of the station's best-known names who later became presenter of the BBC's popular afternoon chat show, *Pebble Mill at One.*

For twenty minutes, I sat in the studio – terrified and in a cold sweat. At one stage, I thought I was going to be violently sick. The manager of Sheffield Wednesday Football Club, Alan Brown, with whom I was to conduct a live interview was led into the studio and spotting my obvious signs of distress, give me a thumbs-up sign and scribbled a kind note to say: 'Don't worry. I'll keep things going if you dry up.'

Bob Langley too, had noticed something was amiss. In the couple of spare minutes between introducing two film reports, he turned to me and said: 'Get your head up Bill. There may be a million people watching this programme but they're all sitting in ones and twos. Most are having their tea. Just conjure up a picture of the most beautiful girl in the world, look straight into that camera and talk to her. Believe me, it works!' It did – though to this day I still cannot fathom how I managed to get Sophia Loren to take such an interest in football!

Bob was one of the most popular Tyne Tees presenters. In the eyes of Tyneside's mini-skirted sixties gals, he was also the most handsome. Autograph books in hand, they would gather at the foot of the steps to the City Road studios waiting for him to depart the building. Some viewers were under the distinct impression that all ITV programmes were made at Tyne Tees. They crowded around the doors hoping to see Clint Walker from *Cheyenne*, Hughie Green from *Double Your Money* or Patrick Macnee, alias British agent John Steed in *The Avengers.*

Each day brought new challenges. It was an invigorating and exciting environment in which to work and I was anxious to find out how everything ticked in the outside world. Emotions surged or calmed dependent on the nature of the next assignment. Hard news or lighter items, this was the perfect journalistic environment in which to cut your teeth.

Inevitably these included disasters. One happened just outside Amble harbour in Northumberland when an RAF pinnace capsized in heavy seas, another on the notorious railway curve at Morpeth when a London to Aberdeen sleeping-car express train was derailed, killing six people and injuring a hundred others. The leading coach ploughed straight into the roof of the station's northbound platform, the others scattering in all directions. At a later inquiry, it was found that the driver had been travelling at 80 miles an hour, nearly double the permanent speed restriction. Called from my bed at some unearthly hour of the morning, I arrived to find the emergency services still trying to extricate passengers from the twisted mass of shattered compartments and dishing out blankets and hot tea to stunned survivors, some of whom were still in their night clothes.

One of the heroines of the night was a nearby resident, Evelyn Dixon, who told of the chaos. Hearing the crash, she hurried to the scene of devastation.

'The odd thing was that there was no sound from the carriages,' she related, 'no moaning and no shouting. I felt there was little I could do so I came back to the house and starting making hot drinks.'

By now I had been accepted in the Tyne Tees newsroom and answerable only to the name of Oor Wullie, which colleagues thought best acknowledged my Scottish roots and my rather eccentric ways which apparently resembled the antics of a wee rascal of the same name and popular cartoon character in the *Sunday Post*. There may have been some truth in that contention though I cannot remember ever endorsing his trademarks of spiky hair, dungarees and upturned bucket! Funnily enough, Roger Watkins, the son of the famous cartoonist Dudley D Watkins who drew the Oor Wullie strips, was a classmate of mine at Dundee High School and I once had the enormous privilege of watching his father's skilful artwork bringing the character to life.

There were certainly characters aplenty in the North East and it was my good fortune to have been given the opportunity to record some of the weird and wonderful situations in which they became entangled ... some of them so bizarre they were also ready made candidates for the 'And finally spot...' on ITN's *News at Ten*.

Brian Gibson, who had replaced Neville Jackson as Head of News, was a master of the art of good script writing. He was also prepared to experiment and try new ideas no matter the risks involved. In the rather staid world of news magazine programmes this was not always well received but I respected both the man and his agenda.

'Get hold of a crew and off you go down to Tynemouth, Wullie.

There's something of a battle royal going on between a couple of old codgers. They're just leaving the court now after being hauled in front of the magistrates.'

If ever a story was ready-made for television, this was the one. On arriving at the coast, I was directed to a village called New York and to a street named Mafeking Terrace. Here, two pensioners – Joe Holcroft, a former miner in his seventies and George Hunter now aged 91 – lived just a couple of doors apart. They had been bitter enemies for years, so long in fact that neither could remember what had originally sparked their feud. Then one day, they emerged through the front door of their red-bricked miners' cottages at precisely the same moment. Words were briefly exchanged before our nonagenarian felt the full force of his neighbour's walking stick smash into his skull leaving an almighty bruise.

I decided to start my report with a 'piece to camera' positioning myself directly between the two houses and with the street sign Mafeking Terrace clearly visible behind my right shoulder.

'According to the history books the Siege of Mafeking ended in 1900. But apparently the news has not yet reached Joe Holcroft who lives in that house (turning to point) and George Hunter who lives in that one. This morning Mr Holcroft was bound over to keep the peace for two years at Tynemouth Court after assaulting his 91-year-old neighbour with a walking stick. So will there now be a relief of Mafeking or is the battle to continue?'

My job now was to try to get the two pensioners together and perhaps instigate a handshake. I decided to approach Joe Holcroft first and knocked on his front door. There was no answer. By now, a small crowd had begun to gather and one young lad pointed to a greenhouse further down the street. 'Yer man's gaan doon-bye mister!'

As we approached, I asked Keith McWhirter, an extremely good-humoured yet determined cameraman with a 'seeing eye', to start rolling. On the other side of the glass, the old boy quite oblivious of our presence was busily walking along a line of clay pots, propagating his plants. Glancing upwards, he grimaced and shook his head in an obvious show of annoyance. To add to his irritation, the rays of the sun shining through the large glass panels provided us with a brightness-enhanced image of the assailant.

Now we could turn to the victim. Same procedure – 'roll camera', a knock on the door – and I could hear the sound of slippers approaching. It was the 91-year-old's son. 'Eeeh man, gan yee caal back in five minutes, George is on the netty (toilet)!' A classic. Five minutes later, we were back on the doorstep. This time George himself answered the door.

'Do you think it's time to let bygones be bygones and shake hands with your neighbour across that fence?' I asked him. Still burning with righteous indignation, he threw his cap to the floor and bent forward towards the camera, pointing to a six-inch scar across the top of his head.

'Tek a lyeuk at that ... divvint ivvor mention eez nyem in me kip!' (Take a look at that ... don't ever mention his name in my house.)

We had clearly reached an impasse. But George had one more card to play.

'Did yee knar, when ah wes just a lad, ah used tuh laik (play) the violin fo' the Duke iv Neerthumberland. Wud yee leek tuh heor it neeo?' (Would you like to hear it now?)

Now why would I want to deprive those devoted viewers of Tyne Tees Television the opportunity to see and hear a virtuoso performance on the doorstep of a miner's cottage? If music can move the soul, it seemed as though this remarkable old man of 91 was finding calm and healing in the midst of his own storm.

Much to my relief, Brian Gibson was delighted with my report and a few days later came hurrying up to my desk holding a handwritten letter whose contents he felt had all the makings of another amusing item.

'Come on Wullie. Have a good read of this and then let's have you on the road again – off to Sunderland.'

This time I thought my Programme Editor had taken leave of his senses and that as a result I would more than likely end the day as a casualty at the Accident and Emergency Unit of the local infirmary. The letter had been penned by a 66-year-old widow, Janet Parkin. She explained how she had fallen in love with another pensioner Stan Kipling and that they were engaged to marry.

'But unfortunately', she wrote, 'there is an impediment to the marriage. Stan keeps a monster in his bedroom. Please can you arrange to have it removed so that we can begin life together.'

Tucking the letter into my inside jacket pocket, I made my way downstairs to the crew room. I had been assigned Jim Hodkinson as my cameraman and knew we might have to call at his home in Gosforth en route as he always liked to check on the welfare of his wife Mirelle Gray, a local nightclub singer. Once on an assignment in North Northumberland, he had insisted in bringing his portable radio into the Kings Arms Hotel in Berwick where we had adjourned for lunch. There, he turned the BBC Light Programme up to full volume so that he could take delight in listening to his wife performing on the midday show. The other diners who had been busy discussing a business proposition were furious that they could no longer hear themselves speak while the hotel manager rapidly summoned to try to calm a spiralling confrontation, got an ear-hole blasting of his own!

When I told Jim about the trip to Sunderland, he demanded to read the letter for himself.

'This is ridiculous,' he screamed but interested in seeing how things might develop, asked me to step inside the Tyne Tees Land Rover as we prepared to head south to Wearside.

Janet Parkin had kindly supplied Stan's address in her letter but without a house number. It turned out to be a high-rise development in Monkwearmouth. Previous experience had taught me that if you are trying to locate someone in a multi-storey, the best method is to take the lift (if it's working) to the top floor and then make your way down the stairs one level at a time, hoping that somehow you end up at the right door.

This time I was more fortunate. Walking through the ground floor entrance to the building, my eye was immediately drawn to the door right next to the lift. It had a little wooden plaque attached with the name Kipling inscribed.

Despite my pleading for some moral support, the camera crew decided they would stay put in the vehicle until such time that any filming might be required. I was on my own. My hands were shaking as I rang the bell still wondering how I would broach the subject of the letter.

'Are you Stan Kipling and do you know someone called Janet Parkin?' I asked nervously.

'Oh Janet ... yes she's my fiancée ... but what business is this of yours?'

I explained how we had received the letter at Tyne Tees and told him that Janet had suggested there was an obstacle to any forthcoming wedding. It seemed he kept something in his bedroom.

'I can't quite make out her writing. It looks like ... no, it can't be ... that you have a monster in there?'

'Oh, yes. Would you like to come in and have a look?' Anticipating that I might be faced with a real skeleton falling out of his cupboard, I rushed outside and whistled to the crew, indicating they should get their gear together and join me at once.

The camera perched on Jim's shoulder, we eased slowly towards the bedroom door. It refused to open more than 18 inches. Somehow, we managed to slide our way inside to be confronted with a giant model traction engine built out of wood and metal. It was jammed hard against the outside wall, towered over the double bed and was just a couple of inches short of the ceiling.

Stan was beside himself with joy to see his lifetime's work being recorded on film. 'I'll just go and turn it on now,' he shouted. I had visions of the whole multi-storey collapsing around us as he made for the switch. Suddenly, the whole room lit up as an electric motor sent the flywheel spinning and light bulbs of every colour of the rainbow began flashing on and off. If that hadn't created enough excitement, Stan's insistence that the engine was now ready for solid fuel conversion, I thought might set alarm bells ringing with the powers that be at the town hall.

The demonstration over, I guessed Stan knew what was coming next. It was time for us to meet his fiancée and bring her to the scene of his personal anguish.

There they stood, hand in hand, as I asked Stan the inevitable question. 'It seems you have got a difficult choice here. You can have one but not the other, so will it be Janet or the traction engine?' Tears welled up in his eyes. 'Oh I do love that lass but how can she possibly expect me to part with this?'

Janet was devastated. It seemed the wedding was definitely off … well, that's until my report, shown at six o'clock that evening, brought a barrage of phone calls to the studio with several tearful viewers even offering their services as counsellors and intermediaries to try to resolve the couple's differences.

One caller left a message for me to ring back immediately the programme was over. I recognized the number. Bill Weeks was a well-known lecturer in agriculture and food marketing at Newcastle University. He was also a dab hand when it came to filling in yawning gaps in programme schedules on slow news days. On one occasion, he had caused consternation in the studio when showing viewers how to cook and then carve an 18lb Christmas turkey. As three cameras zoomed in for close-ups of his deft handiwork, the carving knife was making no impression on the bird. Suddenly, a huge lump of plastic appeared. It wouldn't come out, so Bill had to carve a few more slices whilst heaving at the plastic. When it finally emerged, it turned out to be the bag full of all the innards. In the hasty preparation work before transmission, someone had forgotten to remove the plastic container!

'Wullie, that was great television,' he said, hardly able to contain his usual raucous laugh. 'I'll bet you'd like a second go at that story. Perhaps you have forgotten one of the hats I wear. Why lad, don't you remember I'm Chairman of the North of England Traction Engine Society? I have the perfect plan to resolve this situation and be assured you'll love the results.'

Bill then proceeded to reveal his ingenious blueprint. It amounted to making Stan an offer he felt he could not refuse. If the pensioner agreed to have the 'monster' removed from his bedroom, he would give it a permanent home in a farmer's barn near Consett, 25 miles away. As compensation, Bill would arrange for a real steam traction engine to collect Stan from his multi-storey and drive him to church so he could marry the love of his life.

It all sounded too good to be true and I put the chances of success at 1,000–1. Three days later, Bill was back on the phone.

'It's all done and dusted. The wedding's fixed for a fortnight on Thursday. If you don't manage to get a cracking film out of this one then I'll be very disappointed.'

And so the big day arrived. While Janet, dressed in blue satin, was quietly driven in a conventional way by car to St Aidan's Church, Stan climbed aboard the ancient 70-ton traction engine, Cock o' the North, for his journey into matrimony. At the wheel was the machine's owner, Jack Wakefield, who had earlier set up a record by manoeuvring the engine from John o' Groats to Land's End in just seven days. Little wonder then, he was confident he could get Stan to church on time, this despite the fact that it had been arranged to make the journey at peak hour. Traffic behind idled as the coal-fired engine sped at seven knots along the 4-mile route to Grangetown, drawing curious and amused looks from passers-by.

Waiting at the church in his elegantly styled Jaguar was Bill Weeks, immaculately dressed in top and tails and offering his services as Best Man. Stan was also in his Sunday best, though unfortunately, now covered in oily soot from top to bottom!

After the ceremony, Janet decided to get her hands dirty too. Little encouragement was necessary as Stan helped his wife aboard the Cock o' the North and sounded the hooter as Janet shrieked with laughter.

The couple left for their honeymoon as honorary members of the Traction Engine Society and with Stan clutching his favourite wedding present – a miniature steam roller. As the man who conducted the ceremony, the Vicar of St Aidan's, Reverend Norman Moses, was later to concede, if problem-solving by romantic partners is a delicate process then Tyne Tees viewers – and millions watching my report on ITN – were witnesses to one of the big success stories!

In the 1960s, television had not yet enhanced the world of electronic graphics. Captions were prepared on pieces of 12"×10" cardboard with one of the favoured fonts bearing the rather infelicitous title, Grotesque No.9.

Rather more colourful adjectives were used by programme directors on occasions when I ruined a meticulous half-hour's news production by my inability to manipulate those other essential little studio aids called weather symbols.

In his wisdom – or might I suggest madness – the programme editor decided that with the help of an easel, I should stand in front of a large map of the region and present a weather summary compiled by the local meteorological office. Each evening for 18 months, a taxi would arrive at 5.15 from Sharkeys depot in Byker and whisk me into the city centre for a five-minute chat with whoever was responsible for collating the forecast for the next 24 hours. I would then be handed a full-length version which I had to condense into a script of no more than a minute's duration.

One day, I left it behind in the taxi and I could not recall a single word of our conversation. Frantic calls to the taxi office revealed that the driver had left for another job miles from base and was out of radio communication.

Desperate that no-one at Tyne Tees should discover my dark secret, I offered up a short silent prayer before launching into that familiar British projection of sunny intervals and occasional showers. The problem was I was in such a panic that the adhesive strips on the back of the cardboard symbols refused to stick sending them sliding all the way from Holy Island to Whitby before making a final descent on to the studio floor. I can't remember whether the sun shone the next day but abuse was certainly raining down from the gallery as I made a hasty retreat from the scene of my embarrassment.

Apart from the staff crews, Tyne Tees also employed a number of cameramen on a freelance basis. They shot mute film to which suitable sound effects would be added before transmission – birds twittering, traffic on the move, rain and thunder, metal grinding, screams, moans, laughs or applause. In the early days of regional television everything from flower shows to old folks' outings found a twenty-second slot in the programme.

The freelance cameramen were known as 'stringers' and were paid by the day. Once they had set off on the road, the news editor's job was to work them as hard as possible. After he'd been given his first job, the cameraman knew he'd be chased for the rest of the day. It made economic sense. The 'stringers' had union cards but little else in terms of protection. If lunchtime came and went and they still hadn't been allocated a job, the news desk phone became red hot as they *suggested* assignments. The longer the day wore on, the more desperate those calls became.

Armed with the cameramen's shot-lists and contact numbers for the events they had been covering, I would often be assigned to scripting these films for transmission. I was also given the job of compiling and reading the late-night news from a small continuity studio. This bulletin was very cleverly put together. Films transmitted on the evening news magazine were re-edited immediately after the programme to provide a ten minute offering. At the end, the newscaster would simply say: 'And now over to Bill Hamilton for the rest of the news.' Everything that happened in the region throughout the evening was now earmarked for my slot though, if a major national story broke, it threw everything out of kilter and I would have to summon help from wherever I could find it. Apart from the immediate task of getting the material off to ITN, it meant back to the drawing board as the regional programme would have to be completely overhauled.

For me, there was no such thing as a Black Monday. It was the happiest day of the week. One of my tasks was to look after the players of Newcastle United, Sunderland and Middlesbrough when invited to watch playbacks of the Tyne Tees recordings of their weekend matches in the comfort of the viewing room.

Newcastle Manager Joe Harvey and his Boro' counterpart Stan Anderson used these sessions to learn from mistakes and to help improve the technical aspects of their game.

My impression was that Sunderland took the whole exercise much less seriously, treating it more like a day out at the cinema.

The viewing room had two television screens with rows of seats placed on either side of a central aisle. I had access to a bakelite phone which had a direct line to telecine where the video tape recorders were situated. Hand-held remote controls had not yet been invented so the managers were instructed to let me know if they wanted any particular part of the action replayed. I would then pick up the phone and ask the video operator to rewind the tape.

It was a service of which Joe Harvey and Stan Anderson were more than happy to take advantage. Ian McColl, the soft-spoken manager of

Sunderland, rarely intervened, a point not lost on the video tape operator who saw it as the perfect opportunity to disappear to the canteen for a tea break.

One Monday afternoon however, 'Slim Jim' Baxter, a Scottish football legend, now playing in the red and white of Sunderland, unexpectedly found himself chastised by a red-faced Ian McColl who was furious when watching a costly mistake by his star player.

'Could I possibly see that again?' the manager asked me. But before I could pick up the phone to the video operator, Baxter was on his feet.

'Oh boss, you were watching the wrong tv set … it was a perfect pass on this one!' The whole place erupted with laughter and the manager, in an obvious admission of defeat, asked me to replace the receiver!

Today the City Road studios have gone. A very slimmed-down version of Tyne Tees operates out of a business park adjacent to the Metro Centre in Gateshead. Original programme making was the lifeblood of the North-East. It communicated the region's achievements, its industrial enterprise, its sporting successes and its disappointments. It was democratic and inclusive. Programmes from *The One o'clock Show* to *The Tube* drew huge audiences and were upbeat, vibrant and entertaining.

The whole raison d'être behind setting up regional television companies was to ensure people were given a slice of life from those who lived there and understood its priorities. Now, ITV has established so called 'super regions' where companies have merged their news interests – in some cases, gaining more than twice the area to cover but losing more than half their staff. It all amounts to a serious erosion of ITV's original public service commitment and a huge loss to the distinct cultural identity of our communities.

6

Out of the Blue

De dum, de dum, de dum, de dum, de diddly dum de dum – it's a signature tune which has defied the digital age.

Eleanor Oldroyd, first female presenter of BBC Radio's Sports Report

For a generation of schoolboys growing up in the 1950s, one iconic sporting moment captured on grainy newsreel film triggered a mutual spark of inspiration. I was just eleven years old when Roger Bannister became the first athlete in history to break the four-minute mile and the physical and psychological barrier that had long resisted men's efforts to do so. Sitting in the back row of 'the flicks', this was most definitely a spectacle to savour.

In the gym and on the sports field all my friends suddenly became determined to show the PE Master that there was potential to be tapped. I can vividly recall saving a penny by foregoing the tram ride to school and embarking on a brisk walk occasionally breaking into a sprint.

By now, I had become a regular spectator at Tannadice Park, enthusiastically cheering the erratic antics of Dundee United playing in the B Division of the Scottish League. The ground lay approximately a mile from my home in the suburb of Maryfield and imbued with this new spirit of athleticism, I used the final blast of the referee's whistle as the starting signal for a gruelling uphill run to reach the house in time to hear the evocative sounds of Hubert Bath's famous march 'Out of the Blue', the theme music for my favourite radio programme *Sports Report*.

Gently turning the radio dial to ensure the best possible reception, I quickly grabbed the morning paper and waited for John Webster to begin the reading of the football results, each of which I carefully recorded on the dotted lines conveniently placed next to the list of the day's fixtures. My father was already sitting at the dining room table, pencil in hand to check whether he had predicted a winning line of eight draws on the pools and scooped the top prize of £75,000 which in those days would have bought a castle with all the period furniture to go with it, not to mention the exotic Caribbean holidays that the family could have enjoyed for the rest of our lives.

Dad was one of many who used Horace Batchelor's famous 'Infra-Draw Method' which was supposed to increase your chances of securing a winning line even for a very small stake. Advertising on Radio Luxembourg, the name of the town near Bristol to where you had to write to get his little booklet of secrets was spelt out infuriatingly time and again, letter by letter, K-E-Y-N-S-H-A-M. Dear old Horace may have put Keynsham on the map but regrettably little in dad's pocket!

For me, the pools coupon was an aside. My real focus was on John Webster, the announcer who read the football results in such a way that you could tell immediately from his intonation whether the match had ended in a home win, an away victory or a draw. I became so enraptured by his ingenious style of delivery that every Sunday afternoon I would lock myself in the bathroom for anywhere up to half an hour, trying to imitate his technique by reading out loud every single result, including hundreds from the minor Leagues, which appeared in the *Sunday Post*. I now had an ambition in life – to become the next John Webster. Little did I realise that on his retirement in 1970, I would be invited to step into his chair.

Having learned at least the rudiments of television reporting, it was time to experience life in the capital. BBC Radio was advertising for Sports News Assistants and I decided to apply. I had only made brief forays to London and had always been overwhelmed by the sheer size of the place and the hectic heaving mass of six million souls moving around the city. Packed as they were like sardines on to the tube, squashed against the smudged windows and buffeted up and down the escalators, I admired their fortitude but found their unwillingness to engage in conversation a particular irritant. Maybe they were living in a fantasy world, trying to convince themselves they were not part of this daily chaos.

My application was successful and I was asked to report to an office in Portland Place directly opposite Broadcasting House for an interview and voice test. Arriving at King's Cross Station, I first made my way to the heart of the West End and sneaked past the top-hatted doorman at the Strand Palace Hotel to smarten up and have an extra layer of polish applied to my shoes. This proved a wise decision as I was soon to discover that the man in charge of the sports news department had been in the military and counted deportment and discipline as key elements in running a tidy ship.

Angus Mackay was already a legend both inside and outside the Corporation. A fellow Scot in his late fifties, he knew exactly what he wanted from those waiting nervously for their turn in front of the Appointments Board, a system the BBC had inherited from the Civil Service. There were four people on the panel but only one did the talking, the others it seemed to me were there merely to ensure fair play. Slim in build, with greying hair and a thin moustache, Angus' opening line immediately conveyed the sense of worth and pride in the programmes he oversaw.

'So you've working in television then and you've now come to your senses and want to join the big boys? Do you think you could cut it here?'

As I stumbled my way through a series of answers, I noticed Angus kept applying some salve to his upper lip. I thought it was probably because of dryness caused by talking too much. In fact, I was to learn later that he had received facial burns in a horrific rail crash at Barnes Station near Richmond in December 1955 in which 13 of his fellow passengers were killed and another 41 injured.

I could tell Angus liked my Scottish brogue but I wasn't sure I had done enough to convince him that I was sufficiently conversant with the whole range of sports and, even more important, whether he saw me as the right kind of material to become one of 'his boys'.

In the event, four hopefuls were appointed and I was thrilled to be numbered amongst them. The others all went on to make a name for themselves in their respective fields. They were Des Lynam, one of the most accomplished television presenters of his generation; Christopher Martin-Jenkins, the cricket writer and *Test Match Special* commentator and Dick Scales who later left broadcasting to become a high flier in the business world of Sports PR.

So, in April 1970 I packed all my worldly possessions into a now clapped-out Ford Anglia and headed slowly for West London and a tiny attic bedsit run by an Icelandic landlady in Chiswick. I had never had to cater for myself before and found it a trying business using a single electric ring that took an interminable amount of time to heat a pan of water and finding a shared bathroom locked constantly by the neighbouring tenant who took hours pampering herself in readiness for a night on the town.

Mind you, I thought I was fortunate being able to spend even a few hours in my attic abode having read the conditions laid down by 'Auntie' for my employment.

'You agree to devote the WHOLE of your time and attention to the service of the BBC and to attend for duty at such hours of the day or night as shall be decided by the Corporation.'

Ushered into Angus' office on day one, my first impression was that there was something odd about the place. A second glance revealed all. There was no desk. Angus, jacket off and sporting a white shirt and trouser braces, sat in a high-backed wooden armchair overlooking a low coffee table. A typewriter with loaded paper sat on a shelf on the far side of the room – Angus preferred to stand when typing – and beside the chair there was a bell with which he summoned secretarial support – 'his girls'.

Having decided I could be set loose on the daily sports programmes, I was handed over to 'The Chief', Bob Burrows, a man who carried out Angus' instructions to the letter and whose impeccable contacts and exhaustive knowledge of all major sports meant that the accuracy of every script prepared and every word spoken had to be beyond question.

I was first given the job of reading the racing results for the 6.32 pm spot on Radio 2. This was part of an 8-minute sports bulletin and each member of Angus' team was given an opportunity to either produce or present the programme.

We were also responsible for a sports slot on Radio 2's *Late Night Extra* which was often hosted by 'Diddy David' Hamilton. This spot became a great favourite of mine not only because I shared the same surname as one of the country's best loved presenters – who'd also worked at Tyne Tees Television – but because it gave me the opportunity to broadcast the evening football results. By now my sights were fixed more firmly than ever on climbing into that chair vacated by my childhood hero, John Webster.

Fortunately, someone had taken note and one afternoon I was summoned to Angus' office.

'The Chief tells me you want to read the results on Saturday. Do you realise how many out there are listening ... everyone's waiting for the scores ... do you really think you can do it?'

Filled with a mixture of excitement and dread, I could hardly take it in.

'Yes Angus. I'm ready to give it a go!'

As I left the desk-less room, I knew I had invested my whole broadcasting future on my ability to produce a flawless 5-minute performance in just three days' time. Anything less would spell personal disaster and tarnish the reputation of the nation's beloved *Sports Report*, which began on the Light Programme in 1948 and is still broadcast on Radio 5 Live today, making it the longest-running sports programme in the world. The year before I joined the team, the programme had celebrated its twenty-first birthday and audience figures were on the increase again. Angus was the man who devised the format, guided the policy, moulded Eamonn Andrews into a top personality and his show into a sporting 'must'.

The Sports room statistician, Bill Ross, who kept meticulous records of every professional football and county cricket club, came hurrying into the tiny self-operated studio which had been constructed at one end of the sports room, with the classified results from each division in turn. The signature tune was already playing as he handed me a compilation of the first ten results from Division One, which was then England's top flight. One result was missing. Stoke City were the bane of the lives of sports desks up and down the country as they insisted, along with a couple of clubs from the lower leagues, of scheduling their kick-offs for 3.15 pm. One godsend is that the club's first initial 'S' falls well into the second half of the alphabet. It meant I had time to read the first eight First Division results before the door was flung open and a breathless Bill Ross came rushing back into the studio with confirmation of Stoke's final score just in the nick of time.

Other Saturdays would not herald such good fortune. A couple of minutes of injury time would be enough to scuttle any hopes of getting the result in sequence. Occasionally, it didn't arrive until well after 5.05, which infuriated pools punters sweating desperately to see if they were to pick up a vital eighth draw on the Treble Chance.

I heaved a huge sigh of relief as I switched off the microphone and the airwaves passed back to the *Sports Report* presenter Peter Jones in the basement studio. All had gone well and happily the job was mine for the rest of the season.

It seemed a natural extension to this important weekly exercise to offer my services to interpret the 'running results' for listeners at the conclusion of the afternoon *Sport on 2* programme. As the season wore on, so the tension and excitement began to build. Earlier in the day, I had done my homework, compiling charts detailing all the games being played and jotting down interesting statistics about each side. The facts soon began to accumulate as I started to scrawl across the charts: *Arsenal still on course for League and Cup double; Ray Kennedy scored 24 times; Everton's Joe Royle on 17 goals; Barrow conceded 86 goals; a Carlisle win will lift them into fourth place in Division 2; East Fife need just two more points for promotion to the Scottish First Division.*

By 4.45 pm I had taken my place in front of the Press Association teleprinters as the results and scorers began to appear. A Carlisle victory meant I could declare with absolute conviction that they were now in fourth place, a Ray Kennedy goal for Arsenal had me excitedly announcing that it was now his 25th of the campaign and yes, the good folks of Methil could look forward to visits from Celtic and Rangers next season as East Fife were now assured of First Division football north of the Border. There was just time to gather my breath and race back into the sports room studio as the strains of 'Out of the Blue' heralded the start of yet another *Sports Report.*

My only regret was that by becoming studio bound, I was no longer able to spend Saturday afternoons enjoying the cut and thrust of Saturday afternoon League football, but the thrill of live broadcasting more than made up for that.

Mentally and physically, it was important that Angus' boys were up to the task. Saturdays were stamina-sapping experiences. Everyone would be expected to contribute to *Sports Parade*, a sports review programme that ran for half an hour at lunchtime. Then after the live afternoon show and *Sports Report*, there was still some serious work to be done.

Occasionally, I would be asked to present a regional show on Radio 4 called *Sports Session* or at least, make some positive contribution to the programme. Then it was time to down a glass of water and take the deepest of breaths before we were all on air again this time with a 30-minute weekly sports programme for the World Service called *Sports Review.*

Exhausted from all this frenetic activity, the whole department was encouraged to move across the road to The Langham, now transformed into one of London's most luxurious hotels but in the seventies, housing the BBC Club. On Saturday evenings it was packed with broadcasters, producers, engineers, secretaries and their friends swapping tales while winding down over a glass or two of their favourite tipple.

No matter how busy the place, all would step aside as Angus entered the bar heading straight for his favourite corner stool on which no-one else dared rest his weary legs. Wives, partners and girlfriends would be introduced, only to be told how sacrifices were required until 'their boys' had forged a career for themselves. His own dear wife, he said, understood this fully but when he retired, he would learn how to drive, become a gardener and do the shopping. At the time, I don't think any of us believed him especially when we discovered that Angus' daughter had been forced to arrange her wedding for a Sunday. When, however, he left Broadcasting House for the last time, Angus was as good as his word.

Behind Angus in the bar stood his chauffeur, Mr Smith. I never knew his first name. I don't think any of us did. Each though in turn, was encouraged to buy a round and to make sure we included Mr Smith.

The exchange was always the same.

'...and Mr Smith, what would you like?'

'Oh, that's very kind of you, Bill, mine's a brown ale.'

All very well but by the time the last round had been purchased, Mr Smith's brown ales had numbered half a dozen or more! Whether he drank them all or not I cannot be certain but the thought did strike me that perhaps Angus might have considered the benefits of sitting that driving test a little earlier in life.

The BBC sound engineers loved Angus' resourcefulness that recognised there were a lot of very talented technicians whose enterprise was all too often overlooked by the Corporation's hierarchy.

He believed wholeheartedly in their initiative and abilities and they, in return, rewarded him by coming up with a deft piece of kit called a SOOBE (Self-Operated Outside Broadcast Equipment). Complete with a lip microphone, this portable little box of tricks about the size of a briefcase was issued to reporters attending the games to be featured in *Sports Report*. When you arrived at the ground, all you had to do was find the appropriate socket, open the case, plug the equipment in, put on the earphones and turn the handle. Hey presto, as if by magic, an OB tester at Broadcasting House answered in a such a clear, high-quality voice that it was easy to believe he was standing right next to you. Angus described it as a potent weapon in the war against other forms of communication especially as it meant that players, managers and officials could be interviewed straight from the grounds within minutes of the final whistle.

I used one of these frequently at midweek games. In most grounds the SOOBE point was conveniently situated in the Press Box. There was the odd exception. Arriving at Brisbane Road, I had to indulge in an impromptu game of hide and seek which led to my tripping over a couple of mops and dustpans before finally tracking the elusive Leyton Orient socket to a broom cupboard in the bowels of the stand.

Unlike most producers, the irascible Angus would insist on deserting the control cubicle for long periods of *Sports Report* to sit alongside the presenter in the studio, whispering all sorts of instructions into his ear and often rewriting links while they had already started to be read. It's just as well that Peter Jones with his mellifluous voice and great presence and Des Lynam, the consummate professional who was to follow in his footsteps, had such powers of concentration that they could absorb all that came their way.

It was immensely uplifting to work alongside such a marvellous group of accomplished broadcasters. Football Correspondent Bryon Butler was always willing to offer words of encouragement. One from the old school of broadcast journalists, he was a real craftsman, strikingly eloquent with a very precise style of delivery. Then there was John Motson, the only son of a Methodist minister who, like me, had entered broadcasting after serving his apprenticeship on weekly and daily papers – in his case the *Barnet Press* and *Sheffield Telegraph*.

John had quickly developed the art of radio commentary, not just football but tennis and boxing too. His voice exuded excitement, passion and unbridled enthusiasm and his preparation was without compare.

By now, I was keen to leave my attic bedsit in Chiswick and seek somewhere more agreeable. No sooner had I started to scan the small ads in the *Evening Standard* than John came up with the ideal solution.

'I'm looking for a third person for a flat share in Finchley. Why don't you come and have a look at the place?'

It was the beginning of a 40-year friendship with the man who was later to become a national institution as the 'Voice of Football'. Our co-tenant Jim Currie was forging a career in marketing and was also a keen follower of the beautiful game. They were both involved in the formation of a football club called Roving Reporters and became automatic choices for their games in the Barnet and District Sunday League. With so many Saturday commitments, I too was delighted that the establishment of Sunday football now gave me the opportunity to continue as a referee.

To my surprise, I discovered that my boyhood hero, John Webster, lived just a couple of streets away from our flat in Nether Street. Motty and I paid him a visit. He was a beneficent host, totally unpretentious with a kind and gracious spirit.

The more time I spent in Motty's company, the more I became aware of the lengths to which he was prepared to go to ensure nothing was left to chance when planning for his next assignment. Everything was written down with meticulous attention to detail. He would phone the managers of League clubs in advance of games, desperate for them to take him on trust and reveal their team's line-up for the upcoming match.

About four o'clock one morning, I was awakened by strange sounds emanating from the front room. I was sure we were being burgled. Rushing over to John's bed, I tugged hard at his sheets. 'Quickly, get up and give me some help. Someone's in the lounge, wrecking the place.' There was no response.

Moving stealthily into the hallway, I launched an almighty kick at the sitting room door, trusting that the element of surprise might give me a glimpse of the intruder before he hopefully made a hasty retreat from the scene of his crime.

Instead, I was confronted with the sight of Motty getting in some commentary practice with the plastic heroes from a rather battered Subbuteo set, some of whom had become decapitated after months of being spent spinning across the dining table. '*Mills up field to Robinson ... Viljoen's waiting at the far post ... a clever flick-on ... what a chance for Clarke.*' Not what I or the landlord Mr Eyles – with any luck still asleep upstairs – were entitled to expect in the middle of the night. Returning to bed my only wish was that in future, the manager of Ipswich Town, Bobby Robson, would be more accommodating in furnishing Motty with details of his expected Saturday line-up so the rest of us could enjoy a decent night's sleep.

Little did I think that less than a month later, it would be Motty having the last laugh, this time at my expense and because I had slept far TOO well! In my haste to get under the covers late one Friday night, I forgot to set the alarm with its distinctive bell chime that in the past had never failed to jar me back into the physical world.

When I finally stirred, the time was after 10.30 am and I was due on air to read the world sports headlines at midday. This would normally mean a 40-minute car journey and a further half hour's work examining the huge selection of stories being churned out by a bank of teleprinters and arriving from agencies and reporters right across the globe.

A quick wash and shave and I was on my way to the West End, clutching a bread roll and a banana but a serious accident in Camden Town had led to a series of road closures and interminable delays. By the time I had ascended the lift to the third floor of Broadcasting House, the clock was indicating it was now 11.50. I thought no-one had seen me creep into the room and was about to remove a sprawling mass of material from the printers when one of the sports room secretaries came running towards me with the instruction: 'Angus wants to see you at once.' I asked her to convey a message that I was due on air in a basement studio in ten minutes and that I would go straight to his office immediately I had finished the broadcast.

A minute later, Trish was back, this time red-faced and clearly upset. 'When Angus says he wants to see you immediately, that means right now!' Panic stricken, I followed her into his office.

Angus was tugging at his braces and sweating profusely. 'It's bloody hot in here,' he shouted as he asked me to take a seat. I offered to open a window. Instead he rang the bell and his secretary appeared again with a long pole ready to spring into action.

'What did I want to see you about, Bill?' he asked.

'I'm not sure Angus but I'm on air in five minutes in B9 so can I see you when I'm finished?'

'Oh I remember now,' he said, once again pressing the bell for assistance. 'Girl, can you get me the *Today* scripts for December.' We were now in the third week of August of the following year. Glancing upwards, I could see a box file with the appropriate date on the second shelf. It was quickly retrieved and put in Angus' hands.

My watch showed the time was now 11.56 – just four minutes to go until transmission.

Fortunately, as the box was opened, the offending script was lying on top of the file. A red pencil mark had been circled around the word 'floored'. It referred to a fight in which Joe Bugner had beaten an Argentinian opponent Miguel Angel Paez by a technical knock-out.

Angus threw the script on to my lap. 'You know what that word means,' he screamed, 'and so do I. But I have to tell you lad that there are admirals employed by the BBC and paid a lot of money to spot such slang. I never want to see that word again. By the way aren't you supposed to be on the air?'

Breathless, I grabbed rolls of teleprinter copy and dashed down four flights of stairs to the basement. Des Lynam was already reading the cue for my spot as I rushed into the studio throwing all the material from my pockets on to the desk. I believed this would be my last act at Broadcasting House but somehow managed to make sense of the four stories I had selected at random.

When I had ended, an irate Bob Burrows rushed out of the control room to admonish me for failing to provide a script and said Angus wanted me back in his room at once.

I was fully expecting to be sacked on the spot. Instead a bottle of

Scotch and two glasses were produced and I was congratulated on my ad lib performance then sent back to work with a grim message ringing in my ears: 'Don't ever be late for work again!'

I had survived by the skin of my teeth. Angus put the fear of God into all who worked for him. He was the supreme disciplinarian who demanded only the highest standards and woe betide anyone who dared to cross him. These included some of Fleet Street's finest sports writers under strict instructions to provide a 1-minute report for *Sports Report*. Running over by just a couple of seconds was considered something of a cardinal sin which would be followed by a verbal warning from Angus: 'Do that just once more and it will be your last contribution to the programme.'

I became so frightened of oversleeping again that when assigned to the overnight shift, charged with putting together the sports slot which I would then have to present on the highly popular *Today* programme the next morning, I declined the opportunity to put my head down for a couple of hours in a room that was provided in The Langham immediately across the road in Portland Place.

The current affairs show provided wonderful experience for a young broadcaster. Just to sit at the same table as Jack De Manio and John Timpson was a real privilege. Timpson's unflappable style and De Manio's infuriating habit of giving out the time incorrectly brought a lighter touch alongside some of the more serious issues of the day.

The team spirit engendered among those who worked for Angus was remarkable. One Sunday we were all asked to report to Scaynes Hill, a delightful Sussex village just outside Haywards Heath. A cricket match had been arranged against the local side, one of the most successful teams in that part of the county. Fearing my dreadful inadequacy as a cricketer would be exposed, I asked if I might field at long stop, which seemed to me to be a less vulnerable position. Though wickets tumbled at regular intervals, one of the village batsmen remained defiant and scared the living daylights out of me as he continued to let rip.

After a lunch break at the nearby Farmers Arms, it was decided the BBC should adopt more aggressive bowling tactics and despite my protestations, I was ordered to move to gully. Thoughts of being removed to the local accident and emergency unit had begun to cross my mind when the rapacious batsman suddenly skied a ball about five feet above my head. Ignoring calls from my colleagues 'to get out of the way Bill', I determined that no-one would deprive me of the opportunity to pull off the most important catch of the day.

In the very next over, another batsman got a top edge and the ball floated straight into my hands. Suddenly, the coward had become a hero and with the Sports team able to call on batsmen of the quality of Chris Martin Jenkins and Jeremy Allerton, the result was never in doubt. The après-cricket party was one of the best I can remember. So many fellow revellers wanted to fill my glass that I'm glad someone else was driving home.

In the summer of 1971 I was told I had been chosen to join the Radio Sports team for the Olympic Games in Munich the following year but just weeks later I received a phone call from Border Television. They had a vacancy for a presenter of their highly popular nightly News Magazine programme, *News and Lookaround*. It was an opportunity I felt I couldn't refuse though I was sad to say goodbye to the most professional group of broadcasters I have ever had the privilege to work with.

My most abiding memory, of course, was of being allowed to fill the chair of the legendary John Webster. The role now passed to James Alexander Gordon. His distinctive voice with its noted intonation has brought the football results to the nation for close on 40 years, happily preserving the innovative style of a past master of the art.

7

Border Terrier

Colour television! Bah, I won't believe it until I see it in black and white.

Samuel Goldwyn

Had viewers been counted in sheep then Border Television would have boasted one of the largest audiences on the ITV network. Before the dreaded foot and mouth disease exerted a heavy toll, 6 million of them could be seen grazing on the hills, fells and pastures spilling out across a tenth of the land mass of the British Isles.

Border was one of those oddities created by the Independent Television Authority 50 years ago. The franchise dictated that the company had to provide for the tastes of viewers living in three separate countries – Scotland, England and the self-governing Crown dependency of the Isle of Man. The problem was that there were only 600,000 of them, fewer than the population of Leeds, and straddling an area from Kendal to Stranraer, Millom to Galashiels and Douglas to Berwick-upon-Tweed. Unfortunately, the sheep had more in common than those who watched the programmes.

Given such a culturally fractured region, it might have seemed reasonable to think that the station would end up satisfying no-one. But that was far from the case. Indeed, though it was often mocked for its parochialism, it was this insularity that ensured the viewing figures for the evening news programme were among the highest of any BBC or ITV region in the country. After all, where else could you switch on at six o'clock in anticipation of seeing a report on fireworks night in the Muckle Toon, the crowning of the Eyemouth Herring Queen, the rescue of a Lakeland bull whose head was stuck in a metal fence or a next-door neighbour complaining about a series of late bin collections by the local council?

In the autumn of 1971 my girlfriend and I packed what few possessions we had in a rusty old transit van and headed up the M6 to Carlisle and the Border studios which lay close to the sprawling council estate of Harraby. In nearby London Road, we persuaded Violet, an elderly but galvanic Methodist local preacher, to rent us her two antique furnished upstairs rooms until we could find something more permanent.

Unlike the heavily populated areas of the UK, Border was still transmitting pictures in black and white. It would be some considerable time before they would catch up with the enthralling new world of colour television. Even then, some viewers were under the distinct impression that their existing sets would suddenly burst into colour on day one of the new service. Complaints that they could still only see the programmes in monochrome had to be handled delicately.

'I'm afraid you will need to buy a new television to enjoy the feast!'

Ironically more than thirty years later, Whitehaven would become the first town in Britain to enter a new broadcasting era by having the old analogue signal switched off and going totally digital.

On arrival in Carlisle, I was pleased to meet up again with my old friend from Tyne Tees days, Allan Powell, who was now ensconced as Head of News and Current Affairs. He deployed his staff sensibly. I was one of four presenters. On the days when we weren't required in the studio, we were despatched to all four corners of the region, often battling through mountain passes or dodging tractors and horseboxes in our rush to get footage back for the evening programme. With 35 minutes to fill, losing just one film could spell disaster and spark a series of frantic phone calls to anyone with a guitar and agreeable voice to bridge the gap.

Travelling large distances over difficult and inhospitable terrain meant exhausting journeys. Being driven over stone-littered lanes, hump-backed bridges and hidden potholes is not exactly conducive to enlightened script writing, with notebook and pen flying in all directions.

Back at the studios, the film had to be rushed straight to film processing. Depending on how much had been shot, it took anywhere up to an hour to wind its way through a bath of chemicals, known in the trade as 'the soup'. Trying to speed up the process could have fatal results. No-one wanted to hear that their day's work had 'gone down in the soup'.

If all went well, the film moved on to the cutting room, where the reporter, film editor and the programme producer could view 'the rushes' as the reels were spun through the editing machine before chinagraph pencils, white gloves and a splicing machine were put to use as the film was chopped and stitched together more often than not right up to the deadline.

The edited films would then be laced on to one large reel and loaded on to the telecine machine ready for transmission. The problem was that Border had just one of these machines. This meant the films could only be shown in the order they had been assembled. More worryingly, if the film snapped or the machine should seize up, 20 minutes or more of material would be lost to the programme, inducing mass panic and an immediate recall for man and guitar to strike up again. To prevent total catastrophe, there was a list of half a dozen interviewees in close vicinity to Carlisle who were prepared to leap into a car at a moment's notice and dash to the studio to give their expert opinion on anything from how to lose weight to building a garden shed.

With many 'live' guests and performers, it was important that the studio was of a suitable size to accommodate the programme's needs. The presenting/reporting team were an interesting bunch. Alick Cleaver was twice my age, a father figure sporting a handlebar moustache and a love of gin and tonic. Acutely aware of the nightly struggle to satisfy the demands of a 35-minute programme, he had a canny knack of asking long and detailed questions which put most studio guests in something of a tizzy. Amazingly, Alick and his wife also found time to run the Horse and Jockey Public House in the Cumbrian village of Parsonby.

Eric Wallace had left his first job at Carrs Biscuit Factory to take a three-year course in Film and Television at Durham University. On graduating, he had joined Border as a reporter where he would remain for the next 30 years. An ardent movie enthusiast, he directed and funded several independent films and was himself the subject of a short film, *The One and Only*.

The fourth member of the team, Eric Robson was born in the south of Scotland but had spent his early years heaving furniture around for a removals firm in Carlisle. Eric had got his big chance after impressing as an assistant floor manager and showed all the potential to become another big success from the Border Television stable. Today he is best known as the chairman of BBC's *Gardeners' Question Time* on Radio 4 but his voice is also known to millions as a television commentator on major state occasions including Remembrance Sunday and Trooping the Colour. For the last 15 years, he has run a small farm in the Lake District looking after some of those 6 million sheep!

On the English side of the Border, *Border News and Lookaround* was more popularly known as *Border Crack 'n Deekaboot*. I always viewed that as something of a compliment. It says something about the deep and very real affection that so many viewers had for this gutsy minnow in the gargantuan pond of British television. Yet, when put to the test with major stories like the Lockerbie Air Disaster, the Carlisle floods, controversies surrounding the nuclear processing site at Sellafield and the human – as well as animal – tragedy that emerged from the foot and mouth epidemic, the newsroom reacted with an alacrity and professionalism that surprised many of its sternest critics.

Today, the smallest yet most loyally supported ITV region has disappeared in all but name. Ostensibly, it has been merged with Tyne Tees Television, with the most successful news magazine in Britain replaced with a 20-minute opt-out broadcast from a business park in Gateshead. As for the Isle of Man, they now receive their news from Granada in Manchester.

You could say, of course, that I am biased. Border Television is where I learnt the art of live television. I had read the weather at Tyne Tees and presented the late night bulletin but these were ancillary to my prime role as a reporter. Here, there was the responsibility of anchoring a half-hour programme with all its twists and turns, highlights and uncertainties. What I learned was that you need to be flexible so you can adapt to changing circumstances. At Border, the good thing was that you could make mistakes and quickly learn from them. In many ways live broadcasting is like sport. There's really nowhere to practice and until you're out there in front of a crowd, you can't tell how it will go. You really do have to think on your feet and be prepared to stretch yourself whilst always remembering that at the end of the day, you are no more than a conveyor of the message.

Autocue was still something for another age at Border. This innovation reminded me of the days when I was a naughty youngster turning the handle of the destination board of a Dundee tramcar to give passengers the distinct impression that it ought to have been heading in a different direction! In television terms, the presenter's lines were typed on to a scrolling paper script which through a closed-circuit camera system displayed the image on a CRT monitor, which in turn was reflected off the prompter glass into the newsreader's eyeline. It was amazing how many viewers thought the presenter had assiduously memorised all his lines. At Border though, it was a case of A4 sheets plonked on the desk at the last minute with eyes more often than not cast downward rather than looking directly at the camera.

Border's Head of Production, Derek Batey, was also a genial on-screen performer. During the 1970s, the game show he hosted, *Mr and Mrs*, was the company's principal offering to the ITV network. He began this popular husband and wife quiz in 1967 and hosted it for 21 years. It proved so successful that he took the show on stage and in cabaret. At one time, he was booked at every major holiday resort for the summer season.

Derek was born in Brampton, a small market town nine miles east of Carlisle, where his dad ran a mineral water and 'pop' bottling firm. His leaning towards show business began when at the age of nine, he bought his first ventriloquist doll.

It was to Brampton too that Veronica, now my fiancée, and I headed in search of accommodation. We went by train keen to see whether the station had any memorial dedicated to Thomas Edmondson, its first stationmaster who invented the ticket machine used by British railways for over 150 years. Instead, arriving at Brampton Junction, we found the station still lit by oil lamps and to our dismay, situated a mile and a half south of the town.

To compound matters, no sooner had we opened the carriage door when the heavens opened, the rain so heavy and the illumination so ineffectual that it was like being transported straight into a Frankenstein movie. We were the only passengers to alight there but, on opening the wooden gate at the rear of the platform, we discovered that there appeared to be a rough track heading away from the station, though to exactly where we had no idea. A clap of thunder was followed by an eerie silence. By now the rain was blowing horizontally into our faces and stung like giant needles, the starless sky and thick mist clouding our way to such an extent that it was impossible to gauge whether we were still on the track. It later transpired that we had been following the course of an old railway, nicknamed the Dandy, that had started as a number of wooden wagonways hauled by horses.

At last in the distance through the gloom, we spotted a couple of orange lights, followed by three more. We had arrived. Our mission now was to find Ashmore, a large stone-built house that had been converted into a small Catholic chapel and five self-contained flats. We rang the bell to the caretaker's flat. The door was opened by a smiling round-faced lady with a gentle Scouser accent who was clearly astonished to see a pair of drowned rats standing on her front step, clothing completely saturated and rivulets of water running down our faces.

'We hear you have a couple of flats to rent. Might it be possible to take a look?'

'I think it best we hang up your wet clothes first and than I'll pop the kettle on,' came the sympathetic reply.

Tilly Silvester had a heart of gold, kind and generous to a fault, with a cheery smile and kind word for everyone she met. 'Would you like a poached egg, pet?' was her favoured greeting to all who called by. Apart from keeping her eye on the church's tenants, she provided tea and a sumptuous meal for the parish priest, a Benedictine of French origin, Father Francis Vidal whose presbytery was situated in the neighbouring village of Warwick Bridge. Tilly's husband Joe, who worked at the Blue Streak rocket establishment at Spadeadam, would no sooner return from an arduous day shift at the base than he was at work lovingly cleaning and polishing the little church.

The flats proved ideal. By this time, Veronica, whom I had met in Newcastle where she worked as a therapeutic radiographer, was now employed by an independent travel agent in Carlisle and we had already set a wedding date for the following February. One Friday evening though, I returned from work to find two Fire Engines in the drive with Joe Silvester in a frantic state of alarm desperately trying to prevent the drapers and greengrocers who made up the part-time crews from spraying their hoses anywhere near the chapel. With so few call-outs, they looked a little disappointed at the pleas to curtail their fire fighting activity.

Upstairs, the kitchen of Veronica's flat was filled with columns of choking black smoke. A chip pan had inadvertently been left unattended when the man from Radio Rentals called round to take a look at a television set on the blink.

The embarrassment would have been even greater had not Joe and his alert son Tony dipped a tea towel in water, wrung it out and successfully smothered the flaming pan.

Another possible embarrassment was avoided when my former flatmate John Motson reluctantly decided he could not attend our wedding. Motty had just recently joined the *Match of the Day* team and had been asked to commentate on the FA Cup game between non-League no-hopers Hereford and First Division high-flyers Newcastle United. Everyone expected the result to be a formality but Motty was determined that the West Country and not Cumbria was where he ought to be. This saved me any discomfiture over the choice of Best Man. That role would now go to my other flatmate from Finchley days, Jim Currie. What's more, having been born in Kilmarnock, he was more than happy to don the kilt.

Many of the wedding guests were friends with whom Veronica and I had shared enjoyable times in the North East including more than a sprinkling of Newcastle fans.

As the roast beef was served, transistors were tuned to Radio 2 for the latest news from Hereford's Edgar Street ground. The minnows were holding their own until just eight minutes from time, 'Supermac' Malcolm McDonald headed Newcastle in front. A cheer went up around the tables. By the time, the sweet was served, the whole game had been turned on its head and effectively launched Motty's career.

Ronnie Radford's incredible 30-yard equalizer sparked a pitch invasion and would be endlessly replayed for years to come and when Ricky George, John's lifetime friend, hit the winning goal in extra time, Hereford had pulled off arguably the greatest FA Cup shock of all time.

Originally, it had been planned that the game would fill a short segment in *Match of the Day* following the two main games selected by the BBC, but the programme editor quickly switched the Hereford match to the top of the programme. The audience that night was 14 million and for the first time, John Motson had the lead game.

As the band struck up and the dancing began, our Newcastle guests put on a brave face. As for the bridegroom, well I have to confess, wedding night or not, I could hardly wait to get in front of a TV set to watch Ronnie Radford's spectacular goal and the corybantic Motty capturing one of the most unforgettable moments in sporting history. The thought that I might have robbed Motty of his big day still makes me shudder with fright.

By now I had bought my first new car, a Fiat 500L which was slow, noisy, leaked a little when it rained and required the accelerator pedal to be pressed to the floor to keep it moving. Today, such an antique sells at nearly ten times its original price – pity I hadn't held on to it for it certainly took up little room on the driveway.

In Finchley I had lived in the constituency of the then Education Secretary, Margaret Thatcher. In Brampton, our MP was Willie Whitelaw who was to become her Deputy Prime Minister. His Penrith and The Border constituents gave him one of the largest parliamentary majorities in the country. In the early seventies, he served as Secretary of State for Northern Ireland in Edward Heath's government and came close to achieving a power-sharing deal between Unionists and Nationalists before the Sunningdale Agreement which he negotiated, collapsed in the wake of a Loyalist general strike.

Charm was the essence of the man. Few politicians of his stature are affectionately known by just one name. Wherever he went in the constituency, this endlessly courteous man was simply referred to as 'Willie'. Occasionally, on Fridays, I would be sent to the gates of his mansion at Blencow, near Penrith, to await his arrival from London with ITN keen to acquire an interview about fast-moving developments in Ulster. If he was delayed, his wife Celia, would come bounding down the path carrying a silver salver with a bottle of lager, a glass and some ice. It was the beginning of a firm friendship with Willie Whitelaw. Our paths would frequently cross in the following decade when I was asked to take on the role of the BBC's Home Affairs Correspondent and Mrs Thatcher had put Willie in charge of the Home Office.

One of the Iron Lady's predecessors as Prime Minister, Sir Alec Douglas-Home was also very supportive of Border Television. The Home family's 5-kilometre estate is now designated as a country park lying just to the west of Coldstream which marks the border between Scotland and England. I had met him there one stormy night in the 1960s when we discussed the ending of the Biafran War, but it was to his ancestral home at Castlemains near Douglas in Lanarkshire that I was invited to film a short documentary about his life in politics. He had served as Parliamentary Private Secretary to Neville Chamberlain and thereby was associated with Chamberlain's policy of appeasement towards Hitler and Nazi Germany. In 1951 he had to quit the Commons when he inherited his father's seat in the House of Lords, becoming the 14th Earl of Home, but was given the job of Foreign Secretary in Harold Macmillan's Government.

His wide experience of world affairs made him a much-respected politician at home and abroad. As we talked of the post-war days, Sir Alec broke into fits of laughter as he recalled how he had watched the Soviet President, Nikita Khrushchev, in a fit of pique, bang his shoe on the desk at the United Nations after being accused of double standards by conducting an imperialist policy in Eastern Europe.

'I spotted him taking off his shoe and undoing the laces under the desk so I had an idea of what was coming!'

When Macmillan resigned in October 1963, the Earl of Home became the compromise candidate to succeed him with the party divided over the two leading contenders, Quintin Hogg and Rab Butler. This meant Home had to disclaim his Earldom for life and fight a by-election to re-enter the Commons. Sir Alec was only Prime Minister for a year before losing the General Election to Harold Wilson's Labour Party, but in 1970 he was prepared to take a ministry in someone else's cabinet returning as Foreign Secretary to Edward Heath.

He was eminently suitable for the job and stayed until he was 70.

'I have loved it all,' he told me. 'But at my age flying to the other side of the world can be very difficult. When you touch down at some far-flung place, whether or not you have managed even a few minutes' sleep, everyone wants to get straight on with the business.'

Certainly, few leaders had such a varied insight into the power brokers of the 20th Century. Hitler, Mussolini, Kennedy, Nixon, Khrushchev, Hammarskjöld and Chou En-lai, he had dealings with them all. I could detect though that the ultimate pleasure was to be able to return to the Borders to reflect on major events and unwind in the natural beauty of his country estates.

Sir Alec was also extremely loyal to all who worked for him. One incident he did not reveal to me or anyone else only came to light after his death. During his year as Prime Minister, he had foiled a kidnap plot by bribing his abductors with beer. Two students from Aberdeen University had tailed his car from a conference to the house where he was staying. Astonishingly, his bodyguard was using separate accommodation and when the plotters knocked on the door, they were greeted by a bemused premier.

Told he was about to be kidnapped, he replied, 'I suppose you realise if you do, the Conservatives will win the election by 200 or 300.' He asked permission to pack a few things and was given ten minutes' grace. But then the Prime Minister scuppered the group by offering them beer and convincing them to abandon their plot. He never spoke of the kidnapping because he didn't want to ruin the career of his bodyguard.

It also emerged that before the war he had shot a woodcock which fell into the tender of the Royal Scot. The driver stopped the train at Berwick and gave the bird to the Stationmaster who delivered it to Sir Alec.

If the future Prime Minister enjoyed a moorland shoot then it was his younger brother for whom bird watching had become a lifelong passion. Henry Douglas-Home would spend endless days recording and photographing every feathered creature from robins and wrens to eagles, swifts and terns, exotic birds, waxwings and yellow wagtails. By the early 1970s he had recorded so many bird songs and calls that they had been transferred on to several dozen 78rpm records.

With Border Television always keen to save money, I thought we had all the makings of a good series. I headed north to Berwickshire to meet Henry and his wife Felicity. He was in ebullient mood and eager to please. Photographs, diaries and beautiful combinations of stone carved birds perched on various bases, all self-creations, were handed over for my inspection. I suggested a series of seven 15-minute programmes, the first to be shot at The Hirsel, the others to be studio recordings at Carlisle in which we could feature a variety of bird calls and illustrate these either with a fast changing collection of stills or from archive footage supplied by the RSPB.

Henry was well disposed to the idea but suggested we should design the series for children.

'There's a new generation out there who don't know what they're missing. We've got to get them on board. Let them see what fun they can have discovering so many different song birds their homes play host to each year.'

The outdoor location filming provided some excellent footage but in trying to keep costs to a minimum, it was decided that the six studio programmes be recorded in just two days. Henry arrived with all the necessary accoutrements – a pair of mini plastic binoculars, a little notebook, a couple of pencils, a spotting chart and his invaluable record collection.

We loaded up the necessary film, got the stills in the right order and gave the director a rough script though Henry insisted he wanted to do things off the cuff.

Opening titles, sound, cue Presenter. Having described bird song as one of the wonders of the world of nature, I introduce Henry and ask him what every child requires to take up this fascinating hobby. Excitedly, he produces the notebook and the pencil, swings the binoculars to and fro and announces that everything can be bought at Woolworths for less than a fiver.

Stop recording.

'Unfortunately this is commercial television and we really can't promote the name of a High Street store.'

Off we go again but try as he might, he cannot throw off the Woolies line. Third attempt, better luck but the illustrations and the bird calls start to go badly out of sequence.

When recording time is over for the day, we still haven't got one complete programme together. But it seems there's nothing that a stiff drink can't put right. Next morning he's back ... enthusiasm unbounded, a faultless performance and the resonance of bird song turning Studio 1 into a virtual Amazon rainforest.

Even without a mention, Woolies had a field day ... within hours, stores on both sides of the border sold out of binoculars as Henry acquired a burgeoning fan club of junior ornithologists.

In the little Border Burghs of Scotland each new generation is encouraged to play a part in maintaining centuries' old traditions. These include the annual Common Ridings which are an inescapable part of the Borders' culture. A Standard Bearer known as a Cornet or Braw Lad is chosen from the young men of the town, mounts his horse and leads a cavalcade of riders into the surrounding hills and around the ancient boundaries re-enacting the age old ritual of 'riding the marches'.

One of the oldest of these flamboyant ceremonies takes place at Langholm in Dumfriesshire. Only 2,500 people live there but the town has always occupied an importance way beyond its size.

It's also the home of the Armstrong clan, feared outlaws and reivers, who occupied much of the Debateable Lands, the disputed territory between England and Scotland. Five hundred years ago, the valleys of Eskdale and Liddesdale echoed to the sound of horses' hooves as the raiding clans went about their business when the moon was right. Local historians will tell you that the Armstrongs had a phrase unique to their clan: 'there will be moonlight again'– in other words another raid was imminent.

How appropriate then that the first man to set foot on the moon, astronaut Neil Armstrong, should take another giant leap for mankind by becoming the first Freeman of Langholm in 1972. Researching their roots has become a passion for most Americans and this was a real television bonanza for Border. I found him the most reticent of people, a humble man who was clearly not experiencing any heroic afterglow of his achievement.

The whole town turned out for him, the pipe band in resplendent tartan uniforms with the astronaut and his wife driven through the streets in an open landau. In the parish church, the Commander of Apollo 11 had to swear an oath of allegiance before signing the Burgess Roll. Langholm had claimed him as one of their long-lost sons and he was clearly moved by the whole occasion.

'It's said that the most difficult place to be recognised is in one's own home town and I consider this now as my own home town.'

The congregation broke into thunderous applause.

After his moon walk, Armstrong had asserted that 'pilots take no special joy in walking. Pilots like flying.' Surely an irony then that he should become more famous for his shortest walk than his longest journey. As for the folks of Langholm – a walkabout was most definitely on the agenda. With the pipe band ahead and the Provost on his shoulder, the astronaut strolled the town like a true Borderer, waving enthusiastically and acknowledging – among others – the acclaim of his fellow clansmen.

By now, we had bought our first house, a brand new semi-detached at How Mill adjacent to the Newcastle to Carlisle railway line. It was the pride and joy of a local builder who made frequent visits to check everything was in good order. His timber yard on the other side of the main line became an elephantine hiding place for our newly acquired Siamese cat Meikleriggs Lulabelle. I don't know whether she felt affronted by our insistence on calling her Coco but this previously unwanted 'royal' with an immaculate pedigree would bound across the level crossing and disappear beneath endless stacks of sawn timber. As a child I can never remember being involved in such elaborate and time-consuming games of hide and seek. Siamese may be the most vocal of cats but Coco was in no hurry to give the game away, obviously taking great pleasure from listening to the layers of wooden planks creaking and groaning as my struggle to locate her became ever more tortuous.

How Mill Station was closed to passenger traffic in 1959, 20 years and more after Hedgeley on the old North Eastern line between Alnwick and Cornhill. Yet bizarrely, Billy Houston, who moved into the Stationmaster's house there swore that he could still hear the distant whistle and clatter of the old steam locomotives heading north to the Scottish border.

I decided to investigate this ghost train revelation. When our film crew arrived, there was Billy dressed in his old railway uniform complete with whistle and green flag. He waved and he blew and I swear he could see a Class D20 engine emerging from the early morning mist. Alas it never showed up on our celluloid or at Hedgeley's platform with its beautifully preserved station building of buff-coloured, rock-faced sandstone. The herringbone-patterned wood and glass lean-to structures that once sheltered travellers from the vagaries of the weather were still there too but the passengers had gone, living only in Billy Houston's head. But not all was lost. Our audio library was able to produce the authentic sound of a Class D20 to bring an extra head of steam to his story and no, it wasn't April Fool's Day! Returning to Carlisle, I was forced to admit feeling a little envious of Billy and his wife Evelyn's retirement home though bemused as to why the North Eastern Railway should have chosen to lavish such splendid facilities on a secondary and unremunerative line.

Stories like these were a Godsend not just during the silly season but in the winter months too. When snow storms sweep across the Lake District and the hills of Southern Scotland roads can quickly become impassable. Forced to dig a camera car out of a drift at four in the afternoon made your chances of getting a feature back for that evening's programme a virtual impossibility. Building up a small bank of undated films was seen as the best method to ensure the yawning gaps in the running order could be filled, not of course, forgetting the opportunity once again to call up man and guitar!

On one horrendous day in late February 1973 these judicious measures failed spectacularly. Man and guitar were unavailable, two camera crews were snowbound more than 60 miles from the studios and the film bank had not been replenished for the past fortnight. By late afternoon, Allan Powell and his team were in panic mode. Twenty minutes of a 35-minute programme lay bare. Even the local AA director – an ideal interviewee given the conditions – indicated he could not make it. Every weekly newspaper was scanned in a desperate search to find studio guests with an interesting story to tell.

Turning over the pages of *The Cumberland & Westmorland Herald*, my eyes caught sight of a tiny article about a member of Appleby Women's Institute who had won a national competition for corn dollies, an ancient rural craft symbolising Mother Earth and traditionally made from the last ears of wheat to be cut.

I quickly traced the 'dolly maker' in the phone book and while I was speaking to her, I got a colleague to send a local taxi on its way to her door with strict instructions to the driver to get her to the studio in time for the start of the programme. Her doorbell was already ringing as I ended our conversation with a plea to bring every shape and size of doll she could squeeze into the car – crowns, knots, handbells, lanterns, spirals, whatever – all were required.

The dear lady arrived at ten minutes to six, shaking like a leaf and feeling physically sick. I ushered her into the canteen and ordered a soothing cup of tea and suggested she took a deep breath and tried to relax. I told her someone would bring her into the studio just a few minutes before the interview was due to commence but first, could she get the taxi driver to hand over all her fine craft work to the production assistant.

Fifteen minutes later, into the studio she came carrying only a handbag. Inside was the tiniest corn dolly imaginable. The poor woman was in a dreadful state. Out came her scissors, hankies, purse and finally the doll.

The Floor Manager, Harry King, a delightfully ebullient man, indicated the interview had been allocated five minutes. I knew I would have to work hard.

'How do you feel about winning such a prestigious competition?' I asked her.

'*I don't really know.*'
'What's the secret behind creating such fine masterpieces?'
'*I don't know.*'
You won the regional final. How many were in the competition?
'*Three.*'
'And in the National Final?'
'*Three.*'
'What's the average size of the dolls you make?'
'*Four inches.*'
'Let's take a close-up look at this fine specimen you have brought along ... a very intricate art form...'
'*I wouldn't say that.*'
The interview had yet to run for thirty seconds. I was perspiring profusely, desperately trying to elicit a few crumbs of information. Dialogue was clearly becoming impossible. I had exhausted twenty questions or more when at last Harry King began the count down ... 30 secs, 15, 10 ... and then suddenly a desperate wave of the hands to indicate something was wrong. As I launched into yet another question, Harry was scribbling something on to a chalk board. He held it just under the camera. 'We have lost the next film ... keep interview going.'

I grabbed the miniature doll from the woman's hand.

'Ah, I see now ... if we turn it upside down, we can capture far more of the detail.'

'*Really,*' she said, '*I don't think so.*'

The ordeal was to last another four minutes right up to the closing titles. I said my goodbyes both to the country's corn dolly champion and to Border Television. Running along the corridor, I picked up the public phone in reception and dialled BBC Scotland.

Asking to be connected with the Head of News, I told him I had just experienced the nether world of television.

'Then you'd better get yourself up here lad ... we're holding auditions next Tuesday!'

As I watched the queen of an ancient art disappear up the drive back to Appleby, I really didn't know whether to laugh or cry.

8

Reporting Scotland

Breathes there a man with soul so dead, who never to himself hath said: this is my own, my native land!

Sir Walter Scott

In the early 1970s Glasgow was a city of great contrasts. Prosperity and desperate poverty lived almost next door to each other. The elegant elevated Georgian terraces of Park Circus and the imposing villas and handsome sandstone tenements of the West End stood as a unique memorial to some of the most gifted architects of the nineteenth century. Yet you didn't have to travel far to encounter degradation on an unimaginable scale ... boarded-up buildings, slum dwellings, litter-strewn courtyards and an intimidating atmosphere.

In the outer suburbs, thousands living in huge 1950s overspill developments like Castlemilk, Easterhouse and Drumchapel were facing an accumulation of social problems – high unemployment, damp and overcrowded homes, poor health and poor diet and a lack of affordable child care. I remember standing at the interface of Drumchapel and the leafy Glasgow suburb of Bearsden and announcing the sad truth that being born just a couple of hundred yards on the wrong side of the boundary spelt out a life expectancy difference of 10 years.

I was back working in my native Scotland and adapting once again to city life, a distant cry from the six million sheep and wide open spaces that had been my patrol path at Border Television.

Life at Queen Margaret Drive, the stylish headquarters of BBC Scotland was busy, vibrant and years of fun. The newsroom boss who hired me, Hugh Cochrane, had a real 'feel' for stories, a good journalistic pedigree and was prepared to give me my head.

Fear of failure can be a driving force to help you succeed, and throughout my broadcasting career, as each new opportunity arose, I always felt I was working at the outer limits of my abilities. Nothing builds more self-confidence than turning a negative thought into a positive response and so I returned to life on the road with renewed vigour and enthusiasm.

Alas, the desire to make an early impression meant that I was absent at the birth of our first child. My heavily pregnant wife had stayed behind at How Mill and I was thankful that Tony Silvester who had helped extinguish the chip-pan fire in Brampton should ride to the rescue again by running Veronica to Carlisle General Hospital where our daughter Claire made an unexpectedly early appearance. I was at the bedside within an hour but still too late.

A wise man once said that any man can be a *father* but it takes someone special to be a *dad*. Children certainly bring a new dimension to life and a good dad must surely recognise his responsibility for them. Fatherhood changes your perspective as you try to reconcile life at work and spending time with your children. Unfortunately, journalism does not lend itself to a stereotypical office routine. The profession is no respecter of hours, meal times or the demands of the reporter's private life. Loosen the tie, put on the jeans by all means, but be prepared, at a moment's notice, to be summoned back to the fray.

Apart from breaking news stories which can decimate a carefully prepared running order, the planning of most evening news programmes begins the day before. Diaries are checked to discover what events are already scheduled – press conferences, ongoing industrial disputes, new car launches, royal visits, murder trials – there could be dozens of entries which need to be prioritised.

By arriving ahead of most of my colleagues, I was able to quickly grab hold of a diary print-out of the day's events and decide which story held the most personal appeal. By the time the cut and thrust of the morning conference began, I had formulated a convincing case as to why I was the best man for the job. Surprisingly, this brazen little ploy paid off handsomely for the first few weeks until the News Editor of the day began to see through my shameless shenanigans.

The variety and pace of the work kept everyone on his toes. You could be on the press bench of the High Court in the morning, a picket line at lunchtime then sending the car accelerating towards an afternoon blaze at an industrial workshop. There was never a dull moment with every day throwing oddity and surprise into the journalistic mix alongside stories of political intrigue or industrial muscle.

I had barely settled into this routine when Hugh Cochrane summoned me to his office.

The regular presenter of *Reporting Scotland* Douglas Kynoch had gone on a religious retreat to Ireland and wasn't sure when, if ever, he'd return.

'I would like you to give it a go. I'm sure you'll face up to the challenge. You'll need to think on your feet, be alert at all times and ask the straightforward but tough questions the public expect in these live interviews with politicians.'

This was an opportunity I certainly had not expected. Whatever I had achieved at Border Television, this would be a far greater test of my broadcasting capability and resourcefulness.

Initially, it wasn't the politicians who were giving me problems but my choice of clothes. Having just purchased a new semi at Carluke in Lanarkshire with hefty mortgage payments to be met by a salary that – even proportionally – pales into insignificance against similar jobs today, my attire comprised little more than a couple of well-worn blue suits and a navy blazer.

The introduction of a colour-separation overlay system by the BBC meant that my clothes provided an unacceptable clash with the studio's large blue background. So now, instead of spending the precious minutes running up to programme transmission time checking the scripts that were still racing off the printer, I was engaged in a smash and grab exercise in the wardrobe department battling through chain mail, riding habits, bearskin hats and claymores to lay my hands on anything that resembled a half-decent suit, preferably one that would stay up without resort to belt or braces.

Not surprisingly, the programme's director was none too pleased with my absence from the studio floor at such a vital time. Hugh Cochrane was asked to get the problem resolved and quickly. He contacted the Personnel Department and asked that I be given a little financial help towards purchasing a new suit.

A week later, I received a short note attaching a cheque for £5. I doubt whether that would have bought more than half a dozen pairs of socks at The Barras, Glasgow's famous flea market.

Cochrane was furious, so too the ladies of the Wardrobe Department who were getting rather tired of constantly pressing the grey suits that were required for other more important dramas.

I was marched back to the personnel office, this time to be told that the national newsreaders Richard Baker, Robert Dougall and Kenneth Kendall were not granted any clothing allowance and that if I was not able to make myself presentable then they would find someone else to do the job.

The impasse was a huge personal embarrassment but I could see this was a battle that Cochrane was determined to win. The issue had now reached the desk of a Scottish programme executive. I was told I could purchase two jackets (you don't need to buy trousers, no-one can see your legs!) and the cost must not exceed £20.

The following Saturday morning, my wife and I entered the men's department of C&A in Glasgow's Sauchiehall Street.

The manager approached and said he recognised me from my appearances on television.

Could he be of help? I explained I wished to buy a jacket.

'Certainly sir, this rail has an excellent selection.'

I glanced at the price tags on the sleeves: £45, £50, £60. Humiliated, I was determined to come out with the truth.

'Very smart, I must say. The only problem is that I have to purchase TWO jackets ... oh, and I have just £20 to spend.'

The manager's jaw dropped. All went silent. And then, 'Yes sir, well we do have a few cut price offerings in our autumn sale. If you manage to find anything you like, bring it to the desk and I'll parcel it up for you.'

I found two – one burgundy red, the other a checked sports jacket. The bill came to £21.32p + £2.13 VAT. I had spent £3 more than I was entitled to and told the extra cost would be deducted from my salary. In addition: 'The jackets will, of course, remain the property of the BBC and should the nature of your employment change to make it unnecessary for you to wear them on television, they must be returned at once to our Wardrobe.'

In the early 1970s no-one in Scotland had come up with the simple idea of giving presenters an earpiece to listen to instructions from the programme director sitting in the production gallery. These are wonderful aids which are moulded to fit precisely and securely within the newsreader's ear.

Instead, perched on the studio desk was a Bakelite telephone with a light attached. If it lit up, I knew instinctively that there was something seriously amiss. I'd calmly pick up the phone, hiding any sense of panic whilst listening intently to the instructions given. All of this would take about five seconds but sitting there, it felt like an eternity. The job then was to politely inform the audience that we were experiencing some difficulty with a particular film and that it was necessary for the moment to move on to another item.

In full view of close on a million viewers, talking back to the director was something to avoid at all costs, so too, yielding to a naughty temptation when lifting the receiver to say 'I told you not to ring me at work' – that would surely have resulted in immediate dismissal!

Reporting Scotland was operating a three-studio set-up with the director in the Glasgow gallery able to switch to fellow presenters Kenneth Roy in Edinburgh and Jack Reagan in Aberdeen. It was a time of great political intrigue and debate with an increase in nationalist sentiment following the discovery of North Sea oil. The SNP were able to field a strong line-up of television performers like Winnie Ewing, Margo MacDonald, George Reid and Gordon Wilson, while Labour's former schoolmaster, Willie Ross, the longest-serving Secretary of State for Scotland, always portrayed his tough and uncompromising image in a live studio interview. Opposed to devolution and British membership of the EEC, he was once described by political commentator Andrew Marr as a 'stern-faced and authoritarian Presbyterian conservative who ran the country like a fiefdom for Harold Wilson'. My recollections were of a no-nonsense politician more than capable of running ever-increasing rings round anyone who hadn't properly prepared or researched the topic to be debated. The other parties too, were boasting young politicians heading for high office such as the future Liberal leader David Steel and Tory Foreign Secretary, Malcolm Rifkind. For a still relatively inexperienced presenter, being able to pit my wits against the some of the sharpest analytical minds of the day was an invaluable learning experience.

As the Scottish presenter, I was frequently called on to appear on live injects into *Nationwide* which was broadcast nightly from the BBC's Lime Grove studios but encouraged participation from the English regions as well as Scotland, Wales and Northern Ireland. The programme had something of an appetite for the eccentric, its most famous offerings including the celebrated skateboarding duck and a beer-drinking snail.

One night the focus was on presenters' ties. On sound advice, I donned an extremely wide Kipper with its garish colours and patterns. The sartorial expert from Savile Row, wheeled on to make his judgement, complimented my colleagues in Cardiff, Norwich and Bristol before suddenly launching a savage attack over my choice, dismissing it as an affront to the programme's 10 million viewers.

My favourite recipe for inclusion in the *Nationwide Cookbook* proved a trifle more popular. I plumped for an old Highland favourite Cock-A-Leekie Soup, just the thing to warm the cockles of your heart on a cold winter's night.

My home city, Dundee had a studio too. It was situated on the first floor of Coldside Library in Strathmartine Road, next door to the Odeon Cinema. I used it several times for live reports into *Sportscene*. Dashing there from Dens and Tannadice (respective homes of Dundee and Dundee United FCs), everything depended on being able to locate the off-duty caretaker who held the only key to the self-operated facility. Apart from switching on the power, you also had to remember to grab a cushion or two. With the chair levers long since inoperative, even for someone 5ft 10ins tall, it was only possible to establish a camera eye-line by settling your backside on top of a couple of these moth-eaten offerings.

Guests arriving at Queen Margaret Drive were normally escorted to the Green Room for a discussion with a member of the programme staff. It was situated opposite the tea bar run by Molly, a big Glesga woman with a word for everyone, many of them unrepeatable.

She did not suffer fools gladly and the young assistants under her charge – most of them only recently out of school – changed regularly, having been reduced to tears when criticised for some minor indiscretion.

Molly was no respecter of persons. Whether you were the Director General or the newest floor cleaner, you could expect to become bait for her frequently acid tongue. One African television executive examining the fare available was told to 'get your hands off thae bananas, yer no in the jungle noo!'

When my good friend Motty arrived on the eve of the big Scotland–England international at Hampden Park, I led him past a long line of people waiting to be served and asked Molly to pour him a quick coffee as a car was waiting to take him to the ground as part of his preparation for the next day. She was having none of it.

'I don't care if he's Archie Macpherson (the legendary Scottish football commentator), get him to the back of the queue!'

The news anchor role was only part of my daily responsibilities. I was still very much 'on the road', one of a small team of reporters who ranged over every kind of story. If I was finding life more than a little frenetic at times then I marvelled at the incredible stamina of some of my working colleagues.

David Helme, one of the two staff cameramen allocated to news, lived a double life as a Lanarkshire farmer, rising at four o'clock every morning to muck out the shed of his Hereford cattle. A small man in stature, he had the energy and strength of one of his prize bulls. I first met him when on one of my last assignments for Border Television. We had stopped for lunch in Lockerbie when unexpectedly a BBC Scotland team who had been covering a different story walked into the hotel. As I slipped off to the gents cloakroom, David was asked: 'Did you know Bill will be joining you soon? We call him Harpic because he's clean round the bend!'

I got on splendidly with David. He was kind, considerate and very enthusiastic about his job. We relished working together. Occasionally, I would drive over to meet him at his farm near Stonehouse. One morning, we were about to set off when he suddenly shouted 'hang on a minute. I've got something important to do.' He sped out of the house, heading for an adjoining field. Looking out the window, I could see him dismantling part of a wire fence and driving a bull back into his neighbour's meadow. David had borrowed the beast earlier that morning and left him to service his cow while he went inside for breakfast. It was a successful introduction as the Hereford heifer produced a 'braw wee calf' some months later.

Robert Murison too, was a larger than life character. The Chief Constable of Fife for nearly 20 years, he had his own unique method of getting people to heed his message. The tactics he deployed were often more graphic and thought-provoking than the expensive Government-sponsored television advertising campaigns against smoking, drugs, obesity or drink/driving.

With Christmas and New Year fast approaching, I received a telex from Fife Police HQ then situated at Dysart. It was an invitation to attend a Press Conference the following day in which 'our Chief Constable will be issuing a stern warning about the effects of drink/driving over the holiday period. Mr Murison wishes to emphasise that this will be very televisual. Non-alcoholic refreshments will be provided.'

When I arrived with cameraman Bob Thomson, the approach road to police HQ was lined with staff lying prostrate on the verge. Some were wrapped in blankets with blood, effectively replicated by the use of liberal amounts of tomato ketchup, streaming from a series of simulated head and body injuries.

At the other end of the drive, the Police Chief was waiting. He suggested we might like to attach a radio microphone so he could wander amongst the casualties whilst every now and then glancing up to the camera to ask viewers whether they wanted their Christmas and New Year holidays ruined by this kind of horror. 'Leave your car at home. Don't have this on your conscience. You'll never forgive yourself.'

I can never remember a more effective display of amateur dramatics but the Chief Constable didn't leave it there. He'd also invited along a Senior Staff Nurse from the Victoria Hospital in Kirkcaldy.

'Tell them what it's like in Accident and Emergency on Hogmanay,' he insisted. 'How many road accident victims did you have last year?' And looking around at all the bodies still lining the roadside: 'Is this the kind of thing you have to deal with?'

I couldn't get a word in edgeways. A very effective piece of public relations – when the drink/drive statistics were published the following January, the figures for Fife showed a significant fall.

Another former Chief Constable, Willie Merrilees, was an extrovert of the highest order and one of the finest humanitarians I have ever encountered. He was allowed to continue in post as head of the Lothians and Peebles Constabulary until his seventieth birthday. With a touch of real Merrilees humour, he bought a disused railway station at Dolphinton south of Edinburgh and converted it into a holiday home for old folks and disadvantaged youngsters.

'Look here, I've given the place a new address,' he confided, his face alight with a mischievous smile. 'Just as well there are no trains running now. I doubt whether too many would have alighted here now the station board reads *999 The Nick.*'

As a lad, there was no indication that Willie would become one of the most colourful figures in the annals of law enforcement and crime detection. Starting work in a rope factory, he lost several fingers in a horrendous industrial accident. Despite his dreadful injuries, he was an outstanding swimmer and became the hero in a daring rescue of a number of people from Leith Docks.

Impressed by his courage and determination, Edinburgh's Lord Provost was determined to help Willie realise his ambition to become a policeman. In the event, the Secretary of State waived the minimum height regulation and Willie Merrilees became at 5ft 6ins Scotland's shortest lawman. He quickly established a reputation for cracking difficult cases and became the master of disguise. In September 1940, when dressed as a railway porter, he caught the Nazi spy Kurt Walther in a railway carriage at Waverley Station. The German was carrying a pistol but with his arms pinned to his sides in Willie's crushing bear-hug, he was overpowered before he could draw it.

On another occasion, he used his lack of height to great advantage. Police had been desperately trying to track a man who had been molesting nannies in the streets and parks of the city. Willie jumped into a pram, managed to push his legs up his back, dressed himself as a baby and lay in wait. As the man approached, he suddenly leapt from the pram and caught the would-be assailant red-handed.

Willie's generosity knew no bounds. Long into his retirement, he was still organising events for pensioners and handicapped children. It was not unknown for him to roll up at a children's home unannounced, his driver carrying containers of ice cream and his pockets brimful of sweets, while our cameras would be on hand to film the trips he organised to take children to the seaside. Woe to any taxi driver who refused his request to join the convoy.

If the country's smallest policeman held a captivating appeal then so did the world's smallest underground railway ... a six and a half mile circle to serve 15 stations in Central Glasgow. Incredibly, in 1976, most of the two car trains celebrated their 80th birthday. They were the original carriages which were cable-hauled under Glasgow's gas-lit Victorian streets. In the world of modern transport, they had become an anachronism, a circulating museum of moving parts that all but recreated Glasgow of 1896.

The pleasantly archaic atmosphere gave the system its character and friendliness. With carriages lurching at what seemed crazy speeds and wheels grinding against a particularly tight curve to create the famous 'Cowcaddens shoogle', the constant shake, rattle and roll could match some of the mind-blowing rides at Alton Towers. It wasn't difficult to experience the spirit of the even older tramways reincarnated in the tunnels dipping beneath the Clyde. In these tunnels, a boat was rowed, an eel discovered and 'ghostly' strangers in the night had maintenance men dropping tools and fleeing in panic.

Out of touch, out of cash and out of register, the Subway seemed to be on its last legs. Fearing its demise might not be long delayed, Gordon Casely, the buoyant and irrepressible PR of the Passenger Transport Authority asked all friends of this Lilliputian railway to don the finest Victorian attire so that we could film a re-enactment of its glory days. With our best friends Bill and Rena Fleming, Veronica and I trundled down the staircase to board the train from the island platform at Kelvinbridge on what we thought might be one of the last circuits of the city. Just days later, to everyone's amazement, Edward Heath's Conservative Government who commanded little support in Glasgow, authorised a 75 per cent infrastructure grant for redeveloping the entire underground system.

The modernisation took three years to complete. There were no extensions to the route but the new 'Clockwork Orange' trains won over a new generation of transport aficionados as well as providing a fast and frequent service to stations on both sides of the Clyde.

I spent many happy hours 'downstairs' on filming assignments and was honoured to have been asked to provide the voice-over for an historical documentary on the Glasgow Subway. I found at least 18 nationalities working on the staff of this proud little railway including a former Ghanaian welterweight boxer, Ugandan and Chinese stationmasters and a kilted Pakistani driver – once a bodyguard to the Viceroy of India – whose passengers were entertained on their journey to work listening to the strains of 'I belong to Glasgow' and 'The Bonnie Banks of Loch Lomond' emanating from his driver's cab.

With one of Scotland's best loved presenters, Mary Marquis, returning to Queen Margaret Drive, I was now free to spend more of my time on reporting duties again. It's a role I have always preferred. News presenters are very important for programmes. Viewers associate with them and a bond of trust begins to build with those whom they like and admire. They will always have their critics, of course, which is only to be expected if your face appears uninvited in folks' living rooms night after night. For me though, the real broadcasting buzz is being at the heart of the story, reporting events as they happen and meeting face to face with those who create the headlines.

Some stories have a direct effect on whole communities. Winning the League, the cup or, in the case of Chris Hoy, three Olympic Golds, brings people on to the streets in their tens of thousands, three – or sometimes four – generations of effusive, flag-waving fans. Such events are tailor-made for television.

Communal grief is much more difficult to express in pictures and words as villagers retreat behind closed doors and dropped window blinds.

Normally, it is left to the local minister or the Superintendent from the Fishermen's Mission to relay the sense of loss and trauma experienced by so many families when a trawler is overwhelmed by an unforgiving sea. Not for the first time, on arriving in the little fishing port of Hopeman on the Moray Firth, I felt myself an intruder at a time of distress and crushing bewilderment after word had gone out that one of the village boats, the Acacia Wood, had capsized with the loss of nine crewmen. Fishing is surely the most dangerous of peacetime jobs and such is the outlay required to buy a boat these days, you often find that two or sometimes three families have pooled their resources. If the vessel should suddenly succumb to nature's ferocity, the sacrifice of fathers, sons, uncles, brothers and cousins has a devastating effect on the lives of the widows, children and ageing grandmothers left behind.

Of course, many of the risks undertaken by our fishermen are also endured by thousands extracting gas and oil from the North Sea day in, day out. All too often they have to contend with mountainous seas and gale-force winds and are also dependent on the skills of the helicopter pilots who provide the lifeline transport service which keeps the North Sea working. There's nothing glamorous about these flights and, despite an excellent safety record, when things do go wrong the results can be catastrophic.

I shall never forget flying in a Sikorsky S61 with a group of oilmen's wives who had been unexpectedly given the opportunity to get just an inkling of what daily life was like for their husbands working in the largest of the oil fields. We were bound for BP's Forties Charlie rig, 112 miles off Aberdeen.

In driving rain and buffeting winds, the skill and courage of the helicopter crew to complete the mission without mishap and to land their machine on a helipad just 22 metres wide was a hazardous exercise, yet such feats are carried out frequently with meticulous efficiency.

Defying all the laws of gravity, the helicopter was described by Ivor Sikorsky, that great pioneer of aviation, as probably the most versatile instrument ever invented by man. 'If you are in trouble anywhere in the world, a plane can fly over and drop flowers but a helicopter can land and save your life.'

It is an extraordinary bird and I have never ceased to be amazed at the heroic efforts of the men and women who endanger their own lives to airlift survivors from a sinking ship, pull injured climbers off a mountainside or rescue those trapped by earthquakes or natural disasters. Sikorsky would have been proud to know that the helicopters that bear his name have already helped save an estimated two million lives.

Over the past thirty years the 'black gold' from the North Sea has brought enormous economic benefits to Aberdeen and to the Shetland Isles where the Council's shrewd former Chief Executive, Ian Clark, uniquely won the islands' right to royalties from the various revenues gained from the flow of oil through the terminal at Sullom Voe.

Complaining that the oil bosses appeared to think the council was 'completely bereft of all business sense', he dismissed early offers of compensation for the disturbance caused to the islanders' lives until, as the North Sea boom got under way, he began skilfully manipulating international companies and the government to win millions of pounds for Shetland. It later emerged that Shell regarded Mr Clark more difficult to deal with than Libya's Colonel Gaddafi.

As the money began to roll in, the Council got to work on a whole string of initiatives. Disabled drivers were given automatic Volvo cars and residents living in some of the smaller islands suddenly found their homes being connected to mains electricity.

Taking the five-minute ferry cossing from Lerwick to Bressay, I drove to a little but n' ben where Willie and Violet Leask had lived for over seventy years. As darkness set in, their regular routine was to hang up a paraffin-fuelled Tilley lamp to provide a measure of light and heat. In the corner, there was a peat-burning stove and I could just make out a bed built into a tiny alcove.

Like many of their neighbours, the Leasks were apprehensive about entering this brave new world. To try to suppress their anxiety and offer encouragement, friends arrived armed with a range of electrical gadgets – a television, fridge, hairdryer, bedlight, even an electric blanket to replace the stone hot-water bottle they'd used for almost all their married life. As we filmed the big switch on, Willie and Violet were stunned into silence. It took a good ten minutes before they had recovered sufficient equilibrium to announce that they would 'give it a try'.

Departing for the ferry back to the Shetland mainland, the crew shared my view that if we were to return the following week, we'd be sure to find all the electrical goods banished to the shed and the Tilley lamp reigning supreme once more!

Not that the Leasks' neighbours were any more enamoured by this sudden surge of energy. One threw out his television set believing that just turning it on would be sufficient to blow up the house, while another couple in the east of the island found themselves leaping a couple of feet off the ground in fear every time they flicked a light switch.

There's something magical and romantic about island life. The shame is that as a news reporter you rarely manage to find enough time to sample even a little of what's on offer. On the stunning Inner Hebridean island of Jura that would surely include a wee nip of the island's famous malt. Alas, it was not the distillery to which the BBC despatched me via plane and ferry but to the home of a delightful old lady, Effie MacDougall.

Jura is one of Scotland's last wildernesses. Here, a little over 200 people are outnumbered by 6,000 deer spread out over an island 29 miles long and 7 miles wide. The west is wild and virtually uninhabited, occupied only by the three Paps of Jura which in Gaelic are known as The Mountain of the Sound, The Mountain of Gold and The Sacred

Mountain. They soar to almost 2,600 feet and comprise mainly scree and lumps of quartzite.

From her house in the island village capital of Craighouse, Effie was on call 24 hours a day. In her front room sat the manual telephone exchange complete with plug cords and jacks to enable direct connection to every one of Jura's 30 phones. To reach the outside world, each subscriber had to pick up the receiver and turn the handle furiously to attract Effie's attention. No communication into or out of the island was possible without her. What's more, on a Monday morning all the orders for the shop were phoned through via Effie. If anyone was ill or short of a pint of milk or loaf of bread, then the good lady would see the problem was attended to without a moment's hesitation.

Then consternation ... it was announced that nearly twenty years after its introduction, Jura would finally join the rest of Britain in converting to subscriber trunk dialling. Panic set in with the oldest resident reduced to tears even when sent a magnified number display to be inserted on her new phone. When told she could now phone her son in Dundee all by herself, she became even more upset. Why had life to change? What was the meaning of all these mysterious letters and numbers? Surely it was much easier just turning the handle? A home carer was summoned but the protest persisted as our camera continued to roll.

Returning to the Craighouse exchange, Effie had released her pet parrot Patsy from her cage. There she was, perched on her shoulder listening intently for the bell indicating an incoming call. 'Hello, Jura here,' she squawked, breaking a ten minutes' silence between calls. Then, to our absolute astonishment, with Effie about to connect the outside subscriber, the parrot produced one of those great television moments. 'Wrong number, wrong number – try again later!' was her perfectly timed interruption.

Effie was awarded the British Empire Medal for her services to the island folk and stayed on in the house that had been Jura's lifeline for the better part of the twentieth century. I think Patsy, star of *BBC's Nine o'Clock News*, ought to have been given a medal too.

No creature, of course, has proved more elusive than 'Nessie'. The legend surrounding a dinosaur-like monster resident in a 24-mile stretch of deep, cloudy water has turned Loch Ness into one of Scotland's top tourist attractions. Stories of its existence have been around since a seventh-century account of St Columba rescuing a swimmer from a 'water beast' that rose out of the loch, but it was only after a new road was built along the shoreline in the 1930s that reports of sightings really took off.

Like most schoolboys, I had always been fascinated by the stories and grainy photographs purporting to show the monster and on visits to the Highlands would sit by the side of the loch staring out across the water, 750 feet deep in places, hoping to catch a glimpse of an aquatic predator with humps and a long snake-like neck.

I was discussing this with cameraman Peter Leddy as we drove northwards on the main road that skirts the loch heading for a conference called by the Forestry Commission at Glen Affric to announce plans for the regeneration of the Caledonian Pine Forest.

It was a warm spring evening with not a cloud in the sky. As we neared Castle Urquhart just south of the village of Drumnadrochit, the high ground provided an excellent view over the loch. Suddenly, looking out of the window, I spotted a mysterious object about a quarter of a mile away with an elongated neck and something that resembled a tail. Peter drove the car off the road and into to a lay-by just yards from the grass bank. He grabbed the camera and started filming immediately, afraid that the creature might disappear from view by the time he set up his tripod to ensure a steadier shot.

Zooming in, Peter was convinced this was something most unusual. Having filmed for a good 90 seconds, he then opened the boot to get hold of the tripod. Just then, a car carrying American tourists pulled up. There were cries of 'hi there ... I say, is that the famous Nessie out there you're filming ... we've read all about the monster back home in the States but we never expected to see her!'

I explained that all of us might be mistaken ... that there could be some other logical explanation of what had become the centre of our gaze. Next, a national newspaper journalist heading for the Glen Affric conference veered into the lay-by to find out what all the commotion was about.

'Don't tell me you've caught the monster on film. I'll get on to my office straight away. We'll need a couple of stills for the front page.'

The situation was fast getting out of hand. By the time we reached Glen Affric, a despatch rider was waiting to rush the film straight back to Glasgow for processing while, to the obvious annoyance of the Forestry Commission, it seemed as though their press conference had been hijacked as reporters demanded first-hand accounts of just what we'd seen.

I was afraid that Peter and I would be made to look fools when the film emerged from processing. In fact, the creature was unidentifiable but an aquatic expert invited to give his verdict said it was more likely to have been a Merganser Duck which had created a fast-moving narrow V-wake which is often misinterpreted as something large swimming under the water. Researchers have also noted that if swimming in pairs, the ducks can give a clear impression of the head of a larger animal with their necks even resembling horns.

The film was shown on *Reporting Scotland*, allowing viewers to make their own minds up about the proof or otherwise of Nessie's existence.

Since than, many scientific studies have been conducted including an expedition called *Operation Deep Scan* which used a flotilla of 20 sonar-equipped boats to sweep the loch with a curtain of sound. The operation yielded three underwater targets all reported to be larger than a shark but smaller than a whale.

The mystery of Nessie lives on. Keeping it centre stage has done wonders for Scottish tourism.

9

Making Friends with 257

*When people dub commercial local radio as merely ads, prattle and pop, I remember
lives being saved during late night phone-ins.*

Alastair Pirrie, former Radio Tees presenter

Coughing and spluttering my way up a loose, creaking stairway and
into a first-floor corridor thick with brick and plaster dust, it was
impossible to believe that within a couple of months the old Water
Board building in Stockton-on-Tees would be resonating to the unique
and distinctive sound of one of Britain's most successful independent
radio stations.

It was Spring 1975 and I had been summoned to Dovecot Street to
meet two very impressive and talented professionals – John Bradford, a
former independent film-maker whose clients included the multinational
petroleum company Shell; and Bob Hopton, who had worked for the
BBC before becoming a partner in a record business, building an
exhaustive knowledge of the music industry along the way.

John introduced himself as Managing Director of Radio Tees, the
country's twelfth independent local radio station. Bob had been appointed
Programme Controller. Now they were looking for someone to run the
station's news operation. The big question – was I the right man for
the job? As the dust continued to swirl around the building and the
noise of hammer drills through concrete rendered any sensible conversation
impossible, it was decided we should retire to the pub next door. 'Watch
your feet on these wobbly floorboards,' came a timely warning as we
prepared to carefully descend the stairs and make our way through the
entrance lobby to the street and a welcome breath of fresh air.

I quickly warmed to the two executives, helped no doubt by a tipple
of Scotch they insisted in bringing to the table. The questions started
rolling. What did I know about the area? Did I understand people's

125

aspirations? How successful would I be in recruiting the right sort of journalistic all-rounders who could be moulded within days into competent broadcasters and whose abilities and integrity would be beyond question? How could I ensure a successful mix of the national and international news stories fed to us from London with local news from one of the largest areas in the country? What about sport not just on a daily basis but how best to present a five-hour Saturday show intermixed with music?

Before I could present my plan of action, I needed to have some answers myself. How many journalists would I be allowed to recruit? How many news programmes and bulletins would be required each day? What sort of equipment would we be provided with? What sort of transport would be made available? How much would the station be prepared to pay its newsroom staff?

John and Bob did not hold back. They provided the assurances I knew I required if I was to be offered the job. I saw it as a break from the world of television, an exciting opportunity to take charge of a department for the first time in my life and at a time when I was still young and fit enough to expend the energy that the position would inevitably demand. The other appeal of course, was that the job would allow me to be present at the launch of an entirely new station. If given enough freedom and flexibility, I could hopefully shape the presentation of news and sport in a vibrant and exciting way.

There were other candidates still to see but I felt I had given a good account of myself. I was then despatched to meet the managing director of the *Evening Gazette* based in Middlesbrough. Bill Heeps was a fellow Scot who had risen from messenger boy to a key decision-maker in the newspaper industry and would later become Chairman of Thomson Regional Newspapers. We struck up a good rapport and he seemed enthusiastic about my ideas to retail the news to an expanded market in a complementary way, the spontaneity of Radio Tees allowing us to broadcast news instantly whilst whetting the appetite of listeners to read more background and detail to the stories in the written press.

Before leaving Stockton, I asked if I might take a look at the newsroom. A number of desks had been delivered, so too a dozen chairs and a long bench with rectangular holes ready to be fitted with vital editing and telephone equipment. Wires and cables were flying off in all directions like the arms of a giant octopus. Could all this possibly be completed in time for the start date just over two months away? I seriously doubted it.

A call the following day confirmed the job was mine. I was told I could recruit a team of six journalists, all of whom would become quickly familiar with the meaning of the word 'work'. The station was clearly going to be a voracious animal which had to be fed 22 news bulletins a day with an additional 15-minute programme for lunch and the same again for tea. Sport – and lots of it – was on the menu too, including the marathon Saturday afternoon show.

It was obvious everyone would have to be rotated on a three-shift system to cover a day starting from 5 in the morning to 10 at night and I dreaded to think about how sickness and holidays would wreak havoc with the system.

I was determined that, unlike most of the other independent radio stations already on air, we should not go down the path of regurgitating news packages fed down a Post Office line from Independent Radio News in London. To me, it was an absolute waste of labour. Spending vital minutes re-recording material on to tape, seizing last minute scripts from a teleprinter and then asking one of your own newsroom staff to broadcast a mixture of international and national stories alongside a few offerings of local news was surely nothing more than an exercise in duplication and self-aggrandizement.

My views were not welcomed by most News Editor colleagues across the country but I had not taken this job to court popularity. I was given one hundred per cent backing by the station's management team. A conscious policy decision was taken that our newsroom would be a local one in every sense of the word. To this day, I believe it was the right one.

To emphasise the importance of putting the area first, we decided that the national news provided by IRN should be preceded by the local headlines and followed by a local news bulletin. This meant I could get at least one of my staff out and about every hour of the day ensuring we could get the interviews that mattered on a whole range of topical issues, rather than being stuck in the office trying to determine the priorities between what was going on in Redcar and the latest developments in Saigon.

So now, all that I needed were six people, who understood at least the rudiments of journalism, had an acceptable voice and with time fast running out, would not be tied down by intractable notice periods. The adverts placed, I waited for the replies with keen anticipation, hoping to uncover a pool of untapped talent who would share a sense of purpose and identity.

By now a couple of offices had taken shape and there was a palpable sense of relief that those short-listed for interview would be spared the noise of men and machines not to mention a nasty mouthful of dust before being asked to pick up a microphone and read a self-prepared news script.

I was pleasantly surprised at the quality of the applicants. Some had dabbled in radio before on a freelance basis, others had already established themselves as proficient reporters on weekly newspapers or specialist publications. All were excited at what the future would hold and fired up by the thought of becoming a team of local radio pioneers.

Those worried about a drop in salary were persuaded that here was a wonderful opportunity to climb on to the broadcasting ladder. 'Get stuck in, learn, develop, enjoy … the experience you'll pick up here will be invaluable. Give it a couple of years and who knows what all this will lead to.'

I don't know whether they believed it at the time but all six – John Andrew, Libby Fawbert, Ken Barker, Steve Aylward, Kate Fawcett and Ian Fisher – would later become respected correspondents either with the BBC or in regional television. Those who followed took the same road to success, an impressive range of talent occupying a number of key journalistic posts around the world.

Despite fears to the contrary, Radio Tees began broadcasting as scheduled at 5.58 am on 24 June 1975, testament to the hard graft of the builders and the incredible foresight and planning of the station's Chief Engineer Chas Kennedy. The first offering was the *Les Ross Breakfast Show* which proved so popular with the public that the phones were beginning to light up within minutes of the start of the programme which was transmitted on 257 metres Medium Wave. Two months later, the number of listeners began to spiral when the VHF transmitter at Bilsdale in the North Yorkshire Moors was switched on.

The area was one of the largest of any ILR station. In addition to the industrial belt of Teesside, it ranged from Ripon, Thirsk and Pickering in the south to Durham, Bishop Auckland and Hartlepool in the north and from Barnard Castle and Richmond in the west all the way to the North Sea coast at Whitby.

Audience figures were most encouraging, quickly overtaking the mainly speech-based BBC Radio Cleveland and within months an independent survey revealed that over 50 per cent of adults and children in the area were listening to over 11 hours of programmes each week. That was just the kind of news the advertisers needed to hear.

Like most commercial stations, music was the bedrock into which a great deal of information, a lot of good humour and up-to-the-minute news was inserted. Above all, it concentrated heavily on community involvement with its homely theme of: '*You've got a friend on 257. Radio Tees here with you.*'

The management team knew the importance of the station building a solid relationship with its listeners but were equally aware that, unless they could ensure a 'professional sound' from Day One, then all their efforts would count for nothing. When Brian Anderson, a popular DJ from Radio Caroline, arrived for interview, the Managing Director asked him outright: 'How do you intend to relate to people here when you don't come from this area?'

'By switching on the mike and saying hello,' was his immediate response. 'If that doesn't work, what will?'

It worked so well that Brian, like so many of the other presenters, was in demand to attend functions all over Teesside, South Durham and North Yorkshire. He would later become Head of Music and Training. Among those he trained are two former daytime controllers of BBC Radio One not to mention a host of radio presenters in China where he got caught in the middle of the Tiananmen Square student demonstrations before producing a series of pioneering programmes occupying more than 30,000 hours of airtime and conducting $12 million worth of business.

Radio Tees inspired people and it was true to its original objective to be a local entertainment station with a sense of duty and service. The Chairman of the Board, Jim Robertson, one-time director of ICI's Agricultural Division was to be seen in the building every second day proudly wearing his Radio Tees badge with its prominent red heart symbol which remained firmly pinned to his suit in whichever circles he moved. Other directors included a nightclub owner, a solicitor, a farmer and a housewife. Finance for the station came from 33 investors, none with a dominant shareholding.

Some of that money was invested in a fleet of vehicles mainly for the sales team and to tour local shows and events complete with T-shirts and merchandise of every description.

The newsroom had just one small car at its disposal but I made sure it only became stationary when one of the team was breathlessly running up the stairs, a hardy Uher reel-to-reel tape recorder slung over shoulder, ready to edit another package for the next news programme of the day.

The miles were totting up fast as each reporter in turn was despatched to grab the stories that mattered in an area of such diverse interests. In

Middlesbrough, Redcar and Hartlepool, huge furnaces were spewing out bright orange rivers of molten metal, many of the workers as tough as the steel they manufactured. A few miles away, streams of blue smoke rose from the chimneys of the massive ICI complex at Billingham, wafting their way across the rest of Teesside towards the Cleveland Hills. On the river, cranes were constantly at work coping with the demands of one of the UK's largest and busiest ports while shipbuilding was undergoing something of a renaissance at Smith's Dock in South Bank.

By contrast, North Yorkshire was an area of farms and rich farmland, of real people working a real landscape, with a large National Park and a coast with spectacular cliffs and sweeping sands. With an economy based primarily on livestock, we had other interests to serve – farmers and agricultural workers whose interests lay more in their animals than the latest goings on in a Durham working men's club. To ensure we kept them on board, a special Market Watch feature was included in our morning bulletins giving daily prices from the local auction marts.

This was something that particularly appealed to Willie Whitelaw, Margaret Thatcher's deputy on a visit to the station. The Tories were now in opposition to Harold Wilson's second Labour Government but keen on the idea of expanding local radio. I always suspected that Willie saw this kind of broadcasting as a clever way of keeping farmers talking to each other. After all, in his own area of Cumbria, BBC Radio Carlisle's most talked about programme was *Lamb Bank*, an exchange service set up in response to pleas from farming folk to find a home for orphaned lambs.

If one of the reporter's alarm clocks failed to function, I would receive a call from the security officer about 5.30 am, leaving me just enough time to throw a coat over my pyjamas and dash from home in the nick of time to broadcast the first news of the day. Threatening the culprit with an early dismissal was sufficient to keep such incidents to a minimum! The team jelled well and we had youth and energy on our side. We also had Danny, the best newsroom secretary cum office organiser cum bookkeeping wizard I have ever encountered. I wasn't surprised to discover that today Danielle Lloyd is now Head of Production for BBC's *Question Time*. I insisted that whoever prepared the bulletin should also deliver it at the microphone, concentrating minds and lessening the chances of a major error.

Too many broadcasters are lazy when it comes to seeking out opinions and interviews. *Vox pops* (voice of the people) are easily obtained by striding down the nearest main road to the studio. When it came to reaction to the Budget, the price of petrol or the Cod War, we would hurl microphones in front of the villagers in places off the beaten track with such captivating names as Newton under Roseberry, Coatham Mundeville and St Helen Auckland.

It was all about reaching people with different tastes and needs. Listeners were encouraged to interact with the station by participating regularly in phone-ins, sending in requests or visiting in person. Groups were forever being shown round the building and if Danielle discovered a visitor or two with a special hobby or interest, she would escort them straight to the studio for an immediate on-air interview or at the least, a recorded one.

In the evenings, Radio Tees produced a wide range of programmes including jazz, country and folk through to hi-fi and educational shows. These were the halcyon days of local broadcasting.

When a major story broke – an industrial explosion, a devastating fire or a motorway pile-up, we immediately put into place a well rehearsed plan of action which pooled all our newsroom resources of personnel and equipment and with which the emergency services were more than happy to co-operate.

We also tried to lift the rather dull and uninteresting face of local politics, inviting decision makers to explain their policies in ways that listeners could more readily understand and giving them, in turn, access to the airwaves to air their concerns and grievances.

On polling day, I sent reporters to all the major councils in the area to feel the pulse of the electorate and get the reaction of the various parties and candidates as the votes were counted. In Darlington the council was persuaded to provide funding for a permanent studio which also allowed reporters to more instantly edit and send back reports from other parts of County Durham.

Local MPs and national politicians too, were keen to speak to us at every opportunity. On the warmest day of summer, I drove to Alnwick Castle in Northumberland for a pre-arranged interview with Margaret Thatcher. The Tory faithful had gathered in large numbers for the fete in the castle grounds and all dutifully strolled across the lawns that swept down to the large marquee that had been prepared for their leader's speech. As the temperature continued to soar, it was like walking into a pressure cooker and the first aiders were kept busy as people wilted in the intense heat. My impression was that the audience would happily have settled for a ten minute clarion call but Mrs Thatcher was having none of it and rattled on for the best part of an hour.

'At this point of greatest trouble,' she declared, 'we can find the spirit and the strength to throw off the dead years of decline and stride out again to build a better Britain.' Most, including myself, by that stage, would have been more than happy just to stride out of the marquee and fill our lungs with a breath of fresh air!

When Margaret Thatcher finally emerged she found her chauffeur had done a runner too, leaving her change of clothes locked in the boot.

My interview looked as if it might be the next casualty. It was about to be moved to the back burner until I insisted that a firm arrangement had been made with the Tory high command. At that, Mrs Thatcher relented. 'All right then, Bill. You can ask two questions only and no supplementaries!' It was a cogent introduction to a woman whose tough-talking rhetoric would gain her the nickname of The Iron Lady by the Soviet Press.

One day the station received a call to say an old man was sitting in the reception area of Stockton's Swallow Hotel asking if a Radio Tees reporter was on his way to interview him. When John Andrew and I got there, we recognised him as none other than former Prime Minister, Harold Macmillan. A former MP of the town, he had arrived much earlier than expected to take part in the 150th Anniversary celebrations to mark the opening of the world's first public railway from Stockton to Darlington.

With not a porter in sight, I offered to take his case to a bedroom on the second floor. Gasping on the stairs and clearly out of puff by the time we reached the room, he collapsed backwards on to the bed, took a deep breath and enquired:

'Are we ready to go then?'

What followed was five minutes of magic from a real exponent of the art of oratory.

'Steam ... everybody knew about steam ... right back to the Romans ... but no-one harnessed it until Watt and Stephenson came along. This is what we are celebrating today, a golden age of steam, a great British heritage which fills us all with enormous pride.'

Radio Tees was there to record the big day with a parade of 35 locomotives slowly making their way from Heighington to Shildon. A series of grandstands was erected along the line and tens of thousands turned out to see the cavalcade led by a full-size replica of the original *Locomotion* built by a group of engineering training establishments as a memorial to the pioneers of the railway.

If railways raise passions in the North East then so too, does fierce rivalry on the football field. Competing with the huge audience for Radio Two Sport for whom I had worked five years before, meant we had to discover exactly what the listeners would warm to. Clearly it had to be local sport and lots of it but not in isolation. Followers of Middlesbrough, Darlington and Hartlepool for instance, would also need to know how matches being played in other parts of the country affected the fortunes of their own clubs.

We had no commentary rights but could cross to the grounds at regular intervals for short updates on the progress of the games. We were also in a unique position in being able to promote the grass roots of many of the sports. I sat down and listed them all. There were dozens from darts to ice-skating, wrestling to fly-fishing and I determined to give a voice to as many as was humanly possible. After all, there were five hours to fill, though Dave Gregory who was responsible for the music part of the programme was eager and waiting to ensure the turntable was given more than just a handful of spins throughout the afternoon.

The audience soon began to catch on. One caller, Howard Pillar, wondered why we had ignored greyhound racing. I remembered him well. He used to write about the sport under the pseudonym Trapper when I was working on the *Hartlepool Mail.*

'We're featuring it now,' I told him, 'YOU are going to do it starting next week!'

He sent his wife instead, a good choice as Betty Pillar became something of an institution on Radio Tees. The tips she gave may have been prepared by her husband but she had a tremendous following and local bookmakers reported a big upsurge in bets. They became avid supporters of the programme too!

Horse racing was the domain of Harry Andrews. I made sure he sent in a broad selection of tips from the different race meetings of the day. Appropriate jingles were prepared and a winner would spark an immediate studio celebration as the airwaves were filled with the sounds of a cash register being sprung open followed by a huge bundle of cash cascading to the ground.

The legendary Jack Charlton was now manager at Middlesbrough FC. Each week, I called at his office with a list of questions about team performances supplied by listeners to the programme. As I turned on the tape recorder, I could tell he relished this little exercise. Refusing to sit at his desk, he strode around the office answering each one in turn, becoming very animated in the process as he snatched the microphone from my hand forcing me to follow behind like a dog in tow desperately clinging on to the recording machine.

Harold Shepherdson, trainer of England's World Cup winning side of 1966, was Jack's assistant at his home town club. Both were very supportive of Radio Tees and I was occasionally rung up to come down and referee 'in-house games' in which Jack took to the field and got up to all his old tricks that had for so long marked him out as a no-nonsense, uncompromising centre-half.

A few years before I had filmed his mother Cissie moving into a house, appropriately named *Jules Rimet*, which Jack had bought for her in the mining town of Ashington just after England's World Cup triumph. Now, he had moved her again to a farm in North Yorkshire so she could keep watch over the club's apprentices and ensure some of the first-team squad like striker Alan Foggon were fed the right kind of diet.

The regular updates for listeners from the Boro' games were provided by one of Teesside's most respected sports writers Bernard Gent. It involved an astute juggling act between microphones as he was also employed as DJ for the club's own Radio Ayresome. The television theme tune, 'The Power Game', accompanied the players on to the park and acted as a signal to those still walking up Ayresome Park Road that they had precisely three minutes to get into the ground before kick-off. Bernard's antics behind the mike were something of an alarm clock for everyone in that part of town including Boro's centre-half Stuart Boam. As soon as the first record boomed from the ground's tannoy, the defender with the pudding bowl haircut would rush out of his newsagent's shop and head straight for the dressing room.

My last recruit at Radio Tees was a young man from Hartlepool by the name of Jeff Stelling. He had a news background but fancied trying his hand at sport. One Saturday morning, with Bernard Gent struck down by flu, I asked him to go to Leeds to cover a First Division game. He look terrified but stunned us all with the quality of his reporting.

Jeff is now known to millions as presenter of Channel 4's *Countdown* and ringmaster of Sky Television's six-hour marathon *Soccer Saturday*.

In June 1977 the country celebrated The Queen's Silver Jubilee. Outside our home in Stockton's Greenvale, a fun-filled children's party got under way with bunting strung across the street, fancy dress, parades and presentations. Claire was just a month short of her fourth birthday and enjoying the festivity to the full. As I looked along the tables full of party treats and excited children, I realised just how little time I had spent with my daughter in her formative years.

Downing a celebratory tipple after one of the most exhausting periods of my life, I was contemplating my next move – recrossing the border back into the hands of 'Auntie.'

10

BBC Snowman

There are two seasons in Scotland – June and winter.

Billy Connolly

In these days of sophisticated signalling and an array of mobile phones, it is unthinkable that a main-line train could simply '*disappear*'. Yet, thirty years ago, as blizzards raged across the Scottish Highlands, anxious and overworked railway controllers were forced to admit they had no idea what had happened to the Great North Express or of the fate of its 70 passengers.

Frantic phone calls to station staff, signalmen and the emergency services produced no answers. The Inverness to Wick train was lost in the snow and no-one could establish precisely where it was.

From my earliest years, I loved the thrill and excitement of outdoor treasure hunts but could never find the right square inch of garden to unearth the prize. This time, when it really mattered, came a large slice of journalistic good fortune. The nose for a good story and the sheer bravery of a helicopter pilot operating in near white-out conditions, enabled me to be the first to pinpoint the train entombed in a massive drift and so set in motion the rescue of its frozen and hapless passengers. Their 30-hour ordeal would soon be over – my *scoop* had just begun.

Saturday 28 January 1978 heralded a cold, 'dreich' morning as the Scots would have it. Nothing exceptional for mid-winter and with no sense that anything ominous might be on the way. On my return to BBC Scotland some months before I was despatched to their elegant Beechgrove Terrace studios in Aberdeen as the reporter covering the north of the country, a vast expanse stretching from the Shetland Islands to Tayside.

On occasional Saturdays, I volunteered to provide live reports on football for *Sportscene*. That morning, I set off from my home in the village of Pitmedden to travel to Arbroath whose football team had been tipped to provide a giant killing act in the third round of the Scottish Cup against their more illustrious opponents from Motherwell.

Lying right on the edge of the North Sea, Gayfield Park is arguably the coldest football ground in Britain. Standing on the terraces in mid-winter can be cruelty personified. On stormy days, you can even hear the waves beating on the outside walls. Little wonder then that Gayfield was chosen by a mountain clothing manufacturer as a testing ground for its latest range of hardwear waterproof jackets.

This Saturday afternoon however was as mild as the football. Arbroath were completely outplayed and with little exertion, Motherwell wrapped up a 4–0 win. Returning home in the evening, sleet began to fall and the temperature plummeted sharply. Our home was experiencing faulty electric under-floor heating which had the effect of directing the warmth towards the foundations rather than into the bedrooms, not exactly the perfect scenario for a cold winter's night.

Yet such discomforts paled into insignificance as a telephone call alerted me to an emerging picture of chaos in many parts of the Highlands. Roads were blocked, trains stranded and most worrying of all, a number of people reported missing.

From 900 miles above the earth, a camera had in fact warned of what was to come. Swirling clouds showed how conditions were building up to the worst weather for many decades. They were photographed by an American weather satellite and picked up by Dundee University's receiver. Meteorologists at the university watched the depression build as it moved from Mid-Atlantic. The surprise was that it arrived much sooner than many had thought.

For generations, Scots have had a love–hate relationship with snow. Its beauty can be beguiling but when Mother Nature sends snow to Scotland, your life can be in her hands.

At 17.15 that evening a diesel-hauled train with its six coaches left Inverness on the Great North railway heading for Georgemas Junction where the train was scheduled to divide ... the front half turning eastwards to Wick, the end coaches proceeding to Britain's most northerly station at Thurso. As it proceeded northwards, falling snow and gale force winds meant at times speed had to be reduced to a crawl, with swaying tree branches and even a loose telegraph pole striking the side of the carriages.

British Rail, heeding warnings that things would take a turn for the worse, decided it was wise to double-head the train and ordered driver Stewart Munro and second man Jimmy Forbes to take the Thurso branch engine south as far as Helmsdale in Sutherland to meet up with the Inverness train. By the time they had reached the rendezvous point, conditions were deteriorating fast.

Among those joining the train there were dentist Chris Andrews, his Dutch wife Heleen and their nine-year-old son Duncan. Like teacher Andy Anderson and his wife Olive who were returning from a job interview in Aberdeen, they had been forced to abandon their car after running into a deep drift at a notorious stretch of the A9 road at Navidale.

Grateful for a lift back to the hotel in Helmsdale, they found it in relative darkness due to a power cut but there was a positive ambience about the place with open coal fires in every room and an abundance of hot soup and sandwiches.

Andy was well equipped to deal with emergencies. Having served his apprenticeship as a marine engineer, he had been appointed emergency mechanic on the Fraserburgh Lifeboat serving alongside his uncle.

In February 1953, just a week after the great gale, hurrying to the slip, he missed its launch for the first time by a matter of 30 yards and then watched in horror as the lifeboat overturned in heavy seas at the harbour entrance. Only one of the crew of seven survived. His uncle was among those who died, trapped beneath the upturned hull.

The double-headed train pulled out of Helmsdale shortly after 21.30. Unlike the main road, the railway turns its sinuous course inland and makes a wide circuit over the moors of Sutherland and Caithness. The mountains here tend to stand in isolation rather than run in ranges and the country is wild and bare in the extreme.

At the controls of the locomotive, Stewart Munro found himself battling at once against the ever-worsening conditions. Driving snow rendered the windscreen wipers and headlight useless. Now and then he could pick out a landmark, but most of the time he could see nothing and frequently he would feel a jolt as the nose-plough hit a drift.

As the train continued into the teeth of a gale, some of the passengers likened the journey to being on a frightening carnival ride. At times, the noise reached almost intolerable levels, the carriages were continually being buffeted about with luggage tumbling out of the racks.

The train finally reached Forsinard a full 90 minutes late but the locomotive crew knew the worst still lay ahead. Between Forsinard and Altnabreac the rails reach an elevation of 708 feet. Those who had built the track through this mean and inhospitable moorland had found their work considerably hampered by spongy and seemingly bottomless bogs.

Making their way through the third coach to join the Wick section of the train, the Andersons struggled to stay on their feet as the carriage rocked from side to side with their fellow passengers clinging on to each other as well as their belongings.

Suddenly, there was a horrendous crash and the train came to a juddering halt. Five of the six coaches were derailed and the wheels of the third coach had been running on the sleepers for over a mile when the coupling between the second and third carriages sheared, together with the air-brake pipes. The two parts of the train finished over 150 yards apart.

Though alarmed, all the passengers, including several children and two hospital patients recovering from major surgery, were unhurt. Guard Martin Marke did what he could to calm them and the crew of the two locomotives managed to get a foothold in the snow and erect a ladder to get everyone safely out of the derailed coaches and transferred to the front carriage, the only one to have stayed on the track.

Crammed they may have been but the combined warmth created by so many packed into one coach would prove a real blessing during the ordeal ahead.

Eventually, the train was on its way again, but not for long. About two miles further north, a massive drift brought it to a complete standstill. Looking out the windows, the passengers could see nothing. The snow was up to the roof, an illustration of just how fierce the blizzard was, for only a few hours earlier Stewart Munro had cleared that spot on his journey south.

It was pointless to try to reach the nearest phone at Altnabreac, the next stop on the line, since the white-out conditions made it impossible to see more than a few feet. There was nothing for it but to bed the passengers down for the night. The one consolation was that the heating was working and they had plenty of fuel.

Dentist Chris Andrews had a half bottle of whisky in his pocket but with at least a dozen crammed into his compartment was embarrassed by the thought that there wouldn't be enough wee drams to go round. To his amazement, he found there were no takers. All his fellow passengers were teetotallers!

Yet, no-one in the outside world had a clue about what was happening. Relatives awaiting the arrival of loved ones at Wick and Thurso could get no answers to their questions and news was beginning to spread that a train had disappeared off the map without trace.

In the cabin at Georgemas Junction, signalman Jimmy Miller was becoming extremely anxious. Where was the Inverness train? He waited as long as he could and called the control room in the Highland capital. It was agreed that another loco based at Wick should proceed to Georgemas in readiness to assist. By 01.00, the loco was ready.

With still no news of the missing train, however, more radical action was required. Senior British Rail officials decided to take a huge risk and sent the relief loco into the Georgemas–Forsinard section of single-line track. Though there was a modification to the electric token block regulations to allow for train failures here, it depended on the driver contacting the signalman at Georgemas. In this case, he hadn't.

The crew of the relief loco were instructed to proceed with extreme caution with the headlight on and the whistle sounding continuously. The guard was left behind to man the telephone in the signal cabin and told to contact control at regular half-hour intervals.

Moving very slowly, the diesel loco disappeared into the white gloom, the sound of its whistle soon devoured by the howling wind.

Back in Inverness, outdoor superintendent, Syd Atkinson, couldn't manage a wink of sleep. He got dressed and drove to the control room. There was still no word of the missing train or the search locomotive.

Other problems such as the blockage of the Kyle line at Garve, the Highland line at Carrbridge and the need to divert traffic via Aberdeen, demanded his immediate attention. As daybreak approached, he was almost frantic with worry about the lack of news from the north.

He wasn't the only one in such a predicament. There were reports of dozens of vehicles within a 200-mile radius of Inverness abandoned in impossible conditions with no sign of their occupants.

Rescue services were stretched to the limit. The dilemma for the police was where should they deploy the helicopters first – to the motorists or the train? As temperatures plummeted further to −12°C, there were fears of a substantial loss of life.

By late Sunday morning 13 RAF, Royal Navy and civilian helicopters were being used in the search for victims. Giant snowploughs and blowers were commissioned from as far afield as Lancashire and Northern Ireland and the world's biggest snow-blower, the *Bertha*, flown in from Switzerland.

The decision that the motorists be given priority meant there was still no concerted rescue effort being mounted to reach the stricken train.

At the BBC Studios in Aberdeen, News Editor Arthur Binnie and I were hastily thumbing through our contacts lists. Could there be just one helicopter somewhere in the country that had been overlooked by the rescue organisers? There was, and of all places, it was sitting on the tarmac at Aberdeen Airport. The only problem was getting it airborne would cost the BBC licence payers a great deal of money. For this was a British Airways Sikorsky S61 used for transporting offshore workers to and from the oil rigs in the North Sea.

The cost for hire was £1,200 an hour. I phoned the Assistant Editor in London responsible for the national bulletins. Derek Maude was a brusque Yorkshireman who did not suffer fools gladly. When I mentioned the figure, he almost laughed me out of court till I pointed out that ITN had chartered a Jet Ranger helicopter earlier in the day and were already on their way.

While I was still in mid-conversation, the adjacent phone rang. It was the helicopter captain.

'I'd really like to help you,' he said. 'I'll probably get into trouble for this but let's drop the hourly hire charge to £1,000. How does that sound?'

'Hang on a minute,' I said. 'I'm just talking to Television News in London.'

Derek Maude's tone mellowed. 'Okay lad, off you go. But you'd better come back with summat bl–dy good. Understand?'

I understood only too well. Before setting off for the airport, I rang Highland Police and suggested they have volunteers armed with emergency blankets and supplies of hot soup and coffee standing by at Wick where the pilot agreed he could set down.

Battling against gale-force winds and heavy snow, it took two hours to reach Caithness. On the tarmac, the police and volunteers were waiting. Food supplies, refreshments and blankets were all boxed and ready for an airdrop if we could successfully pinpoint the stranded train.

As we took off again the helicopter crew were confident and determined. With one set of eyes constantly trained on the instrument panel, the other trying to find anything that resembled a railway line, this was certainly an adrenalin-pumping experience of the highest order.

Within a matter of minutes, the navigator spotted what he thought was the booking hall of Georgemas Junction. If he was right, it would be a case of following the tops of the telegraph poles, jutting barely a foot above the snow line, and the hunt for the stricken train would be over.

He WAS right. As flying conditions took a decided turn for the better, we spotted the relief locomotive, which had set off from the north, hopelessly stuck in the drifts.

Then, a few miles further south, through the cockpit window, there it was – the 'lost train' – the outline of the two locos and sole remaining coach barely visible through the drifting snow which in places was now ten feet high.

The relief and sheer excitement of the moment is hard to describe. Some of the 70 passengers were so elated that they temporarily forgot the world blanketed in white outside the carriage door. Down into the snow they jumped, falling over like a pack of cards in the noiseless drift, believing rescue was now at hand.

In fact, all we had planned to do was to give them the necessities to ease the hunger, fear and discomfort of a second night aboard the train. Not for a second had we contemplated that we might be able to land.

By now, cameraman Mike Herd had been strapped to the floor of the helicopter as the side door was opened for the supply drop. We had agreed on a simple plan to ensure we got the best shots. As the helicopter began the first of three loops, a tap on Mike's left ankle would mean the train was about to emerge to his left, a tap on the right ankle indicated the reverse. There was no panic as the boxes were blown slightly off course by the howling gale but as they hit the ground, there was a sudden realisation among the passengers that the food drop indicated there would no swift end to their ordeal.

Our filming was interrupted by a shout from the captain.

'I think there's some harder ground over there ... perhaps it's been an old yard of some sort. I may be able to get down.'

We all held our breath as the helicopter was lowered to blow away the loose lying snow. Now everything would depend on a further descent to discover if there was any significant updraught of snow which could suck into the engine intakes, endangering the aircraft and everyone aboard.

A thumbs-up indicated the captain was happy. With darkness descending, snow still falling and the wind gusting at over 60 miles an hour, we finally set down. On the ground exhaustion gave way to ecstasy. The great escape was now under way. All we had to do was to let the camera roll – the snowbound passengers and a myriad of stories about life aboard the 'lost' train were heading straight towards us.

A seat had been removed from one of the compartments and used as a stretcher for one man with a broken leg and plastered hip who clearly needed medical attention. Others looked pale and bedraggled, fighting to keep their feet in the dreadful, never-ending gale.

Still the line kept coming like a column of refugees fleeing a war zone. For some, reaching the safety of our helicopter was of far more importance than having a microphone dangled next to their cheeks glowing bright red from the cold.

Now we had a serious conflict of interests on our hands. I had a deadline to meet and given the huge outlay on hiring the helicopter, I knew I might well be fired if the story failed to make the air.

Yet imagine the fury that would ensue if we refused to take anyone on board with us. To make matters worse, the passengers wanted to go north while our destination was a flying distance of 85 miles to the south.

In the 1970s television news crews weren't equipped with portable satellite dishes to beam the story back live from the scene. In Aberdeen, they had not even reached the age of the video camera. We were still working with 16mm film which took a minimum of 45 minutes to process on arrival at the studios. Then it had to be edited and a voice-over laid before the film report could be sent down a Post Office line to BBC TV Centre in London ready for transmission.

Again, the helicopter captain came up with the answer to our predicament. The aircraft would have to be refuelled at Wick, allowing him to evacuate the majority of women and children, leaving our camera on the ground. This would give me a half-hour window to interview those left behind including the drivers of the two locomotives. With the promise of a tail wind on the return journey to Aberdeen, I was told we could reach there in little more than 40 minutes.

Fortune was smiling again especially when learning that the Jet Ranger hired by ITN had run into a white-out and had been forced to turn back without reaching the train.

Soon the survivors' accounts began to flow. Most recalled the sheer courage and constancy of the train crew. One engine had been kept running to provide some warmth, but during the early hours of Sunday morning the water to heat the boiler had run out. The temperature dropped dramatically and the passengers had to huddle even closer together to allow their body heat build a human cushion against the bitter cold. As conditions worsened, one of the locomen had volunteered to dig through the snow to try to connect the pipes from the carriage to the other engine. This could only be done by tying a rope round his legs and hauling him back up from the huge mound of snow.

In the meantime, the crew of the relief locomotive which had itself become derailed one and a half miles to the north, trudged through the drifts with two tins of soup and a pint of milk. This was all mixed together, heated at the engine exhaust, and offered in tiny amounts to the passengers via an unsavoury looking tin with jagged edges.

As promised, within half an hour, the helicopter had returned and we set off for Aberdeen with the snow still falling and a biting gale sweeping us south at a great rate of knots.

London had despatched producer Courtney Tordoff north by air. Within minutes of arriving at the airport, the editing was under way and the story of the 'Lost Train' provided a four-minute lead for the National News.

For those passengers we had left behind at Altnabreac, the later arrival of an RAF rescue helicopter seemed to signal an end to their troubles. In fact, they still faced a long and eventful journey home.

Instructions were given that they should be ferried three at a time to the nearest house with a road. On arrival at Scotscalder though, they found the only telephone out of action and the road blocked. Andy Anderson waited for the arrival of the rest of the group and had no choice but to trudge through deep snow across the fields to the railway line and into Halkirk. His abiding memory is of being taken into a railwayman's home and the alluring smell from a huge pot of home-made soup bubbling away on the stove. The taste to frozen, hungry folk was out of this world. He eventually arrived in Wick at seven o'clock that night and was amazed to find there wasn't a drop of snow in the town. His wife, Olive, had been picked up by our helicopter and was home by late afternoon.

Recalling his experience, Andy says the feeling was one of complete helplessness. 'We were cold and hungry and couldn't sleep. Yet we felt someone would come at some time and they did.'

It took a further week for railway staff, supplemented by soldiers from the King's Own Scottish Borderers and mechanical diggers mounted on bogie wagons, to remove the great white sloping mass of snow that had entrapped three locomotives, derailed five coaches and torn up miles of track.

Subsequently, all trains on the Great North line were ordered to carry emergency rations.

One of the train passengers, Dr Ken Swanson, a Dounreay scientist who had been on a recruiting mission in Edinburgh, has a daily reminder of life on the 'lost train'. He had been travelling in the rear carriage and vividly recalls the alarming moments when it left the rails and began to jump over the sleepers. The locomotive crew were at first unaware of the alarm behind them as the train charged onwards for some considerable time before the coach parted company and the air brakes went on.

145

After the track repairs, some of the old sleepers were put up for sale. Among them, those clearly showing the marks of the steel wheels ingrained in the soft oak as the train veered off the track. At a £1 a time, they've been put back into service as timber walls for the cattle pens on Dr Swanson's farm at Bridge of Westfield, just south of Thurso.

Buoyed by my *scoop*, I tucked into a celebratory dinner that evening, the last proper meal I would enjoy for some considerable time. The story of the Highland blizzard still had a long way to run and would bring triumph and tragedy in equal measure. It was time to turn back to the frozen north, this time by car.

Another hazardous journey lay ahead but a combination of steely determination, good fortune and an ear tuned to local radio enabled our crew car to reach the control centre at Inverness from where the huge rescue operation was being coordinated.

Decisions as to where to deploy rescue teams were becoming harder by the hour and calls for help were being funnelled to those with the impossible task of determining which emergencies should be given priority.

A tramp buried in the snow for two nights was dug out on the Culloden road after a passer-by reported having seen something moving under a hedge. He was taken to hospital where he shed six coats, three pairs of trousers and a pair of long johns! Round his waist were strung his pots and pans and other cooking utensils.

Nicholas Quinn, the doorman at The Eden Court Theatre in Inverness was not so fortunate. His body was found after the crew of an RAF helicopter spotted his feet sticking out of the snow beside his abandoned car.

The Sinclair family's railway cottage near Carrbridge became home for more than 65 stranded motorists for three days. The family helped dig motorists out of trouble and prepared hot meals and beds for their unexpected guests. And a kitchen table saved another family from a freezing death. They chopped it up for firewood when trapped for four days in their snow-covered cottage near Tomintoul.

The biggest emergency though was just 40 miles from where we had discovered the 'lost train'. Today, huge improvements have been carried out to one of the most dangerous stretches of road in Britain. The A9 over the desolate Ord of Caithness is a barren, treeless stretch of country. In the winter of 1978 the road followed sheer cliffs, twisting and winding its way north from Helmsdale, the formidable granite mass rising steeply to 652 feet above the sea at Ord Point, a headland on the coast. There is no help or habitation for miles.

In the past, a highwayman known as *Grey Steel* used to patrol this wild and intimidating pass between Caithness and Sutherland. It's said his main objective in life was to waylay travellers on the Ord and demand payment for safe passage over it. If he wasn't satisfied with the amount offered, the unfortunate traveller was thrown over the steep cliffs to his death.

On the Saturday morning, trainee solicitor Jim McGuinness and his girlfriend Barbara were heading home from a short break in Thurso. It was such a pleasant day that they decided to meander south and admire the coastal views.

Approaching the Ord from the north, suddenly the skies opened and snow began to fall with such ferocity that it was difficult to see the road in front. Then, through the windscreen, Jim caught sight of a snowplough struggling on the steep gradient ahead. Looking in his rear mirror, he could see an articulated lorry and another car on his tail.

Twice, the plough came to a halt in the snow and the other drivers helped to dig it out. But once they got it on its way, they returned to their own vehicles only to find them hopelessly stuck. There was now no other option but to stay put and wait for help.

The wind was gusting to gale force and the snow was building at such a rate that Jim found it impossible to open the driver's door. After four hours, conditions were so bad that the cold was beginning to take its toll. He tried to keep up a constant conversation with Barbara but when he noticed the pupils of her eyes widening, panic began to set in.

As evening approached, the snowline had reached the car roof. It was time for some serious thought.

'The one overriding feeling was you can't stay here. I just couldn't believe that snow could entomb you in an area like that and create such terror.'

Both driver and passenger had developed a severe headache and all they wanted to do was fall asleep. But they knew in such awful circumstances, that could be fatal.

By Sunday morning the drifts had reached nearly 15 feet and there was no sign of the blizzard relenting. Keeping an air flow into the car was becoming progressively harder and alarmingly, a fear factor had set in, with the belief that there was no-one out there who could help them.

As yet another day passed, they knew the only way to leave their vehicle was to dig snow into it and head for the lorry behind.

'It was either make it to the lorry or stay and die in the car, so we decided to go for the lorry.'

The snow was heavy and wet as Jim and his girlfriend struggled towards the lorry in a blizzard that raged continuously. The conditions were appalling. Jim's subsequent description gives some idea of this living hell.

'It was like Henry Cooper giving you a real haymaker plus thousands of white hot needles pounding you in the face.'

Trying to find where the car ended and the lorry began was a hazardous business especially as there was no longer any feeling left in their hands. They eventually made it and just catching sight of another human being lifted their spirits, especially as those in the other cars had been silent for so long.

After a few hours, the lorry too, was entirely buried in the snow and the anxieties began all over again. Jim and Barbara were covered in white and remarked that it never seemed to get dark even though they were there day and night. By now, they were convinced that those in the other two cars were almost certainly dead and accepted that their own lives were hanging on a thread.

Suddenly, Jim and Barbara detected movement overhead. It sounded as if someone had driven right over the top of the lorry. The digging had commenced. Survival was now assured. The first rescuers on the scene quickly discovered just how damp the snow had been as it fell, for it had formed a solid mass and had to be cut away in huge blocks. But it was too deep to reach the cars in front of them. Frustrated and exhausted, they were forced to withdraw and await more help from the north. This came in the shape of Police Sergeant Bert McLeod and his team from Thurso who had managed to persuade employees at the nearby Dounreay Nuclear Power Station to produce a set of steel rods 14 feet long. They were to prove ideal tools in the painstaking search ahead.

Incredibly, the team had reached 12 miles south of Lybster before they encountered snow. Here they exchanged their cars for a snowcat with its specially designed rubber tracks. Approaching the Ord, the entire landscape changed. They ran into a howling gale and the drifts were now measured at 20 feet and more.

We had managed to reach the Ord from the south and watched as the rescue teams pierced through the snow with their long poles hoping that at some point they would hear the sound of metal striking metal.

A shout went up as one of the poles hit the roof of George Cameron's car. He was General Manager of the Norscot Hotel Group, in his thirties and returning south to his home in Dingwall after a visit to The Royal Hotel in Thurso. Giant slabs of hard-packed snow were speedily dislodged until the diggers reached down deep enough to open a door. Mr Cameron had been dead for some hours but against all odds, his Cairn Terrier had survived.

Nearby, the police found another car. There were two people inside, the driver behind the wheel and a woman in the passenger seat. Bert McLeod was sent down to check their pulses but sadly, it was too late.

The couple, James Bruce and his wife Christine, died of hypothermia. In all probability, it would not have proved too painful. They would just have drifted off to sleep – for good. The Bruces, who had three young children, had been trying to reach Stobhill Hospital in Glasgow where Christine's father was seriously ill. Unknown to them, he died just five hours after they'd set out.

As darkness descended and another day drew to a close, rescuers accepted that it would take a miracle to find anyone else alive but they resolved to resume digging at first light.

The object of their search was a yellow Mini Clubman and its 63-year-old driver, Willie Sutherland, a man who had a fetish for women's tights! I don't mean that in a disparaging way. To the contrary, these snug, stretchable women's garments were the core product of Willie's job as a travelling salesman. They were also responsible for his incredible triumph over seemingly impossible odds.

Willie had set out in fair weather on his way to Brora and Golspie to relieve a colleague but never arrived in Sutherland. It took 80 hours to find him as his car was at least half a mile south of the others, entombed in 20 feet of snow and perched near the edge of a 200ft cliff. Surely, no-one could survive for four days in such conditions.

None of the police rescuers wanted the job of having to identify yet another body. To the astonishment of Inspector John Morrison, Willie was not only alive, he all but resembled an Egyptian Mummy!

Having run into a drift from which there was no escape, the enterprising salesman first managed to create an air hole through the snow and use melting snow for water. He had no food and feeling his legs going cold, he remembered the boxes of nylon tights he was carrying in the back of the Mini. At hourly intervals, he would split them up and wrap them round his legs, stomach and head until he had built up a four-day cushion against the vagaries of the worst Scottish winter in memory.

Suffering only from mild hypothermia, he was in such good spirits that he amazed staff at Golspie Hospital by bounding out of the ambulance and declaring: 'Thank God. I'll live to collect my pension!' For sure, their bandage cupboard had never been so well replenished.

I don't think on all my journalistic travels, I have ever encountered such astonishing coolness. Here was a reluctant hero whom I fully expected to see on commercial television expounding the virtues of women's tights. What a missed opportunity!

As for the other survivor, Jim McGuinness, it appears there wasn't a shred of sympathy when he reported back to work in Edinburgh.

One of the partners of the law firm where he was training to be a solicitor, called him into the office and demanded to know why he had not been in contact for four days.

When Jim tried to reason that making phone calls is well nigh impossible when entrapped in a giant mountain of snow, his explanation was dismissed as a cock and bull story.

'The last trainee who came up with that kind of tale is now selling stockings in the North of England,' he was told.

Now there's a coincidence if ever I heard one!

Left:
Dad at sea aboard HMS *Montrose* as Commander (Electrical) of the Tay Division, Royal Naval Reserve.

Below:
Primary 1 at Dundee High School in the late forties. The author is seated third from the right in the second row.

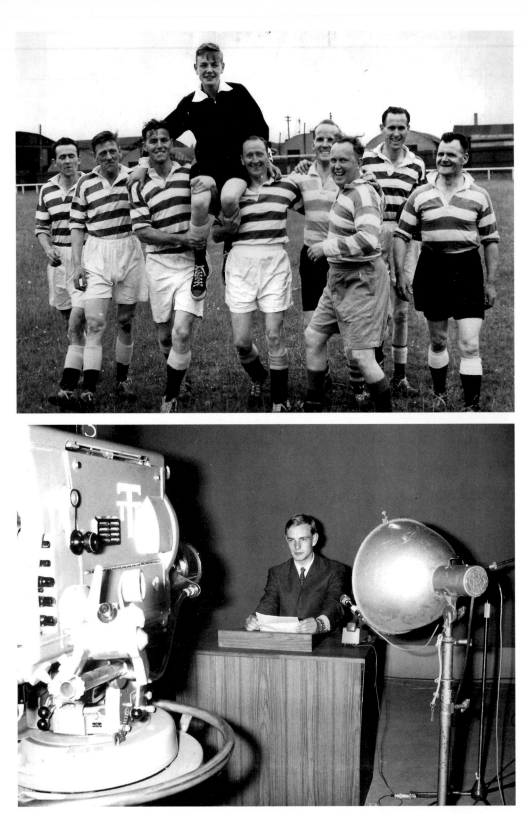

Above: Happy days as Scotland's youngest football referee, aged 14.

Below: Reading the news at Tyne Tees Television in the sixties.

Left:
Celebrating Burns Night in Newcastle
with my future wife, Veronica.

Below:
With 'Big Jack' Charlton and the apprentices of
Middlesbrough FC. Also in the picture, Boro legend
Harold Shepherdson, trusty assistant to Sir Alf
Ramsey in England's World Cup success of 1966.

Above: Mother Teresa of Calcutta receives her Albanian citizenship from President Sali Berisha in 1992.

Below: Steel ring of security suddenly disappears as the kings and presidents of the Arab World take their salute from armed Moroccan tribesmen at the 1982 summit.

Above: In tandem with son David reaching the summit of the Cairn O'Mount on the road from Banchory to Fettercairn in the Scottish Highlands.

Below: First taste of breakfast cereal for the forgotten children of the Shkoder Home in Albania.

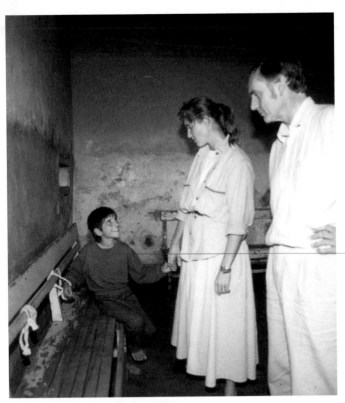

Left:
Introducing the Duchess
of York to the horrors
of a home for mentally
disabled children in Albania's
'showpiece resort' of Berat.

Below:
Scavenging for food among a
mountain of filth ... daily horror
for six-year-old Vera on the
rubbish dumps of Tirana.

Left:
Father Zef Pllumi, miraculous survivor of 28 years of the worst cruelty imaginable after Albania 'abolished God.'

Below:
English surgeon Nick Jacobs examines Albanian children before attempting to restore their sight.

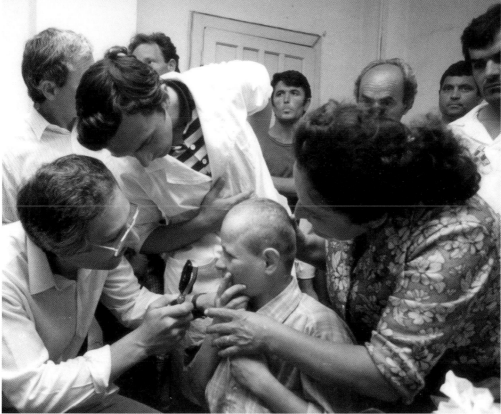

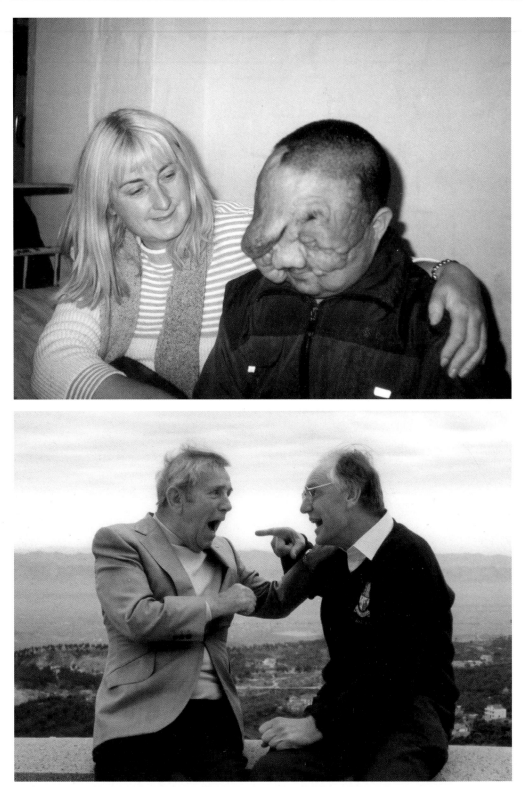

Above: Legacy of misery in Kazakhstan ... Berik, radiation victim of Soviet nuclear testing programme, is consoled by Irish charity director, Fiona Corcoran.

Below: Sparring with Norman Wisdom, 'the luckiest little devil in the world!'

Above: Not the place for a ski jumper! With fellow *Now the Good News* presenter Eddie 'The Eagle' Edwards on the roof of Broadcasting House

Below: Editing a BBC Nine o'clock News exclusive with Louise Kerslake.

Left:
Rescuing passengers from the Great North Express which 'disappeared' in a blizzard in Caithness.

Below:
With cameraman Bhasker Solanki, receiving Albania's highest civilian award 'The Order of Mother Teresa' from President Sali Berisha.

Left:
Aids orphan Silindile prays at the graves of her parents and three siblings in KwaZulu-Natal. At 13, she has assumed the responsibilities of both mother and father.

Below:
Meeting the Batwa pygmies in the Semuliki rainforest on the border of Uganda and Congo.

Above: Interviewing President Yoweri Museveni of Uganda.

Below: Singing along with the founding father of Zambia, former President Kenneth Kaunda.

Above:
Preparing to referee a Zulu
youth football derby ...
some played in bare feet!

Left:
A far cry from an appointment
at the new Wembley.

Left:
Brighton's Grand Hotel after the IRA's daring strike at the Tory Conference in 1984.

Below:
The Brighton bomber, Patrick Magee, is now a Doctor of Philosophy. 'The hope must be that violence is over for ever.'

Above:
Yesterday's terrorist, today's politician ... Martina Anderson working across Northern Ireland's sectarian divide.

Above:
Holding the Football Association's Gold Medal after 50 years 'in the middle' alongside former flatmates Jim Currie and BBC TV commentator John Motson.

Left:
The Salvation Army's Link team who produce films of the organisation's work around the globe.

Below:
All change. Experiencing life at the hub of the BBC's news operation at Television Centre.

Left:
Grandchildren Stevie and Amy developing a love for 'The Beautiful Game.'

Below:
A family occasion. Four generations celebrate mum's 90th birthday in St Andrews.

11

Horror at Westminster

In Ireland, the inevitable never happens and the unexpected constantly occurs.

Sir John Pentland Mahaffy, tutor of Oscar Wilde

That old adage *it's an ill wind that blows nobody any good* has an authentic ring about it. Like it or not, another's misfortune can often serve to advance a broadcaster's career.

In early 1979 the Home News Editor at BBC Television Centre, George Carey, decided it would be a splendid idea to offer a monthly attachment to a reporter from each of the Corporation's regional newsrooms including those in the national regions of Scotland, Wales and Northern Ireland. The purpose was to establish where the best broadcasting talent lay and to give enterprising young reporters the chance to produce material of a standard suitable for transmission on the nightly national news bulletins.

BBC Scotland's Head of News, George Sinclair, was the first to receive the call from London. He beckoned me into his office.

'Get yourself down there Bill and show them what you're made of but don't get into any bad habits!'

Over the years, there had been a history of friction between the London and Glasgow newsrooms and though relations had taken a distinct turn for the better, it was clear that my steely and determined boss wanted me to remember exactly where my loyalties lay.

Working alongside some of the brightest talent in broadcasting was a stimulating experience. Though I grasped every opportunity that came along including an interview with Prime Minister James Callaghan, reports on a national newspaper printers' strike and Bob Hope's first Palladium Show for 25 years, the month passed quietly and I was beginning to feel I would be quickly forgotten on my return to Scotland.

Then on 28 March, following the infamous winter of discontent which

151

seemed to belie the Prime Minister's nickname of 'Sunny Jim', James Callaghan was forced to call a General Election. That afternoon the House of Commons passed, by a single vote, a motion of no confidence in his Government.

The next day, Mr Callaghan announced that the country would go to the polls on 3 May. Immediately, the newsroom was alight, camera crews scurrying in every direction and telephones ringing incessantly. Surely I would have a role to play in this hotbed of feverish activity.

Difficult then, to harbour feelings of disappointment when told my contribution would be a feature for Friday's edition of *News on Two*, forerunner to BBC 2's popular news analysis, current affairs and political programme *Newsnight*. It had been announced that a record number of former Cabinet Ministers from both major parties would be retiring at the upcoming election and I was being challenged to come up with an innovative and colourful way of telling the story.

I decided to look up the latest edition of *Who's Who?* to establish whether some of them might share the same hobby among their list of recreational activities. I discovered Michael Stewart, twice Foreign Secretary in Harold Wilson's government and George Strauss, Father of the House of Commons, were both chess aficionados.

Having got hold of a decent chess set, I set about arranging a keen contest between the two wily veterans in one of the capital's strangest venues – a tiny studio affectionately known as 'The Bunker', built into a wall on the edge of College Green and directly opposite the Houses of Parliament.

Just to give a balance to proceedings, I was also chasing an interview with the well-known MP for Winchester, Morgan Charles Morgan-Giles, a former naval Rear Admiral with a distinguished war record and later commander of HMS *Vernon* and HMS *Belfast*.

I suggested we should film him in an appropriate setting such as the Royal Naval Dockyard at Portsmouth but the newsroom bosses, keen to avoid complications and what they saw as unnecessary expenditure, suggested instead taking him on the short journey across Westminster Bridge and using the River Thames and the Palace of Westminster as an apposite backdrop.

We agreed a rendezvous time of 2.30 on the Friday afternoon. The normal meeting point is at the St Stephen's entrance in the centre of the building, but arriving in Parliament Square on a cursory inspection of my BBC accreditation, I was pleasantly surprised to be allowed through the gates of New Palace Yard for the first and last time in my working life. Driving slowly over the granite cobbles, I brought the car to a halt just a few yards beyond the exit of the Members' Underground Car Park and strolled up to the entrance door to let the police know I was awaiting the MP's imminent arrival. They contacted him on the internal phone. He was running late but would try to get there as quickly as possible.

It was shortly after 2.50 when he appeared, walking briskly into the yard and apologising profusely for running behind time. But no sooner had we exited the gates than there was a loud bang and, as we turned into Parliament Square, a pall of black smoke was rising from the top of the Commons five-floor car park. On the car 'storno' radio system, I contacted the camera crew who were due to meet up with us on the far side of Westminster Bridge.

By the time Big Ben was striking 3 pm, we had already started to film. A metallic blue Vauxhall Cavalier was wrecked about two-thirds of the way up the car park ramp. Its boot and bonnet had been forced up, the windscreen and windows were shattered and the doors blown out.

I contacted Television Newsroom immediately. I said, 'a bomb's gone off at The House of Commons.'

At first no-one believed me. 'There's been nothing on the agency tapes about that,' I was told.

'I'm not surprised,' I replied. 'It only happened a couple of minutes ago right in front of my very eyes!'

Two minutes later came an apology. 'You're right, Bill. The Press Association News Flash is just coming off the teleprinter now. We're sending Chris Morris down there – he's already on his way.'

To say, I wasn't too enamoured by the thought of being replaced by one of the newsroom's established correspondents would be putting it mildly. Yet, what right had I to allow such a sense of grievance and self importance to spring to the surface? What about the unfortunate victim and the grief soon to be endured by his wife and family? Far too often, the journalistic imperative to get a good story can override the Christian ethic of compassion.

My first thought was that a bomb had been placed in the front of the car, either under the bonnet or the chassis. Official papers and sheets of the green and white Commons notepaper used by MPs were scattered over a wide area, the first indication that the victim was a Member of Parliament.

As the Ambulance and Fire Brigade arrived, MPs, secretarial staff,

Commons officials and lobby correspondents began rushing into the courtyard. The police tried to usher them well away from the car park, fearing that there might be a second bomb in the area.

As the emergency services began the job of extricating the victim from the car, word spread quickly that an MP had been seriously injured and was probably dead. Rumours about whom it might be circulated amongst all those watching from a distance, many of them in a state of shock and disbelief. One of the last names mentioned was that of Airey Neave but it was some time before it could be positively confirmed. A police officer had found his wallet containing his Commons identity pass.

When removed from the driving seat, the Shadow Minister for Northern Ireland, was still alive although unconscious. He was taken to Westminster Hospital but died there shortly afterwards.

When the bomb went off, Enoch Powell had risen to speak in the chamber on the Credit Union Bill. Although the explosion had been heard, no-one realised just how serious it was and some considerable time passed before his speech was interrupted and the business of the House of Commons suspended, though for little more than 15 minutes. All parties agreed that, having marked their concern and abhorrence by a short suspension, it was vitally important to continue with the business as it was essential that the work of the Commons should not be stopped whatever the circumstances.

'The House is the symbol of our liberty.'

As my colleague Chris Morris arrived, uniformed police and detectives had already started to question all who had been in the area and in their search for clues were fanning out into the gardens which cover the car park.

I grabbed hold of all the material filmed so far, rushed back to the car and headed straight for BBC Television Centre. The Assistant Editor in charge of that day's national bulletins, Alan Perry, immediately agreed that as I had witnessed this horrific event at close hand, my report would lead both the early evening and *Nine o'clock News*.

It would be my last act on the month-long attachment and help immeasurably towards obtaining a national TV news reporter's job when the next vacancy arose. Returning to Glasgow by train the next day, I would reflect on just how close I had been to the seat of the explosion and my good fortune of having driven out of New Palace Yard just seconds before the bomb went off.

Later that year, Lord Louis Mountbatten was killed by a bomb blast on his boat which had just set off from the fishing village of Mullaghmore in Ireland, a resort favoured by his family who traditionally spent their summer holiday at a nearby castle. A real tragedy – two war heroes murdered in the most cowardly and shameful circumstances.

Airey Neave was famous as the first British officer to make a 'home run' after successfully escaping from Colditz. He later served as an intelligence agent for MI9 and commanded the escape network which rescued allied pilots from behind enemy lines.

His loss was deeply felt by Mrs Thatcher. Neave was the mastermind behind her 1975 victory in the contest for the leadership of the Conservative Party. She led the tributes calling him 'one of freedom's warriors – staunch, brave, true and strong'.

It may well have been the last of these attributes that prompted the Irish National Liberation Army to assassinate him. With Mrs Thatcher's election victory, Airey Neave would have become Secretary of State for Northern Ireland and most certainly a clear-sighted and formidable opponent for any terrorist organisation.

At the time, INLA had been competing with the Provisional IRA for members, with both paramilitary groups attacking the British Army and the Royal Ulster Constabulary. But this attack, killing such a prominent Member of Parliament, was the first action to bring INLA to international attention. They had perfected the use of the mercury tilt-switch bomb. Placed on the underside of Neave's car, it exploded as he drove up the car park ramp. Claims by the organisation that it had inside information from the House of Commons allowing the bombers to infiltrate the car park were never taken seriously. It's more than likely that the device was planted, with a time delay, outside Neave's home where security was lax.

In the 1980s I would make frequent trips to Northern Ireland to report on The Troubles rarely knowing what new atrocity each new day would bring.

Sectarianism and violence are a dreadful combination striking fear into perfectly ordinary human beings caught up in a hell not of their own making. From 1969 to the conclusion of the peace process, more than 3,500 lives were lost, approximately 1 in 500 of the population.

I could never get my head round some of the strange paradoxes of life in Belfast or Derry. One minute, I'd be sipping a cuppa with some of the kindest and most tolerant people anyone could encounter, then in the next, find my every movement monitored by a grim-faced paramilitary wearing black beret, khaki jumper and dark glasses.

Strangely enough, I never felt in any personal danger in Belfast's Falls Road (the Catholic side), or on the Shankhill Road (the Protestant side) of the dividing wall. Yet in some of the buildings decorated with brightly coloured murals, depicting guns and balaclavas and glorifying murderers, I suspected that 'volunteers' were plotting their next move in a horrendous catalogue of violence.

The BBC's Northern Ireland newsroom with consummate editor Robin Walsh at the helm, was a source of great encouragement and constant advice. Living with the story 24 hours a day, they knew the territory well, were steeped in its history and could anticipate how a story might develop. An eagle eye would often be run over a filmed report in the minutes running up to transmission.

One of the most difficult periods was during the Hunger Strike of 1981. It followed on from the 'blanket protest' of the late 1970s in which IRA and INLA prisoners refused to wear prison uniforms and either went naked or fashioned garments from prison blankets; and the 'dirty protest' where prisoners who were not granted political status, refused to wash and smeared the walls of their cells with excrement.

A hunger strike in 1980 was called off before any prisoners died, but a second one began the following year. Bobby Sands, who was 27 and had served four years of a 14-year sentence for possessing firearms, was the first to refuse food and was followed by nine others who also starved themselves to death.

Shortly after the beginning of the strike, the Independent Irish Republican MP for Fermanagh and South Tyrone died. With tensions running high and increasingly strained relations between the British and Irish governments, the ailing Sands was nominated as an Anti H-Block candidate and elected to the House of Commons, collecting over 30,000 votes. But Mrs Thatcher's Government still refused to give into the prisoners' demands with the Prime Minister insisting that they were not prepared to consider special category status for groups of people serving sentences for crime.

'Crime is crime, it is not political.'

Along with Kate Adie, who was already earning a reputation as one of the BBC's sharpest and toughest operators, I was detailed to cover the funeral of the second hunger striker to die, Francis Hughes. In republican circles, he was seen as a determined, committed and fearless IRA volunteer who had carried out a number of successful operations against the British Army until his capture following a shoot-out with the SAS. At one time, he had been described by the RUC as the 'most wanted man in the North'.

After his body had been released from the hospital morgue, several thousand Catholics had assembled in Belfast to pay their respects but the police, no doubt fearing para-military intervention, refused to allow the cortege to pass through nationalist West Belfast.

Mayhem ensued and the driver and undertaker were sent flying in the resultant scuffles, with the driver refusing to hand over the vehicle to the police and attempting to hide the keys in his mouth. Meanwhile, the Hughes family were shouting and screaming at the police as they ordered the vehicle to head straight for the family home near the village of Bellaghy in South Derry.

It took an age to get the convoy on its way but once it had set off with Kate and her crew in pursuit, the intent was clear. Normally, a cortege travels at a snail's pace. In this instance, having cleared the city centre and hit the motorway heading north, it reached speeds of up to 100 mph. I doubt whether any man has been despatched so hastily to his grave. Hundreds fanned out across the hills, fields and glens around the Hughes' home for the wake and funeral. No-one present will ever forget such a chaotic and highly charged day.

One of my favourite retreats in Northern Ireland is The Everglades Hotel in Derry. Astride the flowing waters of the Foyle it offers superb views across the city and the hills of Donegal. In the early eighties, the welcome, good wholesome Irish cooking and a dip in the pool were the perfect combination to revive body and soul after a night of rioting and chaos. Alas, they have now closed the pool to provide more lounge space.

Londonderry or Derry ... whichever you call it ... immediately gives the game away when trying to unearth anyone's Loyalist or Nationalist leanings and likely adherence to the Protestant or Catholic faith. At least in Glasgow, with its significant religious divide, you can find a subtle way of stymieing the most determined of enquirers.

To the loaded question 'Er ye a Rangers or Celtic fan?'

The smart reply is 'Geesa break, Jimmie ... ah've ye no heard of Partick Thistle?' (the city's third professional football team).

From the Waterside, on the east bank of the river, and a Unionist stronghold in the eighties, Londonderry does bear some striking resemblances to an English market town.

But the place takes on an entirely different look when you cross the double-decker Craigavon Bridge into Derry city.

It was here that political gerrymandering by the Unionists, combined with poor housing and high unemployment in Catholic areas, led to the Civic Rights marches of the late 1960s. The demonstrations were declared illegal and suppressed by the Royal Ulster Constabulary. In August 1969 the Apprentice Boys parade led to the Battle of the Bogside when Catholic rioters fought the police for three days. The battle sparked widespread civil disorder in other parts of Northern Ireland and is generally viewed as the starting point of The Troubles.

My first impression, on passing the 'Free Derry' sign to enter the Bogside and the huge Creggan Estate on the rocky ground above, was that the council housing stock looked to be of a higher standard than much of what you could see in my home city of Dundee, in the endless rows of old pit houses on Wearside or the 1960s answer to a housing shortage – those ugly, inner-city, high-rise flats that plunged the architectural profession to such a low level of public esteem.

The Creggan was of particular interest, given that it was the first housing estate built in Derry with the purpose of housing Catholics. It certainly addressed their long-standing complaints of overcrowded and oppressive conditions but also ensured that as many as 15,000 of them were confined to one electoral area of the city.

If you were sent on an assignment here, you always knew that danger was never far away. The name Creggan was to become synonymous with conflict. To recall just how high a price the area was to pay as it became a symbol of Nationalist resistance, I met up with Derry novelist Garbhan Downey who, with fellow author Michael McGuinness, chartered the estate's 50-year history.

It's recorded that as far back as 1936, Archie Halliday, a Unionist councillor in the city, who opposed gerrymandering, made a chilling prediction. He told an inquiry that if justice was driven underground, there was no way of knowing how it might emerge or the havoc it might cause.

After The Troubles began more than thirty years later, dozens who lived in Creggan were killed, hundreds jailed and countless others forced to endure endless raids, gun battles and riots on their doorstep.

Not that the British Army, nor the police for that matter, Garbhan insists, found life any easier in their attempts to establish 'normality' on the estate. Soldiers and RUC officers were blown up, shot, stoned and subjected to endless vilification.

However, the authors highlighted happier times too, as the Creggan was to foster a glut of artistic and sporting talent, including a Eurovision winner, a Top Ten rock band, international footballers and Olympic athletes.

Given all this, surely there was more than a touch of irony in the choice of Dana's 1970 Eurovision Song Contest entry, 'All Kinds of Everything'. When she returned home in triumph, the whole town turned out to welcome her.

There was a similar reception for European lightweight boxing champion Charlie Nash, though his attempt to win the world title in 1980 was ended by Scot Jim Watt whom I used to watch pounding the pavement past my family home on the outskirts of Glasgow in his crack of dawn stamina-building road runs, all before I had even slipped out of my pyjamas!

The Troubles though left the people of the estate much to mourn. Six of those killed on Bloody Sunday when members of the 1st Battalion of the British Parachute Regiment opened fire on 13 unarmed civil rights protesters, came from Creggan and the funerals of all 13 were held at St Mary's Church.

Willie Best, a Royal Irish Ranger, was abducted by the IRA and shot dead whilst on home leave visiting his mother, while his neighbour, Michael Devine, was the last of the ten hunger strikers to die in the Maze after 60 days without food.

The end of the hunger strike saw both sides claiming victory. Northern Ireland Secretary James Prior announced a number of changes in prison policy which met some of the prisoners' demands including the right to wear their own clothes; but just like Bloody Sunday, those of us sent to cover The Troubles quickly became aware that the hunger strike had brought about a vast increase in support for Sinn Fein, hugely boosted IRA recruitment and served to evoke more international sympathy for the republican movement.

Others, many of them victims of IRA violence, were sickened and angry over the worldwide coverage given to the hunger strike. They included a group of Royal Ulster Constabulary widows whose husbands were among the 300 police officers murdered during The Troubles. As they sat down to watch the evening news, their blood quickly began to boil as the television cameras focused on the mothers and wives of the hunger strikers pleading for someone to save the lives of their ailing husbands or sons. In their eyes, it seemed the world was trying to glorify or lionise men who weren't freedom fighters or martyrs as the IRA would have them believe but a group of convicted killers, gangsters and thugs.

In Derry some of the widows decided it was time to act and I was despatched to find out exactly what they had in mind. One of them was Marlene Wilson whose life had been turned upside down some years earlier by a double tragedy that had devastated both sides of her family.

Her brother, Billy Logan, was driving a police Land Rover when it was ambushed by the IRA at Coalisland in County Tyrone. Billy was shot in the head. He was only 23. Just ten months later, her husband Mervyn – also 23 and a Police Constable – was preparing to come home on his tea break. But while he had been on duty in Derry, his car had been booby trapped and when he attempted to drive off from Harbour Square, the bomb exploded killing both Mervyn and his front seat passenger Sergeant Dave Dorset. Two other colleagues in the rear of the car were badly injured.

Marlene was enraged because unlike those who had decided to end their lives by hunger strike, their husbands had been given no choice. And so they decided to form an organisation called 'The Widow's Mite', an analogy with the story told in the Gospels of Mark and Luke. It was one I remembered had made a big impression on me during my Sunday School days – the widow who put two mites into the temple collection, the least valuable coins available at the time. Jesus though, observed she had given all she possessed. Most appropriate, Marlene insisted, as their husbands too, had given everything they had.

As a lasting tribute to their loved ones, Marlene and their friends melted down their husbands' wedding rings. The gold was then turned into a mite and the memorial dedicated at St Martin in the Fields Church in London's Trafalgar Square.

They also travelled to America to meet Congressmen and Senators at Capitol Hill to try to get the US Government to clamp down on the American fundraising organisation, Noraid, which openly expressed its support for the IRA but always claimed it gave money for humanitarian aid, while denying any of its donations were used for the purchase of arms.

For Marlene and the other widows, aspects of the peace agreement are very difficult to bear especially seeing some of those once associated with violence taking an active part in the new government of Northern Ireland. And of course, their grief was compounded when the name and uniform of the RUC was removed. The name now lives on only in the RUC George Cross Widows' Association in which Marlene takes a significant part, organising events and providing comfort for widows and their families.

Football too, got caught up in the general anarchy and it cost Derry City its place in the Irish League. At the height of The Troubles in the early seventies, a visiting team's bus was burnt and the other mainly unionist-supported clubs were reluctant to play at Derry's Brandywell ground right next to the Bogside. For a time, the club played its home matches 30 miles away in Coleraine but diminishing crowds and dwindling finances made life extremely difficult. When security forces withdrew their objection to the use of the Brandywell the following year, things looked hopeful but they got a thumbs down from the other clubs and withdrew from the League.

After 13 years in the wilderness, frustration gave way to enterprise. Desperate to get back into senior football, the rallying cry became: 'If the North won't let us play then maybe the Republic will.'

So Derry were invited to join the League of Ireland's new First Division in 1985. They won the title and were promoted to the Premier Division in 1987 and the following season went on to win the domestic treble.

The League championship meant entry into the prestigious European Cup alongside all the big names in football. All ears to the radio as the First Round draw was relayed from UEFA headquarters in Switzerland. Out of the hat came Derry City ... against ... Benfica, twice winners of the competition, whose Estadio da Luz (Stadium of Light) in Lisbon was one of the largest in the world with 120,000 seats.

The first game in the two-legged tie against the Portuguese was earmarked for the Brandywell. Derry was agog with excitement. Sales of the re-released club song, 'Brandywell Pride' soared. It was the hottest property in town. The singer – Derry City's own Northern Ireland international, Felix Healy.

Diaries had to be altered and meetings curtailed to ensure that the club's most prestigious supporters could take their place. It was a well-nigh impossible task to find a hotel room anywhere within range of Derry. In some parts of the city, tickets were on sale along with the milk and the groceries. The capacity was limited to 12,000 but with the local cemetery offering a free grandstand view, no-one it seemed need be left disappointed.

When Benfica telexed asking for 2,000 seats, Derry replied they only had 600 and sent 50 but promised a warm welcome and hospitality to match anything their illustrious opponents were preparing for the second game in Lisbon.

With 'full house' notices at The Everglades for days in advance, the BBC crew searched frantically for alternative accommodation. Eventually, we managed to obtain rooms at The Glen House Hotel at Eglinton about six miles outside the city.

On the day prior to the game, I was particularly keen to feature the Benfica legend, Eusebio, hero of the club's glory years, having scored

319 goals in 313 League games. He had also been the leading scorer in the 1966 World Cup in England and I remembered him distraught, tears flowing down his face when Portugal lost to England in the semi-final at Wembley. People were so impressed with his performances that his waxwork was immediately added to Madame Tussaud's collection.

Eusebio was now retired of course, but still travelled everywhere as Benfica's special ambassador. Well, that's what we thought until we saw him bedecked in tracksuit, stopwatch in hand, determined to show he could beat any Irish greyhound round the Brandywell track. Derry City had decided they would see quite enough of Portuguese wizardry the following night and escaped across the border to County Donegal and a high-spirited training session on Buncrana beach.

On match day morning I had just sat down to a full Irish breakfast when an agitated and breathless member of staff came rushing into the Glen House dining room.

'Mr Hamilton, there's an important phone call for you at reception.'

My immediate thought was that a bomb had exploded in Belfast or that Mrs Thatcher was about to fly in for one of those unannounced visits to the Province and that the BBC wanted to divert me elsewhere.

I picked up the phone to hear a distinctly Ulster voice blaring into my ear:

'This is Gregory Campbell, DUP Councillor for the Waterside. I just want to make it clear that Derry City is not a bipartisan club and I'm telling you now I don't want to see any stories suggesting anything along those lines. I'll be keeping a close watch on what you're saying.'

My immediate thought was 'how does he know I'm staying in this hotel and who told him I would be reporting on the match tonight?' The caller was not waiting for a response. As soon as he had made his point, Mr Campbell replaced the receiver.

I was shocked and appalled by the nature of the call. One of the biggest days in the history of Derry City Football Club it seemed would not be spared the ghastly echoes of the wider sectarian nature of Northern Irish society. Of course, I completely ignored 'the advice' and determined to report the build-up to the game in the confident and objective way that the BBC has always demanded from its correspondents, whatever the assignment.

Gregory Campbell is now MP for East Londonderry and Minister for Sport, Leisure and Culture in the power-sharing Northern Ireland Assembly. Today, he admits to being 'an interested spectator' of Derry City's progress, though his greater interest is in following the fortunes of Institute FC based in the nearby village of Drumahoe, a club which has emerged from the junior ranks to take its place in the top flight of the Irish League.

As kick-off approached, there was one more vignette to record. We sped off to Eglinton Airport and asked to be escorted on to the apron to greet the arrival of a small Loganair plane from Scotland carrying one of Derry City's most passionate supporters.

In 1972 Father Edward Daly had become an icon of The Troubles. As we watched the drama of Derry's Bloody Sunday unfold on our television screens, his was the image that left an indelible mark, bent double in terror to avoid the flying bullets, he crept slowly in front of a group of men carrying a teenager who had just been shot. In one hand, he was holding a white handkerchief, a desperate signal to the soldiers to allow the group through without further bloodshed. In the event, Jack Duddy died before they could get him to hospital.

Father Daly was to become emotionally exhausted by the events that followed, all the misery and human suffering and endlessly having to console people who were bereaved. He even admitted to feeling helpless with the sheer scale of obscenity – the taking of life and the destruction of homes and jobs.

In 1973 he left Derry to work as a religious adviser in Dublin for the television channel RTE, but he was to return to the city as Bishop of Derry. Trips to the Brandywell became his delight, a release valve from the burdensome responsibilities of high office. The Bishop rarely missed a match and he certainly wasn't going to miss this one!

He had hardly descended the steps of the plane when I hurled a microphone in front of him. Yes, he freely admitted, he had excused himself a little earlier than had been expected from a conference in Edinburgh. On this of all nights, he could not contemplate leaving a seat empty in the stand with so many from the city clamouring for tickets.

'Oh,' I asked him, 'and is it true that you're planning a pilgrimage to Fatima to coincide with the return leg in Lisbon?'

The Bishop's face turned red with embarrassment. 'And who told you that?'

This was one of those occasions when as a journalist I was not prepared to disclose my source. Speaking to him nearly 20 years later, I wondered whether he was still curious about who might have been telling tales.

'Let's keep it a secret,' he laughed. 'Can you remember the score?'

For the record, Derry lost 2–1 at home and 4–0 in Lisbon though judging by the post-match celebrations at the Brandywell, I sensed the city and its Bishop had enjoyed their evening and that a sense of hope had permeated through that dark misty cloud of violence and suffering.

12

Out of a Suitcase

There are no foreign lands. It is the traveller only who is foreign.

Robert Louis Stevenson

Bounding up the steps of Swiss Television headquarters in Zurich, I was greeted by a smiling newsroom assistant waiting to take my film to the processing laboratory. Leaning forward to offer a peck on my cheek, she announced excitedly: 'Gluckwunsche Bill … sie sind jetzt der vater von einem babysohn!'

Though elated to hear Veronica had given birth to our second child and that our daughter now had a baby brother, I was berating myself for my absence, once more unable to lend support or share the birth experience.

Today, of course, paternity leave allows fathers the opportunity to bond with their babies and gain confidence in their parenting abilities. This was not on the cards back in 1980. My anxiety over the possibility of an early birth was not sufficient to prevent the BBC sending me on my first week-long foreign assignment, a state visit by the Queen and the Duke of Edinburgh to Switzerland.

Though Queen Victoria had gone to Lucerne for an extended holiday in 1868, checking in under the pseudonym of the 'Countess of Kent', Switzerland had never experienced an official visit by a British monarch. One of the chief reasons for this surprising omission is that the country changes its President every year just like an English town with its Mayor, so with such a frequent game of 'musical chairs' the incumbent has few opportunities to travel abroad and is just as limited in finding time to arrange state visits at home. Perhaps the perfect question for a quiz down at your local: 'Who's the President of Switzerland?'

This President though, Georges-Andre Chevallaz, a noted Swiss historian, was eager to show the Queen the Alpine country at its best. In the quaint village of Zweisimmen in the Bernese Oberland, hundreds of schoolchildren had prepared a special welcome for the Royal couple before they set off on the privately owned rail line to Montreux.

Next day, as the sun shone brilliantly from a cloudless sky, we were able to board a specially commissioned paddle steamer which discreetly tailed the Queen's vessel across the sparkling blue waters of Lake Lucerne. As the boats negotiated the lake's numerous fingers twisting and turning through the landscape, the villagers of Weggis, Vitznau, Brunnen and Altdrorf lined the banks on both sides, dressed in traditional costumes, the sound of their Alpine horns echoing across the water with each group determined to surpass their neighbours in the warmth of their welcome.

In the cities of Basle and Zurich, the police cordon was much too restrictive. The people turned out in huge numbers and found themselves kept at a distance of twenty yards and more from the royal party. The Queen was having none of it and to her hosts' astonishment insisted in walking over to the crowds to acknowledge their greeting, causing consternation amongst those responsible for the split-second timing of her itinerary and their security advisers.

The Swiss tour over, the Queen and the Duke moved on to Liechtenstein as guests of Prince Franz Joseph II, an extremely popular sovereign who had overseen the economic development of the tiny principality from a poor agricultural backwater into one of the richest countries per capita in the world. Today it's recognised as a nation that has more registered companies than citizens.

Pre-warned of our arrival, the business and financial community arranged for me to attend an evening banquet with cameraman Mike Viney and recordist Steve Morris. All the speeches were in German and, fortified by the finest of wines, brought great guffaws from the prominent British contingent. I could vaguely make out references to the BBC and it was whispered in my ear that a response of some sort was necessary.

Unable to rattle up more than a few words in German, I decided that a Scottish rendition of a William McCulloch monologue might do the trick. I remembered as a wee boy winding up my grandfather's gramophone time and again to listen to comical recitations from a marvellous 1930s entertainer. To my astonishment, this nerve-ridden ad hoc performance drew spontaneous laughter from our hosts who by now had clearly indulged in one glass too many.

Calls home to check on my wife's condition proved fruitless. Our St Albans phone was out of order, but I knew my parents were in situ and would be able to deal with any emergency. It was just as well. Within hours, Veronica would be in labour and on her way to hospital.

After the overpowering security situation in Switzerland, few in Liechtenstein were aware of the Queen's presence. As we headed for the centre of the capital Vaduz, we came upon Her Majesty almost by chance, dressed in casual clothes and meandering down a side road leading from the castle heights to a gift shop from where she emerged with a cuckoo clock.

The BBC had welcomed the pictures of the royal tour which served as something of a light relief in bulletins dominated by the Iranian Embassy siege in London. Embassy police guard PC Trevor Locke and two BBC colleagues, news organiser Chris Cramer and sound recordist Sim Harris who had stopped by to collect visas, were among the hostages held by six Iranian gunmen opposed to Ayatollah Khomeini. They were demanding freedom for the southern Iranian province of Arabistan and the release of 91 political prisoners held in Iran.

The siege at Prince's Gate in Knightsbridge had continued for six days and was the centre of intense media coverage. When the gunmen shot dead the Iranian press attaché Abbas Lavasani and dumped his body outside, the Home Secretary William Whitelaw ordered an attack on the building.

I was just walking through the doors of the maternity unit of St Albans City Hospital to set eyes on my new baby son when the noise of a loud explosion could be heard coming from an old television set perched in the corner of the ward. Heads quickly glanced up at the screen as masked men of the SAS stormed the embassy building from the balcony, throwing grenades through the windows. Once inside they killed all but one of the gunmen and successfully set free 19 hostages.

The real-life drama was watched by millions with the BBC interrupting coverage of the World Snooker Championship to relay the pictures live with Kate Adie reporting unscripted from behind a van door for 45 minutes.

Two years later, it was my turn to report on another siege at the American Ambassador's residence. But this one was not for real. The scene of the action was Heatherden Hall at Pinewood Studios in Buckinghamshire. Having watched the unfolding drama from Prince's Gate on television, producer Euan Lloyd decided it should form the basis for his latest film *Who Dares Wins* in which the SAS would be despatched to deal with a group of terrorists whose demands included the firing of a nuclear weapon at the Holy Loch submarine base.

Lewis Collins was signed up for the lead role as SAS officer, Captain Peter Skellen and Judy Davis as Frankie, the potentially insane leader of the terrorist group. Helicopters buzzed overhead preparing to drop many of the supporting cast on to the roof in this glamorised look at the methods and tactics of the SAS. Soon, as the suspense began to build, they would be abseiling down the building and deploying the full force of one of the world's most lethal fighting units to save the lives of the high-ranking hostages inside. The all-action plot certainly brought a stark reminder of the events of May 1980.

I arrived at Pinewood just after lunch expecting to be wheeled on to deliver a short piece to camera. Cast as reporter Robert Snow, my job was to relay the latest events to the nation, but for five hours as filming continued in various parts of the site, I struggled to locate anyone who had a copy of the prepared script.

Eventually, at about a quarter to midnight, one was finally placed in my hands. It was the wrong one! Told that my contribution would be filmed in about ten minutes' time, I demanded to see the producer himself.

'Here you are Bill. This is what we want from you ... now let's get going.'

The replacement script was succinct but of a style that neither the BBC nor ITN would use. If it went out in that form, I knew I would be pilloried by my employers.

'Sorry,' I said, 'this just won't work.'

'All right then. Change it to whatever you think best but we must get this done now!' Two minutes later, the cameras rolled and I delivered my piece with thirty seconds to spare before the crew's mandatory tea break. A minute later and the film company would have been facing a hefty overtime bill.

It had been nice to meet the stars but waiting around for ten hours before setting eyes on a script and then having to rewrite and deliver it within the space of a few minutes was not quite the introduction I had expected to life on the big screen!

Reporters at Television Centre worked on a shift system – four days on, three days off – at least that's how it appeared on paper. In practice, it often turned out to be something entirely different. The demands of the newsroom were such that a reporter remained on an assignment until the story was over or the news editor decided to send a replacement. That could take days, weeks or occasionally a month or more. A thick black line had to be scored through all those social engagements that had been written excitedly into the pocket diary.

The pool of reporters amounted to no more than a dozen, so some days you could walk into the tacky, end of corridor office and find only one other colleague sitting munching a sandwich, waiting like a taxi driver to be told where his next job would take him – Downing Street, Buckingham Palace or just as likely a murder, a picket line or the closing day of a trial at the Old Bailey. Possessing a cab driver's geographical knowledge of the capital was also a bonus. It saved precious minutes spent flicking through the street maps of the London A–Z.

The room overlooked a run-down inner-city housing estate and the White City Stadium built for the London Olympics in 1908 and which once boasted a capacity of 150,000. Seventy years later, it was being used for little more than greyhound racing and in the mid-eighties would be demolished to make way for the BBC's White City building.

The pace of life was frenetic but all great fun. Whilst descending to the newsroom garage situated in the basement, either to meet up with the camera crew or to set off in one of the small fleet of Ford Escorts issued to reporters, it was common practice to stop the lift on the fourth floor. This was where News Information was sited, a large room manned by librarians who could produce newspaper cuttings on people, places and incidents that had been compiled over several decades. They also kept old scripts and updated biographies on politicians, film stars, sportsmen and a whole string of VIPs, a real lifeline when you were in a hurry to produce an item for the next bulletin of the day.

The news operation was no place for a loner. This was a team effort with the editors of the lunchtime, evening and *Nine O'Clock News* running a very professional operation in which each person knew precisely what was expected, indeed demanded. Before microwave links, vehicles and satellite dishes became common practice, a team of despatch riders was deployed to ensure the film 'rushes' got back to base and into the processing lab as quickly as possible. The sight of a leather-jacketed motor cyclist bounding up the stairs of TUC Headquarters was a sure sign that another deadline was fast approaching.

When I first arrived in London, I was advised by older and wiser colleagues to ensure I had a good breakfast as it might turn out to be the only meal of the day. Many times rushing from home in the early hours of the morning, I was made to rue ignoring such sound advice. Though never a devotee of the fast-food empire, I was grateful that McDonald's insisted their new branch at Shepherd's Bush should remain open until midnight. Too often, the only sustenance came at the wrong end of the day.

In the boot of the car, I kept a small bag crammed with essentials – passport, a toothbrush, shaver, bar of soap and a change of underwear just in case I was running one way up the newsroom corridor ready to provide a voice-over for one story, only to find myself being sent in the opposite direction to get my teeth into another – a bomb at a Paris synagogue, a fatal motorway pile-up or a ship aground in the Channel.

I was still a raw recruit on a very large learning curve when the new Editor of Television News, Alan Protheroe summoned me to his office. He told me John Humphrys was returning from Johannesburg where he had been based as Southern Africa correspondent and that a number of more senior colleagues had applied for his job. Because of holidays and other circumstances, it would be at least six weeks before an Interview Board could be convened and he was anxious that someone should fill the gap. 'This will be marvellous experience for you Bill. Let's see what you can do.'

Arriving at Jan Smuts Airport, I was pleased to see John waiting to take me to his house which doubled as the BBC bureau. I had barely set my case down in the bedroom when he popped his head round the door.

'I hear you're a football referee so presumably you'll want to keep in trim over here.' Throwing a track suit into my hands, he said: 'I'm just off for my morning run and I think it best you join me.'

It was not what I wanted to hear after a twelve-hour sleepless flight from Heathrow but within two minutes, we were off, mostly downhill, for a two-mile run to the gates of Johannesburg Zoo. As we turned for home, I could see John was far from impressed with my level of fitness.

'Never mind, there's only room for one of us in the shower, so I'll go ahead and you can catch me up later!'

All very well but in my zombie-like state, navigating the way back along deserted streets without a soul from whom to ask directions was not the introduction to South African life that I had bargained for.

When exhausted, and not a little humiliated, I finally arrived back at the house in Saxonwold, John had not only showered but finished breakfast, read the morning papers, telexed London and was repairing a wooden rafter in the dining room. Though there was a lot of packing to do before his return to Britain to take up his new role as the BBC's Diplomatic Correspondent, he spent several hours patiently explaining the political situation in South Africa, introducing me to a host of contacts whom he had nurtured over his three-year stay and to the corps of British journalists based there.

If John has earned a reputation as a tenacious and forthright interviewer – one whom politicians often fear to face – he is also a thoroughly decent man who cares passionately about his chosen profession.

No sooner had John left than I found myself covering a strike by 10,000 black council workers in Johannesburg, demanding higher wages and recognition for their newly formed trade union.

Under the apartheid government of PW Botha, they knew they were taking a huge risk. Within hours of other strikes breaking out in the country, blacks found themselves immediately replaced by others anxious to get a job of any kind. Armed police surrounded council depots as services were disrupted and rubbish piled high on the streets. Elsewhere, thousands of black pupils were boycotting classes as demands for better educational opportunities continued to grow.

With South African based-cameraman, Francois Marais – an inspirational figure – I headed for a rural district just 20 miles from the heart of the city. We got there just in time to see the last group of children arriving for lessons at Swartkops School. Despite spending two hours trudging along dirt roads to get there, they simply couldn't wait to get inside. They were the lucky ones. For most in the area there simply wasn't a place available and the school existed only through the generosity of neighbouring white landowners.

It was designed to accommodate 160 but close on double that number turned up every morning with scores of them forced to squat on the floor. Six-year-olds were sharing the same classroom as sixteen-year-olds and in many cases, they were at the same stage of learning. But there was no embarrassment. In a country where the Government was spending nearly ten times as much on a white pupil as on a black, these children had come to appreciate their good fortune.

The municipal workers' strike, meanwhile, lasted for a week. The strikers were asked at gunpoint by police whether they intended to go back to work. Those who refused were ordered to pack their belongings and were bussed back to their *Bantustans* or 'homelands' to which nearly 4 million blacks had been forcibly relocated during the previous 20 years and from where others would be quickly recruited to take their place, all of them in desperate financial straits.

To come face to face with people defined not by their humanity but by the colour of their skin, to see the fear on their faces and feel the vulnerability of their situation, turned my stomach and filled me with deep anger. My mind recalled a Bible Class address by our Boys' Brigade captain, Walter Brown, back in the 1950s in which he predicted that one day the black man would rise up and seek to right all the injustices perpetrated against him.

The following weekend, I was invited to a garden party at the home of a fellow British journalist. There, I was introduced to Desmond Tutu, then Secretary-General of the South African Council of Churches, who would later be awarded the Nobel Peace Prize for his tireless work as a unifying figure in the campaign to abolish apartheid. As we chatted in the sun-drenched garden, he shared his powerful vision that justice would come, freedom was unstoppable and that one day all South Africans would be free. Today, the Anglican Archbishop who chaired the Truth and Reconciliation Commission following the election of Nelson Mandela's Government of national unity, remains one of the country's most important and beloved figures.

I wished I had asked him where he felt God had been during the apartheid years. I was intrigued to find part of the answer in an interview he gave to an American University researcher in 1999. In it, Desmond Tutu described how he saw God intervene in the cause of South African liberation:

And to be able then to seek to uphold the fervour and the faith of our people, being able to say to them that we had a God who was not deaf, who was not blind, who didn't give advice from a safe distance. We had a God who enters the fiery furnace with you and doesn't say to you, 'well you know, when you are exposed to fire, you ought to wear asbestos and protective.' No. God comes into the fire with you, because this is Emmanuel. Incredible. I mean it was almost as if the scriptures were a textbook written specifically for your particular situation. It has been an incredible privilege.*

Returning to the BBC bureau, a telex was waiting.

'We want you to fly with film crew to Zimbabwe tomorrow am. State visit by President Samora Machel of Mozambique. Make sure you find another story there as these trips are expensive.'

If I was sweating over that one, it would not be long before my mind was set at rest. Still in celebratory mode after gaining its independence from Britain just three months before, the next ten days would provide eight major stories for all the *BBC News* outlets. There was hardly a pause to draw breath.

---

*Interview with Mary Marshall Clark from the Carnegie Oral History Project, Columbia University Libraries, USA, September 1999.

We could not have timed our arrival better. Driving into the centre of the capital Salisbury from the airport, we suddenly ran into a traffic jam. Its cause was not what anyone had come to expect. There in the middle of one of the city's most famous thoroughfares, a giant crane was carefully lifting the founder of Rhodesia off his pedestal. There was just time to scramble the camera out of the boot to record a symbolic moment in the changing face of Zimbabwe.

If the contractors were handling things delicately, the same could hardly be said for the crowds who came to cheer. In their unrestrained excitement, some jumped on top of the monument as it was lowered on to a waiting lorry, lunging kicks and beating it with layers of steel coil. The order to remove Cecil Rhodes' statue to the museum came directly from the Government who also asked for the street nameplates to be torn down. In an instant, Jameson Avenue became Samora Machel Avenue in recognition of the part played by the President of Mozambique in Zimbabwe's independence struggle.

Reminders of the days of colonialism were disappearing fast though Prime Minister Robert Mugabe was clearly determined that his friend from across the border should be afforded the kind of treatment once reserved for members of the British Royal Family.

The Boeing 707 of Mozambique Airlines was escorted into Salisbury by four Hawker Hunter jets of the Zimbabwean Air Force and thousands lined the nine-mile route from the airport to the city centre to greet the leader Mugabe regarded as his closest friend and ally who had given refuge to him and more than 150,000 refugees during the Rhodesian Bush War. For the man who allowed his country to be used as a base for the liberation struggle, the guns were firing again but this time as part of an elaborate programme of celebrations that would continue for the next four days – parades, demonstrations and a state banquet.

Returning to the Meikles Hotel overlooking what is now Africa Unity Square, another telex from London arrived unexpectedly. Against all the odds, the Zimbabwean women's hockey team had won the Gold Medal at The Moscow Olympics and were due to arrive home the following evening. How inconvenient ... that was the night of the State banquet for President Machel and all the senior Government ministers were under strict instructions to be there. What's more, none of them was available for interview and most were still unaware of this remarkable sporting achievement.

Next morning, I picked up the Zimbabwean telephone directory from the cabinet drawer in the hotel bedroom. I was astounded at how thin it was. You could skip through the entire book in little over five minutes. I was equally astounded to find a direct entry for the Presidential Office at State House. I dialled the number expecting to speak to some government bureaucrat.

'President Banana here, can I help you?' came the reply.

I asked him whether he had heard of Zimbabwe's Olympic success and whether he would be willing to be interviewed.

'Certainly, what time do you want to come?'

Half an hour later our car sped towards the gates of State House, the former residence of the Governors of Southern Rhodesia. After an initial check by an armed guard, we were waved through. At the end of the drive, we found the place deserted with only a few hens scratching around in the yard and the distant sound of a transistor radio. Finally, we stumbled upon the cook in an outhouse who pointed us in the right direction. A gentle ring of a bell and President Canaan Banana opened the door himself and ushered us into a room still full of the trappings of British colonial life.

A former Methodist minister, he'd been installed as Zimbabwe's first post-independence President, a largely ceremonial role. He held the post for seven years before Robert Mugabe took the job for himself. Banana's later life would be ruined by a sexual scandal. He was imprisoned after being convicted on charges of sodomy though he denied all the accusations against him claiming they were part of a malicious vendetta.

As we spoke, it was clear that the President was highly embarrassed that neither he nor Mugabe would be in a position to welcome the Gold Medallists on their arrival at the airport. That would be left to the Minister for Sport.

To say the Zimbabweans had over-achieved would be an understatement. The invitation to take part had come out of the blue after the USA and many other western nations had boycotted the Games in protest at the Soviet invasion of Afghanistan. The team captained by Ann Grant, a sister of the former England cricket coach Duncan Fletcher, had been hurriedly assembled and flew to the Zambian capital Lusaka, en route to Moscow, in a plane normally used for transporting meat. The stench was terrible. There were no seats so they all sat on the floor of the aircraft. In the round-robin six-team tournament featuring the Soviet Union, Poland, Austria, India and Czechoslovakia, Zimbabwe remained unbeaten. The team included twin sisters and Arlene Boxhall, who mounted the podium at just 18 years and 290 days old, the youngest woman ever to win Olympic Gold in hockey.

If all this added to the mood of celebration in the city then next day events took a decided turn for the worse. I phoned the Foreign News Editor in London to tell them I was on the trail of a senior Cabinet Minister and Secretary-General of Mugabe's Zanu PF Party, Edgar Tekere, whom police wanted to question about the murder of a white farmer. Bill Adams had been shot in the back after a group of armed men had opened fire on his homestead while he was calling for help on his farm security radio.

Arriving at the Minister's house, we were met by armed guards brandishing AK-47 assault rifles. We were clearly not welcome and I was feeling more than a little nervous at the erratic behaviour of the guards, sharp clicks one minute as they cocked their weapons, the next downing arms to indulge in a game of football.

Cameraman Richard Atkinson refused to budge and we were rewarded for our patience when suddenly an E-Type Jaguar appeared out of the mist. Mr Tekere had arrived home to find CID officers waiting on his doorstep. They left without him but minutes later, he rushed out of his front door in combat gear and leapt into the Jaguar, making off at speed, with the guards leaping on to the back of the vehicle determined to keep any pursuing car at a distance. We thought we had lost him but the Minister was enjoying the chase, occasionally applying the brakes and waiting for our car to catch up with him. The police did too. He was charged with murder and went on trial together with seven bodyguards but found not guilty on a majority decision in the High Court. Two assessors sitting with the judge overruled him, holding that while Tekere had killed Adams, he had acted out of a conviction that State security was at risk.

Though dismissed from the Government the following year, the man nicknamed '2-Boy' remained active in politics and ran against Mugabe in the 1990 presidential election as the candidate for the Zimbabwe Unity Movement.

My next confrontation with armed guards was sparked by total ignorance of the beliefs and traditions of the little landlocked African kingdom of Swaziland. By the summer of 1980 King Sobhuza II known to his subjects variously as 'The Lion', 'The Great Mountain' and 'The Inexplicable' had been on the throne for nearly 60 years, the longest reigning monarch in the world. There were suggestions he was in failing health, his public appearances by now few and far between. Discovering that the King was due to open his tiny nation's most ambitious industrial project aimed at turning Swaziland into Africa's second largest sugar producer, I had little trouble persuading the *BBC News* hierarchy that we had all the makings of a fascinating film.

What I had not expected was the arrival of all the King's wives – I counted close on 70 – so many that they had to be brought three to each official car. When the vehicles ran out, the second wave came by bicycle and the remainder on foot.

They sat together along with many of the King's children and grandchildren in a specially cordoned-off area of the outdoor arena which had been thoughtfully prepared for the ceremony. Government officials, always uncertain of what attire their monarch would choose for any occasion, took no chances, taking their places dressed in top hat and tails while the Royal Marines were clearly the role models for the splendidly turned out musicians of The Swazi Police Band.

As they struck up the national anthem out of tune, the limousine carrying the King finally arrived. He looked in surprisingly good health but had decided this was not a day for sartorial elegance. Unlike his ministers, he determined a loin skin and a thin cloth draped over his shoulder were quite sufficient, along with the traditional three arrow-like feathers adorning his hair.

Looking at the spectacle laid before us, it was evident the King's fertility, attributed to the drinking of juices from a secret root, was among his most important virtues. His people held that it was intrinsically linked to the fertility of the land. In all, he was said to have taken over 100 wives – one from every clan – outliving a fair proportion of them, and to have fathered 500 children.

The soldiers protecting the wives gesticulated that filming was prohibited. I tried to deflect their attention momentarily so that Francois Marais' camera could quickly grab a few meaningful shots. Suddenly, I felt an excruciating pain as a rifle butt smashed into my back just below my left shoulder. As I staggered to my feet in agony, the armed guard shouted a further warning in SiSwati which our interpreter translated roughly as 'try that again and you'll be on your way home.'

Intrigued to find out why our indiscretion had caused such a commotion, it was later explained to me during a lavish reception in the red-carpeted marquee, that many believed in those few seconds part of the wives' personalities had passed on to the celluloid and would now be lost to the King.

Sobhuza II, whose reign lasted another two years, turned out to be a delightful old man mixing freely with his guests and giving the assembled crowds lunch boxes and bottles of wine to celebrate the opening of the new British designed Simunye Mill surrounded by acres of productive sugar cane and providing employment for a workforce of over 3,000. The wine flowed so freely that some of the estate workers wanted to experience a little more of the high life. One burst into the King's marquee, wrenched open a pair of meat tongs and crane-like removed dozens of slices of ham before emptying a huge bowl of sherry trifle on the top of his prize haul ... just as well His Majesty was looking the other way!

The excitement over, we prepared to bed down for the night in a small hotel close by. Downstairs, scores of workers were crammed into the bar whose sparse furnishings included little more than a model of a kilted piper, indicating the availability of a wee dram of Dewars Whisky, and a black and white television suspended from the ceiling. All went silent as a smartly dressed announcer read out the Royal Swazi News in impeccable English. It included a filmed report of King Subhuza's speech at the sugar plantation. After the playing of the National Anthem, viewers were told:

'And now we are crossing to London for the News at Ten.'

I could hardly believe my eyes. In 1980, live transmissions of BBC and ITN bulletins to other parts of the world were virtually unheard of.

'Oh yes, maister, we get this every night ... never miss it,' one told me.

I was as transfixed as the rest of the audience and utterly speechless as I tried to comprehend how it was possible for this tiny African kingdom to transmit the flagship news programme of our greatest rivals. It was only when Alastair Burnet in his own inimitable way began to read the football results that the penny dropped. I recognised the scores ... the games had all been played six days before!

The Editor of *BBC TV News* was right. My stint in southern Africa had provided a major building block in furthering my broadcasting experience. Returning to England, I had hardly stepped foot in my own front door than suitcase in tow, I was off again – this time with cameraman Dick Hill – to the other end of the continent.

In early October a devastating earthquake measuring 7.3 on the Richter scale struck the Algerian city of El Asnam. It was the largest in the country's history and there were fears that a fifth of the population of 100,000 had been buried under the rubble. A tragedy of gargantuan proportions accentuated by the appalling revelation that this was a city that had been built to replace another wiped out by a previous quake just 26 years before.

Arriving at Algiers Airport, we were immediately intercepted by officials from the Interior Ministry and held in a Government building for six hours. With roads closed to private vehicles, they insisted in moving everyone by bus.

The journey was painfully slow, the road clogged by convoys of wailing ambulances, bulldozers and earth-moving vehicles. Evidence of the devastation began to reveal itself slowly, first a few damaged roofs, next walls that had collapsed and huge fissures in the road. Then as the bus reached the crest of a hill, the enormity of the tragedy began to unfold. Each village in turn was more severely damaged than the last. As we looked to our left, there was the ghastly sight of a stretch of railway line lifted off the ground, the rails contorted into something more resembling a fairground roller coaster and a hundred yards further on, the remains of the train lying forlornly where it had been hurled off the track, spilling its carriages like pieces of luggage into the fields.

As the coach driver negotiated his way around huge mounds of rubble on our entry to El Asnam, I was reminded of the newsreel pictures of Berlin at the end of the Second World War. Stretched out as far as the eye could see was a ruined and ravaged city. Eighty per cent of the buildings had been destroyed. Two large housing complexes collapsed like a pack of cards. A large department store, the central mosque, a number of schools and the city's four-storey hospital were in ruins leaving the most seriously injured of the survivors facing a 150-mile journey either to Algiers or the north-western port of Oran.

The most modern buildings built after the 1954 earthquake fared no better. They were supposed to be quake-proof but in many cases the elementary rules of seismic-resistant design had been ignored. Their flat roofs of reinforced concrete held together as they crashed down and became tombs forming a solid barrier against the rescuers. One was the city's largest hotel with over 1,500 rooms, another the Cité An Nasr, an apartment-café-market complex housing 3,000 people.

The earthquake happened at noon on a Friday, the traditional Arab day of rest which meant schools, public buildings and major stores – although totally destroyed – were closed. The Grand Mosque was full and the streets and cafés of the residential neighbourhoods teemed with families. Others were strolling in the park.

The first devastating shock lasted 40 seconds and came without warning. Those who survived were overwhelmed and confused.

As we began to film, there was a sense of hopelessness and sheer exhaustion written on every face. Grief stricken and wandering aimlessly among the rubble, most were still in a state of shock. The city offices, police and fire stations had been destroyed too, as were the lifeline services of water, electricity and gas. Telephone lines had been cut.

Despite no contingency plan for earthquake emergencies, the rescue operation was rapid and effective. When the Army teams arrived they found people digging with their bare hands trying desperately to reach trapped victims. By night, under the arc lights, as the harsh din of the excavators was silenced for a few minutes, the moans of those buried alive were still sometimes painfully audible but trapped in a multi-layered sandwich of collapsed concrete floors, saving them had become an increasingly hopeless task.

Mountain dogs flown in from France and Switzerland sniffed among the ruins alerting their handlers to any trace of human life.

Extricating someone alive from such an appalling scene boosts morale and provides fresh hope. It also helps personalise the tragedy for television viewers, many of whom respond to international appeals to aid the victims of such disasters though close-up shots of faces or serious injuries have to be used very sparingly. Nearly 40 hours after the quake struck, a team of Algerian and French gendarmes prepared to lift a young man from the ruins of a café we were filming but first, to save his life, a surgeon had to be sent down to amputate a leg while he was still buried in the rubble.

The grounds of the ruined hospital had been turned into a vast makeshift morgue. The bodies lay side by side where fathers came looking for their children and entire families awaited identification. I had never encountered death on this scale before and was conscious that while we had a duty to convey the horrific reality of the situation, we must be careful not to intrude overtly into the private grief of so many in that sad city.

Returning to the coach to try to snatch our first hour's sleep since leaving London the previous day, we had no sooner found a couple of seats on which to rest our heads than the bus began to shake violently for ten seconds or more. We had been hit by an aftershock triggering further panic on the street outside. The bus was parked next to a school that had been cracked wide open by the original quake and I feared even the mildest of tremors might bring the damaged building down on top of us.

The job now was to find a car and a driver to rush our pictures back to Algiers in time for the 17.30 news feed to Television Centre. Easier said than done. Scores of vehicles lay under slabs of concrete or fallen walls and were flattened to a thickness of little more than a foot.

We would return to the area the following day as the unequal struggle to find survivors continued. Everywhere soldiers and volunteers worked endlessly in the dust, tent cities were being set up to house the homeless and survivors inoculated against any possible outbreak of cholera or typhoid.

Some parents who had been at prayer when the quake struck were still in a frantic state as they continued to claw at the rubble in the vain hope of finding their children whom they had left behind.

The abiding memory is of one old lady, hand over face, sitting by the roadside clutching a portable radio. Breaking the deathly silence of her demolished street came the opening bars of Beethoven's Fifth Symphony, often described as grim and resolute yet charged with conflict and energy as glimmers of hope swirl through a relentless storm.

It was an eerie experience.

The following year, El Asnam changed its name to Ech-Cheliff to mark a new beginning. After two earthquakes in 30 years, work had already begun in rebuilding the city for a third time.

A reporter rarely arrives for work with a preconceived idea of how the day will go. Pre-arranged events that have been entered in the newsroom diary for days – sometimes weeks in advance – can take an unexpected turn. Others provide a sense of fun and laughter that can come as a welcome release valve. There was Bob Hope's flamboyant return to the terraced house at Eltham in South London where he was born and Margaret Thatcher's return from the theatre where she had been watching the satirical play *Anyone for Denis?* Standing on the doorstep of Downing Street, the Prime Minister was waxing lyrical about Angela's Thorne's impersonation of her but less enthusiastic about John Wells' portrayal of her husband.

'Was that the real Maggie Thatcher we saw on stage tonight?' I asked her cheekily. A warm smile gently crossed her face. 'The real Maggie – who knows the real Maggie?' she responded swinging her handbag in my direction before turning to usher her guest Jimmy Savile into a reception Downing Street had prepared to celebrate the charity performance.

Catherine Bramwell-Booth, granddaughter of the founder of the Salvation Army, provided some incredibly amusing moments.

On the occasion of her hundredth birthday, she preached for over half an hour at the Regent Hall in Oxford Street with typical evangelistic zeal. We had just slipped quietly on to the platform to take some frontal shots of the large congregation when Catherine's sister suddenly rose from her seat and started tugging at her Army tunic. Clearly irritated by this untimely interruption, the centenarian turned her head sharply and uttered a stinging rebuke:

'I will sit down when I'm finished, Olive!'

Commissioner Catherine's disarming frankness made her an ideal interviewee for radio and television programmes. At the cutting of her hundredth-birthday cake, I asked her about early memories of her grandfather. She recalled returning from a Sunday School meeting where she had sung a solo to be asked: 'How did you get on today, Catherine?'

'I did my best, grandpa,' she declared meekly.

'Ah,' said General William Booth, '*anyone* can do their best. For God, you have to do *better* than your best!'

It was a tenet that remained with her during her long years of service to God and the Salvation Army.

By 1981 my suitcase was beginning to show signs of wear and tear, but before I had time to invest in a replacement I was airborne again, this time to South America.

I'd just turned 20 when Ronnie Biggs and his cohorts in crime ambushed the Glasgow to London mail train near Cheddington in Buckinghamshire in 1963 and made off with £2.6million in used banknotes. The audacious heist that became known as the 'Great Train Robbery' was a source of great fascination and the names of some of the gang – Ronald 'Buster' Edwards, Charlie Wilson, Tommy Wisbey and the mastermind Bruce Reynolds – are still readily recalled by many of my generation nearly 50 years later.

The robbers were sentenced to jail terms totalling more than 300 years but Biggs escaped from Wandsworth Prison by climbing a 30ft wall and fleeing in a furniture van. Living first in Spain and Australia and then on to Brazil, he survived several attempts to recapture him including one by 'Slipper of the Yard', a reference to Detective Superintendent Jack Slipper of the Metropolitan Police, who flew to Brazil in the hope of bringing him back to England.

Then in early 1981, Biggs was kidnapped and smuggled into Barbados. The kidnappers, two former Scots Guards, had hoped to collect a reward from the British police but the coup was discovered and in court Biggs' lawyer made use of some legal loopholes to prevent his extradition and instead, have him sent back to Brazil.

Despatched immediately to Rio de Janeiro, I was anxious that I might miss Ronnie's arrival but fortunately a tropical storm in the North Atlantic delayed his flight which gave me enough time to meet up with a freelance film crew at the airport. There we found Biggs' young son

Michael at work crayoning a 'Welcome Home, Dad' banner and already the centre of attention of the 'crime hacks' of Britain's red-top tabloids.

Michael's mother was Biggs' then girlfriend, Raimunda de Castro, who had left to pursue a career in Switzerland leaving the boy in the care of his father. Under the country's law, the parent of a Brazilian child could not be extradited, so Biggs could resume living openly in Brazil, untouchable by the British authorities.

Photographers desperate for reunion pictures chased Ronnie and Michael everywhere. They bought him ice cream, took him to the fairground and for a dip in the sea. In the twilight hours Biggs, glass in hand, decided it was time to relax by the swimming pool of a seafront hotel opposite Copacabana Beach He listened intently as the posse of crime reporters kept him updated on the lifestyles of his former criminal associates, most of whom had by now served their sentences and were enjoying the taste of freedom.

The conversation was in full flow when Michael appeared on the scene. After a day of childhood treats thanks to the beneficent photographers from London, he was demanding even more attention. To the chagrin of the 'snappers', before a single camera could be reached from beneath the parasol, quick as a flash Ronnie lifted his son from the terrace and threw him headlong into the pool. As we all looked on in stunned silence, a few bubbles appeared near the deep end and then up popped little Michael seemingly none the worse for his ordeal and being ordered straight to bed.

As the media circus continued, Michael was interviewed on Brazilian television and did an impromptu song and dance routine that a friend of his father had taught him. The head of CBS Records just happened to be watching and invited him to join a children's pop group. Michael was just six when he started performing with the Magic Balloon Gang, bringing a useful source of income for his father denied a work permit by the authorities.

In 2001 Michael arranged for Biggs to return to Britain in a private jet paid for by the *Sun*. It was Ronnie's own desire to return home even though he still had 28 years of his sentence left to serve. He knew full well he would be returned straight to prison but said his last wish was to walk into a Margate pub as an Englishman and buy a pint of bitter. Only when virtually on his deathbed was he to taste freedom again.

Biggs may have shown no remorse for his crimes, cocked a snook at British justice and enjoyed the attention his notoriety attracted but I found him a likeable rogue.

By May 1982 Britain was engaged in the Falklands conflict with Argentina and there had been fears that the planned visit of Pope John Paul II might have to be abandoned. In the end some deft diplomacy in which that modest and quintessentially English head of the Catholic hierarchy in England, Cardinal Basil Hume, played a leading part, saved the day with the Vatican agreeing that the Pope should visit Argentina too, the following month.

The six-day tour of England, Wales and Scotland was a demanding one, not just for a pontiff now in his sixties but for the BBC whose resources were stretched to cover such a punishing schedule.

I was delegated to cover two of the major outdoor events at Coventry and York. At the Knavesmire Racecourse, more than 190,000 people heard the Pope address them on marriage and family life. At Coventry Airport, the crowd swelled to more than 350,000.

Given the political tensions rife at the time, his homily was interpreted by many as an anti-war message.

'You will live in such a way as to make holy all human life,' he declared. 'You will become living stones in the cathedral of peace ... indeed, called by God to be instruments of his peace.'

John Paul II was an impressive man with a real ability to reach out to the masses. No matter how tight the timetable, he refused to be harried or hassled by aides or those organising his security. A warm and humid day did leave him, like everyone else, in need of a drink. Driven in his Popemobile to a lunch with the Bishops and dignitaries, he asked for a refreshment. Their suggestion of sherry was politely refused, so too, gin and tonic. That's when the Polish chef came to the rescue. At the back of the room, there he was holding up a pint of beer. Silence descended for a few seconds as he delicately eased himself through the vast throng of VIPs and approaching the Pope, gently set the glass down on the table and said: 'Polish beer, your Holiness.'

The Pope took the glass, sniffed it and to everyone's amazement, put it down in one!

Arriving back in the Vatican, the Pope's entourage had barely enough time to unpack before taking off again for Argentina. As he was denouncing all wars as 'unjust', the battle for Port Stanley had just begun. A month before, I had watched the men of the 5th Infantry Battalion – Scots and Welsh Guards and Gurkhas – sail on the QE2 from Southampton, but my first confrontation with the horrors of war would come just days later, 8,000 miles from The Falklands.

13

To War in Lebanon

Unless and until something concrete is done about addressing the Israeli-Palestinian issue, you won't get a real start on the war against terrorism.

Bob Hawke, former Prime Minister of Australia

Picnics are great fun and encourage family bonding – all the more important if your job takes you away from home for sometimes weeks at a time. Early June 1982 heralded ideal weather for the outdoors, our garden attracting birds, bees and butterflies in ever-increasing numbers and our children already counting down the weeks to the summer holidays.

A Sunday picnic was certainly on the cards especially when we read that weekend boat trips had just begun on a short stretch of the Grand Union Canal in Buckinghamshire near the foothills of the Chilterns. We had never been there before as a family and for Claire and David there would be the opportunity not just to soak in the atmosphere of a working boatyard but to see how the crew negotiate the various locks along the route. As for me, well, after all the hectic activity of the previous month, surely there could be no better way to wind down than to just sit back and watch the world pass slowly by.

The sandwiches prepared and a couple of bottles of pop safely locked into the boot, I was just about to drive off when I could hear the distant sound of the phone ringing. A dilemma – should I answer it or not? Thinking it might be a family relation, I rushed back into the house.

'Where the hell have you been?' a familiar voice boomed down the earpiece.

'Nowhere yet,' I replied. 'In fact, I'm just off with the family for a picnic on the canal.'

'Oh no you're not! The Israelis have just invaded Lebanon and you're

going with them. You've got an hour to prepare and get to Heathrow
... and you'd better pack for at least a fortnight.'

In reality, that fortnight became two months. It was my first experience
of war, something I had associated more with my father and grandfather's
generations. Reporting conflict, trauma, disaster and human suffering are
unfortunately an integral part of our profession, but for someone whose
only experience of the military was as a junior member of the School
Cadet Force, nothing can adequately prepare you to be an eye witness
to the bombing, shelling and killing of your fellow human beings or to
the systematic destruction of cities, towns and refugee camps.

The 1982 Lebanon War was a brutal and bloody conflict in which
tens of thousands were killed or maimed, the majority of them civilians.

The catalyst for the invasion was an attempt to assassinate Israel's
Ambassador to Britain outside the Dorchester Hotel in London's Park
Lane. As he was getting into his car, Shlomo Argov was shot in the
head and critically wounded. The Israeli intelligence services concluded
that the dissident Palestinian group led by Abu Nidal had been responsible,
but their government decided to strike back at the mainstream Palestine
Liberation Organisation. The Israeli Defence Forces bombed PLO bases
and ammunition dumps in Beirut and the PLO responded with an
artillery and rocket attack into Northern Israel.

On 6 June the Israelis under the direction of Defence Minister Ariel
Sharon invaded southern Lebanon with overwhelming force which during
the months of conflict would rise to 76,000 troops, 800 tanks, 1,500
armoured personnel carriers and over 600 fighter planes. Whatever was
being said publicly, it was obvious that the Israelis could not have devised
and executed an invasion on this scale within 48 hours.

The PLO had been based in Beirut since 1971 after their expulsion
from Jordan and had effectively created 'a state within a state'. By the
late 1970s the number of Palestinians in Lebanon numbered over 300,000
and the PLO had virtually taken over half the country at gunpoint. For
a number of years Israel's northern border had been protected by a
militia run by a renegade Lebanese Christian Army major called Saad
Haddad. Between this border zone and the PLO-dominated Lebanese
territory was a 6,500 strong multi-national United Nations force. The
Israeli columns simply swept past them with impunity.

Television crews could not move so easily and the numbers allowed
across the border were kept to strict limits. Every car had to have an
escort officer aboard and there were never sufficient to meet the demand.
To ensure we didn't lose out, I insisted that my BBC colleagues were

up and on the road north from Tel Aviv at the unearthly hour of 3 am each day to reach the rendezvous point at the border well ahead of the other crews who were all jostling for a permit.

The roads were clogged with tanks, burnt-out vehicles and civilians desperately trying to flee the bombardment. The announced intention had been to advance no more than 25 miles to secure a buffer zone, but it was clear that the Israelis were intent on neutralising the PLO's military capability once and for all as they pushed on relentlessly towards the capital, Beirut.

We headed for Tyre, once one of the great Phoenician cities of Biblical times and more recently a fashionable Mediterranean port. It was unrecognisable, having experienced the full horrors of war. Resistance here had been tenacious. In the sprawling refugee camp on the approach to the city, house to house and hand to hand combat had inflicted a huge number of casualties. Then the heavy armour moved in and the place was reduced to rubble. One officer of the UN peacekeeping force watching from a distance said it had been like shooting sparrows with a cannon.

As we drove further into the city, we passed bewildered refugees wandering in shock, each face expressing the terror they had experienced. The sickening stench of decomposing bodies filled the air. As the tanks blasted their shells into the buildings from the ground, Israeli fighters had bombed and strafed the port from the skies. For most of the 80,000 people who lived there, there had been barely enough time to get to safety. Some had been herded on to the beach from where they could only watch the destruction of what remained.

What consolation can you offer to a mother pleading for help in digging for her children buried somewhere in the rubble? What words of comfort can you express to another watching her baby dying of shrapnel wounds in a hospital unable to cope with the sheer chaos of so many innocent civilians caught up in the fighting ... or a father who has lost both his wife and newborn baby when a maternity clinic takes a direct hit? No matter whose war it is or how strong your faith, the scars will last for ever.

Near the harbour, where boats had turned turtle, hundreds of people were lined up by the roadside. They were being asked to register with the new civilian administration set up by the Israeli Army. Of those who had registered so far, one in ten was being held for questioning. Many had spent four days in shelters without food, 50 or more of them confined in a space just two metres square.

Despite the human cost, the spirit of resilience amongst many of the Lebanese was quite remarkable. One whose hairdressing salon was reduced to a pile of stones, had somehow managed to stick all the pieces of his barber's chair back together again and was busily shaving a client in the midst of the debris. Another group, seemingly oblivious to the devastation all around them, were engaged in a game of poker. It all seemed totally bizarre.

Further up the coast, Lebanon's third city Sidon had also been badly hit. When the Israelis advanced on the city, residents said Palestinian fighters had taken their guns and placed them next to apartment blocks, hospitals and schools. The result was slaughter on a huge scale. In the large refugee camp of Ain-al-Hilweh, Palestinian militia groups fought to the last man. To break the resistance, artillery barrages and air strikes exerted a heavy toll.

Everywhere, we encountered confusion – families pushing carts flying white flags around the rubble-strewn streets, others still trying to maintain the semblance of domestic life, hanging out their washing on balconies that seemed on the point of collapse. Nearby, bulldozers were preparing a mass grave for many of the civilian dead.

'What did we do to deserve this?' was a question being repeated time and again. 'We didn't want the Palestinian gunners here and we don't want the Israelis either.'

One hospital had been untouched in the bombardment but the medical director seemed as traumatised as most of the patients he was treating. Just an hour before, a local PLO commander had burst into his office and placed a horribly injured fighter on the floor, blood from a gaping wound streaming across the laurel green carpet.

'I'll be back tomorrow to pick him up,' was his parting shot.

Our battle was against the clock. Each day, my camera colleague Bill Hanford and I had to cross the border back into Israel where the BBC crew had set up headquarters in the Sheraton Hotel in Tel Aviv. There, a middle-ranking officer of the Israeli Army arrived to censor the edited film before its transmission to London. At first, cuts were limited to demonstrably military and strategic matters but as the world began to see the scale of the destruction being wreaked in Lebanon, the orders to omit certain images began to broaden on the grounds that they constituted propaganda for Israel's primary adversary, the PLO.

With Beirut's satellite transmission station put out of operation, filmed reports from the Palestinian quarter would now have to travel along the dangerous highway to the Syrian capital, Damascus.

Syria, drawn into the conflict, had put up fierce resistance on the ground but lost 86 planes and nearly all its anti-aircraft batteries in the Beka Valley. After agreeing a ceasefire with the Syrians, Israel turned its attention on the PLO forces trapped in Beirut.

The siege of the city, maintained by a relentless barrage of air, naval and artillery bombardment, continued for 70 days. As the PLO leader, Yasser Arafat threatened to turn the Lebanese capital into a 'second Stalingrad', from the hills above the city I watched the daily battering of Beirut which for those exposed to the ferocity of the big guns had reached new heights of savagery, their shells and mortars pummelling buildings, tearing humans to pieces and delivering tragedy to those who survived.

Suddenly thoughts about the recipients of all this massive firepower were temporarily forgotten as retaliatory rockets screeched frighteningly overhead. As panic sets in, thoughts turn inward to keeping life and limb together. The rockets fired from Palestinian truck-mounted multiple launchers were known to be imprecise in reaching their target, not that such knowledge does anything to suppress personal fear. Like a bolt of lightning, one of these deadly pieces of flying explosive can hit anyone, anywhere.

A Lebanese man, clasping the hands of two toddlers, arrived at the top of the hill and signalled that we should follow him. Reaching a building still under construction, we descended two flights of stairs to reach an underground car park which had become home for three of his daughters hit by shrapnel from an exploding shell. A flickering candle provided the only light. The man had done his best to dress their wounds but one had turned septic. He was desperate to get hold of a doctor but felt his family's best chance of survival was to stay put.

Apart from the 6,000 PLO guerrillas holed up in the city, there were also half a million Lebanese and Palestinian civilians and the deaths were mounting steeply each day. Moving around West Beirut was fraught with danger. The Israelis frequently cut off food and water supplies and disconnected the electricity. Hospitals, starved of equipment, were unable to carry out emergency operations. When one of my BBC colleagues, cameraman Don Leggett, was hit by shrapnel in both legs I promised with the help of the military to do everything possible to facilitate his evacuation from the besieged city.

Along with his recordist, Don Nesbitt, Leggett had arrived in Beirut after boarding a cargo ship in Cyprus. The boat was so filthy that the pair of them bedded down for the night in one of the ship's lifeboats stationed under a heavy metal flap. When they woke up in the middle of the Mediterranean, they found the boat had been boarded by the crew of an Israeli gunboat with armed officers standing menacingly over them and demanding to see their identification.

From their base in Beirut's Commodore Hotel, the two Dons captured the images of life and death that pervaded the city. Television become an emotive source of daily reporting and journalists and film crews were able to move back and forth across the checkpoints along the Green Line that divided the Moslem and Christian areas, giving them an opportunity to verify the claims of both sides engaged in the fighting. That's until the passes issued by the civil authorities and, more importantly, the embattled militias, had run their course and required instant renewal. It was then that the two Dons found their normal, and safest, route across the divide and back into West Beirut cut off by Israeli armour. Approaching the crossing point, the taxi driver was flagged to a halt. There was no room for argument.

'You can't go any further. If *we* don't shoot you, the chances are the *Palestinians* will.'

The only alternative route was across open ground and then via the port. Every hundred yards, the car was stopped by first the militia of the Christian Phalange and then their Palestinians enemies. Eventually, they reached a tiny office where the PLO promptly stamped the passes just as the building was rocked by the force of a nearby explosion.

A block of pensioners' flats had taken a direct hit from an Israeli shell and was ablaze. As Don reached for his camera, another shell smashed into the building and shrapnel flew in all directions, punching holes in the taxi and piercing Leggett's right knee-cap and both his legs. Taken to the American University Hospital, he found the place in chaos. There were no bandages; in the next bed a PLO fighter had shrapnel embedded in his back and the operating theatre was covered in blood. Don was given two pain-killing jabs and sent back to the hotel.

The following morning, a Canadian television operative brought him to an Israeli army position on the outskirts of the city. I eased him gently into the back seat of the car but, since he was over 6ft tall, it proved impossible to keep him lying on his back as I set off on the long and arduous journey back to Tel Aviv – complete with a military escort – snaking our way past columns of tanks, armoured vehicles and dangerously overcrowded vehicles jam-packed with people fleeing the ravaged capital.

Don was relieved to have reached the safety of a private clinic but not so enamoured with the strict discipline wielded by its matron, a Russian Jew, more especially after he had complained of being under renewed attack from airborne pests – this time a swarm of flying ants! In the event, a surgeon removed some flesh but found it too dangerous to extract the shrapnel. Given that now well into his eighties, he still plays a mean round of golf, those embedded relics of the Lebanon War don't appear to have dented the lifestyle of one of the BBC's most sprightly pensioners.

By the beginning of August, time was running out for the PLO. Israel's bombardment was becoming more widespread, threatening to level whole areas of West Beirut. Diplomatically, the PLO had become isolated and the Reagan administration in America was pressing hard for an end to the bombing and shelling. Taking advantage of international guarantees of safe passage brokered by the United States and European governments, Yasser Arafat and the PLO withdrew. Guarded by a multinational force, they left Beirut, guns blazing in the air in defiance, and set sail for exile in Tunis.

If the Arab world felt a sense of humiliation and shame in their failure to live up to their long years of pro-Palestinian rhetoric then the welcome they prepared for Arafat at the following month's summit in the Moroccan city of Fez was a potent illustration of their desire to somehow make amends.

With cameraman Mike Viney, recordist Steve Morris and film editor Norman Lowes, I arrived in Tangier at the start of a 170-mile drive to the ancient town of Meknes. It was a nightmarish journey with blinding rain making visibility difficult in the extreme punctuated every few miles by a red light appearing out of the gloom as police on high alert imposed one road block after another. Pull up too late and a block of solid metal spikes was waiting to rip through the tyres.

Security had become such a delicate issue that advisors of Morocco's ruler, King Hassan, determined that the huge press and television contingent should be billeted in hotels 30 miles from the summit venue – the Royal Palace. They also banned the media from using private transport to and from the conference. Ignoring the rule would result in being despatched post-haste on the first plane home, and so each morning a long line of buses formed at our hotel entrance, the engines idling for an hour or more, as officials awaited instructions as to when, and to where, we should set off.

There was but one notable exception to this ludicrous state of affairs and it happened on the first day. Breakfast had to be abandoned as with indecent haste we were ushered on to the first of the coaches, the driver under orders to head directly to the airport. Yasser Arafat's plane was apparently already in Moroccan airspace and a welcome eclipsing that accorded to the kings and presidents had been prepared for him. What's more, the Arabs wanted the red-carpet treatment afforded to the PLO leader to be seen across the world.

This was all very well, but our bus was of an ancient vintage and clearly unfit for purpose. It was a lurching, coughing beast that failed to pick up speed regardless of the valiant efforts of its driver. We had led the convoy on departure, but one by one the others coaches passed us by. Sweating profusely and fearing the consequences of failing to get us there in time, the government officer assigned to our party broke into a frenzy of activity. First, he ordered the driver to move up a gear but to no avail. The engine's constant splutter simply increased accordingly. Next, there he was, stretched out on the floor, pinning the poor driver's foot to the accelerator pedal.

By now, the police motorcycle outriders were speeding up the road in their own race to reach the airport in time to provide Arafat with an escort into the city. A rackety old bus weaving in and out of the traffic was one obstacle too many and the riders were signalling frantically for us to move out of the way and let them through.

On board, a shouting match ensued as the man from the government refused to allow the driver to apply the brakes. The police decided on a two-pronged attack sending two riders down each side of the bus, sirens blaring. Glancing out the window, we watched in almost total disbelief as one of the bikes was hit a glancing blow despatching its police rider in a somersault on to the grass verge.

Still we pressed on, circumventing a road block by veering off the highway and bouncing along a forest track before at last the airport came into view. Grabbing camera and tripod, we raced into the terminal building only to find the glass door to the VIP lounge firmly locked against us and airport security unable to find the key.

No cause for panic.

'Mr Arafat's plane has been delayed,' a member of the King's entourage whispered politely. 'Time for coffee and then we'll escort you on to the tarmac. I hope you had a pleasant journey.'

Least said the better.

Though communiqués were issued on a daily basis, filming of the summit was restricted to two minutes on Days 2 and 3 in which 50 cameramen became involved in an unseemly scramble to place their lenses over a couple of layers of bullet-proof glass on the second floor of the splendidly adorned Royal Palace to grab a few shots of the Arab leaders seated in the Moorish splendour of the marble hall below.

I thought it impossible there could be any more incongruous twists to the week's events. Not so. On the fourth day, our antediluvian bus, now replaced by a slightly more reliable model, set off for an unspecified destination. As a child, nothing provided more excitement than accompanying my parents on one of the local coach company's mystery tours but it's not the sort of indulgence expected from reporters sent at great expense by 'Auntie' to cover events of huge international significance. An exasperated assistant on the Foreign News Desk in London wanted to know my movements for the day and what the likely ingredients would be in my film package for the *Nine o'clock News*. Like the rest of us, he still hadn't got his head round the workings of the Moroccan Government Information Service.

Even the bus driver was sworn to secrecy ... spilling the beans would cost him his job and put national security at risk. Crews of two of the big American television news networks expressed their annoyance but the press officer wouldn't budge an inch, promising only that 'today's event will make good television.'

Oh, maybe we'll actually be able to talk to some of the kings and presidents as they take a stroll in the Palace gardens, we thought, or perhaps Libya's Colonel Gaddafi, who had announced he was boycotting the summit, had suddenly changed his mind and, heaven forbid, we were off to the airport again.

No, this was much more interesting, the bus trundling past farms and olive groves, fruit trees and majestic forests of oak and cedar; and then starting to climb ever more steeply round a series of hairpin bends leading to the Atlas Mountains. As the sun beat down from a cloudless blue sky, the ascent continued to over 5,000 feet towards the winter ski resort of Ifrane. At the summit of the road, we spotted the entrance to an airstrip and driving through the gate, were greeted by a hundred Moroccan tribesmen mounted on horseback and forming a line along the edge of the runway.

No sooner had we set up the camera than a military truck appeared in full view. Its payload – up to 20 leaders of the Arab world standing cheek by jowl and including the Kings of Saudi Arabia, Jordan and Morocco, Presidents Saddam Hussein of Iraq and Hafez Assad of Syria and the PLO's Yasser Arafat. Incredible that after the steel ring of security that had been placed around them all week, they should now be driven out in the open past the mounted tribesmen shooting off their rifles at full gallop!

As the summit drew to a close, no specific mention was made in the Fez agreement of Arab recognition of Israel. The call was for the establishment of an independent Palestinian state with Jerusalem as its capital and with the PLO to play the leading role in negotiations.

At a Press Conference transmitted live on Moroccan television, I was invited to address a question on the outcome to King Hassan. Speaking in French, he had just started to respond when I noticed two of his aides glaring disapprovingly at me from behind the royal table. One of them was writing furiously on a piece of paper. He handed the scribbled note to a journalist in the front row and ordered him to have it passed back to me *sans plus tarder.*

'Coming from the UK, you should know better. In future, you will address the King as His Majesty, not His Royal Highness'.

Arriving at Casablanca Airport, the supervisor at the check-in desk recognised me at once. She had been watching the conference on television and had been equally upset by my behaviour viewed as the ultimate indiscretion. Red-faced, I apologised and asked her for the boarding card – 'please get me out of here!'

Just three days after the summit, Lebanon's new President, the Christian Maronite leader and Israel ally, Bashir Gemayel, was assassinated. A Syrian agent was suspected to have been behind the killing. Thirsting for revenge, Phalangist militias entered the Palestinian refugee camps of Sabra and Shatila to 'mop up' PLO fighters still remaining there. Once inside, they carried out a massacre of Palestinian civilians, including women and children.

The Israelis manned the gates to the camps and did nothing to stop the slaughter, at one point even providing illumination for the Phalangists. Such butchery shocked many ordinary Israelis and thousands took to the streets of Tel Aviv to protest, demanding answers from their government.

A Commission of Inquiry was set up and found that Ariel Sharon bore 'personal responsibility' for failing to prevent the massacre. He resigned as Defence Minister but later became Prime Minister of Israel.

With the PLO out of Lebanon, a new foe emerged from the hornet's nest stirred by the Israeli invasion: Hezbollah, the 'Party of God', a radical Islamic Shi'ite movement inspired by the Iranian revolution.

There would be no peace in the Land of the Cedars.

14

The Home Beat

If you want total security, go to prison. There you're fed, clothed and given medical care. The only thing lacking is freedom.'

Dwight D. Eisenhower

Webster's toy shop in Dundee opened a world of wonder for children, its window display and two cramped floors a veritable showcase for feasting your eyes on the marvels of Meccano, Hornby and Dinky. Not considered old enough at six to earn pocket money, if I'd behaved myself for a few days or done something good, mum might even open her purse to allow me to make an addition to my prized collection.

Despite the encouragement offered by my parents, I was a rather timid and impressionable child and easily upset by anything that deviated from the norm. Grasping my mother's hand as we turned into Whitehall Crescent, the magic of the toy shop had temporarily disappeared, its doorway blocked by a Black Maria. A policeman was leading a young lad out of the shop and into the van, slamming the doors shut behind him.

'That's what happens if you're caught stealing,' my mum said, the tone of her voice indicating just how grave a situation we were witnessing. 'The police take you away and put you in prison.'

The image and the warning remained embedded in my mind. I used to conjure up pictures of what it must be like to be locked away for years on end unable to attend birthday parties, the school dance or cheer on your favourite football team from the terraces.

In the late 1960s I did make a brief visit to Durham Jail with the Salvation Army band from Shiremoor. We had been invited to perform for the prisoners at a Sunday afternoon praise festival which earned our two attractive lady horn players a few appreciative wolf whistles. In television news terms though, prisons were a virtual no-go area. All that would change in the first years of the Thatcher government. The number of people being sent to jail by the courts was spiralling at such a rate that the prisons couldn't cope. 45,000 prisoners were crammed into buildings designed to hold just 37,000 and, to make matters worse, there had been no serious prison building programme since Victorian times. Some were literally falling to bits. Wings had been closed forcing more and more prisoners to sleep three to a cell. Others were being housed in store rooms, police cells and old army camps.

Clearly, something drastic had to be done. Home Secretary Willie Whitelaw was given the go-ahead to order the construction of half a dozen new jails, but his razor-sharp political sense told him that spending taxpayers' money on housing criminals would not be the most popular of policies. There was only one answer – let the television cameras in to show the dreadful state of Britain's jails and maybe the viewer would appreciate why so many millions would have to be spent.

By now I had been appointed the BBC's Home Affairs Correspondent and prisons were right at the top of my agenda. Over the next five years I would visit dozens of jails and youth custody centres across the country and, counting all the hours involved in filming, probably spent more time inside than many of the short-term inmates though I never experienced that dreadful feeling of being 'banged up' for 23 hours a day or having to endure that single most degrading element of imprisonment – slopping out.

It took until the spring of 1996 before the practice was finally abolished. Watching the long queues of men shuffling along the corridors to empty their plastic pots of the night's waste in the sluice rooms would fill anyone with disgust. The stench was so appalling that many prisoners lobbed their parcels of excrement out of the cell windows. Armley Jail in Leeds was the last to install integral sanitation. The irony of that was not lost on prison reform groups. For like most of the other Victorian prisons it had actually been built complete with sanitation systems, only to have them ripped out at the turn of the twentieth century to make room for more cells and to toughen up life for inmates.

During the 1980s the Prison Officers' Association proved itself to be a tough and robust organisation, filling a vacuum caused by bad management, but seen by many as operating jails for the benefit of its own members rather than for taxpayers or the general good of the prison system. Some in government considered the union as the last dinosaur, especially following the defeats of the print unions and the miners.

Prison governors were working under immense pressure imposed by overcrowding and staff shortages which added to their industrial relations' responsibilities and the ever-increasing interest of people on the outside about what went on in their prisons. They were an interesting bunch varying from the Old Etonian and mildly eccentric to the authoritarian, but all charged with keeping a grip on the repositories of the nation's social problems.

Drugs, gangs, a high rate of suicides, too little education and mental-health issues combined to exacerbate the situation leading to a general perception that prisons neither rehabilitate nor deter.

The growing number of young offenders was a particular thorn in the flesh of the government, and so Willie Whitelaw introduced his *short, sharp, shock* regime. The idea was that car thieves, joyriders, young burglars and football hooligans would be subjected to military-type discipline – up at dawn, head count, early morning drill parades, uniforms, working the looms to produce bed rugs for the prison service, circuit training in the gym, no respite till lights out at 21.30. Orders shouted by officers most of whom were ex-military.

A shock to the system? Well, our filming certainly suggested such until we slid a microphone under the miscreants. They explained that the bullets of sweat were much preferable to being locked up in some crumbling, vermin-infested institution. The quasi-military approach received high public ratings but did little or nothing to stem the burgeoning crime rate or the levels of re-offending.

In his determination to discover the problems at first hand, the Home Secretary made frequent visits to prisons to test the temperature. He also liked to see what useful work prisoners were engaged in and offered words of encouragement.

A story he told against himself came out of a visit to an arts and crafts class at one jail where he chatted to one prisoner after another, asking each the same question: 'Hello, what are you doing?'

'Basket weaving, sir,' said one. 'Making matchstick models, sir,' said another.

'Well done, carry on,' he replied to them in turn.

By the time he came to the last in the line, his concentration had clearly wandered.

'Hello, and what are you doing?' he asked again.

'Twenty-five years for murdering my wife.'

'Well done, carry on!'

Only once did I see Willie Whitelaw visibly shaken. Ashen-faced he arrived in Liverpool to tour the smoking ruins of Toxteth where an orgy of violence, looting, burning and destruction had marked the third serious inner city riots of 1981. By then Lord Scarman had already begun his inquiry into an earlier weekend of rioting at Brixton. Inner city decay, high unemployment – particularly among blacks – and heavy-handed policing of ethnic minorities were seen as contributing factors.

In Brixton the disorder was triggered partly by Operation Swamp in which the police flooded particular areas with officers exercising their powers of stop and search in an effort to reduce the very high levels of street crime. This led in turn to accusations that the police were racist in their dealings with young blacks.

When the disturbances began, the police found they hadn't got the equipment to deal with the rioters. Their helmets were inadequate, the shields were unwieldy, too heavy and not fireproof. There were difficulties in radio communication as they came under a hail of brick and concrete. Molotov cocktails were thrown, petrol bombs set fire to two pubs and 26 businesses and hundreds of local residents were trapped in their homes. It was nearly midnight before the police managed to disperse the rioters and seize control of the streets.

As summer arrived so the temperature in the inner cities was beginning to build. One Friday evening, 40 policemen were injured when a street in the West London suburb of Southall was turned into a battlefield as local Asian youths clashed with a group of skinheads outside a pub that was subsequently petrol bombed. No sooner had we ended filming for the night, relieved that our camera had remained intact, when we were despatched to Liverpool. There had been trouble in Toxteth on two successive nights and there were fears that the situation might explode on the Sunday evening.

I suggested to the camera crew that we drive slowly through the area to try to establish any signs of problems ahead. It was then we spotted a group of youngsters wearing balaclavas running out of an off-licence they had raided. They were fuelling their aggression with the contents of the bottles, ready to turn the empties into petrol bombs. Turning to cameraman Gerry Goad, I said, 'Let's go quickly and have something to eat. It may be our last chance for a couple of days.'

We returned to Upper Parliament Street just in the nick of time. Five minutes later and the worst violence seen in a British city outside war time had begun. Masked youths hijacked several milk floats and drove them straight at the police lines. They also set fire to several three-storey buildings which were soon blazing out of control. Within an hour half a dozen shops and businesses had been completely destroyed and police suffering a constant bombardment of bricks, paving stones and petrol bombs found their casualties mounting every time they charged. Ambulances were carrying off the injured, sometimes as many as ten to a vehicle.

Reinforcements had to be called from Lancashire, Greater Manchester and Cheshire, but time and again they were forced to retreat. The situation was so dangerous that the Fire Brigade had to stay clear. Famous landmarks like the former Rialto dance hall were simply burnt to the ground. Liverpool Racquet Club, a bank and a furniture store went the same way. With the fires threatening to engulf a geriatric hospital, a local vicar pleaded with the rioters to allow ambulances in to evacuate the 96 patients. Some were in wheelchairs whilst others had to be carried to safety. No sooner had the rescue mission been completed than the rioters went in to rifle the patients' lockers.

As our film was uplifted at hourly intervals by despatch rider, I was sending updated reports to Television Centre by telephone – a complicated business given that every public phone had been vandalised and people desperately trying to protect their lives and property were in no mood to open their doors to a stranger. I eventually persuaded a dear old lady of 90 to let me use her phone.

'What on earth is going on out there?' she asked, 'are we at war again?'

Her terraced home overlooked a supermarket. Emerging into the open again, I looked across in utter disbelief as a line of Mercedes and BMWs, obviously from more affluent areas of the city, were sitting – boots open – ready to be loaded by their owners who were staggering out of the shop under the weight of their booty including huge cuts of meat straight from the freezer.

Trying to relocate my crew who had moved on to film the next stage of the battle, I stumbled into Lodge Lane. There wasn't a policeman in sight and looters were having a field day. Children were running back and forward with shopping trolleys full of groceries. Almost every shop had been smashed and huge quantities of merchandise stolen. Things had run totally out of control.

Then, at 2.15 am, the Chief Constable of Merseyside Kenneth Oxford, ordered CS gas to be fired for the first time in mainland Britain. It meant after six hours of fighting, the police were able to push the rioters back.

Police injuries ran into hundreds. No-one was able to put a figure on the number of rioters hurt. The miracle was that no-one was killed. It was almost impossible to comprehend that the events we had witnessed that dreadful night had actually taken place in Britain. It was urban savagery of the highest order.

Racial disadvantage, unemployment and poverty would later be cited as underlying causes of the Brixton riots by Lord Scarman but he rejected the claim of 'institutional racism' within the police. In the meantime, the Government rushed through a series of emergency measures and ensured that in future the police would have better protected headgear and fire resistant clothing. Margaret Thatcher despatched Michael Heseltine north to sort out Liverpool's troubles. He created two new regeneration agencies bringing the public and private sectors together and is credited with spearheading the scheme to save the city's Albert Dock.

The Home Affairs portfolio ensured visits to the Theatre Royal of crime, the famous No. 1 court of the Old Bailey. Here justice had been handed down to among others Dr Crippen, Lord Haw Haw, the Kray Brothers and the Yorkshire Ripper. In October 1983 the man who ascended the stairs to the dock was a very ordinary looking, bespectacled Scot who was about to stand trial for a series of ghastly killings that shocked even those with the most morbid fascination with murder.

Eight months before, I had received a tip-off that police were guarding a house at 23 Cranley Gardens in the Muswell Hill district of north London. Snow was falling as I arrived and there was a definite chill in the air. The owner of the upstairs flat, Dennis Nilsen, an executive officer at the Job Centre in Kentish Town, had been arrested on his return from work on suspicion of murder.

The previous day, his neighbours downstairs had complained of an obnoxious smell from the outside drain and called in the specialists. On lifting the manhole cover, plumber Mike Cattran found pieces of decaying flesh and suspected that human remains had been flushed into the drain.

He was right and despite Nilsen's overnight efforts to remove the evidence, his five-year secret was finally out. Finding the police on his doorstep, Nilsen queried why they should be interested in his drains.

'Don't mess about,' he was told, 'now where's the rest of the body?'

Nilsen calmly asked them to open the wardrobe where they would find two black plastic bags. Still ruminating on the grisly find on the way to the police station, Detective Chief Inspector Peter Jay, turned to his back-seat passenger.

'How many bodies are we talking about – one or two?'

'15 or 16,' came the answer.

No-one in twentieth-century Britain had confessed to so many individual killings.

It's been said that people's fascination with murders and murderers stems from a healthy fear of the dark side of human nature which lurks inside us all. This was a story that was going to run and run.

Detectives found the remains of three victims inside No.23, but Nilsen still had much more to tell them. Next day, we arrived at his first home at Melrose Avenue in Cricklewood to film search teams equipped with spades, sieves and rakes, turning over the garden looking for evidence of at least 12 more bodies. The garden was screened with plastic sheeting, the ground divided into neat sections and the painstaking task of sifting the soil went on for a week. Nilsen told the police he had burnt the remains in a series of bonfires. A number of bones were found and removed to the forensic laboratories.

Stories don't come any more gruesome than this but I have to admit I was gripped by the unfolding drama. It was a murder investigation in reverse. Police had the killer but didn't know the identity of most of his victims. That's because almost all were students or homeless men whom he picked up in bars and brought them to his house for a meal, for sex or just for company.

What seemed to me to be incredible was that, for nearly five years, this industrious civil servant was able to hide bodies under the floorboards of his flat, later dismember them and boil their heads in a cooking pot, go to work as though nothing extraordinary had happened, earn promotion and pursue his union activities. Not a single workmate, not one neighbour suspected anything was amiss. Perhaps that said something about his earlier training as a soldier and a policeman.

In the end the police had to rely on Nilsen's power of recall to piece together the names of some of those he killed. Only one of them was listed amongst 8,000 names in the files of the Missing Persons Bureau at Scotland Yard, which shows just how easy it is for someone to simply disappear in London without trace. A reward of £1,000 had been offered by the parents of Kenneth Ockendon. Nilsen remembered his picture in the papers and also remembered the day he had taken the Canadian tourist sightseeing, had dinner with him and then strangled him.

During his time on remand in Brixton Prison, Nilsen started disclosing his innermost feelings about his crimes and his life by writing almost daily to the only man he came to trust, historian and author, Brian Masters. Nilsen agreed I should be given sight of those letters. In them, he expressed his deep remorse, acknowledging that his sins were of enormous proportions and wondering how he could ever make amends.

'I think I am two stark, contrasting poles of man's character. I have played the angel's role unimpeachably, balanced disastrously by momentary and uncontrollable outbursts of primitive evil.'

Two sides to a killer. I was keen to explore further. Time to meet up with Carl Stotter, a drag queen who miraculously survived Nilsen's attempts to kill him. Still shaking with fear as he recalled his time in the Melrose Avenue flat, Stotter told me how Nilsen tried first to strangle him in a sleeping bag and then drown him in the bath. He was pushed under the water four times and believed he was going to die. After passing out for some time, he woke up in bed. Later, looking in the toilet mirror, he saw his tongue was swollen, face bloated and there were red blotches where blood vessels had burst. By then, the other side of Nilsen had taken over. He spent hours rescuing his young visitor, walked with him to the station and suggested he head for the surgery.

In hospital, a doctor enquired what had happened to him. Still fearing for his life, Stotter told them: 'I think I got caught up in a sleeping bag.'

'Come off it,' the doctor replied. 'It looks as though someone was trying to strangle you.'

Nilsen was visited twice by police but, with many of his acquaintances homosexuals, the complaints were dismissed as domestic fights. His luck and survival instincts never seemed to run out.

My next port of call was the family home in rural Aberdeenshire where to my utter surprise, his mother invited me inside. A kindly and deeply religious woman, she wiped away the tears as she explained how she had tried in vain to reason how the Dennis she knew as a gentle schoolboy could turn into a mass killer. By the end of the interview I felt a real sense of sorrow welling deep within. How could any mother come to terms with the enormity of what had happened? I thanked her and prepared to take my leave.

Her tearful face gave way to a kind and gentle smile.

'Nobody leaves my house without a cup of tea and I'm sure you'd like a piece of my shortbread.'

In Court No1 the jury found Nilsen guilty of six counts of murder and two of attempted murder. He was sentenced to life imprisonment without eligibility for parole for at least 25 years. It's thought unlikely that he will ever be released. Of the other nine killings to which he confessed, seven victims remain unidentified.

Right to the end of his trial, Dennis Nilsen remained an enigma. He actually wrote of his own future and was happy for me to broadcast his thoughts.

'The state will wish that I live on and I must make the best possible use of all the time allowed. I have really no idea of what society wants of me. My trial will be a judgement on them. My judgement is long over. I have judged myself more harshly than any court ever could.'

By the late 1980s the prison building programme simply couldn't keep up with the ever-increasing numbers being sent to jail. The situation was so bad that the Governor of Wormwood Scrubs found his patience had finally been exhausted and angrily wrote to *The Times* describing his job as 'the manager of a large penal dustbin' and insisting that he didn't join the prison service to oversee 'overcrowded cattle pens'.

The Thatcher government was now being forced to consider new ideas such as electronic tagging and prisons built and run by the private sector. In America the state of Tennessee had been pioneering this new approach having begun a crusade to implement mandatory minimum sentences to fight the war against drugs. Predictably, this led to tremendous overcrowding and by 1985 the situation reached crisis point with rioting and several deaths. With at least 7,000 new prison beds required and faced with a bill of $380 million to build six new jails, they turned to the private sector to operate and manage them, allowing profits to be drawn out of more efficient use of the state's operating budget.

The Corrections Corporation of America invited us to film their new high-tech prison near Chattanooga and a youth custody centre at Memphis but we were also keen to compare the daily routine with a look at life in the time-worn State Penitentiary in Nashville.

On Death Row, inside the stark, dimly lit cages, 48 men were all awaiting execution. Right next door to the room containing the Electric Chair, there was a 49th prisoner, the only one to be spared the death sentence and someone I was eager to meet. James Earl Ray was the man who assassinated America's most revered civil rights leader, Martin Luther King. For pleading guilty to the killing, he was sentenced to 99 years in jail. Yet within days he recanted his confession and now 20 years later was trying to secure the trial he never had.

At first, Ray was reluctant to speak but then agreed to be interviewed. A prison guard marched him along the corridor in chains until he reached a wall-sized iron bar gate leading into a large room furnished only with a table and two chairs. Ray was then unshackled and along with the film crew and producer Marcus Davidson, I was invited to join him. The guard turned the key in the lock, rattled the gate to ensure it was firmly shut and disappeared from sight.

Ray spoke of his misfortune to have been in the wrong place at the wrong time. He had been on the run from prison in April 1968 when Martin Luther King was shot and killed whilst standing on the second-floor balcony of the Lorraine Motel in Memphis. That same day, Ray had checked into a boarding house directly across the street from the motel. The shot that killed King travelled 205 feet and tore into the side of his face. Police immediately sealed off the area but the gunman had escaped leaving behind a high powered rifle. The authorities said that the fingerprints on the weapon belonged to Ray.

Two months later he suddenly turned up at Heathrow Airport. Travelling under a false name, he was arrested and sent back to Tennessee. There, the swift disposal of the case in just three hours intensified speculation that he may not have acted alone.

I put it to Ray that despite all the talk of a conspiracy, no-one had been able to produce any concrete evidence. He said a Congressional Committee had suggested the likelihood of one but that official government records regarding the assassination were to remain sealed until the year 2027. His last hope, he said, was for another country to ask for his extradition and give him the trial which America refused. So where did he have in mind? 'The Soviet Union or Iran.'

Three hundred miles away at the Martin Luther King Centre in Atlanta, I found Dr King's eldest son equally frustrated by the decision to lock away all government intelligence documents relating to his father for 50 years.

Martin Luther King III did not rule out the possibility of Ray's innocence.

'If he had anything to do with it, then I don't believe he acted alone. That's why if I was to start hating, how many people would I have to hate? I hope one day the truth will come out.'

That's what the convicted assassin was hoping for too. Ray could no longer mix with other prisoners. In one recent attack, he had been stabbed 28 times.

Before departing, I asked him whether he felt he would survive for long if he ever got out.

'Everyone else does,' he replied 'though I'd want to go to a foreign country if I could get someone to accept me ... maybe Ireland. Most of my ancestors came from there.'

His wish was granted but only in death. James Earl Ray was denied his day in court and succumbed to liver failure at the age of 70. He was cremated and his ashes flown to the Emerald Isle.

Whatever the suspicions of the world and those at the King Centre in particular over who may have planned the assassination at Memphis, it appears that a violent death was never very far from Martin Luther King's mind. An archivist produced a handwritten note of a quotation from Dr King's mentor Mahatma Gandhi which he always carried in his pocket – the first time, I was told, anyone had been allowed to see it.

'We're today in the midst of death and darkness,' it read. 'We can strengthen light and life by our personal acts, saying no to violence and yes to life.'

In the 1980s the personal acts of a growing number of young Britons included the taking of drugs. Heroin once arriving in the country from China and South-East Asia was now being smuggled into Britain in ever-growing amounts from Afghanistan and the lawless North-West Frontier Province of Pakistan. The use of drugs was being fuelled by falling prices and the emergence of a youth culture. Brown heroin was very addictive, with users suffering from severe withdrawal symptoms if they were unable to obtain their next fix. This in turn led to an increase in domestic burglaries and street muggings as addicts became more and more desperate to feed their habit.

The war on drugs intensified with a huge increase in the amount of cocaine reaching Europe from Colombia and other parts of South America. Coca had long since been grown in the Andes to satisfy the demand of several million coca-leaf chewers but now large-scale criminal cartels began to move in, processing and exporting cocaine to the new overseas markets.

Spain with its common language was the major transit point with gangs in situ ready to ship supplies to the rest of Europe. In one three-year period the use of cocaine in Britain increased five-fold but police were already suggesting that this was just the start of an explosion.

At £80 a gramme – five times the price of gold – coke was for years the elite of drugs, restricted to the easy money world of film and pop stars. But now, it was finding a ready market amongst Britain's jet setters.

With British criminals living in Spain and setting up trafficking deals across the Channel, the American Attaché in Madrid was adamant that the UK had to take more serious action before it was too late.

At Madrid Airport, I watched the Spanish authorities spring into action. Good intelligence had led to some spectacular successes. As we filmed checks on a flight from Bogota, undercover men were concentrating on a second plane from Buenos Aires. Within minutes a young Argentinian was under arrest. The police paraded him, shaking with fear, in front of our camera. Under his clothes was half a million pounds worth of cocaine hidden in a body belt and a surgical corset.

We were shown X-ray pictures of a woman passenger who had swallowed nine packets of the drug, each holding 66 grammes. The methods used by the carriers were endless. One Spanish bullfighter stuffed the cocaine into the handle of his sword; a British schoolteacher was caught bringing in two dozen cans of beer from Bolivia, five of them contained one and a half kilos of the drug; others had inserted condoms full of cocaine into the rectum or vagina.

If cocaine had become the new social champagne in the UK then, like heroin, it would not be long before the drug explosion would bring its availability on to the streets of Britain for as little as five pounds a sniff.

The 2009 release by the Scottish Government of the only man accused of the bombing of Pan Am Flight 103 over Lockerbie brought howls of protest from the US Administration and many of the families of the 270 victims. Abdelbaset Ali Mohmed Al Megrahi, a former Libyan intelligence officer and head of security for Libyan Arab Airlines, was freed on compassionate grounds following reports that he had terminal prostate cancer and had less than three months to live.

Twenty-five years before, the UK government were facing similar questions and recriminations after allowing 30 diplomats to walk out of the Libyan Embassy and fly home at the end of an 11-day siege which followed the shooting of Britain's smallest policewoman, Yvonne Fletcher.

Eight weeks previously, whilst on a routine visit to Scotland Yard, I had been told of Special Branch intelligence reports warning that Libyan hit squads had arrived in Britain. Fears of violence mounted when a group of revolutionary students seized control of the embassy known as the People's Bureau in St James's Square. The police, believing attacks on exiled opponents of the Libyan leader Colonel Gaddafi could be imminent, took decisive action.

Dozens of armed officers surrounded the London Mosque where a leading Libyan dissident had been gunned down in 1980. Then two bombs went off – one at a restaurant in the West End, the other a controlled explosion of a car bomb in Manchester. Six Libyan nationals were ordered out of the country.

The situation was becoming more worrying by the day and just before midnight on 16 April 1984, a Libyan diplomat drove to the Foreign Office and warned that if an anti-Gaddafi demonstration went ahead the next day, the embassy would not be responsible for the consequences.

The protest did take place, ending in unbelievable horror. Several eye witnesses spoke of seeing smoke and a flaming gun at a first floor window of the embassy. The burst of automatic gunfire put eleven demonstrators in hospital and WPC Fletcher was shot in the back and died shortly after arriving at hospital.

I reached the square just before it was sealed off. Armed police took to the roof tops and a variety of bugging devices and infra-red cameras were installed. As the streets were cleared my colleague Kate Adie and her film crew managed to get into Simpson's store which backed on to the embassy building. They had found they could get a good view from the windows of the lingerie department and so in Kate's words 'we camped there for several hours among the knickers and bras.'

The longest police siege in London's history had begun. Yvonne Fletcher's police hat was still lying on the street at the spot where she fell and within easy sight of her killer.

Britain's terms for ending the siege were that everyone should leave the building; all should be questioned by the police; the killer of the policewoman identified and the embassy searched in the presence of a Libyan diplomat or a suitable third party. Colonel Gaddafi, on the other hand, had called for the police to withdraw and for the 30 Libyans inside the building to be allowed to leave unhindered. He also had soldiers surround the British Embassy in Tripoli.

It was an extremely volatile situation with the Home Secretary, Leon Brittan, chairing an emergency committee of ministers, senior government officials and the Commissioner of the Metropolitan Police, while officers at the scene were faced with the delicate business of maintaining stability in dealings with those inside the embassy including a number of firebrand revolutionary students

The days came and went. Every few hours, members of the Blue Berets, Scotland Yard's specialist firearms team, would be replaced by colleagues, some of them armed with a new sub-machine gun capable of firing 900 rounds a minute. Food and cigarettes went into the building but no-one was coming out.

My attempts to get straight answers as to whether radio and telex traffic was being maintained between the Libyans and their government, the diplomatic status of the occupants, their immunity from prosecution and any demands they had made, proved well-nigh impossible. Everyone, it seemed, feared making a wrong move especially with the British Embassy also under siege in Tripoli and a possible Libyan connection to a bomb which exploded in an unclaimed suitcase in the Customs Hall of Terminal 2 at Heathrow.

Just as the mood in Whitehall appeared to be turning to one of impatience, after being holed up for eleven days, the Libyans finally made their way out of the embassy in six groups of five, with their hands by their sides. They showed no emotion, even as they passed the spot where WPC Fletcher was killed. More than a dozen diplomatic bags left too, one of them thought to have contained the gun used in the shooting. Under the rules of the Vienna Convention, police were not permitted to search them.

The diplomats and students were escorted by van to a waiting plane and flown out of the country, while in Tripoli, the British Ambassador Oliver Miles and his staff left for London. Diplomatic relations between the two countries were severed and would not be renewed for another 15 years.

The departing Libyans left behind enough evidence to suggest they had built up a substantial arsenal which would have enabled them to initiate a large terrorist campaign against anti-Gaddafi exiles living in Britain.

In 1999 Libya accepted 'general responsibility' for the killing and agreed to pay the Fletcher family compensation, but no-one has ever been convicted of Yvonne's murder.

While the siege had been proceeding, the Home Secretary had other problems on his hands, not least the miners' strike which ran not just for eleven days but nearly a year. The dispute was a defining moment in the country's industrial relations, with the Thatcher government determined to break the power of the National Union of Mineworkers whose 1974 strike was largely seen as having brought down the government of Edward Heath.

The NUM leader Arthur Scargill declared a national strike without holding a secret ballot. His move was in response to the announcement that 20 uneconomic pits would have to close, throwing 20,000 men out of work. The impact of this bitter dispute was felt by many and was supported and condemned in equal measure. It came to be characterised by violence and hardship, family splits and daily battles between police and pickets.

I made frequent visits to the thirteenth floor of Scotland Yard where the police had set up the National Reporting Centre. From here at any given moment, a telephone call was enough to move large numbers of police reinforcements around the country with each force providing a daily tally of just how many officers it could readily make available. The perception quickly got around that this vast policing operation was acting almost as a strike-breaking force on behalf of the government and left many Chief Constables feeling uncomfortable. Instead of patrolling the streets of their own town, as many as 8,000 policemen a day were despatched – in some cases 300 miles – to West and South Yorkshire, to the coalfields of Leicestershire and Nottinghamshire and across the border into Wales. Denuded of so many bobbies on the beat, some areas of the country saw a 13 per cent rise in burglaries.

Van loads of police arriving from the Met found themselves sleeping in old army billets, drill halls and former air force hangers. At the end of their mattresses I spotted bags containing everything from spare boot laces to bottles of indigestion tablets. They operated in detachments of 20 men, usually with two sergeants and an inspector. Some were working 16 hours a day, coming off duty at eleven at night and then being woken at 3 am for breakfast before heading for the pithead or under instructions to turn round flying pickets on their way to the Nottinghamshire coalfield where thousands of miners had defied the strike call.

This huge invasion of 'the boys in blue' upset many of the local police who lived in the mining communities and whose relatives, neighbours or friends were on the picket lines. Those drafted in had no such relationships and did not have to contemplate how difficult life might become when the strike was finally over.

For families wondering where their next loaf of bread might be coming from or how they were going to pay their bills, huge resentment was also building when they read of the vast sums of overtime being earned by the massed ranks of uniformed invaders. Insensitive remarks such as one I overheard from a constable in an exchange with pickets that his family was going to have 'a jolly good holiday in the Caribbean with the money I'm picking up here' only served to inflame feelings.

The Battle of Orgreave, a violent confrontation between police and pickets at the British Steel coking plant in South Yorkshire, has been well documented and has been the cause of much controversy over the years, but the level of the police response with riot gear, batons and horses raised major questions about their role, and the use of shields, snatch squads and horses sent in at full gallop was a visible break with the old ways of dealing with industrial disputes. The number of arrests reached 9,500, the equivalent of one in twenty of the NUM membership.

After nearly twelve months, the strike collapsed and the Association of Chief Police Officers began dismantling the National Reporting Centre. Its role in arranging a staggering one and a quarter million police deployments had been a controversial one and some saw it as the beginnings of a national police force. That never materialised, though today with so many specialised squads now operating countrywide in the frontline battle against serious crime, drugs, fraud, money laundering and counter-terrorism, there are many occasions when the police service appears to be operating as one body even if does not formally exist as one. In addition, the Serious Organised Crime Agency, dubbed Britain's FBI, was launched by Tony Blair in 2006 to 'make life hell' for the 'Mr Bigs' of the criminal underworld. It was given a staff of 4,000 and an annual budget of £400 million.

Co-ordination and cross-intelligence have become key words in British policing. With the methods employed by criminal gangs becoming increasingly more sophisticated, staying one step ahead is proving ever tougher for all those involved in law enforcement.

In the West Highland beauty spot of Ullapool the only uniformed law enforcement official I could find in the autumn of 1985 was the town's one and only traffic warden. I'd gone there to expose a major threat to Britain's security. Thanks to a call from a valued contact, the visit to the shores of Loch Broom enabled me to provide an exclusive for BBC News and a sea of red faces at the Home Office.

Those were still the days of the Cold War. Offshore, 40 Iron Curtain vessels lay at anchor and three thousand Communist seamen outnumbered the locals three to one. They were known as the Klondikers – Eastern Europeans who manned the factory ships for months at a time, eagerly snapping up all the mackerel Scotland's fishermen could provide.

Every few minutes, though, small orange 'liberty' boats could be spotted heading for the port with Russians, Romanians, Bulgarians and East Germans slipping ashore in their dozens. When they got there, no-one was waiting. There were no passport checks, no immigration control, nobody to keep an eye on who was coming or going. By withdrawing resources, the government had provided an open door for potential Soviet spies to get into Britain.

The espionage threat was further emphasised by the nearness of so many key defence installations in the Highlands – the main submarine torpedo testing area at Kyle of Lochalsh, the bombing range at Tain, the fast-breeder nuclear reactor at Dounreay and the Nimrod base at RAF Kinloss. Even the Polaris submarine base at Holy Loch could be reached in a few hours.

Pressed for a response, the government insisted that the Klondikers were entitled to enjoy the same privileges and subject to the same restrictions as any merchant seaman provided they left with the ship. At Ullapool though, they were returning after a day's shopping as they came – unnoticed, unchallenged and uncounted.

Officially, it had been left to the ships' agents to make cursory checks, but they had received no training. The ship masters were supposed to give them lists of who was on board but there were hundreds working below deck processing fish for the Eastern Bloc countries. Their names were then sent 160 miles to Aberdeen and it could take days for the list to reach the nearest immigration officer before they were scrutinised.

Further embarrassment followed the next day. One East German had found joining the fleet bound for Ullapool as the perfect way to get over the Berlin Wall. He came ashore from the *Hans Machwitza* and asked to avail himself of an entitlement to travel facilities to West Germany. It had been a circuitous route but a novel way of defecting.

In the coming years, I would witness the Communist curtain fall not in East Germany but in the most repressive of all Stalinist states where a ruthless dictator had isolated his country and its people from the rest of the world.

15

To Kill the Cabinet

Remember we only have to be lucky once. You have to be lucky every time.

IRA message to Mrs Thatcher after Brighton bombing

Whatever the rota may say, as a BBC journalist you are never off duty. Long before the introduction of mobile phones, news editors found all sorts of ingenious ways to track you down no matter where you were – celebrating a friend's birthday, at a supper party, singing in the church choir or taking an afternoon stroll in the woods.

The favourite and most unwelcome interruption is the phone call that comes out of nowhere, in the middle of the night. It normally indicates a big story has just broken and, as you fumble for the bedside light and swing your legs out from under the duvet, there's that instinctive dread that it could be quite some time before you can next enjoy the warmth and security of your own bed.

A 3.15 am call was the last thing I needed on Friday 12 October 1984. I had barely managed forty minutes' sleep after a frenetic 18-hour shift in which I had no sooner completed a filmed package on policing tactics during the miners' strike then I was sent scurrying out of the editing room and on my way through the last of the peak-hour traffic to Wembley Central station.

The 17.54 passenger train from Euston to Bletchley had run into the side of a freight train which had been crossing from one line to another just south of the station. Passengers said the deflection of the trains meant that the force of the accident was gradual as they slid along side by side. The first two coaches of the passenger train overturned and three passengers were killed. There were also many injured including the driver.

It later emerged that the passenger train had passed a signal at 'danger' after the driver had suffered a transient episode of amnesia. As a result, without realising, he had cancelled the AWS warnings at the signals approaching Wembley, a lapse in concentration which was to prove fatal.

My concentration too, in that fraction between dreaming and waking, was not as it should have been as I picked up the phone in the ridiculously early hours of Friday morning.

'A bomb has gone off at The Grand Hotel in Brighton. We've sent Michael Cole down there to join our political staff on the scene. Get yourself into the office at once and start preparing a background report on who's responsible, the vital clues the police will be looking for and the security implications for the country as a whole. *Breakfast Time* also want to interview you live on air ... are you on your way yet?'

On my way? I was still in my pyjamas in a state of shock. The Grand Hotel, Brighton? Of course, that was where the Prime Minister was staying and most of the Tory Cabinet, for this was the week of the Conservative Party Conference.

The one positive thing about driving at such an unearthly hour is that commuter routes to London are virtually traffic free and you can get from A to B in less than half the time of the normal daily grind.

Keeping my ears tuned to the radio, the enormity of the Brighton attack was beginning to emerge. Though the IRA had not yet claimed responsibility, they were the most obvious suspects. Ever since the hunger strikes some three years before, Margaret Thatcher had been the No.1 target for the Provisionals. In May 1981, as 70,000 people attended the funeral of Bobby Sands, the first of the ten prisoners to die in the H Blocks of the Maze, the Prime Minister was being openly blamed for not granting the hunger strikers political status. The IRA pledged revenge at a time and at a place of their own choosing.

In my dash to Television Centre, it became patently clear to me that both the time and the place had now arrived. Such an audacious attack on the British establishment was the clearest possible demonstration of the lethal capacity of the IRA to wreak terror and devastating violence.

Just hours before, with the Tory Conference drawing to its close, Mrs Thatcher and the party faithful had been in good spirits. The atmosphere at the Conservative Agents' Ball was just as everyone had wanted it and the Prime Minister, having beavered away for several hours preparing her big Conference speech to be delivered the next day, was looking remarkably relaxed as she took to the dance floor.

With her husband Denis, she retired to her suite shortly before midnight and immediately got back to work on her keynote speech. At

2.50 am she used the bathroom and then returned to her room to check one final paper. Four minutes later, the bomb went off.

In her memoirs, *The Downing Street Years*, Mrs Thatcher described the moment.

A loud thud shook the room. There were a few seconds' silence and then there was a second slightly different noise created by falling masonry. I knew immediately it was a bomb but at this stage, I did not know that the explosion had taken place inside the hotel. Glass from the windows of my sitting room was strewn across the carpet. But I thought that it might be a car bomb outside. The adjoining bathroom was more severely damaged, though the worst I would have suffered had I been in there were minor cuts. Those who had sought to kill me had placed the bomb in the wrong place.

It was only when evacuating the hotel that the Prime Minister began to realise the seriousness of the blast. One minute asleep, the next blown out of their beds, others who escaped were too shocked to know what had happened. Some were not so lucky, trapped under tons of falling masonry. Others were dead.

The explosion occurred on the sixth floor. It shot upwards, dislodging a chimney which came crashing down through an entire column of rooms.

Mrs Muriel Maclean, wife of the Tories' Scottish Chairman, was in Room 629. She was to die later in hospital. Across the corridor in 628, Mrs Jeanne Shattock, wife of the Western Area Chairman, took the full force of the blast and was killed instantly. Below in 528, Eric Taylor, the North Western Chairman, was also dead; so too, in 428, Roberta Wakeham, wife of the party's Chief Whip. And in 328, the MP for Enfield Southgate, Sir Anthony Berry, also died.

Norman Tebbit, one of Mrs Thatcher's closest Cabinet colleagues was in Room 228. Firemen, using BBC arc lights after cables were cut, took nearly four hours to free him. The Prime Minister scarcely recognised her Trade and Industry Secretary on a visit to the hospital. His face was bloated as a result of being trapped for so long under the rubble. She also talked to his wife, Margaret, who was in the intensive care unit. She had no feeling below the neck and as a former nurse, knew exactly what that meant.

Determined that the conference should go on, Mrs Thatcher removed most of the partisan sections of her speech. As she said, this was not a

215

time for Labour-bashing but for unity in defence of democracy. She had clearly recognised that far more important than what she said was the fact that she, as Prime Minister, was still able to say it. Her feelings and those of the Conference were summed up in a few brisk, robust sentences.

The bomb attack ...was an attempt not only to disrupt and terminate our Conference. It was an attempt to cripple Her Majesty's democratically elected Government. That is the scale of the outrage in which we have all shared. And the fact that we are gathered here now, shocked but composed and determined, is a sign not only that this attack has failed but that all attempts to destroy democracy by terrorism will fail.

While the newspaper headlines testified to Mrs Thatcher's coolness in the immediate aftermath of the attack, the next day the IRA not only claimed responsibility but released a chilling statement of their intent. In a statement directed at the Prime Minister, they said: 'Today we were unlucky but remember we only have to be lucky once. You have to be lucky every time.'

In 1984 I was in my early years as the BBC's Home Affairs Correspondent and still building a list of reliable contacts within the police, the special branch and 'inside sources' that are so important if you are to steal a march over rivals when despatched to cover long and intricate investigations. You also have to be able to differentiate between rumour and fact, between blatant propaganda and honest detail and ensure you are not being used by any particular section of society for its own ends.

For a relatively small police force like Sussex, the pressure to discover exactly who planted the Brighton bomb and more important, how they had been able to breach the huge security cordon was immense. It was inevitable that anti-terrorist officers from the Metropolitan Police would be quickly on the scene. Though the British public have always endorsed the idea of policing by consent and embraced the structure of local county forces, it is vitally important that any joint investigative team works under one central command. The days of 'get off my patch' when it comes to conducting major inquiries have long since gone.

It was quickly established that the 30lb bomb had been planted underneath the bath in Room 629. The fragments recovered convinced the police that a long-delay timer had been used. I conjured a picture in my mind of all the guests in that room who after a hard day had chilled out and relaxed with a good hot soak in that bathtub totally unaware that a bomb was ticking away right underneath them. In the hunt for clues, 4,000 dustbin loads of debris were taken away for examination.

The police had just one real lead. The hotel register was intact. The job now was to trace everyone who had stayed in Room 629 in the previous three months. Needless to say, this caused at least one 'couple' more than a little embarrassment. Scores of people were interviewed all round the world. Ten weeks after the explosion, only one guest had not been found. His registration card bore the name Roy Walsh but no one had heard of him at the address he gave.

Hoping to confirm his hunch that this was the alias of the Brighton bomber, Chief Superintendent Jack Reece of Sussex Police went on BBC's *Crimewatch* to declare that 'the more time elapses, the more significant Mr Walsh becomes.' No one came forward. No one could identify Mr Walsh's distinctive writing.

At Scotland Yard, fingerprint experts got to work on his registration card. Eventually, two distinctive marks emerged – one a palm print, the other the tip of a little finger.

Three months after the explosion at The Grand Hotel, police had positively identified the missing guest, Roy Walsh, as Patrick Joseph Magee, a Belfast man in his thirties and a well-known member of the IRA. What's more, they had wanted to question Magee for the past five years about a series of explosions in the London area. He had one distinguishing feature, a finger missing on his right hand.

Magee had slipped into Brighton three weeks before the Tory Party Conference. For an autumn day, it was surprisingly hot and everyone was in their shirt sleeves, many of them heading for the big football match against Crystal Palace. Though Magee has since denied it, a taxi driver with a particularly keen eye for detail insists he picked him up at the railway station.

Over the years, I've experienced all the tricks the more disreputable cabbies can play. In Algiers I found one who had long indulged in the practice of driving people the long way round to pump up the meter. But even that little ruse seemed to pale into insignificance on discovering your life was now in imminent danger as – pedal to the floor – the driver set off on the mandatory white-knuckle ride, holding you in a permanent state of prayer until the destination was mercifully reached.

Thankfully, Denis Palmer's way was a tad more gentle. In fact, he'd lost count of the number of ladies who'd no sooner pitched themselves into the passenger seat of his cab than they were tugging at the sun visor so they could take a critical look at themselves in the vanity mirror. No matter how many hours are spent pampering and powdering at home, where better than a taxi journey to apply extra paint and filler.

This particular Saturday afternoon, Palmer had a different sort of problem on his hands. On such a warm, autumnal day, he was surprised to find the man hailing his cab was wearing a thick camel coat. He was even more surprised with the weight of the traveller's case – far heavier than anything he ever picked up even on Bank Holiday weekends.

On unloading the case at The Grand Hotel, Palmer jokily shouted at the porter 'you'd better hold on to your nuts with this one. You'll need 'em!' If it was indeed, Magee, then our taxi driver had been carrying 30lbs of high explosive in the boot of his car.

Once in the hotel, Magee paid in cash for a double room. He stayed for three days but none of the staff could identify him. The night porter, though, had an impression that there had been a second man in Room 629. He had received a phone call asking him what he had in the drinks line and then sent a waiter up to the room carrying a bottle of vodka and two cokes.

The second man was never found but, once Magee had been identified, the police kept a careful watch on his associates in Belfast. Special Branch officers discovered that his wife, Eileen, who was still living there was making monthly trips by train to the Irish Republic. Police in the south were tipped off and they soon discovered that Magee was living openly in the Ballymun Housing Estate not far from Dublin Airport, unaware that he'd been linked with the Brighton bomb.

It was now that the police took an enormous gamble. Fearing possible extradition problems, they decided to wait and to watch. They believed the terrorist they had nicknamed 'The Chancer' would return to Britain. The following April, just to ensure Magee's suspicions were not aroused, Jack Reece of the Sussex Police told the Brighton Bombing Inquest that the suspect's description was too imprecise to be released.

But then, consternation! At Connolly Station in Dublin there was no further sign of Magee's wife. Intelligence reports said that Magee himself had vanished. As police grew increasingly worried, his picture was circulated among Special Branch officers through a confidential edition of the *Police Gazette*. By June, the trail was dead. The police knew they'd lost him. Unnoticed, Magee had slipped back into England.

In the shadow of Buckingham Palace, at the height of the Royal Garden Party season, Pat Magee was about to turn hotel guest yet again.

218

The Rubens, built to house the city's aristocratic party-goers, is a much sought-after hotel by scores of wealthy American and overseas visitors who view it as one of the most fashionable spots in London's West End. Eight months after Brighton, Magee arrived there after telephoning to check if a room was available with a palace view. He signed in, this time using the name Morton and giving a Watford address and as at The Grand, paid in advance before being handed the keys to Room 112.

Magee's one-night stay was to signal the start of what the IRA were hoping would be an even bigger coup than Brighton. The room was ideal, directly opposite The Royal Mews, the back entrance to Buckingham Palace. From his case, Magee pulled out a child's lunch box. Its contents, the IRA hoped, would spark off a summer bombing campaign. It was packed with pounds of deadly explosive. There was also a long delay timer, similar to the one used at Brighton. It was already running and meant that the explosion could be delayed for up to 48 days. There were also two booby traps, a micro-switch in the lid and a mercury tilting device. If the box was moved or opened, the bomb would have gone off.

Magee's eye was drawn to a bedside cabinet. He eased it away from the wall and placed the box against the skirting board. Then he screwed the cabinet back to the wall. It was the ideal hiding place and just to leave his own cynical imprint, the lunchbox carried the image of Postman Pat.

It was a chilling experience to enter that hotel room carrying an identical box – minus explosive – and give the viewers an idea of the stealth and cunning involved in the preparation of an act of terror.

After checking out of the Rubens, Magee bought travel cards and rented a flat in the East End, even placing a gun under the floorboards. He had established a base in the capital – yet just four miles away, Scotland Yard had no idea where he was or what he was up to.

To make matters worse, intelligence from Ireland suggested that the IRA, buoyed over their Brighton success, had been gearing themselves for a follow-up strike. In late 1984, Special Branch detectives raided a remote bungalow near Lusk, 15 miles north of Dublin.

The house was empty but under the floorboards they found sophisticated bomb-making equipment. There was also evidence to suggest similar devices had been moved elsewhere. Sleeping bags were piled up, giving police the clear impression that the house was also a training base for bombers.

After a series of such finds, surveillance was stepped up on both sides of the Irish Sea. In late June, a discreet watch was being kept on the arrival of a coal boat at the deserted port of Ayr in South-West Scotland. The man seen scrambling up the quayside ladder had come in posing as one of the crew but Peter Sherry was anything but a sailor. The Royal Ulster Constabulary's tracker unit E4 had been following him for nearly two years after his release from custody on an attempted murder charge when a supergrass trial collapsed. He was seen as a link man between Northern Provisionals and the IRA's high command. Irish police also suspected he was heavily involved in planning a new bombing campaign in Britain.

Using actors, we were able to demonstrate just how Special Branch officers managed to catch an entire IRA cell. First, they tailed Sherry to the railway station. He caught the London train via Kilmarnock with police convinced he was heading for the capital but when the train stopped at Carlisle, Sherry got off. He checked into a hotel and all night police kept a discreet watch on his room. Next day, he was tailed back to the station. It was a busy Saturday afternoon and a courting couple were seated on a platform bench seemingly only with eyes for one another. As Peter Sherry appeared, there were occasional glances in his direction. The couple were actually Special Branch officers and a tiny microphone had been placed in the girl's hair. Sherry's every move was being recorded.

Just before three o'clock, a small bearded man approached. At first, the couple didn't recognise him but then they spotted his right hand. Part of his little finger was missing.

When they looked up, there was no mistaking the face. It was Pat Magee, the man every policeman in Britain was looking for. But where were the two men going? The undercover police kept their distance as the pair of them crossed the bridge and headed for the northbound platform. As they chatted together, they had not the slightest suspicion that anyone was watching. In the event, Sherry and Magee boarded the Glasgow train and the police trail continued across the border into Scotland.

Just after 5 pm, the train pulled into Glasgow Central station. At first, the men were lost in the crowds jamming the platform but were picked up again heading for a bus. It took them south across the Clyde and into Govanhill. A short walk and then the pair disappeared through the entrance of a tenement building in Langside Road. Special Branch officers occupied a flat across the road and through a discreet gap in the curtains trained their binoculars on the doorway. At 6 pm, Strathclyde Police were alerted. Magee had to be lifted. There wasn't a minute to be lost.

Plain clothes officers were despatched immediately. Their job was to watch and wait. For an hour, no-one came and no-one left. As police kept watch, frantic phone calls across the city brought an emergency firearms squad together. But there was a problem. The tenement had seven flats on four levels and they had no idea which one Magee was in.

At precisely 7.40 pm, 23 officers rushed through the entrance to the flats. Three men were to cover each door. All were to knock at exactly the same moment. To their astonishment, Magee himself answered the door to the ground floor flat. He thought it was the landlord. He was seized by the arm, a gun put to his head, shoes removed and then thrown out of the house to other officers who by now were crowding the stairwell.

More officers burst into the hallway. They had orders that everyone in the house had to be arrested. Suddenly, a tall bearded man wearing a soft cap and jeans, emerged from the back kitchen. Under his loose sweater, one officer spotted the handle of a gun. Gerry McDonnell was whisked into the lounge and pinned against the wall. The gun was a loaded automatic pistol and the safety clip was off. Peter Sherry, the man they'd followed for two whole days, was next to be snatched, followed by two attractive women in their twenties, Martina Anderson and Ella O'Dwyer.

The raid could hardly have been better timed. The five had just been sitting down to a meal they had cooked in the kitchen. When I managed to persuade the landlord to let me into the tenement flat a few months later, I was amazed to find the remains of the meal on plates piled up on the kitchen table and a collection of beer cans from which Magee and his fellow conspirators had been drinking as the police broke in. The cell was found to have over £10,000 between them, all in £50 notes. There were false passports, both British and Irish, false driving licences and donor cards, diagrams, a gun in Martina Anderson's handbag and scores of maps and railway timetables.

The cell's commander, Gerry McDonnell, was carrying the most crucial document. In his money-belt, police discovered a bomb calendar. Sixteen explosions had been planned using long delay bombs. They were to hit London and a dozen seaside resorts at the height of the summer season. The first nine bombs were to have 24-day delay timers, the other seven were to have exploded after 48 days. One entry was more precise. Returning from the Rubens, Pat Magee noted all the details – date, time and place – yet it still took police three hours to find the bomb, no doubt having first taken the bathroom apart.

Even if warnings were to have been given, it is terrifying to think of the carnage that could have resulted from this concerted attack. A commercial target, it may have been, but who can say how many families with young children would have been caught up in the mayhem that would have ensued? I could only surmise how the emergency services would have coped with a new explosion in a different venue every day for over a fortnight and the wholesale panic it would have generated.

As the police held the IRA unit at Stewart Street Police Station, their job now was to find out how many more bombs may have been planted. The questioning went on for hours but there were no answers. In the Langside Road flat, they found wigs and sets of matching keys. Police ripped up the floorboards and smashed open the walls. Everywhere they found fingerprints but no explosives.

As concern grew, MPs from every resort on the calendar were summoned to Scotland Yard to be told what they could do to help. Hundreds of hotels were evacuated and searched. Then came another lucky break. A letter found on the cell's commander led police to a house in the Willesden Green area of London. There, they arrested Donal Craig. He was the cell's man in the capital. He also proved its weakest link. Craig had been sworn into the IRA just three months before. An epileptic and manic depressive, he had rowed with the others. He hired a getaway car with only two doors and rented a safe house with only one exit. Now, in his letter he said he wanted to leave.

While the others stayed silent, Craig confessed his part in the conspiracy and took police to another Glasgow tenement in James Gray Street. Underneath a bath in the cellar they found plastic bags packed with explosives, detonators and 15 long-delay timers, most of them already set and running. They also uncovered rifles from Eastern Europe and indications of further bomb targets, a map of Hereford with the headquarters of the SAS marked out and an article on one of Britain's most decorated soldiers of the time, Major General Peter de la Billiere.

There were fears too, for the safety of the Queen. She was due in Brighton on the day of the first planned explosion and in Great Yarmouth on the day after another. Both visits did go ahead amidst massive security. Even though the cell had been caught, there were still worries of reprisal attacks by the Provisionals.

A week after their capture, the active service unit was on the move for the last time to face justice in England. It was decided to fly them south to RAF Northolt, ironically often used by Mrs Thatcher on flying visits to Northern Ireland. As expected, a huge posse of photographers was lying in wait as traffic on the final stretch of the M40 motorway into London was brought to a standstill and a barrier removed to allow the police van to sweep into the fortified yard of the capital's most secure police station at Paddington Green. Together the cell was the most spectacular catch of IRA terrorists there had ever been.

Magee was charged alone with the Brighton bomb, the others with conspiracy to cause explosions. With their trial at The Old Bailey unlikely until the following year, I was assigned to prepare and present a background documentary which would be immediately slotted into the BBC1 schedules as soon as verdicts were returned. So what kind of people were these terrorists? What was their upbringing? Where did they live? What were the motivational factors that drove them into joining the IRA? What other atrocities had they been involved in?

The first surprise was to find that Pat Magee, the man who came so close to blowing up the Prime Minister, was brought up in Norwich. His family moved there when he was just four years old. By the age of seven, he had already taken his First Communion ... a photograph I was able to get hold of showed him kneeling in the front row, eyes shut and hands clasped together in prayer. His classmates recalled a rather unnourished boy who rarely got up to mischief, while his headmaster, Bill Slack, remembered a lad who didn't dive into trouble himself but was gullible and easily led.

By the time Magee had moved to Thomas More Secondary School, he had started getting into trouble. He was put on probation for shop breaking and, by 16, he was in an approved school. Soon after that, he moved back to Belfast to the Unity Flats, a strongly Republican estate. Recruited as an IRA intelligence officer, in 1973 he was interred in Long Kesh for two and a half years. After his release, he got married and fathered a son.

Magee now featured in the IRA's plans to regroup their dwindling numbers into smaller, safer cells. That same year, a London cell, led by Gerard Tuite bombed an oil storage depot at Canvey Island and a gas works at Greenwich. Police hunting Tuite put out a warrant for Magee too. Travelling openly on his Irish passport, Magee left hiding in Ireland for Holland and even managed to persuade a member of the Irish Garda to sign his passport photograph.

We traced Magee's hideout to a barn on a farm run by the Vloet family not far from the German border. They were shocked to hear of his terrorist activities for they had found him an engaging lodger who had been keen to learn Dutch from the girls in the house and in return had spent many hours teaching them English. In fact, he was so successful in this that at school, Daphne Vloet's teacher enquired: 'How come you're speaking English with an Irish accent?' Her sister, Iris, said he did talk to them about the IRA and about Irish history but clearly remembered him saying that the biggest mistake you could make in life was getting caught. But that was exactly what happened to him. Cycling to the job he'd obtained at a metal factory, he was sent flying from his bike by Dutch police and arrested. While Dutch supporters demanded his release, Scotland Yard applied for his extradition. From prison, he issued a statement backing the H block campaign and went on token hunger strike.

In January 1981 the Dutch did release him, as Britain's evidence was too flimsy. The man security forces now dubbed 'The Chancer' felt safe enough to return to Dublin. There he worked as an illustrator for Sinn Fein on their paper *Republican News*. In the office entrance, he was shot twice in the leg by a loyalist gunman and taken to the Richmond Hospital. He lay there for weeks. Police interviewed him but no attempt was made to start extradition proceedings.

Magee's luck never seemed to run out. He had embarrassed British, Dutch and now Irish Police for a second time. Then, in 1983, came his most extraordinary escape. Returning to England, police thought he was involved in a conspiracy to bomb an RAF station near Blackpool. They followed him for days, photographed him but lost him in a chase through Preston town centre. Most embarrassing of all, the pictures they took of him were not passed on to Sussex Police frantically engaged in trying to identify the Brighton bomber. No one had realised that the man they had been following was Pat Magee.

Gerry McDonnell led the Glasgow cell. He was a practised bomb maker, a Belfast Catholic but not a likely recruit. His father had served in the British Army, was wounded at Dunkirk, captured and confined along with Airey Neave and escaped from Stalag 20A in Poland. The circumstances of his son's imprisonment were very different. Interred in the early 1970s, he was later jailed for 16 years for possessing explosives. In 1983 McDonnell escaped in the mass breakout from the Maze. He was married in Ireland in 1984, leaving for a honeymoon in Sardinia before returning to lead the Glasgow team. The security services are thought to have considered him a poor choice as it was he who blundered by having all the bombing targets in his pocket when police broke in.

Martina Anderson was a factory worker, part-time model and, by 23, an accomplished bomb maker. Brought up in the Bogside area of Derry, when she left school she took up modelling. The *Derry Journal* recorded her success in a beauty contest but she was already involved with the IRA. Still in her teens, she was arrested outside a fire-bombed building. Police say she pulled a gun on them. Held for nine months and then released on bail, she promptly disappeared. Just across the border, she lived quite openly in a house at Buncrana in Co. Donegal despite being on the run. In the republic, Martina was taught to make bombs. She fell in love with Paul Kavanagh, convicted of the car bombing outside Harrods department store in London just before Christmas 1983 which claimed the lives of three police officers and three passers-by. They were later to marry in jail.

Ella O'Dwyer was a country girl brought up among the hills of Co. Tipperary in the south of Ireland. For her, there were no soldiers on street corners or slogans on city walls. The youngest of five children, Ella went to a convent school then on to University College Dublin, studying English. She graduated with honours in 1983 and considered a career in journalism. As a student she seemed to take no interest in politics but then the hunger strikes made a lasting impression. She started attending Sinn Fein meetings. Speaking to her father at the family farm, he expressed his shock and bewilderment that she had become a bomber. Police too were surprised. When they arrested her in Glasgow, it took them four days to find out her identity – the perfect terrorist, committed but anonymous.

Peter Sherry epitomised the IRA's ideal. He was a plausible politician and a willing participant in the armed struggle. Brought up at Dungannon in Co. Tyrone, he was jailed for armed robbery while still in his teens. In 1982, on the word of a supergrass, he was charged with attempted murder but the case collapsed and Sherry was released. It was a propaganda triumph for the IRA and he was given the job of running the local Sinn Fein office. The publicity boosted his chances in a local by-election in 1984. He lost but doubled the Sinn Fein vote. In his manifesto, Sherry had named organisations he claimed were discriminating against nationalists. Soon, people were being murdered outside buildings he had listed. One man was shot in a hospital car park, another who worked in the Crown Offices in Dungannon was also gunned down. The SAS laid a trap at another place on Sherry's list. They foiled an IRA attack but a civilian died in the crossfire. Fearing worse to come, the local MP, Ken Maginnis, took the unprecedented step of naming Sherry in the House of Commons. After that, Sherry adopted a lower profile. The Brighton bomb had gone off and he had begun to mastermind the IRA's bid to blitz the British mainland. That bid failed when Sherry led police to the tenement flat in Glasgow. The conspiracy had been foiled partly through good intelligence work and partly through sheer good fortune.

At the end of the Old Bailey trial, Pat Magee, who was then 35, received eight life sentences, seven of them relating to the Brighton bombing. He was sentenced for planting the bomb, exploding it and five counts of murder. The trial judge, Mr Justice Boreham, recommended he serve a minimum of 35 years, branding Magee as 'a man of exceptional cruelty and inhumanity. You intended to wipe out a large part of the government and you nearly did.'

His eighth life sentence was for the summer holiday resorts' conspiracy. The other four members of the Glasgow cell were also jailed for life.

Little did any of us present in the Old Bailey's famous No1 courtroom that day – least of all those in the dock – imagine that just 14 years later, all would be free. A new dawn had broken in Northern Ireland with the ratification of the Good Friday Agreement, a major political development in the peace process. One of its conditions was the early release of paramilitary prisoners belonging to organisations observing a ceasefire.

The biggest beneficiary was Pat Magee. Things had looked particularly bleak when former Tory Home Secretary Michael Howard increased his sentence to 'whole life'. Then, his successor, Labour's Jack Straw, asserting that Magee's early release would be 'hard to stomach', launched an appeal to prevent it but it was turned down by the Northern Ireland High Court.

Though now free to walk the streets of his native Belfast, the Brighton bomber had yet one more mission to complete.

16

War and Peace

Just minutes after driving off in a hired car from Belfast's Aldergrove Airport, I pulled into a lay-by to take a call on my mobile phone. It was the one I had been hoping for, though I was not sure it would ever materialise.

The voice at the other end was that of a quiet, soft-spoken Ulsterman. 'I believe you want to speak to me?'

I suggested lunch. He suggested a pub that is a favourite haunt for republicans just a stone's throw from the city centre.

Shortly after one o'clock on a grey October day in 2008, a small bearded man, stick in hand and limping slightly due to a painful back, entered the downstairs bar. I recognised him immediately and he seemed to have no more difficulty in identifying me from amongst the regulars downing a pint of Guinness, whilst keeping an eye on the afternoon's racing on the huge plasma television screens that created a much-needed touch of colour to the otherwise dull and cheerless surroundings.

My lunch partner was none other than Dr Patrick Joseph Magee PhD, BA (first-class Honours). The Brighton bomber's years in jail had clearly been put to good use.

Condemned to what he thought would be a lifetime in the bleak concrete Special Units of Britain's high security jails, he got down to some serious study and within months of his release had completed his thesis on Irish post-colonial representations in popular fiction. Having studied the 500 popular novels written about The Troubles, Magee saw the IRA as always being portrayed as 'the big bad other' in a modern morality tale, rather like the old archetypal Wild West story. The republicans were the Red Indians and like them, had no voice. At last, he was at pains to point out that Republicans were writing their own fiction, people like Ronan Bennett and Danny Morrison, once Sinn Fein's Director of Publicity, who had helped arrange our meeting.

Of course, Magee had never expected that a visit to one of his favourite pubs would have been a possibility until the last few years of life. I asked him how he had felt when the original 35-year sentence was pronounced as he stood in the dock of the Old Bailey. It had apparently sparked an immediate exercise in mental arithmetic. He was 35 at that stage, so that would mean being in jail until he was 70. Then he remembered his grandfather's age and thought, if he looked after himself, he would still have a few years of freedom to look forward to. As events conspired, Magee was a free man before his fiftieth birthday.

The secure units in which he had been imprisoned usually held seven or eight men living in a concrete-type bunker about the size of a tennis court. Each prisoner had his own cell, and the unit had a pool table, a television and a small exercise yard with the extra protection of a grill across the top to prevent any possible helicopter escape. There was 24-hour surveillance but for Magee study was a way of pushing the walls back and keeping himself sane. It demanded a great deal of self-determination but without it, incarceration would have been a far tougher existence.

'I had to fight for it. I was in Leicester and it was a huge struggle to get the Open University into the unit.'

Once they were in a secure unit, the Prison Service was very reluctant to move Magee and other IRA prisoners to other jails. In some ways this was beneficial as it created a degree of stability with set routines and less disruption to study, but the downside was that with seven men in forced confinement for four years or more, they found themselves in a goldfish bowl and when fall-outs with other inmates occurred, it could pose serious problems.

The real reason that the authorities were loath to move Irish prisoners around at frequent intervals was that it created a huge security problem. Ironically, it could also raise a prisoner's profile and sense of importance to epic proportions as, handcuffed, he would travel in a vast convoy of armour-plated vehicles with three cars in front, another three behind and a helicopter overhead. And every time the convoy reached a constabulary border, a new team would take over. This could be repeated several times as many of these journeys involved travelling hundreds of miles from one end of the country to the other.

A hugely complex operation ... but what about the death, devastation and broken lives Magee left behind at Brighton – did he have any regrets, was there any feeling of remorse?

Given the scale of the explosion, it was hardly surprising to hear that he often reflected on those caught up in the blast including the wife of Lord Tebbit whose life sentence to imprisonment in a wheelchair, her husband asserted, had not yet been commuted to some lesser inconvenience.

'By the very nature of a bomb, you can't be precise about who you're hitting but there's one thing I can say – the timing of the bomb at about three o'clock in the morning was designed to reduce the possibility of injuring hotel staff. We hoped at that stage it would be just the Tories and their hangers-on.

'Now I do have a different view on it. I do regret that it was the wives of politicians who for the most part took the brunt of it. How could I not regret that Margaret Tebbit is in a wheelchair? I do regret that. Whatever I do will not bridge that gap.

'But Brighton was something we felt we had to do. I think we had to target them. We had to go for them. Until we were able to demonstrate to the British political establishment that bombs would be going off in their country while they refused to deal with us, then we had to pursue this course.

'It was the IRA that bombed Brighton. It wasn't Pat Magee. I was a functionary, a very willing functionary, don't get me wrong here. I totally endorsed what they were thinking. You have got to put it in the context of decades of failed initiatives with counter-insurgency agendas regarding the republican movement. In order to combat that, we had to speak from a position of strength and from a position where they knew they had to deal with us.

'One bomb wasn't going to achieve that, no matter the target, the status or the outcome, but a sustained campaign over many years – which is in effect what happened – that is what would change the equation and open up possibilities.

'It wasn't going to get us a united Ireland. It was going to get us to the point where they had to listen to us so that we could move on and pursue our agenda as openly as possible.'

And what about Mrs Thatcher? As she was clearly the target, were there regrets that she escaped unhurt? In retrospect, Magee's answer was a definitive no. The very awareness that things could have been worse, he insisted, actually gave the IRA more leverage than had they killed her. If half the cabinet had died, it might have been impossible for the British establishment to come to terms with them for a generation or more.

Magee would not talk about the planning and operation at Brighton. Though he was the only one identified and punished for the attack, there were others involved.

'Maybe one day, I'll have something to say; maybe never. There are the victims' feelings to be taken into account.'

Though he accepts responsibility for those who died, he refuses to accept that his fingerprint was on the registration card recovered from the rubble.

'If that was my fingerprint, I didn't put it there.'

As we tucked into a plate of fish, chips and mushy peas, I was impressed by Magee's sharp intellect, yet it seemed at times that every word was measured, his discourse at times cold and chilling.

He would like to teach but, with his record, there was simply no chance of an opening. Our conversation switched to the efforts he'd shared with others to help bring some form of reconciliation between victims and perpetrators of violence.

Along with Jo Berry, the daughter of Sir Anthony Berry, one of those killed in the bombing of The Grand Hotel, he set up a healing project called *The Causeway*. Though there was no early take-up, the research involved brought about a lot of subsequent activity on the reconciliation front. Much of it, Magee said, must remain secretive – just below the radar – simply because of the nature of the work.

'People don't always want it known that these meetings are taking place. It can still be quite difficult for them when they return to their own communities but it can only be a source of great encouragement that so much is happening.'

Jo Berry decided she wanted to meet Pat Magee so she could put a face to the enemy and see him as a real human being. At their first meeting she was terrified, but the pair talked with extraordinary intensity as both set out to recover some of the humanity lost when the Brighton bomb went off. As a result, Magee made the calculation that he could now do more outside than inside the republican movement. He and Jo meet up frequently and see the value in continuing with the process. They have spoken at conferences, on platforms and to young people in prison.

'It's an inspiration sitting there talking to them, hoping they'll gain something from what you're saying. I'm under no illusion that going into jail will sort things out but there are a lot of good people working there trying to do good. I was in the system myself with a troubled youth and even though I might not have responded at any given moment to instances of kindness, later on I thought back to them, so it's important to plant seeds even if they're not used at that time.'

As he took his last sip of coffee before slipping away by taxi, Pat Magee indulged in one final act of self-examination, one that revealed another side to his complex personality yet suggested that he had now come to terms with his actions and their consequences.

'I'm torn in some ways because I don't consider myself a violent person. And yet, for a whole period of my life – almost all my adult life – I was involved in violence and it did not come naturally. I often wonder: what if? You ask all those questions, and the very fact that you have hurt people, well you have to carry that but I would still maintain that we had no other choice. Given the context of a 30-year conflict, we stuck to our agenda and did our best to be proportionate in response to what we had to face. As for the future, the hope must be that violence is over forever and given the political processes now in situ, there is no place for it.'

A final handshake and the Brighton bomber disappeared into the anonymity offered by a bustling Belfast street. I returned the empty plates, headed back to the multi-storey car park and set off for Londonderry to meet another of the IRA bomb-makers whose life had taken an even more extraordinary turn.

Perched on a hill offering a commanding view across the city is the Rathmore Shopping Centre and a small industrial estate. The area was once the site of a British Army barracks. Today it houses the expansive offices of the republican party Sinn Fein, and one of its most active and ebullient politicians, Martina Anderson.

The last time I had set eyes on her was in the summer of 1986. Convicted for her part in the English holiday resorts' bombing conspiracy – along with her co-conspirators – she turned, fist raised, towards the public gallery of the Old Bailey and shouted the republican slogan *Tiochfaidh ár Lá* ('Our day will come'). To me, it seemed a show of bravado. The former 'Miss Derry' in the dock was just 23 and facing a life sentence in jail.

Like Pat Magee, she used her time there delving into books and study and, by the time of her release over 13 years later, she had earned a first-class Honours degree in Social Science. If there was anger and resentment among her enemies over such an early exit from prison then there were more shocks in store, for Martina's day *had* indeed come and in a way she could not have imagined in her wildest dreams.

Throwing herself headlong into politics, she had hardly had time to enjoy the first fruits of freedom when, at the instigation of Gerry Adams, she first entered Stormont as a researcher before being appointed Sinn Fein's Director of Unionist Engagement. Her standing in the party was rising fast and in 2007 she won a seat in the Northern Ireland Assembly. To the chagrin of former members of the RUC with whom she had many run-ins, Martina was also given a place on the Northern Ireland Policing Board, became the party's spokesperson on Equality and Human Rights, travelling frequently to Brussels, and chalked up a very respectable vote as the Sinn Fein candidate for the Foyle parliamentary seat at the 2010 General Election.

This was not a fantasy world. This was for real, however impossible it must have seemed to the young woman once locked away in the dire surroundings of Durham Jail. Another example of yesterday's terrorist becoming today's politician. There have been countless examples over the years, not least that of Menachem Begin who organised the bombing of the King David Hotel in Jerusalem and who later became the Prime Minister of Israel – and as such bitterly opposed the terrorists of the PLO.

I was surprised to find that Martina's father was a Protestant, 'neither sectarian nor judgemental', who found himself ostracised from his own family when he married a Catholic. They had ten children, some of whom took part in the early Civil Rights marches. Her mother took a leading role in the campaign while trying to keep her children safely tucked up in bed at home with the door closed. But in the hostile environment of Derry where violence so often became the order of the day, people made choices either to survive and live with everything that was going on around them or to become involved.

As early as 1973 an elder brother, Peter, was arrested and imprisoned in Portlaoise for three years. The Anderson home now became a target for early-morning raids by army and police. Martina was first arrested and put into the back of a Saracen Army personnel carrier at the age of 16. She had already put down a marker and the IRA knew they would soon have a willing and active participant on which to call.

Five years later that involvement would lead to a life sentence. Yet at 23, entering Durham Prison with fellow terrorist Ella O'Dwyer, Martina began to think that she had led a sheltered life compared to those inmates with whom she would have to live cheek by jowl for years to come.

'Some had experienced incest – raped by fathers or uncles – and just flipped, cracked up and had done all sorts of horrific things. There were fights about us coming in and one of the girls sat down beside me, introduced herself and said "I'm a lesbian, a prostitute and I'm in here for murder." Yet in prison, she behaved like a real lady, very level-headed. But I was totally shocked.'

Observing all that was going on around her, Martina's first impression was that she'd been placed in some kind of hospital wing. Many of the prisoners were clearly in need of some kind of psychiatric help.

The high security unit had 40 women inmates but was deprived of the recreational facilities available to their male counterparts. It took a long-running campaign and the arrival of a new governor before the necessary changes took place. Most humiliating of all were the regular strip searches.

Prison, though, did give her unexpected opportunities. She met Buddhist monks and was introduced to a new experience of meditation.

'I got interested in these characters coming in dressed in orange robes, heads shaved and they began to talk to us about Buddhism. We had a friend who was very concerned that our holy souls were going to be taken in a particular direction and we had to be careful here. We entered into and were engaged in the whole process of meditation and touching base with our inner selves.'

Martina was also hungry for knowledge of what was happening in the wider world and was determined to find the space for some serious study, something she readily admitted she simply wouldn't have had either the inclination or the time to do on the outside. She had left school with no qualifications and surprised herself by what she was able to achieve.

'I did A levels first with As in everything and then picked up a first-class Honours in Social Science. I never believed I had that in me so I realised there was something wrong with the system that was producing thousands of people every year who couldn't read, write or get any qualifications. It gives you an understanding of what needs to change when you have personally experienced that.'

As we chatted over a cup of coffee in a small downstairs office, I had to keep reminding myself that this was this same young woman who had once embarked on a campaign that could have resulted in the deaths of innocent families enjoying a day out at the seaside. I conjured up pictures in my mind of little children clasping buckets and spades, young couples leaving for a stroll along the promenade or grandparents preparing to dip their toes in the sea. Had the thought of the horror that could have been wreaked never crossed her mind? Did she not have a conscience about the possible outcome of the plot in which she had so willingly become involved?

Republicans had a conscience about everything, she insisted, and there would have been a constant evaluation along the way. The idea had been to impact the economy and the tourist trade.

'If there was any question of lives being lost indiscriminately, then the world was your oyster when it came to where to plant bombs. That was not the nature of the activity that was going on in England. In the early 1970s there were actions that resulted in a considerable number of people being killed by bombs that had exploded without appropriate warnings being given. That was a learning experience for the entire movement. One is aware that life must not be taken cheaply.'

An admission of regret on Martina's part that many innocents had been caught up in decades of violence but a clear insistence too, that she had committed her future to ensuring such sickening barbarity does not happen again.

'I believe the only way to resolve things is by talking to and engaging your opponents. Conflicts aren't resolved by talking to your friends.'

I was intrigued by her role as Director of Unionist Engagement. Somehow I just could not picture a former IRA activist sitting down to tea with a group of raucous Proddy women from Belfast's Shankhill never mind the DUP leader Ian Paisley, the man her supporters had for so long viewed as a demagogue, rabble rouser and denouncer of all who opposed a Protestant Ulster.

Even more interesting was to discover that Martina had almost at once begun to empathise with the daily problems families were facing in the most prominent but deprived of Protestant strongholds. Life had changed dramatically from the 1950s when Catholics posed no economic threat, with nearly all the jobs in the shipbuilding and engineering industries reserved for Protestants. With such an abundance of both skilled and unskilled employment, education had formed a much lower priority in the Shankhill than the Falls. Until the abolition of the 11-plus exam in 2008, only 5 per cent of Protestant children were obtaining a grammar school place, thus undermining the whole social fabric of the community.

And what about that seat so long held by Nobel Peace Prize winner, John Hume, that she had hoped to wrestle from the SDLP at the General Election. Given her already heavy workload, wasn't this just one step too far?

Not a bit of it. Martina insisted she was up for the challenge. Making up for all those years in prison, she is now a workaholic. She has no children but cares for a mother in her eighties who suffers from Alzheimer's.

'The things that get you up out of your bed at the crack of dawn and not falling back in again until the witching hour, are the people you're meeting and the struggles that are going on in their lives. This is about ensuring that those who have never benefited because of their religion or denomination are given the help they need. No more can we play Peter off against Paul, deploy the sectarian card or make sure the dividing wall is there so that the working class issues are never brought to the fore.'

How difficult it must be for those who looked upon Martina and her ilk as the enemy – heartless and self-glorifying criminals – to see them today holding down several of the top jobs in the new government of Northern Ireland. In particular, I wondered whether the police had privately passed any comments on having a former IRA terrorist sitting on the board responsible for holding them to account and monitoring everything they do.

Indeed, they most certainly had.

'At one Police Board meeting, an officer came up to me and said "How do you think we feel about you being our boss?" That's the world. Change challenges us all. It will no longer be a Unionist police force when one community polices another. Those days are gone. The challenge for us all is acknowledging and recognising that and then trying to build the kind of society we all want.'

And to those who say Martina was an IRA bomb maker?

'One person's terrorist is another person's freedom fighter. And I am very proud of whom I represent. I'm a very proud Republican. I acknowledge that there are people who are proud Unionists and I can accept and respect that. We have to learn to respect difference. I'm entitled to be a Republican and just like any other country or state that had an army, I was involved in a military campaign as part of an army. I have no regrets about what I did in the past and I just hope that nobody has to do all that again.

'There's a window in the Stormont Assembly that I look up at every day and I think of all the people who have died and all that we have come through, where we are now and what we need to do. In my head, I see them all looking in at us and there's a sense that we have to be certain that we can get this done to ensure that what happened in the past never happens again here in the North.'

For three decades and for so many television viewers in the rest of

Britain, stories about Northern Ireland were met with a cold indifference. Unpleasant and unpalatable, they were not the kind of items families wanted to see as they prepared to sit down to tea. Would there ever be an end to The Troubles? To most, it seemed the shooting, burning and bombing would continue ad infinitum.

What a surprise then, when those bitter arch-foes, Ian Paisley and Gerry Adams, met face to face to decide on a new way forward. The transformation was complete as Paisley, firebrand leader of the Protestant DUP, indicated he would enter government with the political wing of the IRA. Here was the man whose stinging sermons from his church pulpit cleverly interwove a political tirade with vivid Bible messages, who had bitterly opposed power-sharing executives brokered by more moderate politicians during the Sunningdale and Belfast agreements of past years, prepared to work with those from across the sectarian divide.

Martina is but one of them, proud of her past, industriously working for a more optimistic future. Before I took my leave, she invited me upstairs to the main Sinn Fein office.

The next five minutes were bedlam. A phone receiver in each hand, notes being hurriedly scribbled in a desk diary, constituency workers dancing round her desk with a list of pressing problems, it could hardly have provided a greater contrast from her previous life locked up in a high security jail. The Creggan and Bogside had come calling and here was a woman single-mindedly determined to make up for lost time.

Glancing up from the growing mound of paperwork, her parting words echoed the new mood of optimism about the place.

'I never thought I would come to a position in my life when I would look at someone like Ian Paisley and think I hope he'll live a little longer. At one time, I would have wished he'd go home and pray for a happy death.'

In Northern Ireland, there have been too many false dawns to take things for granted and politicians on all sides are under pressure to deliver. Dissidents opposed to the political changes have pursued a low level but persistent campaign of violence but have gathered little support for their actions. After decades of deadlock, the pace of change in Ulster is quite bewildering.

17

Albania – Who Cares?

We shall eat grass rather than surrender to imperialism.

Enver Hoxha, Stalinist leader of Albania 1944–85

In the 1950s Albania was the country nearly every school textbook chose to ignore. It was almost as if the place did not exist. I remember being awarded a bar of homemade fudge from a teacher at Dundee High for correctly naming Tirana as the capital, a fact I knew only because memorising capital cities of the world was one of my healthier youthful indulgencies. Little did I know then how big a part this tiny Balkan state, not much larger than Wales, would play in my journalistic career!

Even today, many sixth form geography students find difficulty in placing the country on a map of Europe, a vivid demonstration if ever one was needed of the appalling isolationist policy of its former Stalinist dictator Enver Hoxha. From the end of the Second World War until his death in 1985, he ruled his country through terror, the politics of the permanent purge and a personality cult that verged on the paranoiac.

Those of his subjects who dared to remotely criticise his totalitarian regime were declared enemies of the people, removed from job and home and either liquidated or sent into labour camps with their families for a lifetime. Successive links with Yugoslavia, the Soviet Union and China were severed, all forms of religion outlawed and no opposition tolerated from whatever quarter it might come.

Hoxha even persuaded his people that they had the highest standard of living in Europe and that there were many enemies preparing to take it from them. Nearly a million military pillboxes, standing like concrete mushrooms, were erected across the Albanian countryside. They were to protect every road, every field and every factory from invasion from the West. What his people did not know was that the world was completely

237

indifferent to Hoxha's Albania. The dictator had managed to pull off one of the twentieth century's greatest confidence tricks, and the amount of concrete used for constructing the country's defences was more than enough to have built a decent house for every Albanian family.

My first visit to the place was in March 1989 when the control tower at Rinas Airport had (unusually) to handle two incoming planes at once, the England football team in their chartered aircraft touching down just two minutes ahead of the twice-weekly Swissair flight from Zurich.

The World Cup qualifying competition had drawn England in the same section as the Albanians whose players had a rare opportunity to see how people really lived in the capitalist societies their leader so vehemently condemned. The return match at Wembley though, was still a few weeks away. First, it was England's turn to experience life on the other side of a door that had been closed to most of the world for well over 40 years.

Suspicions about Albanian hospitality (entirely ill-founded) meant their stay would be brief and risk-free. They even brought their own chef and bags of peeled potatoes. The time it took to unload them all was equal only to the inevitable delay caused by the Albanians' insistence on checking inside every suitcase just in case someone might have inadvertently popped in an issue of *Playboy* or *The Times* or, just as offensive to the Marxist-Leninist leadership, a copy of the Bible.

My good fortune to have been allowed in was emphasised by a conversation with the Swissair pilot and stewardesses who could not recall how many times they had landed there yet had never been permitted to leave the airport perimeter.

On the bus at last, the Fleet Street sports writers suddenly found themselves subjected to a non-stop commentary on the virtues of Albanian life as expounded by Ilia Zhulati, a press officer from the Ministry of Foreign Affairs, who could describe in infinite detail his government's policy towards any and every nation of the world from which we had all believed they had totally isolated themselves. Those who had brought earplugs to cope with the change in air pressure on the incoming flight now had a decided advantage, being able to concentrate instead on the traffic jams caused by donkey and oxen carts carrying workers home from another tiring day in the fields.

Forty minutes later we had reached the Hotel Tirana where a crowd several hundred strong had gathered to await the team's arrival. Mr Zhulati however, had still not finished espousing the virtues of the country's former dictator, Comrade Enver Hoxha. The bus doors remained firmly shut until his speech was finished.

Anywhere else in the world, football fans as passionate as these Albanians would have made a rush for the steps of the bus, armed with cameras and autograph books. In Tirana, they had neither, not even a pencil or a scrap of paper. Instead, the crowd stood behind the police in orderly lines, staring at the England players as if sighting aliens from another planet.

England won the match 2–0 and left immediately for the airport. I was not due to leave until the following evening, but attempts to make my own way on foot around the city were frustrated by a sullen-faced man who followed me everywhere. By Albanian standards he was very well dressed, wearing a smart grey suit and well-polished leather shoes. Twice, I felt his arm drop on my shoulder as he brought my wandering to an abrupt halt and insisted on accompanying me back to the hotel where he made enquiries about my room number and the purpose of my visit from the receptionist. It was my first encounter with a member of the Sigurimi, the Albanian secret police.

Later that night, I finally managed to give him the slip and got the merest of glimpses into everyday life in this forgotten part of the world. What I saw made me determined to return at the first possible opportunity.

For a whole year, I sent a barrage of telexes in the direction of the Department of Foreign Affairs. Each one was ignored, so too scores of telephone calls that remained unanswered. The longer the sequence continued, the more determined I became.

On the night of 9 November 1989, the Berlin Wall – the most potent symbol of the cold war division of Europe – came down. In the same year, the communist regimes of Eastern Europe were falling like a pack of top-heavy dominoes. Soon Albania, under the control of Hoxha's hand-picked successor Ramiz Alia, would find itself the continent's last bastion of hard-line communism.

As Christmas 1990 approached, a report by a Yugoslav news agency appeared in the British Press stating that a group of Albanian students had been found hanging from lamp standards in the port of Durres. Knowing the animosity that existed between the two countries, I was extremely sceptical, but I telexed Tirana once more to tell them what was now being written about their country.

'It serves you right,' I said, 'because you are the rudest people I have ever come across. I have contacted you so many times as a responsible journalist asking to visit Albania but not once have you extended the decency of a reply.'

To my amazement, John Mahoney, the Foreign News Editor of the BBC called me into his office the next morning.

'This came through for you in the early hours,' he said. 'The Albanians say they want to see you and you've to leave at once to pick up a visa at their Paris Embassy.'

An incredible state of affairs – be polite and be refused; be insulting and be accepted. But then, as I was soon to find out, nothing in Albania followed a logical pattern.

More than a hundred years after the invention of the motor car, Albanians were still banned from owning one. Only party officials could be seen driving on the roads which were, in consequence, a pedestrian paradise. From my hotel room window I could hear the water splashing in the fountain nearly half a mile away and the soft whispers of people huddled together in conversation in Skanderbeg Square below. Hard to believe on a recent visit to the country that Albania is now the most dangerous place in Europe in which to drive. Especially at night, you take your life in your hands when you venture forth in the company of those who sit behind the wheels of ailing Mercedes and Volvos – many of them MOT failures – brought into the country from Germany, Italy and Greece. Easily distracted, always on the phone and ignorant about seat belts, they overtake on dangerous bends at high speed as if they were still riding horse and donkey carts.

As the first Western television news team allowed into the country, we were allocated a Government car, a driver and two guides, both of whom I presumed were members of the Sigurimi reporting back our every movement and turn of the camera. I had experienced this before during my visit with the England team. One minder was never enough. There had to be two so that they could watch each other. If you could get them embroiled in an argument all the better, for it meant that as the temperature began to rise, so their guard dropped momentarily allowing precious seconds for a spot of clandestine filming.

The good news was that on this trip one of our minders turned out to be none other than Mira Shuteriqi, a producer in the Foreign Affairs Department of Albanian Television, who not only had an excellent grasp of English but an impressive contacts list. Along with cameraman Bhasker Solanki, I had a clear idea of where we wanted to go and what we wanted to see. To our utter surprise, we found Mira totally committed to our cause and shocked almost to the point of disbelief with what she was confronted as we systematically began to unlock the door to reveal the dreadful legacy of the Hoxha tyranny.

By now the government was on the point of collapse, the country in economic chaos, its people queuing sometimes for hours just to get bread. To watch the excitement of children walking home with a loaf under each arm, you would have thought they were carrying bars of gold. At night, they were being sent on to the streets by their parents to set rubbish alight to keep themselves warm. Firewood was fast running out. Along country roads there was hardly a tree left standing, such was the desperation. The shops were empty – no meat, no fish, no coffee.

At one stage the railway network had to be closed down completely. The general manager feared a disaster. Railway sleepers had been removed to be used as a source of fuel and signalling wire torn down by those who had thought of an innovative way of connecting electric supplies from street lights into their homes.

Nearly 70 per cent of the adult population were out of work. There were no raw materials for the factories. Machines stood idle and resilience was wearing thin. One electrical worker trying to mend a severed cable was machine-gunned to death by an angry mob.

If this was what daily life had been reduced to for those living in the cities then what must the situation be like, I wondered, for the former enemies of Enver Hoxha? Some of them were still entrapped in the same labour camps to which they had been sent nearly half a century before.

The world knew little of such places. In the eyes of the Albanian authorities they did not exist. Human Rights groups could gather no information save from a few survivors who had managed to flee abroad.

I was determined to find one of these camps and discover the truth for myself. With the communist government now on the brink of collapse, the chances of success had increased considerably. Discontented members of the military were risking all by allowing more than a few state secrets to pass their lips.

And so it was that we were able to negotiate the filth-strewn dust tracks that took us right into the heart of Gradishte Camp, in the southeast of the country. By now, the guards knew their number was up and were already stripping the place of its watchtowers, machine guns and electric fences.

For hundreds of internees, the chance to leave had finally come, yet there was simply no escape. There they were, still trapped and abandoned in their ramshackle huts crudely put together with mud, a few pieces of old timber and animal excreta allowed to dry in the sun. With no money, no home and no family on the other side of the fence, their prospects for a new life were virtually non-existent.

Unravelling their backgrounds and their stories was a distressing experience even for a hardened journalist. Just sitting and listening to their accounts left me mentally and physically drained. The reality of a lifetime's experience in such grim and barbaric conditions had left many of them in a state of permanent shock. It would be a long time before they could fully trust another human being again. This was the dreadful legacy of the Hoxha years.

Take the Dosti family – before the Italians and then the Germans occupied Albania during World War II, they had enjoyed all the luxuries the country could afford. Hasan Dosti, was the Chief Justice of the Supreme Court and a fierce nationalist. He was one of the founding members of a resistance movement called *Balli Kombetar* which fought alongside Hoxha's Communist partisans. Then, at the end of the war, secure in the knowledge of backing from both Tito and Stalin for their revolutionary goal, the Communists decided to liquidate their nationalist opponents.

Fearing the consequences of Hoxha's triumph in the brutal and bloody civil war that followed, Dosti fled to America with his second son Luan, leaving behind four sons and three daughters. He would never set eyes on any of them again. What's more, all efforts to discover their whereabouts came to nothing. For 47 years he could not be sure whether any, or all, of them were alive or dead. When contact was finally established in 1991, Mr Dosti had reached the ripe old age of 96 and was just weeks from death.

On the very day of Tirana's liberation from the Nazis, Hasan's wife, Fetije, was shot dead by the Germans, who then set fire to the Dosti home. The Nazis gone, it was now the Communists who turned on the family. The eldest son, Victor, was arrested at a students' rally for denouncing the Soviet Union as 'red imperialists'. The original sentence was five years' imprisonment, but for being the son of a nationalist he was condemned to a further 42 years in labour camps.

The rest of the family fared no better. They were all rounded up, accused of being traitors of the State, stripped of all their money and possessions and sent into hard labour for life.

During their 47 years in internment, six of the family were married and fifteen children and six grandchildren were born in the prison camps. Even the third generation was forced to endure the unspeakable horrors of what came to be known as 'Hoxha's Hell'. As a family they had to look to each other for the strength and courage to withstand a regime intent on breaking and dehumanising even the most hardened inmate.

The work began at 5 am and continued until dark. It was physical, constant and exhausting and always carried out under the eyes of guards looking for the slightest excuse to round on their subjects and indulge in an orgy of violence.

Children born in the camps were given only elementary schooling. They were 'non persons' with no hope whatsoever of higher education or a release into the outside world. For the 'crimes' of their grandfathers, they were forced into the same cruel and sorrowful existence, beaten into submission at every turn, deprived of the joys of their youth and faced with a life of hopelessness and despair.

Proper medical care was non-existent. A doctor or nurse was summoned to the camps only when the guards deemed it necessary and then it was mostly to tend the needs of their own families.

Victor's wife, Hyrije, gave birth to their daughter on a dirt track. Her child survived but many born in similar circumstances did not. As we talked about the experience, her daughter, Arta (meaning 'golden'), lowered her head, tears streaming down her face.

'Poor thing, she feels she has no birthplace and she's never been to a proper school,' Hyrije explained, 'but I tell her to cheer up for she means everything to us.'

In the labour camps human tragedy became part and parcel of everyday life. Illness or disease were ignored as if they did not exist. Those from persecuted families reporting sick would still be rounded up by the guards and sent out into the fields or the marshes or down the mines. Old men collapsed under the weight of the extra loads the police kept piling on to their backs, people were drowned in the swamps to terrorise others, while savage beatings were the inevitable result of failing to fulfil the quota of work for the day.

For their hard labour the internees could earn a maximum of 80 pence a month, barely enough to buy bread. Women forced to till the land by hand were given just one hour's break in their dawn to dusk workload. It was usually spent knitting something for the children.

Returning home in the dark to their crumbling windowless shacks, the only nightly protection against the cold winds that swept through the makeshift roofs of sticks and plastic sheeting was a threadbare blanket.

The cycle of terror was never ending. Frequently the guards would call someone out by name and ask him to run an errand. Some never returned from such missions. Others were taken to a hostel and tortured for days and then asked to undertake a spying mission for the Sigurimi.

Men were forced to look on helplessly as their wives were paraded before them. A cat was placed inside their dress which was then bound tightly at both ends.

'Imagine', Victor Dosti asserted, 'what a cat will do to try to free itself in such circumstances. It was just insufferable.

'In one camp the authorities forced a wife to give a false testimony against her husband to whom they had taken an obvious dislike. Afterwards she strangled herself with a sheet, her husband died in the interrogation room and their five children were orphaned.'

After close on half a century of internal exile, the Dosti family finally moved into the top floor of a multi-storey block in Tirana. Even that was only made possible by the arrival of their brother, Luan from the United States. While they had languished in their living hell, the brother who fled to America had become a business high-flyer in charge of international relations for a big armaments factory in Los Angeles. Visiting the rest of his family in the squalor of Gradishte Camp just before their release, he could not come to terms with what confronted him. He did however, have some exciting news – their father, Hasan Dosti, was still alive.

At 96 years of age, Mr Dosti picked up the telephone to take the most important trans-Atlantic call of his life. At the other end of the line the eight children whose voices he'd last heard in 1944. At first, there were only tears, and then... 'Where have you all been? Are you all well ... still alive?'

'Yes, father ... and you now have fifteen grandchildren and six great grandchildren, all born in prison camps. You must know, Dad, that we never regretted for one minute that we suffered for your sake. On the contrary, we have always been proud because we know you were cherishing a noble ideal for which you sacrificed mother, yourself and your family. This is what made all the suffering worthwhile. We just hope you will live long enough to see us.'

He did not. Such was the shock of speaking to his family again after 47 years of silence that Hasan Dosti collapsed within a matter of weeks. He died though, in the sure knowledge that each and every one of his children had miraculously survived.

Alas, not all were so fortunate. Three years after Hoxha's death, political prisoners were still being executed for attempting to escape from internal exile. One of them, Havzi Nela, a schoolteacher, had spent 19 years in labour camps followed by internment for openly criticising Hoxha's campaign to destroy religion and then attempting to cross the border to Yugoslavia with his wife.

Before going to the gallows, Nela who was 54, penned the following verses which were smuggled out of the camp and handed to his relatives. Alex Standish, a UK economic consultant based in Tirana in the early

1990s, was moved to tears on receiving a copy and, having translated the teacher's words into English, said the family would be proud to see their father's verse in print.

WHEN I DIE

When you learn that I have died,
When you say 'he's been forgiven,'
Do you know what I have passed through,
Me, the poet with a burning heart?

When you ask ' where is his grave?'
When you search to find me,
Say, he hated the cruelty of man,
Say, the earth won't consume him.

Say, life he loved,
But life through hate destroyed him.
Say that he had defended right,
And could not endure the tyrant's fist.

Say, he hunted for freedom,
As a hawk in flight,
He knew chains, and dark cells,
For others had ignored the call.

Say, he searched for light,
But never saw it with his eyes,
Say that for humanity he sang,
While for himself he mourned.

I thought it impossible to believe any fate could be worse than that experienced in Hoxha's labour camps … that is until I endeavoured to locate the prison of Burrel. Even in the height of summer, it takes hours to reach the place, travelling along a winding pot-holed road and climbing ever steeper through tunnels cut into the granite rock that straddles the mountain passes of the north. The journey is one of the most breathtaking in all Albania, passing through a magnificent landscape of virgin forests, shimmering lakes and sheer cliffs before finally levelling out on entry to Burrel itself.

The prison is just half a mile from the town centre, but here inmates were condemned to a life of unspeakable horror. One of those I met, Sadiq Poda, spent a life of unending pain and utter degradation in the place deemed 'the prison of extermination'.

You have to go back to the early days of 1945 to find the 'crime' for which he was responsible. Like 40 other young volunteers from his village he joined the ranks of the nationalist forces which were drawn into the civil war against Hoxha's victorious partisans.

Defeat meant that Poda and his friends now joined the many thousands of 'war criminals' whom Hoxha, through a series of show trials, wanted dealt with expeditiously. Many were summarily sentenced to death, the others condemned to prison or the special labour camps set up to deal with such 'enemies of the people'.

Of the 440 prisoners held within Burrel's white concrete walls on the day he entered, Poda claims 300 did not survive. Starvation, an endless cycle of torture and beatings, disease and the sheer cold sapped the strength of even the most hardened men. Death became inevitable. In case anyone had the slightest doubt about the prison's purpose, a huge sign was hung over the gate. It read: 'This is Burrel where people enter but never leave.'

Poda survived on 500 grams of bread a day plus a little salt. To get water, he and his three cell mates were sent to a well inside the prison compound. The men linked their towels in rope-like fashion and then lowered them slowly into the well in the hope that a few drops of water would soak into the material. When the towels came up they were completely red. The water was polluted. Yet without a mouthful they knew they would surely die. Back in their cells they squeezed the towels into a dish. The filthy sediment eventually dropped to the bottom and each man in turn took a sip from the top of the dish.

The beatings continued daily, weakening body and spirit. Such was the desperation for food that, when a prisoner died, those sharing his cell would try to keep news of his demise from the prison guards so they could share his daily ration. A favourite trick was to put a lighted cigarette in the dead man's mouth to allay any suspicions. Next day they would put him under a blanket, pretending he was asleep, but when the smell became overpowering, they had to hand the body over and suffer another beating for their pains.

Poda told me he buried several inmates with his own hands. Many prisoners have no known grave, for the hole their colleagues dug was just 40 centimetres deep. Placed in such shallow graves, the bodies were savaged by the prison dogs.

Listening to experiences like these is a real test of one's faith. I must confess I found myself frequently asking 'God, how could you let this happen?' But of course, that so much of Albania is soaked with the tears and blood of the innocent is not God's doing. We cannot chalk it up to Him. Cruelty and brutality perpetrated on the orders of a ruthless despot is a great travesty and a dreadful stain on our shared humanity. But that is no reason not to believe.

Indeed, it was his unswerving faith that allowed Peter Arbnori to survive the worst moments of Stalinism Albanian-style. A teacher and writer, he was sentenced to death for his part in forming a Social Democratic organisation based on the principles of Western countries and pluralism. The sentence was later commuted to 28 years' imprisonment as the authorities hoped Arbnori would lead them to catching other ringleaders.

Having survived two years of interrogation and torture, Arbnori was eventually incarcerated in Burrel for longer than any other man who survived. Every winter, for at least a month, he was confined to a cell, dressed only in his underwear. Barefoot, he was forced to sit on a cement floor with the temperature minus 15°C. Buckets of water were thrown over the floor, which froze almost at once. He was then tied into position using ropes suspended from hooks on the cell wall. The barred window was open to the elements and the door hatch was also left ajar to cause an icy current of air to encircle the entrapped prisoner. The pain was excruciating. There were no blankets and a daily ration was just one piece of bread weighing half a kilo. Arbnori ate only half, placing the other half against his ribs so he could use it as a prop to shield him from the ice-covered floor. That way he managed to turn on to his side and try to get a few minutes' sleep.

At other times of the year, the prisoners were cast into overcrowded cells. Every now and then the guards would burst in and begin drawing pencil marks across the floor. They wanted to make life even more unbearable and did so by designing precise areas in which each man must sit. The most fortunate was offered 66 centimetres, the unluckiest 38. When the inmates quarrelled among themselves, the guards would simply open the door and throw in an additional prisoner. That meant they had to sleep virtually on top of each other.

One of the ways Arbnori preserved his sanity was to write at every given opportunity. He would scribble using the tiniest possible lettering along the margins of the Communist Party's newspapers and magazines which the prisoners were given to read and he came up with an ingenious method of getting his writings out of the jail right under the noses of his prison guards.

His mother visited faithfully every month. After waiting, sometimes for hours, she was taken into a grim, concrete room just inside the prison walls. The door to the inner compound remained firmly locked. No visitor was ever allowed to see what lay beyond.

In the middle of the room stood a small table. On the visitors' side a bench, on the other a wooden chair on which the prisoner was already seated. Standing abreast of the table was the prison guard who listened to every word and monitored every action. He was under precise instructions to ensure no physical contact took place between the prisoner and his visitor at any stage.

'My mother was ordered to put her bag of food on the table. The guard immediately checked each item inside and then ordered me to put my empty one alongside. A wink in my mother's direction was the only indication she needed. You see the empty bag she was handed had a double bottom and inside I had hundreds of small strips of paper torn from magazines on which I had superimposed my own script. Month by month the story was taking greater shape.'

Just in case his plot was ever discovered, Arbnori had cunningly woven an intricate pattern of deceptions into his writings designed to throw the authorities into total confusion.

One of his favourite ploys was to hide behind the name of an internationally known novelist and pretend he was translating an original work into Albanian. John Creasey, one of England's most prolific writers, fitted the bill perfectly. Creasey had published so many novels that Arbnori thought it highly unlikely his captors would bother to check the hundreds of titles available.

He was right. So from his prison cell, *Brighton, A Summer's Lightning* was conceived. It was, of course, entirely Arbnori's own work but under the title he penned the words 'by Xhon Krizi' and *perkthyer nga Anglishtja* ('translated from English'). The protagonist is an Irishman living in Brighton. He longs for a new life. The *real* character is Pjeter Arbnori fighting for his freedom.

Finally released at age 54, Arbnori had no sooner tasted the first fruits of freedom when he became the target of an assassination attempt during the last throes of the Communist government. He wanted a teaching post but had to settle for a job as an apprentice to a carpenter.

With the first free ballot, Arbnori stood as a Democratic Party candidate and was elected to Parliament and became its Chairman, equivalent to the Speaker of the House of Commons. He was determined to make up for lost time, married Susanna twenty years his junior, and they had two children.

To me, his appointment seemed a first significant step towards addressing the growing feeling of national guilt over the years of Communist oppression. Meeting him in his elegantly furnished office, a stark contrast to the horrors of Burrel, I was struck by his humility, integrity and intense compassion. It could have been such a different story had he chosen retribution over forgiveness but amazingly, there were no thoughts of revenge.

'Every day I see people who spied on me, who accused me, who interrogated and tortured me, judges who brought false evidence and witnesses to testify against me, and I turn my head on the other side so as not to show contempt.

'I don't say I forgive or forget them but the Albanians have a greater aim which is establishing democracy in the country and re-unity with Europe. That is where we must invest our energies and this will minimise the suffering I have passed through, turning the head and mind towards the future.'

In 1997 his party lost the elections to the Socialists led by Fatos Nano, following the turmoil caused by the disastrous pyramid investment scheme that caused the financial ruin of thousands. From the benches of the opposition, it soon became clear to Arbnori that there was a risk that the censorship of the old communist regime might be reinstated. So when the state-owned television station refused to broadcast the statements and initiatives of the opposition party, he went on hunger strike.

It was here that the fame of 'The Mandela of the Balkans' claimed the attention of many Western governments whose support forced the majority coalition in Parliament to approve a formal guarantee of independence of the Press from state interference.

It was just one more battle in the life of a remarkable fighter for social justice but the energy expended in his new life after the physical cruelties of his long years in one of Europe's most notorious prisons, was beginning to take its toll.

Peter Arbnori died of a brain haemorrhage in 2006 but not before his book *The fight to remain a man* was finally published. It had been typeset for some considerable time but raw materials were so scarce there wasn't enough paper to get his volume into print.

The privilege of being the first Western broadcaster to be given free rein in the country was now sitting heavily on my shoulders. It was clear that for some the physical and mental damage that wrecked their lives could never be repaired, but being able to freely talk of their experiences was, in itself, an almighty release.

In the back streets of Tirana we found an old building being lovingly restored to its former use as a Catholic church. Mothers, their young children in tow, were endlessly dusting and polishing while their husbands nailed the timbers of the old pews back together again.

But it was the parish priest whom I was desperate to meet. His name Zef Pllumi, now an old man who against all the odds, had survived one of the worst cycles of sustained cruelty perpetrated in the second half of the twentieth century.

By the beginning of the summer of 1967 Enver Hoxha's final onslaught on religious practices had begun. The results were devastating, the persecution relentless. Hoxha was to act in a way no other leader, including Hitler and Stalin, had dared. *He abolished God.* Albania became the first self-proclaimed atheist state in the world and Hoxha would describe it as one of his greatest achievements.

Teams of party activists were whipped up into a frenzy and despatched the length and breadth of the country to cajole, bully and intimidate people into giving up their religious beliefs. By the end of the year more than two thousand mosques, churches, monasteries and seminaries had been shut down. Many were demolished or burnt to the ground. Others were turned into warehouses, cinemas, basketball courts or gymnasiums.

Hoxha called on the 'sharp knife of the party' to be used in the class struggle against religious ideology.

'Religion is opium to the people and we must do our utmost to ensure this truth is understood by everyone, even by those who are poisoned by it. We shall have to cure them.'

The Muslim community, who accounted for 70 per cent of the population, lost 1,300 mosques, had twenty *haxhis* (imams) tortured to death and several others hanged themselves or committed other forms of suicide in jail.

It was to be the Catholic Church though which would experience the regime's savagery on a scale as yet unprecedented. Its clergy, almost without exception, were scholars and highly cultured people. They had studied abroad in Austria, Italy and Germany and the Church had run seminaries and schools in its northern stronghold, the city of Shkoder, two for boys and one for girls. They had also published their own newspaper and a whole range of religious books and literature. All this,

Hoxha rightly considered, presented a very difficult obstacle to his policy of 'wiping them off the face of the earth'.

Zef Pllumi's life as a young Franciscan was subjected to the first onslaught of the fanatical and remorseless campaign to destroy Catholicism as early as 1946. The police laid siege to the seminary which the Order used as their own living quarters. One man only was allowed out once a day with the police to buy food and bring it back to the dining hall where the Franciscans were being kept hostage, incommunicado with everyone.

As the days passed, so the pressure was stepped up relentlessly. First despised, then ridiculed and physically abused, their ordeal was, as yet, only in its early bearable stages.

The Sigurimi and government officials burst through a back door carrying arms and ammunition. They opened cupboards and cloakrooms, hiding bullets under piles of books and slipping rifles into wardrobes full of cloaks and cassocks. Then, in the middle of the night, they surreptitiously crept into the church, stacking the vestry and ante-rooms with as many weapons as they could muster.

At Sunday Mass the Sigurimi returned, displayed 'their find' in front of the congregation and accused the clergy of conspiring to overthrow the Hoxha government. 'What more evidence do you need of your priests' intention to kill our leaders?' they would scream at the terrified worshippers.

Father Pllumi prepared for the inevitable. He was just 22 years old when he was arrested, charged with the possession of arms and plotting an insurrection.

With the Franciscans held hostage in their own seminary, the secret police were content to deal with them right where they were. The sacred building was turned into a prison overnight. The dining room became a torture chamber.

'The agony ... the screams ... went on day and night. Hundreds – believers as well as priests – were tortured inside the House of God. There was no mercy. It was as if the Sigurimi were competing with one another to find ever more ingenious and dastardly forms of torture.'

One of the most common practices was to tie the prisoner with a rope under his armpits and then suspend him from a plum tree, rather like a trussed chicken in a butcher's shop. This torture was reserved especially for stifling summer days and presented the only occasions when the unfortunate victims were allowed to leave their inner prison. More often the priests were suspended from the stair railing, their toes

251

only partially touching the ground. This was called 'the break or the resting'. What they meant by this, Pllumi says, was 'think it over now'.

'We were tied up like this for days on end. There was no respite. We had no food, and all the time an armed guard was standing over us. It was impossible to sleep in this position and even if we tried, a bucket of water would be thrown over us. Twice a day we were dragged to the toilet just for a couple of minutes. We wanted to lengthen the time but they dragged us back again. Sometimes we were suspended like this for well over a week.'

After the Franciscans were untied, they were taken to the investigation room for 'intensive interrogation'. This began with hour-long beatings with batons and iron bars. Their bodies became so bloodied that many of the priests were unrecognisable, even to their friends, when they were thrown out of the room.

The beatings over, the prisoners were then subjected to the electric shock treatment. Live wires were attached behind both ears, and the guards used the handle of an old fashioned telephone to generate the current.

'It was terrible. They wanted to terrorise us because they had no proof. "We know everything," they'd shout, "so let's have it out or you will die under torture." Those who could take no more and admitted things they had not done were treated in one of two ways. Some were executed at once but for others there was no relief, the torture just went on.'

Another particularly cruel form of torture was to place fleas on the prisoners' shaven heads while their hands were tied up to prevent them scratching themselves. Under such conditions, some just broke down completely.

The psychological torture took just as heavy a toll. One method was so simple to administer, yet it drove most of its wretched victims to insanity.

'I was asked to stand upright against the wall. A guard then drew a circle at the precise point which corresponded with the position of my nose. A small hole was drilled and my nose pushed into it. I was then ordered to stand there without moving for ten days. I was given neither food nor water and sleep was forbidden. If I collapsed, I was beaten and then pushed back into position. Mentally, I don't know how I survived. Many of my dearest friends went mad within a week.'

As soon as the Sigurimi believed a prisoner's spirit had been destroyed they threw him a piece of paper and waited for his signature to the charges they had drawn up. Pllumi could not be broken. He was released after more than three years of interrogation under the most sadistic torture.

'At that time, freedom meant absolutely nothing to me because it was also prison on the outside.'

Hoxha's campaign against religious beliefs was entering its second stage. Yet intimidation and threats had failed to clear the pews. People were turning up in greater numbers than ever. Churches destroyed during the first stage of the persecution were being rebuilt by believers who were prepared to make all kinds of sacrifices to keep them going. Far from 'throttling the Church at source', Hoxha's persecution was helping to deepen the faith of many Christians for they saw his regime was ever bending them.

By 1967 Hoxha had become exasperated. There was now no other answer than to shut down the churches and mosques completely.

Zef Pllumi was arrested again, accused this time along with several other priests as being 'spies of the Italian Embassy'. Pllumi refused to accept the accusation, so the authorities came up with another one. They said he was preparing to flee to the United Nations to protest about Church closures. The tortures and beatings started all over again. The sentence this time – 25 years' imprisonment with hard labour.

It seemed almost impossible to me that any human being could withstand such a litany of sheer barbarity. By now Mira Shuteriqi, my interpreter, was struggling to keep her emotions in check. I suggested a break, perhaps a cup of tea but yet another power cut had left the presbytery without electricity and the room was damp and cold. Father Pllumi tightened his cassock and pressed on with his account determined that his sufferings and those of his fellow priests should be made known to the world. I promised I would not let him down.

Life in the camps, he insisted, was worse than internment. The work was back-breaking, the torture and punishments indescribable and the living conditions inhuman. The most crucial factor in the fight to survive was the attitude of the camp commander. He could either make life 'a living hell' or ease the suffering. The camp rules stipulated eight hours' work a day, but many forced prisoners to work twelve and sometimes sixteen hours. Some commanders saved the lives of their prisoners, others speeded their deaths.

'At Vlora Camp we had to drain the swamp with our bare hands and a few basic implements. There was no modern equipment. We were beaten black and blue if we did not work hard enough.'

Many who were sent to the labour camp at Spac died as physical and mental wrecks. There the prisoners were made to work like animals in the copper mines. The 16-hour shifts – in appalling conditions, with little food and often nothing to drink – took a heavy toll. The supply of water to the camp flowed from the mines. It was polluted and undrinkable.

'Can you imagine working sixteen hours in such dreadful heat without a proper break, with inefficient machinery and living under terror ... and there isn't a drop of water to drink? Our bodies couldn't take any more. We were going mad just for a sip of water.'

That week Pllumi was moved to another camp. The transfer saved his life. Just three days later, now at their wits' end, the prisoners at Spac rebelled. The army was called in and five of the ringleaders were executed in front of the other inmates.

Conditions in the other camps were equally bad. Suicides were commonplace.

'God kept me alive. I wanted to die. I just could not endure any more. Many times I was on my knees begging God to give me death. I watched many of my fellow prisoners break down completely. They usually said even if we were to be released, we would be better off dead. So they just threw themselves on to the wire fences around the camps where they were instantly machine-gunned by the guards. This was their release.'

In 1984 Father Pllumi began to experience serious health problems. One morning just before roll call, he suffered a major heart attack. He slumped to the floor of his cell, unable to summon help or move even a few inches towards the door. Death, he believed, was now only minutes away.

Under prison rules, anyone failing to present himself for roll call had to be in possession of a doctor's note. Guards were ordered to check each cell in turn to ensure that everybody was out. Pllumi's door was pushed open. Towering over him was the most brutal guard he had ever encountered, a man whose inhumanity was notorious.

'I can see you are dying. Does the doctor know you are like this? I'll have to finish my rounds but then I'll go to the doctor and tell him to come and see you.'

Though in great pain, Pllumi felt at ease for a few short moments because for the first time he was witnessing a brute showing a spark of compassion. Death, he prayed, would come quickly, but now with life ebbing from him, the sad and saintly Franciscan had no inhibitions about speaking his mind.

'It is such a surprise to see you behaving like this, for you have always been a monster to other people. Think of all those prisoners as humans … they all have families.'

The guard stiffened, his tone of voice displaying a dismissive arrogance.

'I do everything according to the rules.'

'Whose orders are you following?'

'The orders of our great leader, Comrade Enver Hoxha.'

'But don't you know Hoxha is a madman and all the world has ostracised him? Yet here you are, following the orders of a madman.'

'These are also the orders of the Party,' the guard insisted.

'Surely you know', Pllumi continued, 'that when Hoxha dies, the Party won't continue two days without him. When that happens, all these prisoners will come out and demand justice.'

With evidence like this the guard could have had Pllumi executed almost at once. Instead, he left the cell in silence and returned with the prison doctor. The priest's life was saved and the guard's general attitude showed an immediate and dramatic change.

Two years after his final release in 1990 and his appointment as parish priest at St Anthony's in Tirana, Father Pllumi was just preparing to retire for the night when he was disturbed by short, intermittent rings of the presbytery bell. Opening the door, he found a tall, middle-aged man in obvious distress. He was shaking all over, his face pinched and pallid.

'It was only when he stepped into the sitting room that I recognised his features. The sadist who once beat and tortured me and then had saved my life was now begging for forgiveness. I listened, I counselled and I forgave. Even in my most difficult moments, I had never harboured thoughts of revenge. Indeed, I prayed to God to influence the minds of my persecutors … to turn those animals into human beings.'

That prison guard was to become a regular attender at Sunday Mass – so too, members of the Sigurimi, the police and the army, all of whom had been prime players in the job of eradicating religion from Albanian soil.

The full horror of what happened may never be known. One priest was executed for daring to baptise a baby, four Franciscans were burnt to death when a church and convent were set on fire and an untold number of priests, *haxhis* and ordinary believers laid down their lives for the faith.

In December 1972 Pope Paul VI said the Church in Albania 'seems relegated not only to the peace of silent suffering but to the peace of death. With the shepherds stricken and the flock dispersed, one cannot see what human hope remains for the Church.'

If it was a remark designed to try to focus worldwide attention to what was happening in Albania, then it could also have been shamefully construed as indicating a distinct lack of faith on the part of the Vatican.

Little wonder then that the most revered of his successors, John Paul II, was moved to tears as Christian and Muslim alike filled the streets of Shkoder to choking point as he processed triumphantly to the nineteenth-century Catholic cathedral loving restored from its Stalinist years as a basketball court. There, he ordained four new bishops who between them had spent 44 years in jail for refusing to renounce their faith. Franciscan Pllumi was not counted among them.

He had other work to do, not just as a parish priest, but teaching fifty Albanian boys who had entered the Shkoder Seminary to train for the priesthood and writing his trilogy *Live only to tell*.

The Pope described the occasion as a 'glorious resurrection'. The evidence clearly supports that assertion. New churches and mosques have sprung up all over Albania. Christian missionaries and Muslim imams have arrived in large numbers and, in Shkoder Cathedral alone, more than 2,000 people are drawn to a single Sunday Mass.

In 2007 Father Zef Pllumi finally passed away at the age of 83, now a national hero. His home town's religious renaissance proves that faith cannot be wiped out by decree, bulldozers or bullets.

18

Just Call Me Sarah

You can take everything away from someone but you can't take away their spirit.

Sarah, Duchess of York

A referee friend of mine, John Wynne, is a driver on the Northern Line of the London Underground. Though I have always been a train enthusiast, I wouldn't have his job for the world. The only time the poor chap gets to enjoy a bit of daylight is on his days off. Somehow, I would find it difficult retaining my sanity spending hours navigating one of the longest tunnels in the world, the 17 miles from Morden to East Finchley. Little wonder he relishes his Saturday afternoons on the football field.

In comparison, working overnight for *BBC Breakfast* might be considered more conducive to a healthier lifestyle. Not a bit of it! Tackling the night shift can wreak havoc with your sleep. For some, it can lead to other nasty disorders such as gastrointestinal complaints, depression, mood swings and fatigue. Daytime sleepers have to contend with noisy neighbours, building works, children, traffic and the telephone. Ah yes, the phone – why do I never switch it to silent mode? Perhaps, it's because as a journalist, you're never *really* off duty.

If afternoon is your preferred time for getting under the covers then of course, you have to contend with the children arriving home from school. One Thursday afternoon in September 1993 I had no sooner dozed off when my son David came bounding into the bedroom, tugging at my pyjamas and shouting that a lady called the Duchess of York was on the other end of the phone and desperately wanted to speak to me.

I told him to stop winding me up and to please leave me in peace for a couple of hours.

He returned to the phone and indicated that his grumpy father did not want to be disturbed. The caller was determined not to be rebuffed, insisting that this was not a hoax and that the matter she wanted to speak to me about was of the utmost urgency.

And so, half asleep, I picked up the receiver.

'Is that Bill Hamilton?' a familiar-sounding voice enquired. 'This is the Duchess of York. I have just been watching a report of your last visit to Albania. The state of those children you showed in that orphanage is the worst thing I have ever seen. You know I run a charity, Children in Crisis. We must get out there straight away. When can we go?'

I explained that things were not that straightforward. Though her marriage to Prince Andrew was in difficulties and the couple had gradually drifted apart, she was still a senior member of the royal family with an HRH title and her security would be a major problem in a country where lawlessness was all too common and where bandits were roaming the country roads as soon as darkness fell.

We arranged to meet up at her home at Romenda Lodge near Ascot. Cameraman Bhasker Solanki and *BBC Breakfast* producer, Bob Wheaton, came too, along with the Director of Children in Crisis, Theo Ellert. The Duchess ushered us into her front room and opened the flap of the VCR machine attached to the television. She wanted to see everything we had filmed in Berat, Albania's oldest city, where we had encountered this 'home from hell'.

Bhasker and I had been there just days before. Set in a valley between mountains rising to over 6,000 feet, Berat was such a favoured spot of the Communist dictator, Enver Hoxha, that he invested millions in turning the place into a showpiece resort and left his inscription chiselled into the boulders of every hillside so that the world would recognise the fact.

What he didn't show his selected visitors was an odious, crumbling building well off the beaten track where he locked away the city's orphans and disabled children. Two years after the collapse of communism, Berat still held its dark secret.

Behind the bolted doors, we discovered naked and ghostly figures deprived of even the faintest touch of human dignity. It was hard to comprehend how such horrors could be visited upon the innocent and most vulnerable even in Europe's most impoverished country. These children were not the casualties of war or civil strife but the victims of sheer neglect, for the most part left only to console each other.

Mealtime provided little respite from the daily agony. There was not even a table at which these pitiable little children could sit. Covered in flies and filth, many of them were scouring the dirty stone floor for every scrap they could find. When lunch was over, there was further indignity. We found tongues lapping at dirty water in an old bath tub as the children tried to quench their thirst.

Upstairs, all was silent. Younger children, in rusted cots, were seemingly unable to comprehend anything going on around them. Others risked suffocation, using plastic sheeting – meant to protect mattresses – to provide warmth and security. Faced with this on a daily basis, the staff were in a state of despair. One nurse came running up to me to express her shame over the situation and compared it to life in the Middle Ages. A Christian group from Sunderland had recently brought some new beds but, distressed incomprehension in their eyes, some of the traumatised children simply refused to abandon the floor. Other pathetic looking figures were tied to their cots. Asked why, the nurse said it was to prevent them injuring themselves.

We confronted the Albanian Health Minister, Tritan Shehu, himself a doctor. Why were such atrocities allowed to happen? He too was shamefaced but with a health budget equivalent to the price of a cup of coffee for every Albanian and desperate requests for help from an endless stream of hospitals and institutions cluttering his desk, sorting out priorities was clearly going to be an unenviable task.

Just hours after our pictures were broadcast around the world, an order was issued for an immediate closure of the Berat home and an evacuation of the children. Our job now, with the Duchess on board, would be to find out precisely where they had been taken.

My initial worry had been that details of our secret mission would be leaked and that we would be surrounded on the plane by members of the paparazzi or unwelcome hacks from the 'red top' tabloids. Ever since a well-documented and photographed indiscretion, 'Fergie' had been frequently disparaged and vilified in the popular press and I feared that all attempts to improve life for the unfortunate children might be seriously compromised by cameras being trained on the royal visitor's every move.

It was a pleasant surprise then to find the Duchess and her charity director boarding the Swissair flight to Tirana via Zurich with not a Fleet Street photographer in sight, but my heart sank again as I spotted two television crews on the ground as the plane made its final descent on to the uneven runway at Rinas Airport. Fortunately, the rush towards the apron was not to welcome the first member of the British Royal Family to step on to Albanian soil but a reception party for the Belgian Agricultural Minister, who was also on board.

As ever, the luggage was piled case upon case in the arrivals hall, necessitating an eagle eye to be trained on every movement lest someone should decide to make off with our belongings. It was not a fate we wished our fellow traveller to experience.

To help protect her security, I had made arrangements for our party to stay at the villa of the former Communist Party leader Ramiz Alia. At least, this way, I thought the Duchess would be assured of getting a few welcome drops of hot water when the supply came on briefly just twice a day. Unfortunately, she was not there to use it. Unable to wash properly for three days, she had to manage with the few bottles of mineral water she had brought with her.

I wasn't sure how she would appreciate travelling around in a rusty old transit van, but a brief glance at the alternative four-footed transport of donkey and cart was enough to convince her that in a country of such dire poverty she could count herself among the most fortunate.

It was also immediately evident that she wished to abandon all royal protocol. 'Just call me Sarah,' she insisted. It seemed to me to be eminently sensible, for our time in Albania would be limited to just four days and we had prepared a heavy schedule of frenetic activity across the country that would require every member of the team pulling together.

There was just time to offload the luggage before we set off for Tirana's Dystrophic Hospital. Albania was the only European country with a network of these supposedly specialist hospitals to look after the desperate needs of badly malnourished children. Yet it was hard to find a specialist. Even harder to find an aspirin or any form of antibiotic, never mind proper food for the babies.

When I first visited the place, I found children aged 6 months weighing a pound less than when they were born. Babies were doubled up in most of the wooden cots which seemed in imminent danger of collapse. The only heat was provided by a brick laid on the floor. It had a single electrical element sunk into a central cavity in the baked clay.

Bare wires dangled over two of the cots where babies were engaged in a desperate fight for life. The sheets in the room were grey with age.

As if all this was not bad enough, night after night the hospital was being plunged into total darkness. Without heat or light, there was little the medical staff could do to comfort suffering children. There were no emergency generators, not even a candle. Despairing nurses were forced to set fire to pieces of newspaper so they could patrol the wards and monitor their patients' progress.

For many babies, survival in such appalling conditions was simply impossible. Some had dystrophia, others hepatitis or gastroenteritis or bronchial pneumonia; a considerable number were suffering from all four.

The Duchess was shocked. Her immediate impression was that the place was more like a jail than a hospital. Later describing her visit in the pages of *Hello* magazine, she talked of doors falling off their hinges and still no light inside.

'I felt my way up six flights of stone stairs in total darkness and eventually saw a chink of light. A door opened and I was suddenly bombarded by a horrendous smell of unwashed bodies, stale food, old, sick and unchanged nappies.

'One single bulb lit the whole ward but in the gloom, I could see rusting cots falling to bits, each holding one or two sobbing little babies. There was an overpowering ammonia kind of smell from urine around them. And when I went looking for the loos I turned pale. They had not been cleaned in a very long time and were covered in flies.

'I went back into the ward and picked up one tiny little boy. As soon as I did, his sodden nappy drenched the front of my dress. He hadn't been changed for five days.'

The Duchess carried the baby over to a changing mat and gently lifted his sopping, blood-stained clothes to discover open, weeping sores covering his entire body. His nappy rash had become infected and spread right up his back to his neck and even into his hair.

I could detect at once that Sarah was a practical person and a knowledgeable one too, when it came to recognising many of the symptoms of the children's afflictions.

She found some rusty-looking water in an old jar and cleaned the little lad up the best she could. Then one of the nurses found a dry rag. It was as stiff as a board but at least it wasn't wet, so on it went. All the babies were in a similar condition.

Theo Ellert looked as if she wanted to cry, but Sarah felt the babies were doing enough crying for all of us. There was no point in joining them. They just had to get on with doing what they could to settle them down for the night.

The choice of restaurant in downtown Tirana was not difficult to make. There were only two where you would even consider taking a visitor. We settled for the fish restaurant where the kindly owner ran out of the kitchen holding two rather odd-looking specimens – one in each hand.

'Which would you like your Highness, fish from lake or fish from sea?'

Though I can't remember the choice, it was the right one. All of us slept soundly that first night, our slumbers interrupted only by an early morning alarm call.

I wanted Sarah to see how aid and practical support from the British public had helped transform lives in a home for mentally disabled children. This lay in the northern city of Shkoder but, on the way, we made an unscheduled stop at a bread factory in the industrial town of Laç.

The Duchess had no sooner stepped out of the transit van when she spotted a huge rat sitting on a heap of garbage outside the main door. But there were more surprises in store.

The factory staff were all smoking heavily as they mixed the dough for the bread and piled it into ancient, grimy-looking tins. Cockroaches were climbing the walls. At times the conveyor belts that fed the ovens came to a standstill, which was hardly surprising, as they had been in place since the early 1950s. Every few minutes workers were scurrying back and forth with an assortment of screwdrivers in a frantic effort to keep the production line moving.

Sarah, too, was pressed into service, helping carry the loaves to a window from where they were transferred on to an old wooden cart and covered with a dirty grey blanket.

Arriving at last in Shkoder, we made straight for the children's home. 'This is like a dream compared to what we saw in Tirana,' was Sarah's immediate reaction. If only she had seen the conditions that Bhasker Solanki and I had come across on our first visit to Albania, she would have realised just how great a miracle had taken place.

All in authority had tried to persuade us that the place did not exist. Yet it lay just 500 yards from one of the city's main thoroughfares. It might just as well have been 500 miles. No one visited and no one cared.

I recalled how, as our vehicle sped through the entrance gate of the stark, ugly-looking building, a cloud of dust swirled around the filthy forecourt that provided the children with their only experience of the world outside. A handful of them, clad in striped pyjamas shabby and holed, ran down the stairs, staring in disbelief at the mere sight of a visitor.

Others on the upper floor, their necks craned through the distorted iron bars, looked every bit as bemused. One boy, a little older and taller than the others, beckoned us to step inside. Even with such an eerie welcome, we had still been totally unprepared for what lay on the other side of the door.

Children, some as young as three, were huddled together on cold stone floors, many completely naked and covered in their own excrement. The matron had called it the sitting room. But there were no seats … no toys, no books, no comforts, not even a lick of paint on the walls.

In the dark, forbidding corridors – the nearest thing they had to a playground – tiny, shadowy figures, their hair cropped back to keep the lice away, were running aimlessly back and forth. Most, though, appeared to have little inclination for exercise. All they wanted to do was sit, sometimes up to a dozen crammed into a room resembling a prison cell. There were various degrees of handicap. Some were totally illiterate, others badly brain-damaged. In a corner, one older boy was banging his head continuously against the wall.

Some members of staff tried to offer love and affection. They seemed frustrated at every turn, with no resources to call on. The majority seemed uninterested in the children's needs. They stood in a corner, smoking and sullen-faced. It was hard to take in. Most, I presumed, were mothers with children of their own. Yet here attitudes were hard and cold. They did not play with their charges. There were no hugs and no attempt to stimulate the children.

Hygiene was non-existent. Some of the children had open wounds, but there were no ointments or bandages. Some had serious infections, but there were no medicines. Others in a dank and dirty dormitory further down the corridor were so weak they found it impossible to summon enough energy to wipe away the flies.

The showers were inoperative. Using the alternative was a traumatic experience. I could barely watch as one little girl was subjected to the 'bucket treatment'. This involved having a pail of freezing water poured over her head from a few feet away. The rush of water engulfed her tiny fragile frame, her piercing screams ample and painful testimony of the agonies of taking even a wash. Without hot water or a bar of soap, the whole wretched exercise did little more than remove the dust from her hair.

In the kitchen the sight of a new ladle to stir the bean broth, sent round from the General Hospital nearby, was enough to raise flagging spirits. The last wooden one had been thrown into the stove when the logs ran out. Nobody was looking forward to winter. Apart from the twisted bars, there were only a few scraps of hardboard on the windows.

The rain poured in whenever the frequent storms blew in across the mountains.

Everywhere the stench was terrible. Like everything else in this dreadful place the toilets did not work. Faeces littered the stone floors. The matron and the more willing nurses had to double as cleaners.

David Grubb, then Executive Director of the charity, Feed the Children, penned two poetic sketches, after watching our BBC Television News report, from this ghastly home.

THE HOME

The flies are always ready to play,
darting between darkness and silence and the
stench of scars.

The children hunch in remote coils of
desolation; they perch between stranded ideas,
dream junk, no longer remembering what
anything is meant to be.

There are no toys, no games, no names;
there is no colour.
Tides of torture relentlessly lap on crooked dreams.

One boy stretches into space,
recoils, springs out again,
as if there were somewhere to fly.

In the same cold cage, two others squat,
frozen in despair, too tired even to rock,
to continue pecking at their chains.

THE ROOM

This is the sitting room. This is the room
where we sit all day. This is the floor.
These are the walls. This is the window
where there is no glass. This is the ceiling.
This is the useless radiator. This is the

264

place where the light bulb hung. This is
the door. It shuts. It is closed. There
is nothing either side. This is the sitting room.
The sitting down in silence room. The nothing room.
The all life room. The room where we are.
The room where we will remain.
This is the entire world. This is the total existence.
This is the no room. The don't room. The cannot room.
The never ever room. The will never room.
This is the sitting room.

The Duchess shook her head in disbelief as I recounted the appalling situation with which we had been faced. I told her that on this occasion, I had to defy one of the most important journalistic codes – to report a story impartially without ever assuming a personal role in it. I had made promises of help though worried that honouring such pledges might prove extremely difficult at a time when there were so many other pressing needs in the Third World. Yet to have known and not to have responded would have been unforgivable.

Bhasker Solanki had been less anxious. He knew his camera had recorded some heartbreaking images of those pathetic children whose limbs were as thin as the catheters the hospital so badly needed. Bhasker's belief was that, given the strength of the pictures, the international community would react. He was right, though neither of us at that stage could have contemplated the size of the response from the British public alone reaching over 8 million pounds.

Two of the smaller British-based charities, Feed the Children and ADRA (the Adventist Development and Relief Agency) had been operating inside Albania for the previous four months but were experiencing problems in generating interest in what was happening there. Their fears were that the public's general ignorance of the place would count heavily against their aid efforts.

The film, however, was transmitted worldwide and proved the catalyst for a huge international aid effort delivered by air, land and sea. Newspapers carried appeals, thousands of schoolchildren donated their pocket money, lorries laden with tons of supplies set off across the continent, specialist doctors and physiotherapists were flown in to pass on their skills and expertise, and builders and decorators arrived to transform the place into something resembling a hospital.

I have to admit I shed more than a few tears especially when boxes laden with shoes arrived, bringing a look of bewilderment on the faces of children who had spent their entire lives barefoot. One little boy, overjoyed, leaned forward, lifted each foot in turn and kissed his shoes. In that fleeting moment, I suddenly realised how much I take for granted. God gives abundantly but how often do we pause to say thank you?

The Duchess toured the refurbished rooms in turn, talking to staff and organising games for the children. Suddenly I spotted one young boy who had moved north from the squalor of the home that had now been closed in Berat. Sarah picked him up and cradled him in her arms. He look terrified, probably afraid that he would be sent back to the dreadful place from which he had so recently escaped.

As she looked around, Sarah repeatedly asked the staff what had happened to the other children there. There were no answers. Clearly, we would have to go to Berat to find out for ourselves.

It had been a long, tiring day without a break for lunch and as we pulled out of the gates, the Duchess was suffering from a migraine. Theo took off her coat to provide a pillow and Sarah quickly fell asleep at the start of the long, arduous journey back to Tirana. Then, about an hour into the trip, the van ran into an enormous pothole, throwing us all violently out of our seats, hitting our heads against the roof of the vehicle and then back down again. Not exactly the mode of travel a royal might expect but not a murmur of complaint from Sarah. Instead, she enquired, 'what time have we got to set off tomorrow?'

'5.30 latest', I said, 'as we don't want to become a target for the bandits.'

Any thoughts that we might be pushing our VIP guest beyond reasonable limits were quickly forgotten as I rose at the crack of dawn next morning. Shaving the stubble off the underside of my chin, I was interrupted by a sharp knock at the door.

'It's Sarah here. Can I suggest you get a move on. Just to let you know, I'm packed and ready for the off!'

A horrendous thunderstorm erupted as we got under way. We reached Berat by mid-morning and drove up to the home for mentally disabled children. It had been boarded up awaiting repair but outside we were mobbed by a crowd of gypsies and poverty-stricken locals without work or money to buy food for their families. To our surprise, not all the children had been evacuated. In one disgusting room, Sarah found twin girls, ten years old. Their mother had simply abandoned them there because she had too many children and couldn't cope.

We tried desperately to glean any scrap of information as to where the majority of the children had been taken. The general consensus was that they had been moved to Vlora, Albania's second largest port city on the Adriatic Sea. Getting there would prove a hazardous business as the rain continued to lash the area throughout the day. At one stage, our van got stuck in a huge rut. There was nothing else for it but to get out and push. Sarah joined the rest of us helping heave the mud-splashed transit out of the hole and back on its way.

Conscious of the time and the dangers that would ensue after dark, we were anxious to trace the children's whereabouts as speedily as possible. But, arriving in Vlora, we spent hours driving around the city, knocking on the doors of various institutions, without success. Theo, noticing how tired and hungry Sarah looked, urged us to turn back. The Duchess was having none of it.

'We've come this far and we're not leaving until we find them.'

One last institution, one last door. It was opened by a nurse wearing a nose mask suggesting conditions inside must be grim. Yes, the children were here in a couple of stone-floored rooms of an adult psychiatric institution.

Some of its inmates had spent a lifetime in this dreadful place, having been pronounced insane for daring to mutter the mildest word against Enver Hoxha. They shared the same Spartan existence with those suffering from acute mental illness.

It was like walking straight into a blackened railway tunnel ... filthy, freezing and funereal. Existence in this forbidding place must surely rank as one of the nearest things to hell on earth.

In the children's rooms, most had attempted to dress themselves. Their clothes were unbuttoned and upside down. Startled by the appearance of strangers, they cowered in a corner. Shooing everyone else out of the room, the Duchess crouched down on the floor and began dressing the children properly. She fed and played with them for over an hour and they were clearly pleased that someone had the time to provide a little stimulation.

Bhasker and I moved along the corridor to discover yet more horror. The adult patients were being forced to sleep on broken wire-mesh bed springs whose jagged edges lacerated exposed limbs. Sarah begged for just ten more minutes to visit the locked women's ward. Half the patients were naked, the rest only half-dressed with shaven heads. A nurse explained they had not been issued with mattresses or bed linen because most of them were incontinent and there was no water to do the laundry. One young girl shivering in the freezing conditions was lying on her makeshift bed with all her worldly possessions – a pair of flip-flops – in a wet plastic bag beneath her head in place of a pillow.

Reaching into her bag, the Duchess pulled out a *Children in Crisis* tee-shirt she had brought along to wear in case her clothes became dirty. She put it on the girl and comforted her until she fell asleep.

In another corner, she found one old lady confused and anxious, mumbling something to herself. Her face was cut and bruised. She had either fallen or injured herself or perhaps been attacked by some of the other patients. The nurses ignored her as if she didn't exist.

Sarah knelt down, gently clasped her hand and wiped her brow.

Outside it was still raining and darkness had already descended. I was getting extremely nervous about the four and a half hour journey back to Tirana. There had been reports of several muggings and carjackings in recent months and of people held at gunpoint by robbers determined to take anything they could find. For Sarah, though, the emotional impact caused by coming face to face with the desperate plight of those around her was so profound, there was simply no question of hurrying away.

In another ward, she found a young girl traumatised by two dreadful experiences, first having been raped by her father and then by her uncle after the authorities had put her in his care.

The return journey was a sombre and muted one. I arranged a meeting with the Health Minister, Tritan Shehu for the next day, the last of the Duchess' brief visit.

A three-point plan to improve conditions was discussed. The first was to arrange safe warehouses to ensure that aid delivered could be secured. With so many malnourished infants, the second priority was to construct a baby-food factory and the Duchess agreed to help implement the third vital part of the plan – a health clinic for which the *ADRA* charity was already attracting Europe-wide funding.

Her next stop was a visit to President Sali Berisha, who thanked her for her concern. He told her she had been the first member of the Royal Family to visit Albania and that he saw it as a welcome opportunity on which to build a new and meaningful relationship with the UK.

On our return to the airport, Sarah's compassion for the disadvantaged led to one last charitable act, albeit a little misguided.

'Stop the van,' she shouted at our driver. 'Look at that poor little mite with just one leg, begging by the roadside.'

Out she jumped and opening her purse, lovingly placed a dollar note in his hand.

'Actually, Mam, that lad is one of the best rewarded children in all Albania,' I said as she resumed her seat in the transit. 'He's a real little acrobat. You see his other leg is tied behind his back!'

'Never mind, Bill. Just imagine what it would be like being sent out by your parents to beg every hour of the day. He needs our love and support but more importantly, so do all those desperate children we've seen this weekend. I promise you I won't abandon them and I'm going to get as many others as I can to join me in saving them.'

She was as good as her word. In the succeeding months, Children in Crisis made several trips to Albania and particularly to the Dystrophic Hospital delivering a range of aids and equipment that have helped improve the lives of many malnourished children.

As a member of the Royal Family, the Duchess of York has often been maligned and misunderstood. It would be a great pity if we overlooked her boundless energy and compassionate heart.

A few weeks after her visit, I took another phone call from the Duchess. She asked if my wife and I would come round to Romenda Lodge for an Albanian reunion evening. When we arrived, we discovered many of the British volunteer lorry drivers and aid workers she had met in the Balkans were there too. There weren't enough seats for everyone and the host crouched down on the floor.

Everyone in turn offered her his seat. She declined.

'It's such a joy to have you all here ... and please, just call me Sarah.'

19

Wit and Wisdom

As you get older three things happen. The first is your memory goes, and I can't remember the other two!

Sir Norman Wisdom

My fears about the Duchess of York's safety on her trip to Albania proved to be unfounded. Her care, compassion and generosity may have made their mark but the simple truth is that no one recognised her. Not so the next VIP clamouring to get into the country. The voice on the other end of the phone this time was none other than Norman Wisdom. One of the great enduring names of British comedy had but one unfulfilled ambition – to visit the country where he had become a household name.

At a meeting in a London hotel, businessman André Axford and Norman's agent Johnny Mans discussed the possibilities of Norman accompanying us on our next visit to Albania. It didn't take long for me to persuade the BBC that viewers back home would warm to the antics of the little man with cloth cap and ill-fitting suit let loose in this remote corner of the Balkans.

And so we were airborne again! Norman was by now in his eighties yet his athleticism remained as sharp as his wit. For four hours he had kept the crew and passengers of the Austrian Airlines plane in fits of laughter until at last the front door was flung open and down the steps he came, literally tripping over himself in his rush to get into the country.

The fun and laughter packed into his 65-inch frame had turned Norman into an Albanian folk hero, his films the only ones from the west to have escaped the censorship of the Stalinist ruler, Enver Hoxha. The dictator may have abolished God from his country but not Pitkin or Puckle.

Indeed, it was Hoxha, who, paradoxically, ensured Norman would enjoy cult figure status by decreeing that his comedy films like *A Stitch in Time*, *The Square Peg* and *Trouble in Store* were acceptable entertainment for the masses. Norman put his appeal down to the absence of sex, violence and crime in his films. But for Hoxha and his sycophantic cronies it was the struggles of the working-class hero Pitkin against his boss, Mr Grimsdale, that served to replicate the glorious revolutionary victory of the proletariat.

Norman's Albanian fan club spans three generations. You don't need to understand English to appreciate his timeless humour. Some of his films were shown twenty times over or more, and it seems that, during the long years of repression, those who flocked to the local cinema or watched on state television found a rare opportunity to set aside their worries for an hour or two and laugh heartily at the adventures of an irrepressible Englishman.

Rinas Airport in the early 1990s was a chaotic scene at the best of times with passengers desperately trying to get through immigration to retrieve their case before someone else made off with it. Norman's arrival had security running round in circles.

As Albanian television crews rushed to the foot of the aircraft steps, Pitkini as the Albanians have affectionately come to know him, suddenly started darting off in all directions pretending to run away. The armed guards gave chase with Norman screaming 'I thought you liked my films. Don't tell me you're going to haul me off to the slammer!'

Outside the terminal building, hundreds of people had turned up to get a glimpse of their hero. 'Mr Pitkini, Mr Pitkini!' they roared. Taxi drivers jostled with one another as they attempted to persuade him to enter their clapped out and battered vehicles for the 13-mile drive to the capital, Tirana. Tears welled up in his eyes. This was as good as any reception he'd ever experienced back home in Blighty, reminding him of the newsreels of the Beatles arriving at London Airport back in the sixties.

If we'd kept our previous royal visitor secure in one of a series of former Communist villas then we were able to go one better with Norman. His popularity demanded only the finest of surroundings and so our driver proceeded straight to the palatial home that was once the residence of the former tyrant, Enver Hoxha. For over 40 years only members of his inner circle were ever allowed to walk within 500 yards of the house, which was hardly surprising as it boasted among other luxuries two large outdoor swimming pools, now drained of water. I have seen families out for a Sunday stroll making a point of showing their disdain by lifting their children on their shoulders and watching as the little ones attempt to turn the pool into a sea of spit.

If anyone should enjoy the splendour of the inner sanctum of the place then why not the man who had long since become the 'Clown Prince of Albania'? The job now was to keep an octogenarian from being pressed into accepting too many invitations to appear on stage and screen in what had been planned as a relatively short visit.

Easier said than done. Norman wanted to be on the go almost every waking minute of the day.

'Bill, I'm the luckiest little devil in the world. Where are we going next?' was his constant inquiry.

I suggested we might start by taking a look at an entertainer who had been receiving rave notices for his performances at an arts centre just a few blocks away.

In no time, our 'little devil' was up to his tricks. Not for him a seat in the packed arena. Oh no, straight down the aisle he ran and leapt on to the stage, to raucous laughter from the audience. Norman's trademark slapstick routine left Albania's top comic in a state of bewilderment. Not content with that, he then dislodged the pianist from his seat and began to accompany his own singing of '*Don't Laugh at Me 'Cos I'm a Fool*'.

Whenever Norman ventured outside, a near-riot ensued, so eager were ordinary Albanians to get close to him. Within minutes of him being spotted strolling down *Bulevardi Deshmoret I Kombit* (*Avenue of The Martyrs*), the main boulevard of the capital, crowds grew to dangerous levels, thousands clamouring to shake his hand.

At times we lost him in the general melée, and on several occasions there was no alternative but to call the police to arrange his evacuation. The problem was that the forces of law and order were just as keen to get hold of his autograph. We suggested bundling him into their car might be the best way to achieve their wish and to ensure that Pitkini escaped the disquieting stampede.

Finding a quiet but respectable restaurant also proved quite elusive. The waiters' delight at the opportunity to serve him was tempered by their despair at being unable to dish up his request for Lancashire Hot Pot or Shepherds Pie. I suggested Spaghetti Bolognese might be a safe choice but did not expect to find Norman having a laugh at my expense by indulging in a two finger trick of spinning pieces of spaghetti off the edge of his plate and on to mine!

I was pleased to note his table manners had improved immeasurably by the following evening when Albania's Minister of Culture, Teodor Laco, held a lavish dinner in Norman's honour.

'Mr Pitkini's art is above all politics,' he said. 'Totalitarianism is very dark. But the humour that comes from him is like a light, a joy for us all. It is well known that people need humour in their times of difficulty, and for twenty-five years he has been giving us that humour.'

For Norman, it was the ultimate accolade.

An informant, a cheerful young interpreter organised by the welcoming committee, certainly had a feel of things in the world outside which, following the fall of communism, was by now extremely unstable. The Albania mafia had become a serious threat and pushing an unhealthy line in drugs and arms dealing.

'Mr Pitkini, you can buy a Mercedes here for just $5,000. Except that you cannot take it out of Albania. It will have been stolen from Germany or another European country and brought in here illegally. You will be arrested at the border. Or you want a fully automatic Kalashnikov assault rifle? Easily purchased for just a few dollars on the streets of Tirana.'

Quick as a flash, Norman spurned all invitations to become involved in the seamier side of Albanian life.

'Blimey,' he said. 'Thanks, but no thanks.'

The humanitarian side of his visit though, he took very seriously. Four charities, Feed the Children, The Adventist Development and Relief Agency, Task Force Albania and Mencap were eager to show Norman how young lives had been transformed thanks to the generous support they had received from appeals to the British public.

The visits amounted to an emotional roller-coaster for a man who had himself grown up in horrendous circumstances. Norman's own childhood has drawn inevitable comparisons with Dickens' *Oliver Twist*.

He came from a broken home, was ill-treated by a drunken, violent father and, when his mother fled the family home, Norman found himself walking to school in his bare feet and fending for himself, stealing food to survive. Little wonder then, he was able to empathise with the dozens of Albanian children huddled together on the pavement's edge, forced on to the streets to beg for a bread crust or a few *lek* to help feed themselves and their siblings.

In the Dystrophic Hospital he pulled faces at the infants, made unintelligible noises and then burst into song. When it came to soothing the pain, there was no greater tonic than the sight of Albania's beloved Pitkin.

ADRA even named their new health clinic and aid warehouse The Pitkini Centre. Unveiling a plaque though was not enough for Norman. Looking across at the huge boxes of humanitarian aid that had arrived from all over Britain, he discovered so many exciting props that the aid workers and their charismatic director, John Arthur, were treated to an hour's impromptu performance.

Then it was on to the 'No 1 Hospital, Tirana', a misnomer if ever there was one. Norman could hardly believe his eyes looking at a grey, crumbling slab of a building that passed for the country's largest medical facility. He was even more horrified to find doctors virtually chain-smoking when doing their rounds.

'As for the equipment, it looks as if it's inherited from Florence Nightingale and it certainly makes our National Health Service seem like *Shangri-La*.'

Task Force Albania Director, John van Weenen, whipped him off to a crowded ward where Albania's leading eye surgeon Sulejman Zhugli was checking on the progress of his patients. The quality of Zhugli's work had been described as outstanding by a visiting British surgeon who was staggered by the primitive conditions in which he was forced to operate. Zhugli's remuneration like so many of his colleagues in this dire hospital amounted to just 25 US dollars a month.

Even with one eye completely bandaged up, patients' recognition of their distinguished visitor was immediate.

'Mr Pitkin, Mr Pitkin, how marvellous to see you!' was the universal cry.

In a kindergarten built by volunteers from Jersey and named Corbière after the island's most famous lighthouse, Norman introduced a hundred children to a new dance routine before succumbing to the temptation of the new playground slide. Guess who was shouldering the kids aside to get up the ladder and whizz to the ground?

Albania's new Democratic President, Dr Sali Berisha, was as anxious as anyone to meet the man that had raised so much laughter in his own household ever since he was a young boy. What he didn't expect was Norman marching military-style back and forth over the newly-hoovered green carpet of the Presidential suite demonstrating how the Army had helped model his career.

Much to our relief, the President could not contain himself. He burst into spontaneous laughter.

'Welcome to our country Pitkini,' he said in excellent English. 'You are so funny! I can do with audiences like you. Perhaps you could take over as President!'

At that, agent Johnny Mans interrupted.

'I have no doubt Norman could do *your* job but unfortunately, you couldn't do *his*!'

From there, it was off to the 'Pyramid of the Pharaoh', the name Albanian students have given to the multi-million pound museum, a last gasp of self-congratulating communist architecture built to hold everything Hoxha ever possessed. It was designed by his architect daughter Pranvera and dominated by a giant marble statue of the dictator. It used to have an illuminated star on the top and the building's sloping shape represented rays from the star's light. The museum was closed within three years, turned into a night club and is now used as an exhibition and arts centre.

Here, Norman became only the third person after US President Jimmy Carter and Mother Teresa to be awarded the Freedom of the City of Tirana. It was a moving occasion, though this time Norman refrained from rolling around on the floor. The Albanian *raki* flowed in large amounts but, like Pitkini, I steered well clear of it. The invitation to take a glass, fill it and down it in one, may be trumpeted as a cure for all ills including toothache and dizziness but it's about as potent as vodka and should be treated with respect.

Everywhere Norman went, the 'Gump' suit went with him. It has always been his trademark – tweed flat cap askew, with its peak turned up, a suit at least two sizes too tight, a crumpled collar and a mangled tie. If this character known as 'The Gump' was the perfect antidote to the bleak austerity of post-war Britain, then he did wonders for the repressed people of Europe's poorest country.

The last night was a memorable one. Recalling it in his memoirs, Norman describes it as 'unforgettable'.

When did I ever sing 'Don't Laugh at Me' with bats swooping around in the ceiling like swirling leaves in a squall? It happened at the Academy of Fine Art where the students put on a special performance for me, everything from opera to comedy.

The building itself, with its peeling wallpaper and cracked plaster pillars, had seen better days. But the show had a youthful zing about it that was totally captivating, and judging by what I saw I couldn't help thinking there was hope for this small country with its resilience, optimism and creative talent.

My turn … I had nothing rehearsed but they were shouting so insistently that I had to go up on stage to say a few words and thank them. I climbed the steps hesitantly, faced the black curtain in apparent bewilderment, then turned to face the audience and recoiled with mock stage fright.

Finally, I managed a small speech of appreciation, interrupted when I appeared to slip and bang my head on the mike (yes, they did laugh), made sure Jimmy Noon had found the piano in the corner ... and launched into 'Don't Laugh at Me'.

That was a scene I won't forget in a hurry. The students cheered Pitkini to the echo, the bats buzzed me one last time and I reckon I found myself a new fan club that night.'

Such was his appreciation for that fan club that Norman was in no mood to fly home next day. After saying his goodbyes at the airport, he had one more trick up his sleeve. As the rest of the party were slowly ascending the aircraft steps, down below a diminutive figure was up to his antics again turning on his heels and heading back to the terminal building. It took the combined efforts of two armed and burly guards to lift him on their shoulders and bundle him on to the flight for home with Pitkini screaming at the top of his voice, 'I don't want to go. I want to stay another fortnight.'

The trip might well have been prolonged as a rigorous check of Norman's luggage in the transit lounge of Vienna Airport revealed two ceremonial swords he'd bought from a street hawker outside the ancient fortress of Kruja. The security chief who was hurriedly summoned was furious that they had not been spotted at the point of embarkation. He was quite obviously unaware that in the immediate post-communist days, Albania's airport scanners were still examining goods coming *into* the country rather than anything going in the opposite direction!

Norman's impromptu demonstration on how the swords may have been wielded against the Ottoman invaders did nothing to calm an already inflamed situation. Fortunately, the cabin crew of the London bound aircraft happened to pass by just as the row was at its height and after exhausting several rolls of reinforced anti-tampering tape to provide maximum security, the swords were allowed to leave in the personal possession of the airline's captain.

In the same year Norman was finally awarded the OBE for his services to entertainment and he extended an invitation to me to join him at a celebration party. There he related how in the year following the Queen's Coronation he been invited to Windsor Castle to do a private show for the Royal Family's Christmas staff party. All the senior royals were present

– the Queen, Prince Philip, the Queen Mother, Princess Margaret plus an audience of Castle staff and their friends.

Norman had done a pre-show recce, checking the acoustics, any blind spots and the stage. It was a bit on the small side so he would have to make sure he didn't fall off the end. There were three steps down at the front and on either side, flower displays that looked lovely in priceless ceramic vases.

Wilfred Pickles was the compère and led the royal party in a chorus of 'Have a Go, Joe'. When Norman's turn came, he leapt out on the stage, went through a fast 20-minute routine and was relieved to hear the great hall resounding with laughter. But then, oh dear … his big mistake.

Instead of staying on stage to take his bow, he wandered down the steps and passed along to the middle of the front row where Her Majesty was sitting.

I gave her a deep, sycophantic bow until my head almost rested on the royal lap. She smiled at me with those brilliant blue eyes and nodded an acknowledgement. It was time to go but I suddenly realised I was stuck! Protocol requires that you always keep your face turned to the royal personage. I couldn't turn my back to the Queen!

So I started walking backwards, fumbling my way up the steps with a fixed smile … straight into the flower arrangement. There was an almighty crash as the vase broke and flowers and plants spilled out on to the floor. I rolled over backwards in the debris. The Queen had a hand to her mouth in concern, most likely on my behalf.

There was a deathly silence as I struggled to my feet, surveying the wreckage. Then I looked at the Queen and said: 'Don't worry, Your Majesty – I'll pay!'

The Queen led the laughter as Norman recalled how he scurried away, red-faced but in one piece. Maybe, I thought, that was why he had been kept waiting so long for his 'gong' though a knighthood too, would soon follow.

Norman was determined to return to Albania, and six years later events conspired to provide the perfect opportunity. Along with a number of charity directors, I was visiting morning assemblies at a host of schools across the UK and describing the appalling conditions that still existed in a country just three hours flying time from Britain.

I wish I could have invited along some of those who constantly criticise the younger generation as being apathetic, unmotivated and selfish. Thousands of children had raised funds to purchase their own infant ventilators for children's hospitals in the most critical areas of Albania. Each one of the machines, doctors said, could save the lives of up to 400 children a year. Schools, setting a target of a few hundred pounds, collected six thousand and more. There were *non-uniform* days, *fast* days, *marathon* days and *sit in silence* days ... all were *highly profitable* days.

In addition, pupils saved up their own pocket money to pay for the cost of sending books to a new children's library established by the Task Force Albania charity.

Not only was Norman champing at the bit to go and examine the results of all these efforts for himself, he was equally keen to see the England football team in action in yet another World Cup qualifying match against Albania which had been arranged for a Wednesday evening in March 2001.

Having by now officially retired from the BBC, I contacted Gary Rogers, the ebullient Head of News at Channel 5, the relatively new terrestrial channel, who had won the right to transmit the game live from the Qemal Stafa Stadium in Tirana. Would he like a special feature on Norman's visit to coincide with the big match? It took him just a few seconds to give a thumbs-up.

As agent Johnny Mans sought sponsorship for the trip, I could see we were confronted with a serious dilemma. Norman wanted to offer his support to the England team but being a national hero in Albania everyone there would be expecting him to back the underdogs in their bid to make history. What could possibly be done to resolve such a pressing conflict of interests?

Johnny summoned me to his agency offices at Hoddesdon in Hertfordshire. We talked and talked without resolving anything and were just about to part when he suddenly had a moment of inspiration.

'What we must do is to purchase both international shirts – England and Albania – and send them to the best seamstress in town. She can split the shirts and stitch half of each together. The same thing with the shorts and Norman can wear one white stocking and one red one.'

It was the perfect solution but we decided we wouldn't tell Norman about it until the evening of the game just to ensure our little secret didn't leak out to the dozens of English sports writers expected in Tirana.

On the eve of the big match we had arranged a hectic day of activities for the much awaited return of Mr Pitkin. First, there were the doctors to meet who were involved in the daily fight to keep Albania's newborn babies alive. One in ten was a premature birth in a country where the infant mortality rate was four times that of Western Europe and the health budget so tiny that the babies' lives were dependent on help from abroad.

Tears streamed down Norman's face as he saw the life-saving equipment purchased by British schoolchildren and then it was on to the children's library stacked with 50,000 books all sent from UK schools. Task Force Albania's Director, John van Weenen, explained that it was not considered a handicap having all the books written in English. Indeed, the thirst for knowledge was so great amongst Albanian children that learning English was seen as a passport to the world outside.

Albania's new television stations whipped him away to draw the winning lotto tickets live on air, perform on the trumpet and saxophone and to be swept off his feet on the dance floor by the country's finalist in the Miss World contest.

With tickets for the football international costing the equivalent of a week's wages, hundreds of Albanians decided that watching the England team's training session at the stadium was the better option.

Every girl around made a dash towards David Beckham as he appeared from the dressing room tunnel. But then with perfect comic timing, Norman burst upon the scene and suddenly 'Becks' was booted out of the limelight for the first and perhaps the last time in his illustrious career – for the tabloid journalists, this really was a Norman conquest!

The England manager, Sven Goran Eriksson looked bemused by the impish little grey-haired figure waddling on to the pitch and then falling over his own feet in his time-honoured trick. Assistant coach, Peter Taylor, famous for his Wisdom impersonations, studiously kept out of the way despite being urged by the players to meet him.

Local television crews pressed Norman for a prediction of the score.

'There won't be too much in it. I expect England to win 15–0.' Then remembering his divided allegiance, he added: 'On the other hand, I might just be a devilish little liar!'

His favourite players? 'Er, there's that Beckham and erm ... Michael wotsisname?'

'Owen' came a helpful prompt.

'Yes, that's right, him.' said Norman. 'I'm terrible for names. The trouble is when you get to my age three things happen to you. The first is your memory goes and ... I can't remember the other two!'

On the afternoon of the game Norman decided he'd like to take a couple of hours nap so he could recharge his batteries. I sneaked out of the hotel and walked to the headquarters of the Albanian FA. I suggested that perhaps they might consider allowing a national hero the chance to run on to the pitch before kick-off so he could wave to his fans.

'Are you talking about Mr Pitkin?' they asked. 'We can go one better. He can provide the half-time entertainment. Come on the pitch, do what he likes. The crowd have paid good money for tonight and they need to see the stars.'

And so when Norman awakened from his slumbers, a surprise was waiting at the foot of his bed ... the twin-coloured England/Albania shirt all neatly embroidered with the national badges and ready for his delectation.

'I can't go wrong tonight ... one of each!' He slipped the shirt over his head. 'And look at those shorts and stockings ... what would Mr Grimsdale say?'

England won the match 3–1 but dear little Norman helped make up for Albanian disappointment. In fact, most of the home fans made him Man of the Match. As he ran past them, the cry rang out: 'Pitkini, Pitkini.' And as he turned to the end of the ground where the 2,000 English fans were gathered, with one voice they broke into song: 'There's only one Norman Wisdom!'

Later that year, Norman now a Knight of the Realm, found himself in Albanian company again when arriving at the the Grosvenor House Ballroom in London's Park Lane for a lifetime tribute luncheon laid on by Comic Heritage. Seated at the top table right next to Sir Norman was none other than the Albanian Ambassador, Agim Fagu, a former basketball international.

Getting to his feet, the ambassador in grey suit and pink tie, paid a remarkable tribute of his own:

'Mr Wisdom is one of the greatest artists that Albania has received in recent years. I myself was dismissed from school for seeing Mr Pitkin and lying to the headmaster that I had been to the dentist. The enjoyment that Pitkini gave me not just that day but all my life was bigger than the punishment from my school. This lunch will be one of the most remarkable days of my life.'

In a career spanning over six decades, Norman Wisdom brought laughter to millions, but nowhere was it appreciated more than among the repressed subjects of Hoxha's Albania. For me, it would be impossible to forget the sheer pleasure of spending a week in the company of 'the luckiest little devil in the world'.

20

In The Presence of a Saint

Being unwanted, unloved, uncared for, forgotten by everybody – I think that is a much greater hunger, a much greater poverty than the person who has nothing to eat.

Mother Teresa

The wooden floor was bare even of a rag carpet, the rudely plastered walls unadorned by paper or paint. Two roughly hewn chairs and an old second-hand table were the sole furnishings apart from an antique Bakelite phone sitting forlornly beneath the broken window frame. The guest room was exactly what I had expected. Along the corridor I could hear the faint sound of soft footsteps.

In through the open door came a tiny woman in a simple white cotton sari with blue borders. Her face was wrinkled but her dark eyes commanded attention and her reassuring and kindly smile lit up the room. She stretched out her hand in welcome. As I clasped it, my only fear was that I might cause her an injury, so brittle were her tiny bones.

It was a meeting I had been eagerly awaiting. For this was Albania's most famous daughter, Agnes Gonxha Bojaxhiu who, as Mother Teresa of Calcutta, had for so long embodied the gospel of love that asserts it is more blessed to give than to receive. She had practised it through the daily toil of those same fragile hands and had understood it with every fibre of her indomitable spirit and every ounce of her frail body.

The year was 1993 ... the venue – an old house on the outskirts of Tirana which Mother Teresa's Missionaries of Charity had acquired as a home in which they could tend to the needs of the homeless and destitute in the Albanian capital. As yet, there were no showers and no running water but an abundance of care and compassion. More recently, the place has expanded into a combination nursing home for the terminally ill, a health centre, and a safe haven for women and children.

I could immediately sense the joy that Mother Teresa was experiencing of being able to begin her work in her own country. She had tried several times from the early 1960s to get the government's permission to visit Albania, but every request was turned down by the country's Stalinist dictator Enver Hoxha. He had adopted a hostile attitude towards her, with his continuous persecution of the Church ending in the complete abolition of all religion.

We had been told in advance that though Mother Teresa would be pleased to meet us, there would be no question of her doing an interview for the BBC. But when her aide was called away to take an urgent phone call, I politely asked Albania's revered expatriate whether we could now retrieve the camera from the outside corridor.

Without a moment's hesitation she nodded her agreement.

'Being a journalist, you will understand when I say we are all pencils in God's hands,' as (dare I say it!) a mischievous smile crossed her face.

She wanted to hear about the huge response from Britain to the plight of the poor in her country and particularly the help that had been offered to so many vulnerable and innocent young children. I told her how the television pictures we had shot had become a catalyst for an enormous humanitarian aid effort.

Given that neither country had enjoyed any sort of relationship for over half a century, we agreed that it was remarkable that so many wanted to become involved.

'But you must know Bill that it's not how much we *do* or how much we *give* that matters. It's how much *love* that we show in the process that makes all the difference.'

I thought of all the marvellous fund-raising efforts of the schoolchildren I had met; the old ladies who had spent days on end knitting clothes and blankets; the haulage drivers who'd given up their holidays to drive thousands of miles across Europe to deliver aid to the desperate and disadvantaged; the doctors, nurses, carers and therapists who'd offered practical help. In my mind the *love* that Mother Teresa was describing had been vividly demonstrated by the great personal sacrifices made by so many who had answered the cry for help.

She knew precisely what I was thinking.

'I want to thank all the British people for what they have done to help the people here. It is very much appreciated. You can see it on their faces. They are much more at peace now.'

As I listened intently, I recalled the observation of India's former Prime Minister, Indira Gandhi. Of Mother Teresa, she said, 'she is tiny to look at but there is nothing small about her.' Certainly, her integrity and humility were striking. No soaring rhetoric just a simple central message designed to leave its mark. The success of that can be judged by the incredible expansion of her work. By 2010 the Missionaries of Charity numbered approximately 450 brothers and 5,000 nuns worldwide, operating 600 missions, schools and shelters in 120 countries.

Mother Teresa was keen to talk about Britain too, expressing her shock at the scale of the homelessness problem there and her determination to address the need especially with the provision of more soup kitchens.

Then in a spirit of reflection, she added: 'what is very beautiful is that many people thank me for the opportunity I've been able to give them to do something for the poor. We must thank God for giving us the chance to serve. Jesus said very clearly whatever you do to the least of my brethren, you do it to me. If you give a glass of water in my name, you do it to me. If you receive a little child in my name, you receive me.

'We have given in adoption over 3,000 children. One little girl has grown big now and is married. She wrote to me and said give me a little child. I want to give that child all that you were able to give me.

'We must do everything possible not to spoil God's work. If we do it like that, we are sure to do it well.'

It's amazing how certain individuals can arouse compassion in us. It is almost as if they have the ability to remind us of our true nature as spirits experiencing life in the form of human beings.

As we were talking, the sisters were preparing to take Mother Teresa to the home of the country's new President, a former cardiologist, Sali Berisha. Cameraman Bhasker Solanki and I had covered Albania's first free elections for nearly fifty years which had brought his Democratic Party to power. He had decided to set an example by refusing to move into the Presidential Palace or the less pretentious villa used by his predecessor. Instead, he insisted in staying put with his family in their two-bedroomed flat in a rundown Tirana housing estate.

In an earlier audience with Dr Berisha, Mother Teresa had received her Albanian citizenship to sit alongside her Indian one. Now he wanted her to visit his modest home to share tea with his family. Not wanting to offend her in any way, he had politely inquired of her sisters if she followed any special diet. Taking hold of the telephone herself, she told the President that she had no need to eat or drink but whatever he calculated would be the cost of the food, it would be appreciated if he handed the money to her nuns to help look after the poorest of the poor in his country.

If Dr Berisha felt humbled then he may well have recalled that when Mother Teresa was awarded the Nobel Peace Price she refused the banquet in her honour and asked that the £4,000 cost be given to the poor in Calcutta.

A few fleeting moments spent in the company of the saint of the gutters. Along with Bhasker Solanki, I was very honoured to have received *The Order of Mother Teresa*, instituted as Albania's highest civilian award, from President Berisha on behalf of all those who had contributed to the huge humanitarian aid effort at a time when the country was on its knees. Every time I glance at the silver medal, I think of that frail petite body that belied a remarkable power within.

Mother Teresa also had a unique way of appealing to individual conscience. To one aid worker overwhelmed by the pressing needs of others, she gave this advice: 'If you can't feed a hundred people then feed just one.' That is something any one of us can do. We can help change the world, person by person.

How the face of Albania has changed. The body of the ruthless dictator who abolished God from his country has been removed from the guarded marble tomb at the Cemetery of the Martyrs of the Nation and placed in a common grave with a headstone bearing little more than his name. As one observer noted: 'it is quietly terrifying to consider that the neurosis which kept three million people locked up was inside the head of one man.'

By contrast, Mother Teresa is now remembered everywhere in a country where only 16 per cent of the 3.6 million population are Roman Catholic. Albania's only international airport at Rinas has now been renamed Nene Tereza Airport, the largest hospital in Tirana bears her name, so too the city's second largest square while statues, schools and mosaics have been dedicated in her honour. Albania also has a new public holiday, Mother Teresa Day, on 19 October which marks the anniversary of her beatification by the Vatican.

Agnes Bojaxhiu was actually born in Skopje, now the capital of the Former Yugoslav Republic of Macedonia, to Albanian parents Nikolle and Drana. They had moved there from the predominately Catholic city of Shkoder in the North of Albania where Nikolle was a merchant and actively involved in politics. Father Martin Thompson, a British priest now based in the city, says Mother Teresa is venerated not just by Catholics but by Muslims as well. Indeed, she herself once said: 'If in coming face to face with God we accept Him in our lives, then we are converting. We become a better Hindu, a better Muslim, a better Catholic, a better whatever we are ... what God is in your mind, you must accept.'

Despite years of strenuous physical, emotional and spiritual work, Mother Teresa refused to retire. Though frail and bent, she continued her mission right up until her death in 1997. The BBC sent Bhasker Solanki to film her funeral in Calcutta. Among the many tributes he found written in a book of condolence was one from the hand of a young woman: 'I am going to try to live a better life in remembrance of you.'

Bhasker himself was moved to help initiate a new Leicester-based charity helping some of the most disadvantaged children in India. The Rushey Mead Foundation is named after the secondary school he attended in Leicester and the trustees include the former Head, a teacher and the Vice Chair of the school governors. The main thrust of their efforts has been to build a new school in Nagor village near Bhuj where a devastating earthquake brought hundreds of buildings to the ground like a pack of cards. Filming the wholesale destruction brought tears to Bhasker's eyes as he observed mass funeral pyres being set up to cremate the thousands killed and the erection of temporary houses in tents by the roadside. It was a terrifying experience and he remembers being woken up several times by the aftershocks whilst camping in the grounds of a hotel.

The Bollywood superstar Aamir Khan launched the charity which has been the catalyst for bringing together those in Leicester professing many different faiths – Hindus, Moslems, Sikhs and Christians – in a city with a sizeable ethnic minority population.

By 2009 a new Rushey Mead School – 4,500 miles from Leicester – had risen from the village ruins of Nagor, catering for 120 children aged from twelve to sixteen. In addition, the charity is supporting a project in a shanty area of Bhuj where local people have been trained to run classes for children who have never had access to basic education before. Being taught how to read and write has given many deprived children an unprecedented opportunity to join mainstream schools.

In Albania, too, the only country in Europe where at the dawn of the twenty-first century there were more children than adults, it was imperative that a huge transformation took place in the educational system to bring it into line with the general social and political changes.

Gone are the days when the role of the school was simply an information and propaganda transmitter. Instead of becoming passive recipients of knowledge, students now have to apply themselves to constructive action and critical thinking so as to acquire the skills and opinions needed to become active and responsible citizens.

Subjects like History of the Party of Labour of Albania and Moral and Political Education have been driven out of the curriculum to make room for new offerings like Knowledge of Society and Citizenship Education.

Thanks to the work of the ADRA charity, country schools and clinics are being transformed by grants offered by foreign governments and financial contributions from a range of donors. Much work still remains to be done. Even in 2010, up in the remote mountain areas, I was surprised to see pupils as young as five and six entering classrooms through a gaping hole in the wall. Even more surprising was to find them willing to stay behind at the end of lessons to dust the cupboards and scrub the floors. The thought struck me that if they tried that little exercise in Britain, we might have a youth rebellion on our hands!

In secondary schools, English has now replaced Russian as the first foreign language.

When I first visited Albania 20 years ago, it was a rare privilege to be invited into a classroom where English Literature was part of the curriculum and where 14-year-old pupils were reciting whole scenes from a Shakespeare play in perfect English without as much as a fleeting glance at the one textbook shared by over 30 students.

I was greeted by shouts of 'please sir, take me to England. I want to see Stratford, Liverpool Football Club, The Royal Opera House.'

'Oh,' I said, 'some of us come from another part of Britain, that magical bit right at the top of the map.' At that, a young girl stood up, folded her arms, approached the camera and immediately began to recite:

> *My heart's in the Highlands, my heart is not here,*
> *My heart's in the Highlands, a-chasing the deer;*
> *A-chasing the wild deer, and following the roe,*
> *My heart's in the Highlands, wherever I go.*

You could have knocked me over with a feather. The poems of Robert Burns had long since had a prominent place in Albanian thinking. Alas, these had also been the heady days of Albania's association with the Soviet Union to whom the school books attributed every scientific discovery.

Teachers would tell their charges George Stephenson was not the first man to make a steam engine that ran on rails. He pinched the idea from Pollsunov. The miner's safety lamp wasn't Davy's invention, it was developed by Jablotchov. Edison was a thief too, as was Marconi ... everyone knows Popov first discovered radio waves could bend around the spherically shaped earth. So Marconi's Nobel prize was a fake.

Whenever some Russian hero was discredited, the textbooks had to be changed. Teachers told me there was no shame expressed on this ... some books were rewritten not three times but seventeen times! And each new publication said that the previous one had lied. It wasn't a laughing matter either, for some people were arrested and spent years in jail for not accepting it. When Albania split from the Warsaw Pact and threw its lot in with Chairman Mao, suddenly the Chinese spiralled to the top of the inventors' league.

Sadly, when Mother Teresa first arrived to take soundings about the possibility of restarting her work, a huge slice of the country's youth were fleeing in the opposite direction. With the social and economic fabric disintegrating, many were abandoning all hope for the future. Food shortages were worsening by the day, factories were on strike and noticeably, the students were even more brazenly bringing their protests on to the streets.

The rush to the ports became unstoppable. In Durres and Vlora, ships large and small were overrun by frenzied refugees demanding to put to sea at once. The first exodus to the Italian port of Brindisi amounted to 20,000 people. The vast majority of them – after much vacillating by the Italian Government – were allowed to stay.

The next Albanian invaders in search of *la dolce vita* would not be so fortunate. By the time one rusting freighter, the *Vlora* set sail there were 10,000 aboard fighting for space, food and water. The boat was soon lurching under the combined weight of a vast army of stowaways hanging precariously from the masts and packed like sardines into the holds. Several died after gang attacks or after being crushed by a derrick which snapped on the upper deck.

On arrival in Bari, everyone was marched to the football stadium which was surrounded by the carabinieri. Deprived for the most part of food or drink for three days, the Albanians became a picture of human dejection, misery and shattered illusions. It was not a pretty scene to film and few had little energy left to vent their feelings. Bedraggled, exhausted and humiliated, they accepted defeat as the Italians sent them back from whence they came.

In the case of six-year-old Vera Naci that meant a return to a life of squalor and disease. Every day since she first learnt to walk, she had hurried to the hillside rubbish dump on the outskirts of Tirana to await the arrival of the first of the day's refuse lorries provided through funds from the European Union.

I looked on in horror as the driver started to discharge tons of festering household waste, the signal for Vera and her young friends to leap excitedly into the sea of litter to scavenge for anything that could be salvaged or sold for a few lek to put towards a loaf of bread.

A keen eye and a heavy metal scraper was enough to uncover a discarded jotter and broken crayon, the perfect gift with Christmas just a few days away.

The undignified scramble demanded the children's full attention. Anything missed became a ready target for the sheep, the dogs and the goats, all of them competing in the melée.

Every day from first light till dusk, Vera, her parents and her brothers were putting their health and their lives at risk, just one amongst scores of families determined to eke a living from the dump. Some had been taken to hospital with lung and respiratory problems, others were bitten by rats.

The stench, the smoke and the constant threat of disease were compounded by the dumping of lorry loads of sewage just yards away.

Most of the families had been forced south from the mountainous settlements of the North-East where unprofitable and unworkable land, rising prices and a suspension of social assistance payments had made it impossible to survive.

Portraying the agony of such desperate people is hardly a dignifying business, but it's important that those of us who are fortunate to enjoy life's comforts here in Britain should gain a little insight into the kind of degradation that confronts more than just a tiny minority who live in our own continent of Europe.

One mother of three, Sanije Danaj, asked why we should deem to film in such a place.

'We know it's filthy work here but unlike governments we're not stealing anything. We have to live somehow and occasionally we come across something we can sell. Bottles can bring us a few lek and throw-out vegetables can be cleaned up and used to make soup. When you have five mouths to feed, you need to be up here almost every hour of the day.'

As we chatted, I heard an excited scream reverberating across the smouldering piles of rubbish. It was little Vera. Deep down amidst the rotting garbage, her friend had found his treasure ... a TWO-wheeled tricycle! Any three-year-old in Britain waking up to that on Christmas morning would doubtless feel short-changed by Santa.

The Albanian story never seemed to come to an end. Every time I thought people would lose interest in the place, another unexpected development would plunge the Balkan state back into the headlines. That old adage of one step forward, two steps back, aptly describes the Albanian experience.

Just as long sought-after improvements were beginning to take hold, anarchy descended on the country in early 1997 bringing it almost to the point of collapse. In the eyes of many, the frenzy of murder, riots and looting in which thousands of Albanians freely indulged was viewed as a spectacular own goal. In all 2,000 died and ten times that number were injured.

The crisis was sparked by the collapse of pyramid investment schemes which in the absence of savings banks found it easy to exploit the desperation of tens of thousands of impoverished Albanians by offering irresistible interest rates ranging from 10 to 50 per cent a month.

These ridiculously high returns were paid to the first investors out of the funds received from those who invested later. Most of the schemes were insolvent with liabilities exceeding assets from the day they opened for business. Yet they did flourish initially as news about the high returns spread. Encouraged by the exceptional payouts, still more were drawn in by the promise of similar windfalls until the interest due to the early investors exceeded the money paid in by new ones.

People sold their property, their livestock and most of their possessions to invest in the schemes. The economy of Europe's poorest nation became nothing less than a gigantic lottery with a huge proportion of its people living off their dreams of unbelievable profits and interest rates.

Eventually, the high rates began to arouse suspicion and the schemes were unable to make interest payments. When investors tried to get their money out, they discovered the truth about the schemes whose demise was swift and in many cases accompanied by acts of outright theft.

This exploitation of greed and gullibility is estimated to have deprived domestic savers of over $1billion, a staggering 43 per cent of the country's GDP. The Democratic Party government ignored the warnings, acted too late and paid the ultimate price.

It was frightening to watch the consequences. Tens of thousands went on the rampage as the Government lost control. The angry protesters swept into military bases and stole nearly a million weapons – rifles, machine guns, grenades and ammunition by the boxload. It was virtually impossible to sleep at night. From my hotel room, all you could hear was the constant noise of gunfire. The number of Kalashnivkovs in circulation was the equivalent of one for each Albanian family. The gun became a toy and also a symbol of power. Many slept with one under their pillow. In the streets, in the backyards and along the boulevards, angry and disillusioned people were firing their newly acquired arsenal day and night.

Needless to say, senseless deaths resulted from this crazy lifestyle. Some treated it all as a game but surely, I thought, everyone knows that when you fire off a volley into the air, what goes up has to come down and hardly a night went by without a stray bullet falling out of the sky and hitting some poor instant bystander on the head. One visiting Orthodox priest was even offered some bombs.

'What for?' he asked.

'To protect yourself. One bomb can take care of an entire gang. Just throw it out the door and that's it.'

Needless to say, he passed up the offer but many took these bombs not just for protection but to play with them as if they were fireworks. In one village, a young lad threw a hand grenade but it didn't go off. So he went and picked it up. Then it exploded. Similar incidents occurred on a nightly basis.

All this was the consequence of a confidence trick that had ripped off over a million people in a country of just over 3 million by pretending money could be plucked out of the ether. As one financial commentator put it: 'nothing stupefies like money. Even the savviest investors tend to look the other way when extraordinary returns are being made.'

I was anxious to find out how the government intended to recover the stolen weapons. With so many missing, surely the whole security of the country was now at peril.

Stripped of all their savings, many Albanians sold their guns for ready cash so they could feed their families for a few days. Defence Minister Ilir Gjoni acknowledged that the stolen arms posed a threat to regional peace and arranged for me to visit an Army barracks near the city of Elbasan. There, to my astonishment, I was shown 100,000 guns which had been destroyed, lying in piles more than six feet high. The weapons had originated in over a dozen countries and even included a Russian cannon dating from before the Bolshevik Revolution.

Foreign governments anxious to see an easing of tension in the Balkans financed a nine-month amnesty, but by now, towns – especially those bordering the then Serbian province of Kosovo – had become literal arms bazaars. All types of small arms were available from AK47s to machine guns and mortars, all from the looted arsenals and police depots. Smugglers bought large quantities of weapons and arranged for them to be carried northwards across the border and delivered to the Kosovo Liberation Army, a guerrilla group fighting for autonomy from the Serbian regime in Belgrade.

Often it was peasant farmers who did the smuggling, carrying the weapons across, two or three at a time, on the backs of pack animals. But there were dangers. Serb forces realised what was happening and laid mines along the frontier. As a result, many villagers and farmers were killed or wounded.

By the spring of 1999 NATO missiles were targeting Belgrade and other Serbian cities in an attempt to end the nightmare many had long predicted. It was a belated response to the years of civilian repression that ethnic Albanians who made up 90 per cent of the population of Kosovo claimed they had endured at the hands of the authorities. When their liberation army fought back and NATO intervened, the Yugoslav President Slobodan Milosevic determined to throw them all out.

Thousands were marched to the train station at Prestina and taken straight to the Kosovo–Macedonia border which soon developed into one vast and sprawling refugee camp. In this humanitarian catastrophe, as many as 800,000 streamed across Kosovo's borders within days. It was a pitiful sight with rain, mud and physical exhaustion compounding the refugees' misery. Families were split up, some unable to ascertain who was alive and who was dead.

Amidst the turmoil, the Adventist Development and Relief Agency was commissioned by the UNHCR and the World Food Programme to play a leading role in the massive relief effort. As they crammed into tents, sports halls and warehouses, the agency fed a third of the 450,000 refugees who then set off by foot, by horse or by tractor and trailer across the border into Albania. Despite the country's acute poverty, the plight of the Kosovar Albanians touched the hearts of many who, without a murmur of complaint, were prepared to share what little rations they had for themselves. The government too spared no effort, organising humanitarian relief and putting the entire country at the disposal of NATO.

Yet the determination of the Kosovans to return home was nothing short of remarkable. Within three months of the Serb retreat, hundreds of thousands were already back, the unprecedented pace of their return taking even NATO by surprise.

Alas, many found their homes in ruins or burnt to a shell. Others returned as widows discovering that husbands and sons left behind had been shot or mutilated in the campaign of terror. Evidence of the atrocities committed could be seen right across the Kosovan countryside with entire communities razed to the ground and mass graves by the roadside, some of them containing the bodies of pregnant women and children.

Several families I met were inconsolable. Hysen Rafizi and his son Bedri had toiled every day for two years to build a family home in the village of Komogllave about 35 kilometres from Pristina. It was destroyed by the Serbs in just twenty minutes.

Nearby, Ferdinard Njue, one of four water engineers flown in from Kenya, was preparing to clear one of the village's wells 65 feet deep. Dozens gathered, all hoping their worst fears would not be realised. A pulley had been set up. The first object to be dredged up was a smashed television set, then came a fridge and part of a cooker. Hysen recognised them all. The Serbs had thrown everything from his house down the well before setting fire to the building.

The onlookers heaved a huge sigh of relief. There were no bodies, human or animal, found at the bottom of the well. In another one, not many miles from there, a young man had been pulled out along with three dead cows and a dog. The Kenyan team had cleared over 300 wells but there were still hundreds more to be tackled and some had been booby-trapped.

As schools began to reopen, children were learning of friends killed or missing. I was shown into a classroom by a junior school head teacher where a group of half a dozen twelve-year-olds were busily constructing scale models showing how they found their own homes on their return … carving, filing, sandpapering … meticulous in every detail. There were bodies spreadeagled on the bedroom floors, charred timbers strewn across the staircase and hallway, bullet holes in the exterior walls. Teachers said it was important that they relived their horrendous experiences. One girl, tears rolling down her cheeks, had used blackened matchsticks to demonstrate the burnt rafters and sculpted miniature figures to show where her father and uncle had been shot before the rest of the family fled in desperation.

My eye was drawn to another model given pride of place right at the front of the display. The children called it their 'dream home'. This one had everything – birds on the roof, apple trees and flowering hydrangea in the garden, even a Tellytubby wading in the paddling pool! The children told me it was all part of necessary therapy to work their way through darkness into the light. The horror of what they witnessed will haunt them for years but now that they are free to do the things they always wanted, they know they cannot forever dwell in the past and are looking optimistically towards the future.

A highly respected humanitarian, Australian Paul Dulhunty, working with ADRA on restoration projects, came running over to me clasping a painting depicting another young girl's feelings about what she had witnessed.

'Look, this half of the picture is the dark side representing evil. The other half is the light side symbolising good. And as you can see, a hand has come across from the evil side and has attacked and grabbed the young brother and the father and has killed them. This picture portrays the feeling, the emotion, the sadness and the horror that young people have had to experience in this conflict.'

The whole experience left me cold and uncomfortable. Surely, none of us can afford to underestimate the trauma and mental stress that witnessing the horrors of war brings to children or for that matter, the long-term impact of having encountered such dreadful sights and sounds.

Mother Teresa could certainly empathise with such suffering.

'If we have no peace,' she once said, 'it is because we have forgotten that we belong to each other.'

21

I am Somebody

No war on the face of the earth is more destructive than the AIDS pandemic.

Colin Powell

For the past thirty years, no four-letter word – or more correctly, acronym – has struck such fear into the human race as AIDS. We see its devastating impact on television, we read about it daily in our newspapers. We have been swamped with statistics which show that the pandemic is deadlier than war, silently tearing nations apart and throwing millions of families into turmoil. Fathers and breadwinners have been killed in their tens of thousands, mothers all too frequently following them to their graves. With a whole generation wiped out in large swathes of sub-Saharan Africa, children and the elderly have often been left to fend for themselves.

In South Africa alone, ravaged by the disease like few other places on earth, AIDS has been responsible for close on one and a half million orphans. Indeed, it has claimed so many victims that cemeteries are running out of space. In parts of the continent's wealthiest nation, people spend more time at funerals than they do having their hair cut, shopping or holding barbecues.

There are deep psychological wounds to be healed especially among the youngest survivors of this catastrophe. You need only spend a few hours in their company to discover just how marginalised, stigmatised and psychologically damaged they have become.

With producer/cameraman Brian Staveley – unusual for the news business, a deeply sensitive man with a compelling urge to respond to the plight of others – I was despatched to South Africa to film a BBC documentary on this lost generation to be screened on World AIDS Day.

We set off for KwaZulu-Natal, the epicentre of the AIDS pandemic.

297

In a clearing among the thicket and bushland we found 60 scantily dressed children playing excitedly outside a primitive looking primary school. It had been hurriedly built and equipped through funds provided by a British-based charity in a laudable effort to try to provide some elementary education for the ever-spiralling number of AIDS orphans.

As the teacher, grasping a hand bell, rang out the summons to lessons, her young charges suddenly formed a ring and began to chant in happy unison, 'I am somebody. I am special.' The one-line chorus was repeated time and again as the children took turns in stepping inside the circle, singing their names and performing a unique dance designed to inculcate confidence and self-esteem.

Among them were Silindile and her three younger brothers all of whom had walked barefoot through the bush, their feet torn and blistered from negotiating the thorns and loose stones strewn across the dusty pathway.

Their determination to get to school was nothing short of remarkable. For all had been up since the crack of dawn – the elder children already having trudged the best part of ten miles to get a day's supply of water.

I tried to imagine how the children must have felt to see their parents slowly die before their eyes, leaving Silindile to bury them and then to raise and care for all her siblings. The poor girl was just 13 when she assumed the responsibilities of both mother and father.

Home was a one-room shack made of mud and straw and topped with scrap aluminium. Two of the children had to share the tattered mattress on the dusty floor, the few clothes that existed hung from a couple of nails while some vegetable scraps were on the boil in an old pot that sat atop a ground dug stove in the middle of the hut.

Outside sat the children's granny, frail and unable to summon up enough energy to assist in the daily chores. Silindile called each child to the basin of water in turn, washed their hands and face, gave them a few spoonfuls of watery broth and got them ready for school. Her constant fear was that one of them might fall ill, resulting in her needing to stay at home with an important day's schooling missed.

As the children prepared to leave, I noticed three large mounds of earth towards the back of the hut. Tears streaming down her face, Silindile indicated they marked the graves she had hurriedly dug to bury three other siblings who had died from malnutrition.

Each was buried within the hour ... no ceremony, no coffin ... just laid to rest in what space could be found in the unproductive garden. One could only begin to surmise the heartbreak she must have endured. Such tragic events had robbed her of her childhood innocence.

Fortunately, Silindile's plight and those of hundreds like her had been discovered by the Adventist Development and Relief Agency. They had now been able to apply on the family's behalf for a Government child-support grant to supplement the old grandmother's pension. Yet thousands of orphans were still being denied that help because they had no birth certificates and a disconcerted government simply didn't know who they were or where they lived. What a sorry state of affairs!

Thandi Masuku, ADRA's project leader, was angry not only over the inaction of so many in authority but because family after family in this part of the bush were in denial about the deadly disease in their midst.

'If they find out they're sick, they always say they've been poisoned or are the victims of witchcraft. It makes it so difficult for us as we try to convince them by every possible means that HIV/Aids is there. Now what is surprising is that they can see neighbour after neighbour dying in the same way, yet they don't ask themselves the question why. They just say there's no such disease.'

There are many reasons behind the epidemic's grip on South Africa. Apart from widespread denial, there's the legacy of apartheid which disrupted so much of family life, limited access to antiretroviral drugs, resistance to the use of condoms, the low status of women in society and within relationships, good transport and high mobility allowing rapid movement of the HIV virus around the country and social norms that accept high numbers of sexual partners especially among men. But above all, there is poverty. This reduces children's chances of attending school, lowers their chances of getting a job and increases their risk of infection. Many are selling their bodies to survive, to gain an income, to support younger brothers and sisters or to secure their next meal.

The African tradition which embraces the concept of *Ubuntu*, calling on the support of the extended family and the local community to look after orphaned children, is rendered powerless in the face of such dreadful poverty and malnutrition.

I was impressed by the self-sacrifice of many who are in the front line of the work with AIDS orphans, desperately trying to prevent a whole generation of children ending up on the streets. A number of them have gone through a life-changing experience. Confronted by the scale of the problem, they feel they cannot walk away. They are prepared to give up everything – a comfortable home life, a well-paid job, children's schooling, luxury holidays – to perform extraordinary acts of generosity.

Heather Reynolds was one whom I was determined to seek out. I had heard that her response to the orphans' crisis was fired by her religious beliefs having experienced a dramatic conversion to the Christian faith. Like the Apostle Paul, Heather's transforming experience came when on the road – not to Damascus – but at a stop sign in Uganda when her brakes failed and she ran straight into a brand new Jaguar sports car. It was a write-off but, instead of berating her, the owner offered up a prayer. It blew her mind. A clear sign, she thought, that there must be a God.

Having seen the devastating effects of the AIDS virus on children in Uganda, Heather was determined that when the disease spread to her home country, she would not stand by as a helpless spectator. Her conviction was clear. Whatever God directed her to do, she would obey and no obstacle would be allowed to stand in the way.

With her husband Patrick, a sculptor of considerable note, she bought an old run-down farmhouse in the bush high above Cato Ridge in KwaZulu-Natal. She turned it into *God's Golden Acre* with the clear intention of engineering new families from those torn apart by AIDS. Here children could find sanctuary from abuse, poverty and starvation.

God's Golden Acre ... sounds like heaven on earth ... so would there be a Peter type figure on the gate? No, instead a young man bearing the name of the Saint's brother, Andrew, signalled us inside the compound. Andrew was a volunteer worker from Toronto in Canada, one of an incredible number of young people who'd heard through the grapevine what was going on in this remote part of the world and decided he had something to offer the cause.

No sooner had we pulled our vehicle to a halt than we were surrounded by an excitable pack of dogs leaping at the open doors and licking our bare hands in an obvious show of affection. I guessed they were probably from broken homes too.

Andrew led us to the office where Heather was busily trying to sort out the latest problem to hit her desk, the refusal by the authorities to let one of the boys in her charge sit his school exams because he wasn't able to pay.

I had two completely contrasting visions in my head of Heather. One was of a resolute and assertive headmistress whom you would cross at your peril. The other, a cherubic type figure dressed in long, flowing robes whose posture and charm would melt the iciness of even the most hardened of opponents.

I was completely wrong. Here was a larger than life character, intensely loquacious and voluble with beaming face and an obvious capacity to cope with the multiplicity of challenges and quandaries that come to the fore at almost every minute of every day.

Her desk was piled high with papers and lists of important contacts with whom she was endeavouring to get in touch. The computer was playing up, the sweat pouring from her brow.

She broke off a hundred and one other conversations with volunteers, grandmothers traditionally known as '*gogos*' and an array of helpers all clamouring for attention, to welcome us and hand over the keys to a house in the grounds that had been prepared for our needs including a pot of chicken and rice placed on top of the oven.

Behind the office lay her own living accommodation, a double bed barely visible beneath a myriad of books, lamps, curtains, clothes, toys and every conceivable gadget and novelty necessary to look after the needs of 97 children for whom God's Golden Acre had become home.

She glanced up at my blazer curious to know the origins of the badge that adorned my buttonhole. I explained that like thousands of others, I had been a member of The Boys' Brigade which had been around for well over a hundred years and is part of the boyhood experience of many adults.

The BB is a Christian youth organisation with over half a million members worldwide. It offers a wide range of activities including games, crafts, sports, Christian teaching, music and holiday camps. It also embraces the Global Fellowship of Christian Youth whose object is the advancement of Christ's Kingdom, the promotion of education and the relief of poverty among the youth of the world.

It seemed to me that the movement Sir William Alexander Smith had founded in Glasgow all those years ago was just what Heather needed to help catch the energy and enthusiasm of youth and to channel it purposefully. She readily agreed.

When it came to interviewing Heather, I found her oddly shy and diffident. It was as if the experience held a terror for her. She understands the needs of the media but had been tricked in the past and now delivers her message in a way that leaves no room for misinterpretation.

Kindness is second nature to Heather whether to strangers or when conversing with her own staff and volunteers. She has a knack of being able to talk to people at their own level, especially useful when suddenly switching from a heated debate on how best to fix an ailing fax machine to dealing with a cut knee a child has sustained in the adventure playground.

Her relationships with government, both national and regional, are nothing if not fiery. At first, it seems Pretoria took a dim view of her 'cluster foster' experiment because it did not fit in readily with their idea of *ubuntu* or care in the community. Indeed, some in authority went so far as accusing her of uprooting orphaned children from their own areas and engineering new families. But they're now softening their line, at first grudgingly and now enthusiastically supporting her idea of placing AIDS orphans in the care of foster mothers, many of them grandmothers. The grants that she receives though, fall well short of what is needed to keep God's Golden Acre afloat.

The children often referred to as the 'Khayelihle Kids' live in family groups. Each of these has a gogo, aunties and a house parent who is responsible for overseeing their general care, welfare and education. The gogos and aunties are all from the local communities and the children are encouraged to maintain connections with their Zulu roots. They are served traditional Zulu meals and communicate in their native language.

Heather often receives calls from people in hospitals or others in the valley when an abandoned baby has been found. The circumstances are often horrific. Some of the children have been sexually abused or have watched their parents die. One little girl was shot through her spine by her father. A surgeon managed to save her leg, operating on Heather's kitchen table.

She has never had to advertise for volunteers. They just keep on arriving – and from all over the world. We met a Canadian and an Australian but Heather has had groups from the UK, Japan, Germany and the Netherlands.

God's Golden Acre is a place of great contrasts. There are noisy, excited kids roaming the grounds challenging every visitor to a game of football but there also some very traumatised children, some of them terminally ill. Inevitably, with so many of them HIV-positive, pain and death are issues which have to be faced. Heather's strong Christian conviction has helped her through many difficult moments, holding a dying child in her arms and painting a picture of a place where there is no more pain.

Some call Heather a maverick but, then, she willingly courts controversy in defence of her aims. She's also a great believer in chasing money from the private sector to ensure survival. Contrast the rather Spartan surroundings where children spend much of their time to the Young Zulu Warrior Theatre which rose from the dust and to which dignitaries, businessmen and celebrities are frequently lured to watch her dance troupes perform. There's method in this seeming madness, for these are the very people Heather wants to sponsor her cluster fostering project and they cannot fail to notice it. Dance Link, a forum of dance companies regularly send professional teachers to train the youngsters who have recently completed successful tours to Germany, Holland and the UK.

Heather's relationship with the Zulu people in the villages that straddle the Valley of the Thousand Hills is perhaps the best indicator of her success. Traditional leaders, witchdoctors, ministers and countless families salute her missionary zeal. She speaks Zulu fluently and is accepted as one of their own. The Outreach Programme which she runs supports 600 families and 4,500 children in the valley.

For someone who has been witnessed so many harrowing scenes across the world, a heightened sense of detachment and compassion fatigue can be very real. But it's hard to keep your emotions in check when you see the utter devastation inflicted on families by the AIDS crisis and come face to face with the reality of their overwhelming pain and helplessness.

Negotiating a treacherous path, we arrived at a tumbling shack, home for Nonhlanhla. The place looked as if it was about to collapse at any moment. There was no running water or power available for washing, warming or cooking. Now 19, she had a baby of her own and was looking after two younger brothers. All were on the edge of starvation.

Nonhlanhla's teenage years had been one sorry tale of hunger, degradation, misery and abuse. Shaking with emotion, she told me how as a ten-year-old during a time of political violence, she had watched as her father was 'necklaced' by having a rubber tyre filled with petrol forced round his chest and then burned alive. Three years later her mother, thought to be AIDS infected, died of pneumonia.

Nonhlanhla held the family together for six years but in desperate poverty, had become involved with a 'sugar daddy', selling her body to someone able to give her the material things she needed. 'Gift sex' is not seen as prostitution and is extremely common in many societies. Lacking every basic need, children are unprotected against those who would want to abuse or molest them.

Inside a tiny fly-blown room, Nonhlanhla shared the only bed with her baby. The two boys slept on the floor. Heather approached and gave her a bear hug. Tears flowed down the poor girl's face. The years of begging door to door for food were over. The help offered was beyond her wildest dreams – six chickens, five fruit trees, a wheelbarrow, food parcels, school uniforms and fees, clothing and a building team to demolish and replace the family home.

As we set off again, it was easy to see why the prejudice, cruelty and indifference that Heather had faced in the early years of her mission were now melting away. One minute she was comforting a little girl giving palliative care to her dying mother whilst praying and singing Zulu hymns around the bedside, the next arriving at the home of another bereavement.

Parts of the province are in a state of perpetual mourning. So high is the daily death toll that friends and neighbours are having to choose which funeral to attend. Despite their suffering, the people are clinging to their faith, something not lost on the Government which sees a vital role for the church.

Sizani Magwanyana's farewell was a moving occasion and continued for over three hours. Because of the stigma attached to HIV/AIDS, family members often tell you that their loved one passed away from tuberculosis or the flu. Sizani's death certificate cited pneumonia as the cause. Traditional Zulu custom requires the deceased's family to accommodate and feed people coming to pay their respects. Dying is an expensive business for the living.

Plastic seats had been brought into the mud house while big pots of chicken were cooking on a fire for the feast that followed. Long before the service began, the ladies were in full voice and dressed in white, not black. The ceremony itself was in three distinct parts – first, the wailing and spilling of tears, a deep cleansing crying, a real exorcism of grief.

Then came the eulogies, some from relatives, others from a row of clergy from churches of differing denominations. Occasionally, the mourners would burst into song and envelopes of support were placed on the coffin, each bearing a name or short message.

The burial like so many in the valley took place in the garden outside. As the coffin was lowered into the freshly dug grave, the mood changed dramatically, everyone bursting into spontaneous song, the lovely harmony taking on a poignant quality as it echoed across the valley ... another soul bound for heaven.

Courage and vision are great attributes. Heather has them in abundance.

'I hear you've brought your referee's gear with you. Well hurry up and get changed. There are 22 of my best players waiting to start a game down there on the village sports field.'

Arriving at the ground, there they were, proudly wearing the new kit donated by a private sponsor but someone had forgotten to include boots on the list of necessities. Not that the eager youngsters gave it a moment's thought. Off they went, in their bare feet, displaying many of the skills more associated with the professional game.

To my surprise, my match was one of a dozen being played in this remote part of KwaZulu-Natal. Determined that so many AIDS orphans should not end up as a generation of street children sucked in, through desperation, to a life of crime, desolation and abuse, Heather had formed an entire football league engendering team spirit and helping promote habits of obedience, discipline and self-respect. Already, one of the top sides, GGA African Sporting has made it to South Africa's Third Division.

When she discovered a former BBC colleague of mine, Dale Le Vack, counted the President of Manchester United, Martin Edwards, among his close friends, she was straight on the phone to the biggest club side in the world. He has since honoured his promise to advance her vision for enriching the children's lives through organised sport.

He sees her as the modern embodiment of The Bible's Good Samaritan and insists it has been a humbling experience to play just a small part in her eventual triumph following so many years of great challenge and hardship.

Other donors touched and challenged by the spirit of *awethu*, the Zulu word for 'Our Mother' have also stepped in to answer the call.

Heather's relationship with her husband Patrick is an intriguing one. He has his own workshop where he sculpts exotic and interesting pieces of art. Some attract notable buyers and money from the sales helps not just keep the Reynolds afloat but provides much needed income for God's Golden Acre too.

My visit amounted to little more than a couple of days but long enough to get a feel of the place and of the person who runs it – chaotic, eccentric, vibrant and God driven. Whenever Heather feels low, she turns to read the slogans she's plastered across her office wall. 'Do you say Our Father on Sunday,' one reads, 'and act like an orphan for the rest of the week?'

But it's another which best encapsulates her single-minded determination.

'Obstacles are those frightful things you see when you take your eyes off the goal.'

That's something Tony Moll certainly can't afford to do. As a young doctor, he realised his dream by moving out to the sleepy little village of Tugela Ferry with its Church of Scotland Hospital, the perfect place to settle down and raise a family. Little did he know how things would change. Today as the Chief Medical Officer of the hospital, now in Government hands, his life has been completely taken over by the medical demands of the killer virus.

Even if they were to work 24 hours a day, doctors there say they'd still make no impact. For the hospital is right in the heartland of KwaZulu-Natal where the disease is devastating lives, families and whole communities and placing overwhelming demands on medical staff.

As we arrived at the hospital, the queue of patients waiting to be seen snaked all the way along a huge corridor and into the courtyard outside. Relatives were slumped against an outside wall waiting for news. Patience is a necessary virtue in a place like this. It would be several hours before they would hear the results of their spouses' tests for HIV.

Dr Moll was in constant demand, colleagues chasing him with endless queries, outpatients anxiously awaiting his arrival at a series of clinics, in-patients clamouring for attention ... yet through it all, he exuded a calming, quiet and influential presence. As we set up the camera by a patient's bedside, I was concerned that we might be using up too much of the doctor's precious time.

If I hadn't already fully comprehended the scale of the pandemic then Dr Moll's first words left no room for doubt.

'What's happening here is the equivalent of dropping a bomb on a High School every single day. In our Province, this virus claims 300 lives a day.'

With the upward trend continuing unabated, we were invited into the wards to see the human toll for ourselves. Fathers expressed concern over what would happen to their children when they were gone. Mothers, vulnerable and powerless in the face of the onslaught, felt shame and feared their families would suffer discrimination and rejection.

In the paediatric ward too, tiny and piteous figures were fighting for life, many of them victims of malnutrition because their infected and impoverished parents had been unable to provide enough food.

We met a little five-year-old boy, Danisa, who had been infected by AIDS at birth. The complications were mounting fast. Roger Holland, a GP who had arrived from America, explained how the boy essentially had the lungs of an old man – just like someone who had contracted emphysema from a lifetime of smoking. Apart from his respiratory distress, he was now experiencing heart failure. Sitting by his bedside, Danisa's mother was overcome by a sense of helplessness and guilt.

So intolerable was the medical workload at the hospital that potential recruits had been frightened off by the extent of the human tide and low pay. Scots doctor, Jean Leckie, was a notable exception. Long after most of her age would have chosen to retire and enjoy their golden years, she was busily examining a young child in obvious distress and a mother fearing the worst.

Why was she still working at 83?

'Just knowing that so many here endure great suffering with so much courage compels me to help and care for them.'

A doctor true to her calling and someone in whom a beleaguered community felt safe to share their pain.

With so many fathers having succumbed to the disease, women were wondering how they could feed their children. As the Government vacillated, the hospital itself stepped in, recruiting volunteers to train mothers in how to grow crops to sustain their families. Good nutrition is vital to the effectiveness of antiretroviral drugs which prolong life and reduce the chance of an HIV-positive pregnant woman passing the virus to her baby.

Just days before our arrival, in a dramatic U-turn, the Government finally promised to make the drugs widely available, effectively ditching their President's policy of denial. But a much greater and faster distribution of the drugs is necessary to make a real impact and prolong the lives of millions.

Sadly, there are many cases of newly born babies being abandoned by their mothers who have recently discovered that they are HIV positive and simply cannot bear the thought of what that may mean for their children. We had no sooner arrived at the Salvation Army orphanage in Johannesburg than another such emergency was under way.

A baby girl had been discovered inside a shopping bag on the street behind a city centre bank. Hurriedly brought to the orphanage known as Ethembeni, a Xhosa word for 'place of hope', the staff had named him Nhlanhla which means 'lucky'.

The South African Government has never favoured the idea of institutions as a long-term solution to looking after a parentless generation, nor does the Salvation Army. But someone has to look after the most desperate cases where not a single relative can be traced. Many of those tucked into little cots next to Nhlanhla's had been found in dustbins, toilets, taxi ranks, shebeens or left on buses or in bushes.

No expression of anger here about such a cruel abandonment. Instead, the Salvation Army officer in charge of the country's AIDS programme, Major Lena Jwili, looked me straight in the eye as she challenged me to 'put yourself in that parent's shoes. How would you feel if firstly you had been rejected by family and friends and are now told you have a disease that can't be cured. Then you're told there's a distinct possibility that you may transmit this to your child and all this is upon your shoulders. What are you going to do?'

It takes up to three months for tests to show whether babies like Nhlanhla have contracted the virus. But hope does lie within Ethembeni's spotlessly white stucco walls. Up to 40 per cent of the babies who originally test positive can turn out to be negative by the time they reach 18 months when their own immune systems start working.

It's also surprising what loving care and a nutritious diet can do. One baby was given just weeks to live by a visiting doctor. At two years old, Lesego was still healthy, then aged seven was told he could attend school. At 11, such was his boundless zest for life, he had become the brightest pupil in his class.

The home employs social workers and nursing staff to look after the babies night and day. Students and surrogate mothers also visit regularly to stimulate, feed, wash and play with the children.

A visit to Ethembeni is certainly an emotional roller-coaster, a journey through the science of feelings. One minute, I found myself laughing at the toddlers standing in their cots, impatiently awaiting release into the playground with the older children. The next, I was standing in an office that had been converted into a simple chapel, my eyes immediately drawn to a collection of embroidered squares sewn together to form a quilt and prominently displayed above a wooden cross.

Major Jwili, keeping her own emotions in check, pointed to each square in turn.

'At Ethembeni, we have a rule that no-one is to be forgotten, especially those who battled with HIV and have passed on. Some of these babies lived only a few weeks, others two or three years but each one was important to us and to God. We have tried to express the personality of each child through the embroidery. We made a difference in Simon's life, in Joy's life, in Julian's life. This child here had someone he could look up to and smile, this one felt the hug, the cuddle, the warmth ... he had a sense of belonging and that makes me feel really happy.'

Those who do survive and graduate from Ethembeni have found themselves part of a bold exercise to overcome the discrimination and stigma which in South African society is as virulent as the disease.

It was encouraging to see parents in the huge sprawling township of Soweto willingly sending their children to another Salvation Army centre to share schooling and mix freely with orphans like Bonisiwe who contracted AIDS at birth and whose parents' deaths sparked a heartless display of cruelty and rejection. She was told by her uncle to get out of his house lest she infect the whole family.

I met her in the bright, colourful and welcoming surroundings of

Bethesda House. It is home to 36 children, the majority of whom are HIV positive, having been abandoned by mothers who realised their own status and the risk to their child.

Yet this is not a place of gloom or sadness. Bonisiwe took me by the hand and led me to her dormitory simply but brightly decorated. Her pride and joy was a toy telephone. She lifted the receiver and started speaking to an imaginary friend in England. Like the others here, she was receiving antiretroviral medication and was happy, energetic and full of life.

She attended Bethany School which is another of five different and complementary elements to the centre. It also caters for children from a second residential home situated within the grounds, this one for children who are orphaned or unable to live at home because of parental abuse.

The aim of the Home however, is not to keep the children there forever. There is a team of counsellors and social workers who work with families and children to rebuild relationships. Reuniting them can take anything from two to five years but getting children back into the family environment is thought to be best wherever possible. The social workers also run a programme of fostering and adoption for those who have no family or for whom reunification is not possible.

Next door is the crèche and pre-school which accepts children from six months to six years, their antics always a draw for anyone holding a camera. 'Watch me!' was the familiar cry from the confident, friendly and adventurous children keen to demonstrate their prowess on the climbing frame. Not only does the crèche accept children known to be HIV positive but it has done a marvellous job in educating parents to develop an understanding and tolerance of the virus. Following workshops to explain the policy and the lack of risk to uninfected children, not one child was withdrawn.

These are the lucky ones, rescued when at their weakest and most vulnerable, finding love and care from those striving to make a difference. Other children of the pandemic, overcome by grief, have already lost the joy of their childhood and wonder whether there'll ever be an end to their suffering.

My abiding memory of this the saddest of assignments is of 13-year-old Silindile. Every day, between fetching water, cooking and washing for her younger siblings, consoling them at every turn and leading them through the bush to school, there she is, head bowed, kneeling prayerfully for a few silent moments at the graves she was forced to dig for her parents and three other brothers and sisters who succumbed to the killer virus.

When I think of her resilience in the face of such overwhelming odds, I am humbled ... a child mother whose work is never done. Yet each morning – along with tens of thousands of other AIDS orphans who have experienced fear, denial, sadness and abandonment – she has to convince herself '*I am somebody.*'

22

Reason To Remember

I've never tried to block out memories of the past, even though some are painful.
Everything you live through helps to make you the person you are now.

Sophia Loren

My first memory as a child was running gleefully around the back garden of our council house in Dundee waving a Union Jack. I was just twenty months old and didn't understand the significance of the occasion except that I had been told my daddy was coming home. The date was 8 May 1945 – Victory in Europe Day.

As the 50th anniversary of this momentous day approached, Tim Orchard, the exceedingly affable and innovative editor of *BBC Breakfast News*, called me into his office. The government had planned a host of major events to commemorate the anniversary and the Corporation was preparing a number of documentaries. In all of this, Tim felt that the stories of ordinary British men and women might too easily be overlooked.

'Millions of people experienced this day in a myriad of different ways – some overjoyed, others sad that their loved ones would never return. I want you to find some of them and to discover just what VE Day meant after six years of war.'

I liked the idea immensely and was eager to get started straight away, even more so when Tim told me he wanted no fewer than 23 films to be transmitted every weekday running up to the anniversary. There was only one problem. Where was I going to find these 'ordinary people' with a story to tell? The Imperial War Museum was unable to help. At the National Newspaper Library at Colindale, I flicked through a hundred and one publications. There were plenty of accounts of VE Day and references to a number of interesting individuals, but there were no addresses. In any case, I surmised that many of these people would no longer be alive and even those who were, would probably have moved house several times since the end of the war.

My initial enthusiasm was slowly giving way to despair. For three nights, I hardly managed more than a few minutes' sleep. Then at 3 am one morning, everything – including my powers of reasoning – unexpectedly fell into place. The answer was so simple that I was kicking myself that I hadn't thought of it before. Next day, I spent nearly a couple of thousand pounds of licence fee payers' money placing a boxed advert in the small ad columns of 20 evening newspapers in a vast geographical spread including the Channel Islands, Northern Ireland, Wales, Scotland and the English regions.

The advert was headlined: *VE Day – The BBC Needs You!* The text was short and simple, asking people to write in with their memories of VE Day and asking for what photographs and mementos they possessed. At the end of the ad, a PO Box number was given to where all replies should be addressed.

Nearly a week passed and I had not received a single reply. Tim Orchard asked how things were going and I did what I could to deflect any thought that we might be heading for an unmitigated disaster. Then I put a call through to the Royal Mail. Could there have been an administrative error when setting up the PO Box? There had. A huge sack of mail was sitting at the local delivery office just opposite Television Centre and awaiting collection.

Experiencing a sense of both relief and excitement, I hurtled down six flights of stairs and dashed across the road to see exactly what lay in store. The bag was lifted on to the counter and struggling under the weight of the letters, I decided the return to the *Breakfast News* office would require the lift to take the strain.

Replies had come from every part of the United Kingdom and my first cursory glance at the letters provided the best news of all. I had expected perhaps a dozen illuminating stories. Surprisingly, more than half the respondents had first-rate tales to tell. Some were colourful depictions of celebration, others poignant, many wrote of very moving experiences.

It was clear too, that a significant number had been involved in some of the major events of World War II. This meant that, allied to personal photographs, we would be able to use archive footage to illustrate some remarkable reminiscences, stories of selfless courage and sacrifice. Millions of Britons were also heroes on the home front. They built the ships, the planes and the tanks that went into battle while the Bevin boys worked the mines and women tilled the land, kept the railways running and toiled in the munitions' factories. Some wrote of the hardships and privations they suffered but thanks to their indomitable spirit, they somehow came through and had much to celebrate when the guns fell silent and the victory parties could begin.

Eventually, with producer Brian Staveley, I was able to whittle the list down to the required 23. In filming their accounts, my wish was that the series would serve as a fitting reminder of how much we owe to the generation who bore the brunt of the war.

First stop was Coventry which was hit by one of the worst bombing raids on mainland Britain. On 14 November 1940, 450 German bombers attacked the city, destroying 2,000 buildings including the medieval cathedral. More than 500 people were killed and thousands left homeless as entire streets simply disappeared. That night thoughts of an allied victory in Europe were inconceivable.

Avril Woodward was just a young girl at the time and remembered emerging from the bomb shelter with her brother to see the factory across the road reduced to a pile of rubble. On the mantelpiece of her home, her mum had placed a shilling piece which remained untouched for the duration of the war. It was there for a very specific purpose – to feed the gas meter.

'If Hitler crosses the Channel, you two will go in the oven first and then I shall follow.'

However chilling the thought, Avril believed it would have been a last act of love on the part of her mother. The shilling though had been so tempting sitting there day after day.

'You could get threepence worth of chips, some scratchings and a big bag of sweets for that, but we were never allowed to touch the shilling no matter how hard up we were and we'd dodged the coalman several times till pay day. Then on VE Day, it suddenly disappeared to be spent on treats for the street party.'

Intended or not, house names such as '76 Trombones' scrawled across the top of a letter are bound to attract the reader's attention but it wasn't just the address that had me heading in the direction of the Cambridgeshire village of Wimblington. The contents spoke of a great personal embarrassment, one from which, fifty years on, Dora Emery had still not completely recovered.

It was her husband George who had put pen to paper, a soldier who was to make his own piece of military history. As a Sergeant Major in the 11th Hussars, he had served in most of the desert campaigns and by May 1945 had been posted to Berlin. Sitting just outside the city, he was approached by his Colonel, who told him a Desert Rat was wanted post haste at Luneburg Heath in Lower Saxony. To his astonishment, George arrived in an armoured car just in time to witness Field Marshal Bernard Montgomery accepting the German surrender.

If that was momentous enough, he couldn't believe the role the BBC wanted him to play in VE Day. George was introduced to war correspondent Chester Wilmot, and told he had been chosen to speak to the nation following broadcasts from King George VI, Winston Churchill and Monty.

George stopped in his tracks, dumbfounded, asking: 'Why me? Who am I? I'm just an ordinary squaddie.'

'Exactly,' said Wilmot 'that's why you're here. You are the voice of the troops in the front line.'

I asked for a search of the audio library at Broadcasting House. A few hours later, a librarian rang to say they had located a recording of George's speech. His wife Dora was overjoyed to hear the news. For in May 1945, as her husband climbed aboard an open truck, microphone in hand to describe how he had seen 'the Germans crack in Tunis, the last corner of Africa, and I knew they would fall again in the northern corner of Europe,' Dora was not among the millions glued to the wireless. Having listened to the King, Churchill and Montgomery, she thought, 'That's it ... the war's over,' and went off to the pub to celebrate. One can only begin to imagine her dismay when she returned home to be told by all her neighbours that she had missed the biggest moment in her husband's life.

The joy of finally being able to hear George's historic broadcast meant everything to Dora. I was glad we were able to make it happen and join them in that same village local for a celebratory drink, especially when hearing that just weeks later George had succumbed to a heart attack.

I had hoped for a good response from the Channel Islands whose capture by the Nazis in June 1940 represented a propaganda coup of enormous proportions. To the Germans back home it was presented as the first step in their conquest of British soil. Hitler determined the islands should never be given up. On Guernsey alone he stationed 13,000 troops, erected enormous fortifications and locked up a reinforced infantry division for the whole of the war.

Ruth Walsh was one of those eager to tell what life was like for the island children. She remembered how stoical and resilient everyone was, convinced that one day the British would come and the Germans would be gone.

When the allies launched the invasion of Normandy in June 1944 they decided to bypass the Channel Isles. If D-Day shortened the war in Europe, it also severed the vital German supply lines to the islands. Shops were emptied of everything, even scraps were hard to come by. Hunger and illness took hold. By early 1945 Ruth's family were in dire straits. Covered in impetigo from head to toe, she was moved to hospital. Deprived of medical supplies, there was little anyone could do.

Waking up on Liberation morning, Ruth heard the British ships were just outside the harbour. In her excitement, she summoned up enough strength to abandon her hospital bed and make her way to the quayside. There, she watched the troops coming ashore. The soldiers were carrying oranges and bananas, fruit she had never set eyes on before.

'One little boy bit straight into an orange completely unaware that you have to peel the skin off first.'

Guernsey is now an island of plenty but if you've experienced real hunger, it's something you're unlikely to forget.

On the largest island of Jersey, the Nazi propaganda machine sprang into action from Day One of the occupation. Films shown in German cinemas portrayed the island as a place of sea, sun and plenty. With the expected invasion of Britain just around the corner, here was an opportunity to show that the Germans were model occupiers. Those who had to endure life under the jackboot tell a different story.

I found Dixie Landic, an interpreter for the civilian government, dismissive of those who wondered why the islanders had not acted like the French resistance and involved themselves in acts of sabotage. Impossible, he said, on an island just nine miles long and held by forces armed to the teeth. There was simply nowhere to run to.

Dixie defiantly channelled his resistance by digging up a16mm camera and some ancient film out of the ground and making a photographic record of a wedding attended by all the members of the civilian government – a clear violation of the German law.

Just a year later, the whole island qualified for the ultimate celebration … liberation not just for Jersey but for its furtive cameraman. He had to use his film sparingly. There was little left.

'Everyone was laughing, weeping, cheering, waving, embracing, smiling. They wanted to re-enact those scenes for all the major anniversaries to come but believe me, if they had a cast of thousands and everyone was an Oscar award winner, they could never reproduce that feeling of rapturous joy.'

It was the tiny island of Alderney which the Germans decided to turn into the most heavily fortified gun platform in the Atlantic Wall. The SS were there too and hundreds of prisoners of war, among them Russian slave labourers, were forced to build gun emplacements, batteries and vast underground tunnels. Many died in the process.

I flew in to meet an incredibly resilient couple, Dan and Iris Godfray, who had their home at Quesnard Point on the eastern tip of the island for over 80 years. In June 1940, training their binoculars on France just nine miles away, they had glanced the awesome threat of the German army. They got away just in time, among the 1,200 islanders who were evacuated in the space of three hours and facing first a terrifying sea crossing to Weymouth and then a bewildering train journey to Glasgow. If the second city of the empire provided accommodation, food and a job at the shipyards, no-one had expected this introduction to urban life to drag on for six years.

By the end of the war, Alderney was in such a state that only a few islanders were allowed to trickle home. When the Godfrays finally returned in 1946, they found their house a heap of rubble.

'We couldn't find a single thing, not even a spoon but we had to carry on. At least we hadn't lost anyone in the war, which was something, wasn't it?'

The couple were determined to handle their feelings in a positive way. They found the remains of a shingle hut which had been used as an office by the Germans.

'We thought we'll fix it up somehow and live out here again.'

It's been said that the sea has bred people with an independent spirit and the determination, even stubbornness, to safeguard the things they love. Having rebuilt both their home and their lives, the Godfrays' will to survive was as strong as Hitler's Atlantic Wall.

The more respondents I visited, the more I discovered about the rollercoaster of emotions that people experienced on VE Day. One Royal Marine decided to mark the end of the war with a short back and sides in Hamburg. The hairdresser's shop was just a darkened shell and when the barber approached with a cut-throat razor, the marine suddenly thought: 'What happens if he cuts it rough? Maybe life was safer on the front line!'

There was a mother in Staffordshire who gave birth to twins just as the party was getting under way outside her front door. I wasn't a bit surprised to hear she named them Victor and Winston.

Alas, the currency of joy has sadness on the reverse. Of all the letters I had received, the one from Dorothy Williams was perhaps the most heartbreaking. By May 1945 six years of fighting were coming to an end and thoughts on both sides of the North Sea were rapidly turning towards the homecoming. Yet Dorothy could not bring herself to share that feverish sense of elation, convinced in her own mind that her husband wouldn't be coming home with the others.

Inexplicably, a picture of *Bubbles*, famous through its use as an advertisement for Pears Soap, fell off her bathroom wall. As she went to pick it up, Dorothy saw an apparition of her husband standing right in front of her.

'There was blood pouring out of his head and chest and I put my hand up to try to stop it but he caught my wrist and said it's too late for that.'

Her premonition turned out to be correct. On the very last day of the war, her husband, a Seaforth Highlander, was crossing a bridge at Bremervorde in Lower Saxony when the Germans suddenly opened fire. He was the only one killed. Holding back her tears, Dorothy explained how her faith had been severely tested.

'He had survived Dunkirk. He had survived D Day. He had fought bravely right through the war. I said to myself I don't know how you let him go through all that God and then let him die right at the very last.'

In 1951 Dorothy married Len Williams, a naval hero aboard HMS *Amethyst* in the famous post-war Yangtze River incident. VE Day memories for him had been equally sombre. He had been a Japanese prisoner of war for three and a half years and, whilst celebrations were taking place back in Britain, he was one of thousands forced to build the Pakan Baroe railway through the inhospitable jungle and swamps of Sumatra.

That conflict against a ruthless enemy still had three months to run. Those who took part described it as the forgotten war, fought in distant places in the most alien conditions. It seemed only right we should film a second series running up to the 50th anniversary of VJ Day. Again, the BBC invited viewers whose lives had been changed immeasurably by those shocking events to get in touch. I found myself overwhelmed not just by the volume of the response but by the contents of the letters. Many said that they had become so psychologically damaged by what they had been through that this was the first time since the end of the war that they had felt able to express their feelings.

Some had been involved in the construction of the even longer 'Death Railway' connecting Burma with Thailand which included the famous bridge over the River Kwai. Some 16,000 prisoners of war died in its construction alongside 100,000 Asian slave labourers – one death for every sleeper laid.

One who was determined to survive, John Hamilton, resorted to eating maggots from the latrine and spoke of his anger when arriving home to find that few knew about the unspeakable horrors to which they had all been subjected.

Sitting in his Northamptonshire garden, listening to a namesake unburden himself of fifty years of suppressed anger, frustration and resentment, it seemed to me incredible that the country had done little or nothing to address the post-traumatic stress of so many broken men who had been ground down to little more than living skeletons.

Our conversation in midstream, out of the corner of my eye I caught sight of a large snake appearing from the undergrowth. John picked it up and placed it over his shoulder. 'Ah, this is a reminder of one of the best moments on the railway. If you found one of these ... this was a real treat ... you had to kill it first but very tasty for someone with an empty stomach. I told you about my will to survive but I've also got to tell you that vast army of dead behind me still crowd my dreams and I want their story told.'

Five of those came from one North-East family. The Cranmer brothers went straight into the record books by joining the Sunderland-based 125th Field Regiment on the same day. They vowed that if war broke out, they would fight and if necessary, die together.

There was a sixth brother, Jimmy, who defied his mother's will by joining a different regiment whose campaigns were fought in mainland Europe. It proved a slice of good fortune. His brothers, hurried to bolster the desperate and faltering defence of Singapore, were captured without firing a shot and sent to the Japanese work camps. Two perished, three returned unrecognisable, soon to die from the cruelties inflicted.

Jimmy, now living in Sheffield, was so overcome with grief that he had never returned to Wearside to visit their graves. Fifty years harbouring feelings of shame and regret finally prompted him into writing, in the hope that we might include his story and more important, find the exact location where his brothers had been laid to rest. We found a map of the cemetery and pinpointed the spot. It bore no headstone, not even a marker. The collective bravery of five brothers whose faces once beamed proudly from the centre pages of *Picture Post* had sadly been forgotten in death.

Jimmy looked gaunt and pale, and tears streamed from his eyes. We withdrew for a few minutes to allow him to grieve in private and to contemplate the horrors of a war that had left him the family's sole survivor.

In peacetime too, personal lives are often marked by tragedy, but the appalling events that visited the little Perthshire town of Dunblane on Wednesday 13 March 1996 were almost beyond belief.

I had been staying with my elderly parents in their retirement bungalow in St Andrews and woke up early that morning to clear 14 inches of snow from their front path. About the same time, a balding and bespectacled namesake, Thomas Hamilton, was observed by a neighbour scraping ice off his white van parked outside his home in Stirling. An hour later, armed with two legally held, semi-automatic pistols, two Smith and Wesson revolvers and 743 rounds of ammunition, he arrived at Dunblane Primary School and after cutting telephone wires with a pair of pliers, entered the building through a door beside the gymnasium.

In three minutes of carnage, the deranged gunman, wearing a woolly hat and earmuffs, shot dead 16 children from Primary One who had just entered the gym along with their teacher, Gwen Mayor, firing 105 rounds from a Browning automatic before using one shot from a revolver to end his own life.

I knew Dunblane well, having a few years previously participated in a service to mark the Salvation Army's Scottish Centenary which had been held at the town's medieval cathedral. It was the last place on earth one could ever imagine such unimaginable horror taking place. As the first reports of the massacre began to hit the airwaves, I was left stunned and speechless. Given the proximity of the town, I was there within the hour, under instructions to make my way to the BBC outside broadcast point that had already been set up and to prepare myself for a series of live transmissions.

On the ring road which bypasses the town, several motorists listening to the news on their car radios were in such a state of shock that they had turned into a lay-by and were offering a silent prayer, just a small part of a world that was trying to comprehend the enormity of the tragedy. Entering the town, I quickly caught sight of the BBC OB van, but before I could reach it, right in front of me, a Ford Fiesta suddenly pulled up in the middle of the road. The driver was slumped across the steering wheel, her head buried in her hands, tears streaming down her cheeks. As I approached to see if I could help, I noticed that every few seconds, the woman sat up and turned towards the back seat where a little boy, satchel strapped to his back, was fiddling with his pencil. Yes, he was alive. He had escaped the gunman's bullets. For his mother, each fresh glance provided reassurance and relief. Her haste to get away from the school was understandable but now the shock had set in, followed no doubt by a feeling of guilt that her child had survived the massacre unharmed. She simply couldn't drive any further.

That night, I gazed upon the photograph of Primary One which the police had issued to every journalist in the hope it would prevent reporters knocking on the doors of grief-stricken families and friends. Every parent knows the joy and innocence that a child brings into the world. There was life and hope in each of those innocent faces. The suffering for their parents, the enormity of the tragedy and the depth of their loss is beyond our experience.

Some things happen in life which are so awful, so monstrous, so unfathomable that we all struggle to find any words to describe them. There are no words that can adequately express the loss experienced by a mother and father who have had their healthy, happy, smiling child deliberately taken from them in an instant and for ever.

The next day brought a never-ending procession of people winding their way to the school gates to lay their floral tributes. I noticed many walked hand-in-hand as complete families ... grandparents, mum and dad and their children, many of whom attended Dunblane Primary and would have to return there when the school reopened. Most understandably, did not want to speak. Some found talking a form of therapy. One mum told me that by coming as a family unit, it would be easier to explain things to her children.

For many of course, this senseless slaughter of young children was the ultimate test of faith. Where was God when the killing was going on? How could He allow this to happen? For the clergy in Dunblane, the pressure was intense – parents to comfort and console, funerals to conduct, services to arrange and most of all, questions to answer.

The Minister of the Cathedral, Reverend Colin McIntosh, emphasised that God does not engineer the actions of each of us and that His finger was not on the trigger. He places us here on earth on the basis of trust, and when that trust was betrayed in the gymnasium, He was there, and God's heart was the *first* to break.

Hamilton had been a disgraced former Scoutmaster who had been investigated by police following complaints about his behaviour around young boys at a number of clubs that he ran. He also held licences for six guns, a fact which brought considerable criticism of the police for not questioning what he used them for, but Lord Cullen's Inquiry concluded that his actions on that day could not have been predicted.

The Snowdrop Campaign launched in the aftermath of the massacre attracted 750,000 signatures on a petition calling for the banning of the private ownership of handguns across Britain in the hope of preventing such a tragedy happening again. Within a year, its aim was enshrined in law.

In Dunblane, even for the most hardened journalist, it would have taken a heart of stone not to experience some of the pain and terrible sadness that had enshrouded all in that desperate place. Still today, I experience a chilling numbness every time I reflect on such a senseless carnage of tiny innocent lives carried out by someone bearing my own surname.

Every day, stories emerge of ordinary people who have found themselves swept up in a maelstrom of extraordinary events over which they have no control. Unlike the massacre at Dunblane, they make a fleeting appearance in the headlines in the morning paper and in most instances are never spoken or heard of again. News operates like the rapid turn-round schedules of a low-cost airline. It sets down briefly before taking off again to a new destination, leaving readers and viewers in the dark as to how things eventually work out. You can feel cheated when deprived of the final chapter.

With this in mind, I set off in pursuit of some of the headline makers of the previous twelve months. Had the unexpected happenings in which they'd become embroiled altered their lives in any significant way? Tim Orchard liked the idea and, with producer Brian Staveley on board again, a new series entitled *Reason to Remember* was under way. A defining strand soon began to emerge from these filming encounters with a very diverse group of individuals, namely the kind of daring it takes to survive and, most of all, the courage it requires to endure.

In Oxford's South Park, I encountered Chris Kitch as she walked her dogs whilst looking out across the 'dreaming spires' of the city where she had been accepted to study for a Master's degree. A remarkable woman now in her late fifties, she had descended to the lowest of the low. Banished from school and home as a young teenager in Bradford, Chris fled south to London and took to alcohol and drugs. She became a bag lady, a prostitute and a heroin addict. She had children by three different men and injected heroin into fellow prostitutes in the toilets of Piccadilly.

The last vestiges of humanity seemed to have disappeared when a policeman urinated on her while she was sleeping in her cardboard box. It was a moment that changed her life.

Seething with anger, Chris determined to earn respect. Kicking the habit was a hard and eventful struggle but eventually her willpower began to win through.

'I knew I was dying,' she insisted, 'so I had nothing to lose and, with the help of people, I put down the drugs and the drink and at long last could take to books and study.' At 55, Chris realised her dream by graduating as a BA with Honours at the University of North London.

'Stepping on to the red carpet, I felt about 10ft tall. I thought to myself I deserve this. I have legitimised myself. No-one can call me these names any more.'

The degree ceremony had earned the former bag lady a page lead in the red-top tabloids but I was eager to find out the sequel to this amazing story. That's when I traced Chris to an Anglican convent in Oxford where she was working in the kitchen and earning the support and encouragement of the convent Sisters. She needed to be in a safe place to make the mistakes that would be inevitable and had become a Christian of her own choosing.

For me – and I hoped for the viewers too – this gripping insight into the extremes of life reached a truly inspiring conclusion as we filmed Chris, surrounded by students less than half her age, concentrating intensely in an English Literature tutorial as she determined to extend her academic horizons. The prize – a Master's degree at Oxford Brookes.

'I see a Master's as the gift to the child that was denied so much. This is me making amends for the harm that I've caused myself. I hope that people will see that no matter how far you have fallen, you can still change your life.'

Andy Wilson fell too, in totally different but even more chilling circumstances. He had been cross-country skiing on the slopes of Glenshee then vanished in white-out conditions as blizzards engulfed the Scottish Highlands. Nearly a hundred men from seven rescue teams scoured the mountainside without success and on the fourth day decided to scale down the search in the knowledge that no-one had ever survived that long in such atrocious conditions.

They hadn't counted on Andy's awesome determination and will to live. To the astonishment of a helicopter crew, he was spotted making his own way down the mountain after cheating death for three days and nights at over 3,000 feet on just a frozen Mars bar and a prayer.

Just months after an unimaginable ordeal, I joined Andy and his Glaswegian wife Marion back on the very same slopes on which he had pulled off one of the most remarkable escapes in the annals of mountaineering. I thought it quite incredible that he'd want to relive such a nightmare but it seemed the lure of the Scottish mountains and the first snow of the winter were an irresistible combination.

Andy put his survival down to climbing into his bivouac bag and lying low until a weather window appeared. Once he was out of the wind, the snow built up to form what he described as an insulated coffin which served to keep him warm. When I suggested the use of the word 'coffin' might be slightly inappropriate given such a near-death experience, he explained that the whole episode had put his faith to the test.

'I didn't want to die without meeting God. It was then I decided to pray and afterwards I felt very relaxed – not that I was any happier about the chances of walking out alive but if I didn't, there wasn't going to be a disaster on my death. I was convinced I was going to meet God.'

Then came one of those great television moments when a good slice of Glasgow humour coalesced with the candour of two really genuine people to produce a real insight into the emotional trauma that Andy's wife had experienced, with hopes fading fast of ever seeing him alive again.

'What did I think when I heard he was alive? I'm too much of a lady to repeat what I actually said. I did doubt his parentage. I thought what a swine to put me through that!'

The quick-as-a-flash response from Andy was a classic.

'I'm beginning to get the impression it would have been better if I hadn't come back!'

All in jest of course, though I left with the distinct impression that Andy was unlikely to be let loose again unescorted on the Highland slopes for some considerable time!

For me the time was fast approaching when I would join the ranks of that august body of people called the BBC pensioners. I took a good look at myself in the mirror. One or two grey hairs, yes, but not too many wrinkles, most of my teeth still intact and still fit enough to continue refereeing in England's Feeder Leagues. No noticeable memory loss, little confusion and still blessed with good health. I decided to plead not guilty to the charge of ageing and to ignore that destination stop called retirement.

23

Retirement . . . What Retirement?

Don't count the days, make the days count.

Muhammad Ali

I have never been a great fan of carpet slippers and I have no intention of donning a pair now. After all, it may give the wrong impression that I want to spend my retirement years ensconced indoors. Thank goodness, I still have some sensible friends who have convinced me that the experience gained in the university of life can open up new horizons of opportunity.

No sooner had I walked through the swing doors of BBC Television Centre for what I feared might be the last time than my erstwhile colleague, Brian Staveley, was anxious to find out whether I still had an appetite for adventure. Brian was now operating as a freelance producer and had developed his own distinctive style and imaginative skill in mastering the operation of a video camera.

Within days my journalistic fire was rekindled. Destination – Kazakhstan, a country whose name is more recognisable from the cinema caricature of Borat than its place as the largest landlocked nation in the world. What has largely been forgotten is that it was here in a huge area to the east of the country that, hidden from the world, the Soviet Union carried out one-third of the world's nuclear tests in total secrecy. Some 500 explosions took place over 40 years. The legacy of devastation and radiation sickness is incalculable. Over a million people were subjected to the effects from the equivalent of many thousand Hiroshima bombs.

An Irish charity, the Greater Chernobyl Cause, one of very few western organisations operating there, had approached Brian to film its endeavours in the hope of attracting more financial support from donors back home. Would I like to come aboard as the reporter?

Brian had first met the charity's doughty and tireless director, Fiona

Corcoran, whilst producing a documentary for the BBC on the haunting legacy of the world's worst nuclear catastrophe at Chernobyl and was deeply moved by her work with the children of Ukraine and Belarus. Though Kazakhstan, bordered by China and Russia, is in another continent, Fiona accepted that the cry for help from the innocent and most vulnerable victims of nuclear testing should form a natural extension of her work.

We set off for the large industrial city of Semipalatinsk which lies just a hundred miles from the Polygon (the Russian word for firing range) and then on across the inhospitable steppe, a vast and desolate landscape whose scattered population had been cast into a new and sinister role as unprotected witnesses of the Cold War arms race.

I remembered that as a child I had an inbuilt fear that one day the Russians might attack the west with a nuclear bomb. My distinct impression today is that the Soviets probably thought they were in far greater danger from a strike by the Americans. After all, it was the USA which had bombed Hiroshima and Nagasaki to bring the war in Japan to a close and in so doing had Stalin champing at the bit to obtain the same technology.

Driving on across the vast snow-covered plains where the only signs of life were provided by shepherds on horseback prodding their sheep to more acceptable pastures, we reached the once secret city of Kurchatov, named after the enigmatic physicist who headed the nuclear project and where he gathered his team of scientists. A new railway had been constructed but no locals could get within miles of the place. They preferred to call it Konetchnaya, 'the end of the line'. That might have been a preferable term for Ground Zero where the Soviet Union detonated its first atom bomb on 29 August 1949. The world now had two nuclear powers and the Cold War had begun.

With a military scientist aboard, we headed for the test site which was subsequently used for more than a hundred above-ground explosions. I was extremely apprehensive, especially as we were not issued with any protective clothing.

We were told to look out for what the scientists nicknamed 'geese'. They were easy to spot, large concrete buildings that had faced the blast. They were a hundred metres high and housed much of the monitoring equipment. We were allowed out of the vehicle to examine them. Nearby, there were old artillery posts where the guns had melted in the blast and the reinforced concrete stripped down to a twisted wire skeleton.

Finally, we reached Ground Zero itself. It was little more than a large grassy crater, covered in a thin layer of the early winter snow. Here, half a century before, *Operation First Lightning* lit up the overcast skies and 500 mph winds carried away the livestock and tore the trees from the soil, dumping huge quantities of radioactive material on people, fields and houses miles from the test site.

I wasn't too keen to hang around for long. 'Fifteen minutes maximum,' our military escort shouted, 'and then we're off.' He produced a Geiger counter from his pocket and handed me a pair of rubber gloves to pick up some particles of soil. Twenty years after the last explosion in the Polygon, readings were still showing radiation levels up to 400 times above normal.

Fiona was visibly upset. The landscape evoked powerful memories of the Chernobyl tragedy that had propelled her into charity work. We had just time to record her thoughts as she walked through the epicentre of Ground Zero.

'A haunting experience,' she described it, 'knowing that the land would be contaminated for years to come. Chernobyl was one dreadful accident but here, the Soviets used their own people as human guinea pigs.'

In the village of Znamenka, just one of a number of isolated communites spread out across the steppe lands that surround the former testing site, I was introduced to three generations of the Bekartekenov family. It was like revisiting a scene from Albania where the women of the household went without food for days so that they could entertain their guests with a little horse meat, cheese, bread and onions. Not to have eaten it would have been the greatest of insults. Elsewhere in the country, being the eldest guest at dinner, I had been served a sheep's head complete with carving knife and told to feast royally before distributing the remains amongst the others. The consequences of refusing to take part in this ritual were too serious to contemplate!

Salamat Bekartekenov ushered me outside to the spot where he had witnessed one of the nuclear tests. He said the Soviet Army had arrived one morning and ordered everyone on to the street.

'Suddenly there was a loud explosion and the ground shook just like in an earthquake. When I looked up there was a huge mushroom cloud which filled the whole sky.'

The villagers' dread had been compounded by the arrival of the country's chief radiologist, Dr Saim Balmukhanov. Discovering alarming levels of radiation sickness, he set off for the Kremlin with twelve volumes of evidence. Sitting before a panel of Red Army Generals, all his meticulously recorded detail was dismissed out of hand. Instead he was told that the problem was of the Kazaks own making. They were dirty, badly fed and had lots of TB and brucellosis. The generals then seized his books and sent him away empty-handed.

When I met Dr Balmukhanov, now an octogenarian, he was beaming from ear to ear. After the fall of the Soviet Union, he had returned to Moscow and managed to recover all his confiscated data.

One of the first actions of the Central Asian republic when gaining its independence in 1991 was to shut down the test site, but the deadly legacy lives on. Znamenka's school lay directly in the path of the fall-out and there are still huge anxieties over the health of its pupils. Radioactive contamination carried in the wind and defiling the land, the water and the food chain is an invisible enemy.

Nothing had prepared me for our next port of call. Behind a wooden gate in an ice-covered backyard, we encountered a young man cranking the handle of a well as he fetched some much needed water. Berik had grotesque facial disfigurements and had undergone two operations to remove huge folds of skin but they just kept returning. Totally blind, he was one of an alarming number exposed to the highest levels of radiation.

Today, babies are still being born with horrendous deformities. Sadly, scientists say the tragic consequences could continue for six generations. Many have joined other physically or mentally disabled children abandoned by poverty-stricken parents and left in orphanages so poor and dilapidated that they threaten their very chances of survival.

Fiona was astonished at the level of neglect. Children left to rot in state institutions. A national disgrace! Five minutes inside one of these God-forsaken places was quite enough to convince me of the importance of exposing the dreadful fate of so many unfortunate children to the watchful eyes of any potential sponsors.

Kazakhstan struck me at once as a country of the 'haves and have nots'. It has enormous gas and oil reserves and is rich in mineral deposits. Its new capital Astana has provided something of a paradise for builders and architects with its granite and marble palaces, towers, theatres, parks and government buildings.

In the largest city Almaty, the roads are choked by vehicles which include a growing number of Mercedes, Audis, and Land Rovers while beautiful women stroll the streets in very expensive-looking finery. Others crowd the railway stations, jostling each other in their efforts to reach carriage windows and exchange a kebab or an apple or two for a few *Tenge* in the daily fight for survival.

328

I thought it shameful that the 'haves' were seemingly indifferent to the fate of so many unfortunate children in their country and had left it to people like Fiona and her supporters to try to transform such wretched young lives.

At the Semipalatinsk Orphanage, a new washroom, refurbished playrooms and dormitories were taking shape. The charity had sponsored trained therapists to relieve some of the symptoms which were causing the babies so much distress. Sadly though, there were others for whom little could be done. We sat by the cot of Anwar, a little boy with hydrocephalus – water on the brain – a result doctors said of his mother's defective gene, thought to be caused by radiation fall-out. He had already undergone one unsuccessful operation and no-one wanted to take responsibility for a possible second failure.

If some of the sights had been distressing then far worse was yet to come. We moved on to the place Fiona rightly described as a 'hell hole'. By order of the state, orphans are automatically transferred to a second Home at the age of five, no matter their physical condition. We found it 200 miles away in a dismal town called Ayagus where temperatures plunge to minus 35 in the bitter winter months. The place was grey, grimy and falling apart. There was little or no stimulation for the children, many of them seriously ill.

Tanya was sitting upright in bed. She was twelve years of age. I had mistaken her for a boy of five. Though she was content to be filmed, her face failed to reflect any interest at all, not even the merest glance in the direction of the camera. Even holding her hand and calling her name brought not the slightest reaction. We were told no relative ever visited. She was surviving within a world that offered nothing. Unless something not yet tried could lift her from her cocoon, she would sense less and less as the days and years merged between the liquid meals and the heavy doses of medication that were keeping her docile. Tanya was suffering from cerebral palsy and oligophrenia (mental retardation). We were told she could not be taught and would never walk.

One in ten of the children in Ayagus die every year, victims of the bitter cold, disease and in many cases radiation illness. They are buried in a local cemetery, mostly in unmarked graves. Sadly, such is the poverty in the area that the metal plates which bear a number and occasionally a name, had been stolen and sold as scrap metal.

None of us like to see children suffer, and coming face to face with such distressing scenes presents a challenge to anyone's faith. Yet, I was still glad I came, for without the intervention of Fiona's charity, the fate of many more of these children would have been too horrific to contemplate. Single-minded dedication to her work and the use of vast resources of energy, selfless determination and courage give real weight to her slogan that 'every child deserves a childhood'.

The film proved successful. Even in hard, economic times, Fiona found new sponsors and instigated fund-raising in a variety of ways. Schoolchildren showed their willingness to become involved. We decided to make a return visit to see what steely pertinacity and remarkable generosity can provide. At Ayagus, out of the grime and dust, a new orphanage building had emerged. The charity's Irish supporters provided most of the construction costs of half a million euros and the East Kazak Government contributed the rest. The filthy and degrading outside toilets had been swept away while a brand new kitchen gave staff every incentive to provide healthy and nourishing meals to sustain the children over a much fuller daily timetable. The charity was also funding the services of specialists able to understand and treat some of the debilitating illnesses that had thwarted the progress of even the most courageous children.

Sadly, several of those we had filmed on our first visit had passed away, including Tanya who succumbed to a bout of double pneumonia. Anwar, the little boy with hydrocephalus had died too, within days of being transferred from the baby orphanage in Semipalatinsk.

We visited his grave, laid some flowers and stood for a few minutes in silent contemplation, angry at the way the system had treated him but relieved that he would suffer no more.

In such a vast country, I was surprised to find that travelling even a few hundred miles involved an overnight journey by train. The cost of booking sleeping berths is very expensive but don't expect to find your bed empty if you join the train at an intermediate station. Other passengers will almost certainly have bribed the attendant to ensure they get a few hours under the covers! Expect, as we did, to pay a second bribe if you want the attendant to oust the night intruders and lay claim to your own bed. Neither can you expect the train to take a direct route to your destination. As the presence of the secret police still operating across the rail network signifies, old Soviet habits die hard and these include hundreds of miles of track diversions via Russia. So a journey we could have accomplished – had it not been for a snowbound road – in two and a half hours by car, took us 19 hours by train, more than ample time to read that latest novel!

The internal flight from Almaty to Semipalatinsk also proved quite a hair-raising experience. Most of the country's ageing fleet consisted of aircraft inherited from Aeroflot on the break-up of the Soviet Union. A local airline was operating a SMK 1447 with three air crew and around three dozen passengers who had to load their own luggage on to the plane. The one male steward, who supplied a plastic cup of carbonated water during the flight, was struggling to store as many cases as he could on three rear shelves covered by protective netting. He then sat down on top of the rest to prevent them from moving and putting the plane and all the passengers in some considerable danger. On our return flight, there were too many passengers for the number of seats available. No worries – standing room was provided!

Charities are part of our way of life. There are nearly 180,000 of them in England and Wales alone, ranging from small groups meeting local needs to the well-known major ones with budgets running into millions of pounds. I have been a regular collector for the Salvation Army and have been amazed at how few refusals I have received when knocking on the door. That cup of tea in the war has been repaid a million times over but, even with a new generation, there is a realisation of what the organisation stands for, aptly summed up in its war cry 'Faith in Action'. Its double strand as a Christian church and the largest provider of social services in the UK next to the Government has always commended itself to me, especially as its officers work for everyone in need, regardless of their background or beliefs.

Along with a young and vibrant Captain, Kerry Coke, I have been privileged to co-present the Salvation Army's quarterly *Link* programme which gives viewers across the country an insight into the organisation's wide range of activities from caring for the victims of human trafficking to helping the homeless, alcoholics and drug addicts rebuild their lives or easing the hurt of broken families. Under director John Anscomb's guidance, the film unit has engaged at the sharp end of life and with a Chilean producer Enrique Berrios bringing a keen international eye to the programmes, they have concentrated minds on life's big issues both at home and in the 121 countries in which the Salvation Army now operates worldwide. The standards have been incredibly high and in many respects match those to which I had become accustomed at the BBC. This acute sense of visual dynamics, demonstrated amongst others by cameraman Neil MacInnes, has earned the unit a fine reputation.

I also travelled widely with Oxfam, accompanying Liberal Democrat MP Simon Hughes to drought-stricken Zambia and Zimbabwe and the party's former leader, David Steel, to Uganda. Both visits produced a series of films for the BBC who, I'm pleased to say, would still occasionally call on my services as a freelance just to ensure I wasn't wasting away in some moth-eaten armchair.

In parts of the Muchinga Escarpment of Zambia, we trekked for a whole day to reach a village on the south side of the Luangwa river. In the normally stable Eastern Province, the maize crop had been wiped out by the drought and we found families in desperate straits, being forced to cut bush weed for survival. They burnt it into ashes which were then, in turn, used to form a kind of salt. One bowlful had to last a family of 12 for three days.

The Luangwa, normally 50 feet deep in places, was the nearest point for water. Such was the desperation of the locals that they were running enormous health risks drinking and washing in the same pool shared by their animals. Just before we waded across, we were told of the horrific death of an eight-year-old girl. Just a few days previously, she had been eaten by a crocodile whilst attempting to draw a bucket of water.

Across the border in Zimbabwe, the situation was even worse. South of the capital Harare, nearly ever river had dried up and much of the countryside resembled a desert. People were on the move from waterless boreholes and withered harvests. To illustrate the extent of the country's drought, I addressed the camera whilst standing on the cracked bed of Lake Kyle, the second largest stretch of water in the country. In normal times, I would have been submerged under 100 feet of water.

Back in the Zambian capital of Lusaka, I managed to arrange a meeting with ex-President Kenneth Kuanda whose father had been a Church of Scotland missionary. After we talked about the country's new privatisation policies, I found him intrigued by my Scottish accent. When I told him I had grown up in Dundee and had been a member of the Boys' Brigade, he sent his aide back to the house to collect a guitar. Asking me to join him, he rested the instrument over his thigh and began to strum the familiar melody of Crimond, singing all five verses of 'The Lord's my Shepherd' in the local Nyanja dialect.

In Uganda too, I had an appointment with the President. After the pain and dreadful government mismanagement of the Amin and Obote years, Yoweri Museveni had cultivated a lot of friends in the developed world by bringing relative stability and economic growth to his country. I had watched him being interviewed on Ugandan Television the previous evening and was alarmed to find his answers rambling on for ten minutes or more.

After being escorted into his office, I explained the various privatisation and world debt issues which I wished to pursue in the interview.

332

'I would appreciate if you could keep your answers short, sharp and to the point.'

'Not a problem,' he responded.

I have to admit I was pleasantly surprised. Each answer got straight to the heart of the matter and not one ran for more than 25 seconds. Considering his programme for the day was running two hours behind schedule, I thanked him for finding the time to accommodate us.

'You are no different to my own people, you exploit me!' he laughed, before extending an invitation to relax for a few minutes over a cup of real Ugandan coffee. With a temperature of nearly 110 degrees Fahrenheit outside, being allowed to secure a prime place under one of the President's two high-speed revolving fans as we chatted about football was an even more welcome gesture from a genial host.

It was the last act in what had been a particularly distressing week. With cameraman Bhasker Solanki, we had flown north to Arua in a chartered single-engined Piper plane. Arriving at Entebbe Airport, I was alarmed to find the Dutch pilot wearing a crash helmet. 'Normal practice,' he informed us. Then before speeding down the runway for take-off, he asked if we would bow our heads and join him in prayer for a safe flight.

Only later did we discover he was an active member of the Mission Aviation Fellowship, a marvellous charity whose crews fly across jungles, swamps and mountains to bring essential medical supplies and the Word of God to many of the developing world's most inaccessible and inhospitable locations.

Our destination was the Koboko refugee camp in Northern Uganda which had become home to 68,000 refugees fleeing from Africa's longest-running civil war in Sudan. Traumatised by years of instability, many had arrived bedraggled and exhausted. Deaths had reached appalling proportions with many children succumbing to diarrhoea, malaria or measles. The camp's emergency child-feeding centres were under enormous strain.

We determined to trace the refugees' trail back into Southern Sudan and were the first outsiders to reach the town of Kaya for eight months. Once home to 30,000 people, there was now hardly a soul to be seen. The place was in ruins, its inhabitants having fled as the Khartoum government stepped up its bombardment against the mainly Christian south. The local SPLA commander pleaded with us to summon outside help.

This had been a very dangerous corner of the war, for the border with Zaire (now the Democratic Republic of the Congo) lay just eight miles away. Soldiers there showed us the remains of an artillery shell

333

that had overshot its target – the Sudanese town of Bazi, a place we found totally deserted, eerie and ghostly where the papaya fruit remained unattended and was rotting on the tree.

We were also first-hand witnesses to what the fleeing refugees didn't see. No sooner had they left town than the intensity of the aerial and artillery bombardments set off a chain of uncontrollable bush fires. With not a fireman or a single hose pipe to be found, their homes were now nothing more than a mass of charred ruins.

Whilst in Uganda, I was anxious to find the Batwa, a pygmy tribe who live in the Mountains of the Moon, an area that straddles the Equator and close to the border with the Congo. It involved a long and tiring journey over rough, dusty roads full of pot holes and I was getting anxious that we might not get there before darkness set in. Suddenly, there was a loud bang and our van veered off the road. One of the tyres had blown out. There was a spare but no jack. After ten minutes, we caught sight of a vehicle and signalled the driver to stop. He helped us replace the tyre but it had virtually no air in it and no-one could find a pump. Just as it seemed all our efforts would be in vain, the one bus of the day pulled up. To our amazement, though old and rusty, it had an air pressure pipe used for the braking system. We were able to connect it to the tyre and a minor miracle meant we were on our way again.

Two hours later we finally arrived at the Semuliki Rainforest and soon encountered the pygmy tribe who had lived and hunted there for generations. Their methods were still primitive. We found them moving stealthily with bows and arrows between the trees, at times lost in the luxuriant thickness of the undergrowth, with a poisoned tip ready to slay any unsuspecting wild boar. Yet, animal migration had meant food was more difficult to come by, forcing them to travel greater distances, exposing their families to greater dangers and weakening their resistance to disease. In just ten years, their numbers had dropped dramatically from 5,000 to just 400.

We were accompanied by John Arthur, Director of the British-based charity ADRA, with whom I had worked in Albania several years before. At the invitation of the Ugandan authorities, he had despatched agriculturalists to teach the pygmies new survival skills. At Bundibugyo on the edge of the forest, they were being trained to grow potatoes and root vegetables which would soon supplement their meagre diet. Basic aluminium-roofed shelters had also been built to protect mothers and children from wild life and the cold. The Australian Government was helping fund the project but adapting to the new methods was clearly going to be a slow and cumbersome exercise.

The clan chief, just over 4ft in height and a little older than the rest, beckoned me to sit down. He wanted to talk.

'All my forefathers were born in the forest. They lived in the forest and they died in the forest. It's the only life we know. I'll die in the forest too.'

John Arthur insisted the agricultural programme was not designed to impose western culture on the Batwa. Indeed, the whole aim was to ensure their own culture would survive another generation. A fire was lit ready for the latest wildlife catch but it didn't arrive. Spirits though, were high. At the steady beat of the water drums, the pygmy families broke into song and dance, the polyphonic sounds reverberating around their encampment and their bodies going through the most extraordinary contortions. We quickly learnt that this was not a spectator sport and were cajoled into joining in. Swivelling those hips to the drumbeat of the Batwa is an experience I'm never likely to forget!

The children were masters of the art but when looking at their smiling faces, I noticed that several had huge gaps in their teeth. On enquiring the reason, one mother said it was a common tribal practice to extract teeth to relieve diarrhoea. Sadly as a result, some children had actually died of blood poisoning.

In recent years, I have built up a firm friendship with Jim Tryon, surely St Albans' most sprightly octogenarian. Having spent 47 years working for Smiths Industries, he was looking forward to a comfortable retirement but after his wife Peggy died in 2002, he decided it was time he found a useful outlet for his many talents. Helping out at a church youth camp run by relations, one of the leaders asked, 'What are you doing with yourself Jim?'

'Sitting in the garden watching the weeds grow,' was his meek response.

The leader of a small charity, Christian Relief Uganda, was standing nearby and urged him to come out and join them at an orphanage they'd built in Kamuli, one of the poorest regions of the country. Jim thought he was too old but went to see his doctor and told her he'd been invited to go to Uganda to work.

'What a great idea,' she said, 'go for it!'

Since that red-letter day, Jim has been back on ten occasions, helping provide a school and education for over 300 children, assisting with crop-growing and animal husbandry and a whole series of programmes which promote self-sufficiency and dignity.

He's also the charity's top fundraiser, visiting schools, churches and voluntary organisations all over the south of England. Such is his infectious enthusiasm that people can't say 'no' to his requests. I was able to help him out at the microphone with the visit of one of Wales' finest male voice choirs as they performed before a packed hall on three separate occasions. The 50 choir members from Cowbridge even paid their own expenses for the trip. It brings to mind a famous Bible verse in Paul's letter to the Galatians:

'And let us not be weary in well doing for in due season we shall reap, if we faint not.'

At 85, Jim shows no signs of keeling over.

When it comes to courage and fortitude then my thoughts immediately turn to a trip I made to the ski slopes of the Austrian Tyrol. My fellow travelling companions were all young British servicemen who had experienced personal tragedy. Soldiers who one minute were in their prime and at the peak of fitness and in the next, blown up by a bomb or landmine in the service of their country.

It's hard to imagine the physical pain or emotional trauma they must have endured on their return from the battlefield. Now though, instead of wallowing in self-pity, they were off to the roof of Europe on an adventure designed to restore confidence and morale. Having been tipped off by a helpful contact, I had no difficulty in persuading *BBC News* that this was a story they couldn't afford to miss.

Our destination was the ski resort of Solden for a week of ski-bobbing. With its bicycle-type frame, the ski-bob may provide a seat but let loose on mountains towering to 10,000 feet and fraught with danger, would test even the most accomplished skier. I was cajoled into taking part though only on the nursery slopes and found it both an exhilarating, yet at the same time, a quietly terrifying experience.

There were no such problems for Paul Burns, who was just 18 when his patrol was ambushed by the IRA at Warrenpoint. Eighteen of his paratroop were killed in the most devastating attack the British Army suffered in Northern Ireland. Paul was one of only two survivors from the first blast and had his left leg amputated. After more than twenty years of pain, he feared he might have to lose his right one too. Yet such was his courage, it seemed there was never a challenge too great. With his artificial leg, he had done over 700 jumps with the Red Devils and had circumnavigated the world as a member of the first disabled crew to participate in the BT Global Challenge.

He told me how he had long since ignored the cynics who scoffed at his sense of adventure.

'I never thought for a minute that I'd be able to come up into the mountains like this. It has opened up a new world for us and it's a beautiful world. We're able to participate and do a lot better than many of those around us.'

Even more remarkable was that the instructor was a man closing in on his eightieth birthday. Henry Wuga, a German Jew, fled from Berlin just in time before the Nazi crackdown and had been interred by the British as a potential spy even though he was only 15! He later settled in Glasgow and ran one of the biggest catering organisations in the city. Now here he was – his years of experience on the mountains allowing him to pinpoint all the hidden dangers – putting the young veterans through their paces.

'To see these lads with sheer determination, enjoying life again is worth everything. That's why I come back year after year.'

The après-ski at the little chalet Neue Post Inn in the village of Zwieselstein allowed the amputees to swop tales of their Alpine feats and set their goals for the year ahead. The organiser of the trip, Ray Holland of BLESMA (British Limbless Ex-Servicemen's Association) asked me to take a good look round the tables.

'This has transformed many young lives. Some came here depressed. Look at them now. Laughing and joking and in eager anticipation of what tomorrow will bring.'

I didn't need to be told. Pushing themselves to the edge of their possibilities, the young veterans had turned tragedy into triumph. I was only too pleased to raise a glass to their amazing courage.

Retirement has opened up new horizons. For over sixty years, I had an inherent fear of water. I put it down to having been pushed into the deep end of an open-air swimming pool when I was just a toddler, but I had tried to persevere. On school trips to Dundee Swimming Baths, I found myself attached to a hemp rope which the instructor cruelly whipped away without warning, while on holiday trips I signed up for a swimming lesson or two but all to no avail. Then one afternoon, on a visit to Cannons Club in St Albans, I was introduced to Catherine who had earned quite a reputation for teaching adults to swim.

'I wonder whether you would be prepared to take on your greatest ever challenge?' I asked her rather sheepishly. 'Despite all their best efforts, no-one has yet managed to get me to swim.'

'You leave it to me, Bill,' she replied. 'Six half-hour lessons starting next Thursday. They won't come cheap but if you're not swimming by the last one, I'll give you all your money back. Are you up for it?'

Every week for the next month, Catherine stood by the side of the pool and bullied me into submission. Shouts of 'that's pathetic ... I wish I had a camera to show you ... what did God give you arms for? ... do you ever listen to anyone?' accompanied each lesson but by week six, I was off – snail's pace at first – but gradually gaining confidence. Pounding the water gets the endorphins flowing and gives you a high.

Cycling too, has been on my agenda for some time. With my friends Aubrey Foddering, Ian Johnston, Nigel Crump and Steve Pickard, I have pedalled leisurely by the Danube, the Mosel and the Dutch bulbfields and have also taken to learning the rudiments of that most frustrating of sports – golf.

Football though, remains the number one love. *BBC Football Focus* and *Sky Sports* both filmed me in action in my fiftieth year in the middle and were intrigued to find that the tide of ducking, diving and cheating which was distorting fair competition in England's Premier League was being repeated in the lower echelons of the game. What featured on *Match of the Day* on a Saturday night was often seen as fair game by many of those less well gifted in the art of the striker.

Should I still be refereeing at 66 years of age? A fair question and one, if I'm honest, that perhaps I prefer to ignore. I have striven hard to maintain my fitness but the legs are not what they used to be and I am becoming more and more reliant on the experience and sense of humour built up over so many seasons in the game.

Before a recent derby game between Bedford and Ampthill Town, one of the team captains in a rather demeaning manner, questioned whether I was in charge of the match.

'I'm afraid so,' I blustered, 'and I hope you'll be able to keep up with me!'

In truth, I am retiring gradually, reducing the number of weekends in which I am involved and have now become an FA qualified assessor trying to offer help and guidance to a new enthusiastic generation of match officials from whom football will draw its top referees of the future. I also help out on the administration side of the Spartan South Midlands League which is one of the finest Feeder Leagues in the country. Its referees' appointments secretary, Mick Ewen, a former Soho beat bobby, has maintained an enviable reputation for his remarkable ability to recruit, encourage and develop young referees destined for the top. Woe betide anyone who steps out of line!

My grandson Stevie, a fervent Arsenal supporter, is now playing regularly in youth football and his little sister Amy has donned the goalkeeper's gloves for her school side.

Alas, my son David has shown no aptitude for the game but professionally shares my interest in communications, being one of the youngest local authority middle managers in the country. As a family, we are also proud that he was named as the country's Young Communicator of the Year. Our daughter, Claire is a communicator too, running educational and inspiring music classes for babies and toddlers and has produced a sprightly CD of self-composed nursery songs.

Communications is a rapidly changing business, none more so that in the field of journalism and broadcasting. New technology and new techniques have transformed the whole face of the industry. This is the age of the video journalist, of multi-skilling, of the web and 24-hour news. The challenges are enormous. Newspapers are being reinvented in the digital age.

It all seems a million miles away from the day I first entered journalism in 1962. It has been an exciting journey that has taken me from humble beginnings in Fife to major events across the world and opened horizons I could never have imagined. It has brought me into the company of kings and presidents, superstars and convicted terrorists; allowed me to experience the gold and marble splendour of palaces and the dark, dingy cells of prison; to witness the brutality of war and to convey the courage and resilience of the victims of conflict, persecution and disease.

My enthusiasm has not wavered. In my profession, you are only as good as your last story; in football, only as good as your last game. Retirement? I don't think so. I keep telling myself: I'm not growing OLD. I'm just growing UP.

Index